Comintern and Peasant in East Europe, 1919–1930

East Central European Studies
of Columbia University

Comintern and Peasant
in East Europe
1919 – 1930

GEORGE D. JACKSON, JR.

COLUMBIA UNIVERSITY PRESS

New York and London 1966

George D. Jackson, Jr., is
Assistant Professor of History at Hofstra University.

East Central European Studies of Columbia University

The East Central European Studies comprise scholarly books prepared under the auspices of the Institute of East Central Europe of
Columbia University or through other divisions of the University.
The publications of these studies is designed to enlarge our understanding of an important region of the world, which, because of its
relative inaccessibility in the recent past as well as because of the
linguistic problems it presents, has been somewhat neglected in
serious academic study. The faculty of the Institute on East Central
Europe, without necessarily endorsing the conclusions reached by the
authors, believe that these studies contribute substantially to knowledge of the area and should serve to stimulate further inquiry and
research.

East Central European Studies

The Communist Party of Bulgaria: Origins and Development, 1883–1936
Joseph Rothschild
Yugoslavia in Crisis, 1934–1941 *J. B. Hoptner*
The First Partition of Poland *Herbert H. Kaplan*
Czechoslovak National Income and Product, 1947–1948 and 1955–1956
Thad Paul Alton and Associates
Polish-Soviet Relations, 1932–1939 *Bohdan B. Budurowycz*
Hungarian National Income and Product in 1955
Thad Paul Alton and Associates
Politics of Socialist Agriculture in Poland: 1945–1960
Andrzej Korbonski
Polish National Income and Product in 1954, 1955, and 1956
Thad Paul Alton and Associates
Comintern and Peasant in East Europe, 1919–1930
George D. Jackson, Jr.

Preface

The early history of the Third or Communist International is a challenging and treacherous area for research. Challenging because it offers an extremely rich interplay between ideas and cultures, men and political power, revolutionary experience and revolutionary aspirations. Treacherous because it involves an excursion into relatively unexplored territory with little reliable guidance from scholars or sources. Yet the rewards are great for those who undertake the study, because the early history of the Comintern reveals a great deal about the mechanics of international Communist organization, the appeals of communism, and its drawbacks as a revolutionary movement.

The history of the Comintern makes unusual demands on the investigator. Like most organizations which combine conspiratorial with legal political activity, the Comintern scarcely ever revealed its real intentions and actions in the published records of its meetings and conferences. To study the Communist International one must be both archivist and detective. The methods of research probably have more in common with those used in the study of the early Middle Ages than of modern political history, because, like the medieval scholar, the historian of the Comintern has to rely heavily on internal evidence and scant bits and pieces of external evidence, which can be brought together only by deduction, imagination, and even intuition. As a result, the end product is unquestionably more a work of art than a scientific accomplishment.

It is possible, of course, to confine oneself to the history of Comintern theory and doctrine, relying on the printed evidence and indulging exclusively in exegetical analysis. Such research—the least hazardous and the least subject to error—is therefore the most common in English. But by failing to venture beyond revolutionary oratory and pronouncements one runs the grave risk of performing only a pallid academic exercise.

In this book I decided to be both brave and foolish and examine Comintern theory and practice. The subject is Comintern policy toward the peasantry and peasant political movements in Eastern Europe. Part I describes the general social and economic problems of Eastern Europe and the solutions offered by communism and agrarianism. Part II, the core of the book, describes the development of Comintern policy toward the peasantry in the 1920s. In Part III I have brought theory and practice together in five of the East European countries where Comintern peasant policy was applied. The sequence of countries is determined by that point in time when the peasant political movment had its strongest grip on political power. Part III is not intended to be a definitive analysis of the political history of the five countries or their respective political parties in the 1920s. Except in a few instances I have not attempted to draw on the voluminous source material in the native languages on the local Communist parties. Indeed, I could not use such sources because I do not know most of the languages of Eastern Europe. Instead, in most cases I used the abundant secondary sources and documentary material available in Western languages and Russian in order to describe significant examples of Comintern peasant policy in practice. By examining not only the genesis of Comintern policy but also the context within which that policy was applied, it is possible to view the scholastic debates of the Comintern in their proper perspective.

The system of transliteration from Cyrillic is that of the Library of Congress with a few modifications. Most proper names follow the form in the language from which they are derived. For example, the Belorussian names Tarashkevich and Hramada are given in direct transliteration from Belorussian rather than the more familiar Polish versions, Taraskiewicz and Gromada (or sometimes the Ukrainian Hromada).

I would like to take this opportunity to thank the Institute on East Central Europe for publishing this book as part of its series of East Central European Studies and to express my gratitude to Professor Henry L. Roberts, Institute Director, for his warm support and encouragement during the difficult years of preparation. The first version of this study was written as a doctoral dissertation at Columbia University under the supervision of Professor Roberts as Director of the Russian Institute there. I was indeed fortunate in being able to draw upon his wide knowledge of East European and Russian history and his fine sense of style. More important, perhaps, it was Professor Roberts as a teacher and writer who first kindled my interest in the subject of this study and strongly influenced my approach to it. Professor Alexander Erlich of Columbia University acted as second reader on the dissertation manuscript and gave it several careful readings, contributing valuable comments on the Polish chapter and the sections on economics. Professor Joseph Rothschild of Columbia University was kind enough to provide me with a bibliography at the beginning of my research on the Bulgarian Communist Party and to give the Polish chapter a very critical reading. All of the above read the manuscript for my final examination for the doctorate along with Professors Victor S. Mamatey of Florida State University at Tallahassee and Oscar Halecki of Fordham University. I would like to thank Professors Mametey and Halecki for their comments at that time which were used in preparing the present version.

Three of my colleagues in the Department of History at Hofstra University took time from their own crowded schedules to read the manuscript for style and consistency, Professors John L. Rawlinson, John T. Marcus, and Gerrit P. Judd (chairman). William F. Bernhardt, my editor, has done his utmost to prune and trim the text, frequently in the face of stubborn resistance. His work has unquestionably made the prose more fluid and lucid. Finally, I would like to thank my wife, not only for enduring the delinquencies of a writing husband, but also for reading the manuscript for tone and balance. The final responsibility for style and content is, of course, entirely my own.

GEORGE D. JACKSON, JR.

Hofstra University
November, 1965

Contents

Tables

PART I

IDEOLOGY AND REALITY

CHAPTER I

The Dilemma of Peasant Societies in Transition

Communism, an ideology which exalts the mystery of the dialectic, may itself be turning into its opposite. In the nineteenth century Marx imagined that he was giving voice to the aspirations of the dumb and brutalized industrial working class. In doing so he imparted to them the revelation that beyond industrialization lay the proletarian utopia. To the workers of England and Germany he offered the immediate hope of the millennium, for their countries had already traversed the necessary preliminary stage of economic development. But in the twentieth century Marxism has won its greatest victories not in England or Germany but in Russia and China, that is, not in the most industrialized countries of the world but in two huge countries just beginning the modernization process, in two peasant societies in transition. And everywhere in the world today the same paradox is apparent. It is not the urban worker in the already industrialized West, but the victim of incipient industrialization in Asia, Africa, and South America who invokes Marx's incantations.[1] Does this mean that Marxism, a political philosophy designed to give direction to the industrial working class in economically advanced societies, has become the "natural" creed of the underdeveloped peasant nations of the world?

[1] Though concerned more exclusively with Communist efforts in Asia, the essays in John H. Kautsky, *Political Change in Underdeveloped Countries: Nationalism and Communism* (New York, 1962) seek to explain the appeal of communism in countries where its doctrines would seem inappropriate. Adam B. Ulam, in a provocative essay in *The New Face of Soviet Totalitarianism* (Cambridge, Mass., 1963) and in *The Unfinished Revolution: An Essay on the Sources of Influence of Marxism and Communism* (New York, 1960), argues that Marxism is the *natural* ideology of underdeveloped societies in today's world.

RED AGAINST GREEN

One answer to this question may be found in the historical approach. The early experiments of the Comintern in peasant societies produced certain formulas which have become permanent features of Communist strategy in backward countries, and the successes and failures of the 1920s laid bare some of the strengths and weaknesses of the Communist attitude toward peasant societies and peasant political movements. What is more significant, perhaps, in the first ten years of its existence the Communist movement faced a formidable rival for the affections of the peasantry in the movement loosely affiliated to the so-called Green International in Prague.

This study examines the development of the Comintern's strategy and tactics for winning the peasantry and its leaders and the implementation of those policies within a narrow geographic area. My investigation of Comintern agrarian policy is confined to Eastern Europe [2] for two reasons. After World War I Eastern Europe was deceptively similar to prerevolutionary Russia and seemed to offer a laboratory for the application of the lessons of the Russian Revolution. Also, events in Eastern Europe deserve special attention in any study of the early history of the Comintern because the experience of East European Communists had a disproportionate influence at the highest levels of the Comintern. I have focused on the decade of the 1920s, since this is a formative period in the history of the Comintern, and because the peasants' own political movement offered impressive competition during these years. Finally, by concentrating on one geographic area and period I have been able to provide a more complete and detailed examination of both the origins and the effectiveness of Comintern policy than would otherwise be possible.

Just as in many countries today populism or the populist mentality offers the greatest obstacle to Communist penetration, in the 1920s the peasant political movement in Eastern Europe enjoyed far more success in winning popular support than either the Communists

[2] In general, the term Eastern Europe as used in this study will follow the precedent established by Hugh Seton-Watson in his *Eastern Europe Between the Wars* (Cambridge, 1946); see especially p. xiv. Thus "Eastern Europe" will mean Czechoslovakia, Poland, Rumania, Hungary, Yugoslavia, and Bulgaria. I have rashly chosen to sidestep the important, but interminable, debate over the function and inclusiveness of the label, although I will try to make it clear as I proceed why I have chosen this definition.

or the older liberal parties and frequently gained decisive influence at the highest levels of government.[3] The agrarian parties seemed about to emerge with a new and original political ideology uniquely adapted to the needs of their economically backward countries. Much of the agrarian program of the Comintern was formulated in response to the challenge posed by these peasant political parties.

Many of the distinctive features of Lenin's Marxism are a product of the conflict between Russian Marxism and Russian populism (that is, the political movement of the Russian peasants known as the narodnik movement).[4] The competition between populism and communism was by no means a new one in 1919. Before World War I each camp had offered its own plan for future political and economic development. Both movements were inspired by the conviction that certain "evils" had accompanied the industrial development of Western Europe. The Russian prerevolutionary Marxists regarded most of these evils as inevitable and saw the solution only in the distant future after Russia had reached a higher state of industrial development. Their answer lay in part in more rapid industrialization. The Russian prerevolutionary populists hoped to diminish the evils by reducing the scale of industrialization and achieving more balance in the rate of growth between agriculture and industry. Their answer lay in part in less industrialization. In the 1920s each movement tended to adopt some features of the other's position.

In the decade after World War I the two movements had much in common. Both attempted to create organizations in order to consolidate and strengthen their efforts at the international level. The populists created a Green International at Prague in 1922, and the Comintern created a Red Peasant International, or Krestintern, in Moscow in October, 1923. Both promised their supporters a more equitable distribution of the goods produced by their own nations. Like all movements appealing for mass support, both tried to broaden their political programs in order to win members from social classes

[3] The pioneering study in English of the struggle between Marxism and agrarianism (or populism) in Eastern Europe is David Mitrany, *Marx Against the Peasant: A Study in Social Dogmatism* (Chapel Hill, 1951).

[4] For example, see Richard Pipes, "Russian Marxism and Its Populist Background: The Late 19th Century," *Russian Review*, XIX, No. 4 (Oct., 1960), 316–37.

other than those they claimed to represent. Both failed to maintain themselves in power when they had the opportunity to do so.

The fundamental difference betwen the two was the fact that the Communist movement became a disciplined army at the disposal of the Soviet government while the agrarian movement remained essentially indigenous. For the East European peasant, when he became aware of political programs, the most important difference between the two movements was that the Communist movement was directed toward the ultimate destruction of the peasant landholder and the establishment of a highly industrialized society, while the agrarian movement, in most cases, was directed toward the preservation of what the agrarians termed "the best features of a peasant society" and only a moderate development of industry.

An analysis of party programs is not enough, in any case, to explain why communism or agrarianism succeeded in any part of Eastern Europe. Neither the doctrines nor the tactics which these movements adopted at a given moment were inherently persuasive to the peasantry. Rather, it was the special social and economic conditions in Eastern Europe in the 1920s which made peasants and their political leaders responsive to communism or agrarianism. It is unlikely that either movement would have attracted a wide following in stable peasant societies. But in the 1920s all of the East European countries, with the exception of some already industrialized provinces, like Bohemia, were peasant societies in transition, that is, traditional agrarian societies that were being transformed by industrialization and contact with the industrialized world. In general, the process seems to have begun earlier and progressed further in the northwest. As a result, the weight of the peasant population tended to increase as one moved from the northwest to the southeast.[5] A society undergoing this kind of change finds the answer to its problems neither in its own traditional values, which it is throwing off, nor in the new values which it has imported from the industrialized world. Unlike Western liberalism, agrarianism and Soviet communism seemed to provide not only economic solutions but also psychological satisfactions for the peoples of underdeveloped countries. It is useful, there-

[5] For a discussion of this see R. V. Burks, *The Dynamics of Communism in Eastern Europe* (Princeton, 1961), pp. 71–72.

fore, to identify some of those characteristics of peasant societies in transition which might nurture the new ideologies.

ECONOMIC TENSIONS

In the long run, the political problems of East European states must be considered in their economic setting, because the enormity and urgency of the economic problems kept politics in perpetual crisis. The economic backwardness of the peasantry perpetuated its political and cultural backwardness. This was fertile ground for demagoguery and revolution, but not for democracy. Politics in Eastern Europe, in the 1920s, like politics in prerevolutionary Russia, was given pace and direction by conspicuous economic needs.

In Eastern Europe after World War I as in the world after World War II, the language of liberalism seemed somehow remote and irrelevant to the peasantry and to many of its political leaders. Although every East European state except Hungary adopted democratic institutions and enfranchised the peasant, these innovations only served to heighten his frustrations. When the peasant first acquired a voice in politics and became eligible for courting by politicians, he probably did feel that he had acquired a new dimension as a human being. Since the peasantry constituted the majority of the population in most East European countries (see Table 1), it was natural for the peasant to assume that his interests would be given first attention. But the impressive glitter of the new political machinery began to fade when he discovered that it did not meet his most

Table 1

Proportion of Total Population
Engaged in Agriculture

Country	Year	Percentage
Czechoslovakia	1921	40.3
Hungary	1920	58.2
Poland	1921	75.9
Yugoslavia	1920	78.9
Rumania	1913	79.5
Bulgaria	1920	82.4
USSR	1926	86.7

Source: Louise E. Howard, *Labour in Agriculture, an International Survey* (London, 1935), pp. 42–43.

pressing problems. Skepticism about the effectiveness of the existing political system made him more susceptible to apocalyptic programs which called for the establishment of an entirely different order of things. Lurking always in the back of his mind was the conviction that in Russia the peasant had solved his problems by seizing the land he needed.

"Land hunger," or the feeling on the part of the peasant that most of his problems can be solved by the acquisition of more arable land, is one of the most dangerous sources of tension in peasant societies in transition. Indeed, the Bolsheviks attributed their own success in seizing power in Russia partly to their exploitation of the peasant's desire for land. Bolshevik arguments were not lost upon East European politicians, and, if only to stave off a Bolshevik solution in their own countries, all East European governments instituted major land reforms. The Bulgarian peasant leader, Stamboliiski, said, "In order to combat Bolshevism I have, as one shifts ballast, added so heavily to the social reforms and ordered so many of them that I can rightly say that I have vanquished the Communists on their own ground, being more audacious than they and deflating their ideas with deeds." [6] One prominent ex-Communist writer attributed the containment of Bolshevism in Europe to the effectiveness of the Rumanian land reform.[7] Certainly in 1920 the danger of Bolshevik exploitation of the East European peasant's land hunger seemed very real. Hungary had its Bolshevik Revolution in March, 1919, Poland almost had one forced upon her by the Red Army in July, 1920, and the Communists attracted significant electoral support in Yugoslavia and Bulgaria in 1919.[8] However dubious the claim that these successes were due in part to the Bolshevik agrarian program, that explanation was widely accepted.

But something more than anti-Bolshevism was needed to inspire sound agrarian reforms. The other considerations that influenced the shape of East European agrarian reforms in the 1920s, however, had very little relation to the peasants' real problems. Votes had to be

[6] Quoted in Pierre Jousse, *Les Tendances des réformes agraires dans l'Europe centrale, l'Europe orientale et l'Europe méridionale, 1918–1924* (Niort, 1925), p. 55.

[7] Franz Borkenau, *World Communism: A History of the Communist International* (New York, 1939), p. 99.

[8] Jousse, p. 56.

won, and political obligations to be met. Although large landed estates continued to dominate the countryside only in Hungary,[9] the political influence of vested interests often led to the preservation of significant large-scale holdings elsewhere (see Table 2). Except, perhaps, in Hungary, these large-scale holdings could rarely be justified as model mechanized farms in which advantages of scale were employed. Where the large landowners were generally of the same

Table 2

Distribution of Land in
Eastern Europe around 1930[a]

	PERCENTAGE OF HOLDINGS			
Country	Dwarf holdings [b]	Under 5 ha.	5–50 ha.	Over 50 ha.
Bulgaria, 1934	27.0	63.1	36.8	.1
Czechoslovakia, 1930	28.2	99.1		.9
Hungary, 1930	71.5	84.0	15.1	.9
Poland, 1931	25.5	64.2	35.3	.5
Rumania, 1930	52.1	75.0	24.2	.8
Yugoslavia, 1931	33.8	67.8	31.8	.4

	PERCENTAGE OF AREA			
	Dwarf holdings [b]	Under 5 ha.	5–50 ha.	Over 50 ha.
Bulgaria, 1934	5.3	30.0	68.4	1.6
Czechoslovakia, 1930	2.3	80.4		19.6
Hungary, 1930	10.9	20.1	33.5	46.4
Poland, 1931		80.1		19.9
Rumania, 1930	12.8	28.0	39.8	32.2
Yugoslavia, 1931	6.5	28.0	62.4	9.6

[a] This table was originally compiled and evaluated by Alexander Erlich and distributed in mimeographed form. There are various discrepancies and inconsistencies, but the most pronounced have been taken into account (that is, the figures for distribution by area for Czechoslovakia, Poland, and Yugoslavia are his adjusted figures for agricultural area excluding forests). His sources were S. D. Zagorov, Jenö Végh, and Alexander D. Bilimovich, *The Agricultural Economy of the Danubian Countries, 1935–45* (Stanford, 1955), pp. 48–49; *Statistisches Jahrbuch der Tschechoslovakischen Republik*, 1937, p. 53; *Mały Rocznik Statystyczny*, 1938, pp. 68–73.

[b] The dwarf farms are defined differently in each country. In Bulgaria, Poland, and Yugoslavia the upper limit for dwarf farms is two hectares; in Rumania and Hungary it is three, and in Czechoslovakia one. The percentages in this column are also included in the next column—land under five hectares.

[9] Wilbert E. Moore, *Economic Demography of Eastern and Southern Europe* (Geneva, 1945), pp. 231–36.

nationality as the inhabitants or the newly dominant nationality, as in Hungary, Croatia and Slavonia, Galicia, Russian Poland, and the Rumanian Old Kingdom, their interests were taken into account. In the other former provinces of Austria-Hungary and in Prussian Poland the landowners were primarily German and Hungarian,[10] and their land could be confiscated in the interests of national unity. Paradoxically, in some areas where large holdings were broken up toward this end, as in Prussian Poland, their preservation as model farms could have been justified. In the redistribution of the confiscated land very often the desire to reward members of the national liberation armies took precedence over the critical needs of peasants with dwarf holdings. With the exception of Bulgaria, all East European countries introduced clauses giving priorities to veterans of national liberation armies, to wounded veterans, and to the widows of veterans.[11]

Although all the reforms stated or implied that the peasant was entitled to the land he tilled, that landless peasants were to become landowners, and that a certain minimum size of holding should be created and protected by law, these ambitions were frustrated. With the exception of Hungary and parts of Poland, the net effect of the reforms was to enlarge the system of small peasant properties without appreciably improving the conditions of the peasantry as a whole.[12] Desired norms were set. In each country they depended on the terrain and the mode of cultivation. In Hungary, because of the strictly limited nature of the reform, no more than three arpents (1.72 hectares) could be allotted to a landless peasant, and in the case of land allotted to small households the combination of allotted land and previous holdings could not exceed fifteen arpents (8.6 hectares). In Bulgaria, Rumania, and Yugoslavia five hectares was regarded as the desired minimum property, while in Czechoslovakia the desired minimum generally ranged between six and fifteen hectares, and in Poland was fifteen hectares except in the sparsely settled eastern regions.[13]

---

[10] Seton-Watson, p. 78.

[11] Jousse, pp. 37, 40, 46, 48; Jozo Tomasevich, *Peasants, Politics, and Economic Change in Yugoslavia* (Stanford, 1955), pp. 340, 348.

[12] Seton-Watson, p. 80.

[13] Jousse, p. 48; Tomasevich, p. 371; M. Ts. Bouroff, *La Réforme agraire en Bulgarie, 1921–1924* (Paris, 1925), p. 90; *Agrarian Reform in Czechoslovakia* (Prague, 1923), p. 12.

Given the amount of land available for the reforms and the fact that the landless peasants were offered first or second priority, these norms were unrealistic. In most countries the net result was an increase in submarginal holdings.

The extent of the changes wrought in the land tenure systems of the various countries under discussion may be seen in Table 3 which indicates the percentage of agricultural land affected during the period 1919-30 by the land reforms. While the land laws in question limited the sale of allocated land, all of them were inadequate with regard to permanent limitations on splitting property and on the problem of consolidating scattered strips.

Table 3

Agricultural Land Affected by the
Agrarian Reforms, 1919–1930

Country	Percentage
Rumania	29.7
Czechoslovakia	14.1
Hungary	under 10
Poland	6.1
Yugoslavia	under 10

Source: Royal Institute of International Affairs, *World Agriculture, An International Survey* (London, 1932), p. 149.

The unpleasant truth, which few politicians were willing or able to recognize, was that land redistribution, even if soundly conceived and executed, could not have solved the problems of the peasantry in Eastern Europe. The initial impact of Western medical standards created a lag between the fall in the death rate and the fall in the birth rate. Therefore in all East European countries except Hungary and Czechoslovakia one finds a high density of population side by side with low unit yields (see Table 4). The simple fact is that there were more people living on the land than could be supported adequately under the prevailing mode of cultivation. No mere redistribution of land could solve this problem.

Although "rural overpopulation" makes itself evident in the form of "land hunger" and social and political unrest, the degree of rural overpopulation in any one country is extremely difficult to measure. One of the most useful and at the same time most controversial

estimates was made by Wilbert E. Moore for the year 1930 or thereabouts (see Table 5). In his careful discussion of the term "overpopulation" Moore indicates that there is no absolute measure of
this condition and that his estimate, like all such estimates, requires
an assumed "reasonable" level of average per capita product, as well
as other statistical devices, to make possible a comparison of different
types of agricultural land and different agricultural products. The
difficulty inherent in any such standard is the assumption that within
a given economy there are other forms of employment available to

Table 4

Some Indices of Economic Backwardness

		PERCENTAGE OF TOTAL POPULATION DEPENDENT ON AGRICULTURE	NUMBER OF PEOPLE		AVERAGE YIELDS (QUINTALS PER HECTARE)	
	Year	*Per-centage*	*Per 100 ha. of cultivated land*	*Per 100 animal units*	*Wheat*	*Potatoes*
Yugoslavia	1931	76.5	140	141	10.5	58.8
Russia	1930	75.0	105	44.5 [a]	6.22	. . . [b]
Bulgaria	1934	73.2	116	102	11.5	53.0
Rumania	1934	72.4	94	142	9.0	87.8
Poland	1931	62.8	106	112	11.7	112.9
Hungary	1930	51.8	76	115	13.1	61.3
Czechoslovakia	1930	34.5	85	79	17.0	127.2
Denmark	1930	31.2	42	21	28.9	165.5
France	1931	28.0	48	51	15.5	110.5
Germany	1933	20.8	63	44	21.5	160.0

　　Sources: Russian data from Serge N. Prokopovich, *Histoire économique de
l'U.R.S.S.* (Paris, 1952), pp. 22, 110, 164. All other data from Jozo Tomasevich, *Peasants, Politics, and Economic Change in Yugoslavia* (Stanford, 1955),
p. 309.
　　[a] Russian data for number of people per hundred animal units are based on
the population and number of head of cattle for the year 1928, not 1930.
Therefore these figures are not strictly compatible. Unfortunately, it was not
possible to obtain data from each country for the same year.
　　[b] . . . = not available.

the portion of the population found unnecessary for agricultural
production.

　　The same difficulty of measurement arises in any assumption of "symptoms of overpopulation." And yet, it is clear that the indices of overpopulation which are normally used are symptoms of a social and political malaise which demands some form of radical economic readjustment. It is generally assumed that the prevalence of extremely small holdings, of a high proportion of cereals or other food crops with respect to arable area, of low unit yields, of low density of livestock, of undernutrition, of falling wages and farm income, of expansion of secondary sources of income among the rural population, or reduction of area for pastures, meadows, and fallow, of cultural stagnation, and, of course, of underutilization of labor may all be signs of agricultural overpopulation.[14]

Table 5
Proportion of Surplus Agricultural Population
to Total Rural Population

Country	Percentage
Bulgaria	35.7
Czechoslovakia	11.7
Hungary	2.9
Poland	29.4
Rumania	23.1
Yugoslavia	38.8

Source: Wilbert E. Moore, *Economic Demography of Eastern and Southern Europe* (Geneva, 1945), pp. 71–72. Actually Moore has calculated the "theoretical" surplus population for the year 1930 or thereabouts, since his method is based on the assumption of French productivity per hectare of "arable-equivalent" land and European per capita level. Nevertheless, his figures come surprisingly close to those of a study group under Dr. Rosenstein-Rodan which tried to calculate the real surplus population in Eastern Europe for 1937 using methods which were not based on some extraneous standard and which took into account the special conditions prevailing in each country. The latter figures were: Bulgaria, 28 percent; Czechoslovakia, 13 percent; Hungary, 18 percent; Poland, 24 percent; Rumania, 20 percent; and Yugoslavia, 35 percent. Nicholas Spulber, *The Economics of Communist Eastern Europe* (New York, 1957), pp. 275–76.

The standard remedies suggested for relieving agricultural overpopulation are birth control, internal colonization, emigration, an increase in the amount of land cultivated, intensification of agricultural production, development of cottage industries, reduction of

[14] Tomasevich, pp. 318–19.

livestock herds, war, and industrialization.[15] The last, of course, was the long-run panacea offered by the Communists, while the agrarian parties, once the land reforms had been initiated, concentrated rather on increasing the amount of land cultivated, intensifying agricultural production, and developing cottage industries.

In the opinion of Moore, it is extremely unlikely that the problems of overpopulation in Eastern Europe could have been solved by measures which primarily emphasized agricultural production (that is, the agrarian solution).[16] The rapid expansion of population resulting from contact with the West simply could not be matched by a corresponding increase in agricultural productivity unless there was a shift of population to the city, a shift which would produce a change in the demand pattern and the reproductive pattern. The advantages offered by an industrial solution are, first of all, increased national productivity and economic opportunity. Another beneficial aspect is the avoidance of the risks faced by the development of specialized economies.

But, in Eastern Europe after World War I most politicians felt that there were too many risks in the industrial solution. Paradoxically, the peasant probably would have been as dissatisfied with the industrial solution to overpopulation as he was with overpopulation itself. Without the regimentation of the whole country, rapid industrialization probably would have generated as much social unrest as the prevailing "land hunger," in part because of the pattern of industrialization in countries which "arrived late." Instead of developing slowly from commerce and small crafts, industry in Eastern Europe rapidly assumed the Western form of large cartelized undertakings.[17] The fact that the West had already reached a high level of

[15] *Ibid.*, chap. XVII.
[16] Moore, p. 118.
[17] "To the extent that industrialization took place, it was largely by application of the most modern and efficient techniques that backward countries could hope to achieve success, particularly if their industrialization proceeded in the face of competition from the advanced country. The advantages inherent in the use of technologically superior equipment were not counteracted but reinforced by its labor-saving effect. This seems to explain the tendency on the part of backward countries to concentrate at a relatively early point of their industrialization on promotion of those branches of industrial activities

industrial development made it difficult, perhaps even impossible, for the East European countries to pursue the same path. Actually, there was very little reason to assume that they would do so; Russia, and to some degree Germany and France, had already deviated widely from the British pattern.

In Imperial Russia, for example, economic development had followed a pattern very similar to that which later occurred in Eastern Europe. In the first place, the state, for military reasons, initiated the trend toward industrial development.[18] Secondly, those industries were developed most which involved the heaviest capital outlay and which depended on the most advanced technology of the West.[19] The result was that the high cost of industrialization had to be met by both foreign loans and increased taxation at home. Finally, the advantages of industrialization—a rising standard of living and a higher real income—were passed along more slowly to the general population than they would have been if the English pattern of industrial development had been followed.

Therefore, even the industrial solution to the agrarian question involved tendencies toward social and political instability. In spite of some inherent advantages in "starting late," the disadvantages weighed heavily in the balance. In order to develop native industries it was necessary to set heavy protective tariffs, which boosted the prices of consumer goods to fantastic levels. Although advantages of scale and "borrowed technology" existed for some industries, extremely heavy capital outlay was required to profit from these advantages, an outlay which could ordinarily be met only by state control of industry, by mortgaging part of the nation's resources to foreign investors, and by imposing heavy taxes on the already indigent peasant class. Last, although industrialization required the beneficial transfer of part of the population from the country to the city, the displacement process invariably led to another kind of social unrest. If advantages of scale were employed, cities became large

---

in which recent technological progress had been particularly rapid." Alexander Gerschenkron, *Economic Backwardness in Historical Perspective* (Cambridge, Mass., 1962), p. 9.

[18] *Ibid.*, p. 17.
[19] *Ibid.*, pp. 9–10.

agglomerations of ill-fed, ill-housed, poorly paid, semiskilled laborers. This was most fertile soil for Communist agitation.

These are some of the reasons why no country in Eastern Europe dared to embark on a large-scale industrialization program during the decade after World War I. Rather, all East European governments and even the Soviet government, toyed to a greater or lesser degree with the agrarian or peasantist course of development.[20] Consequently there is little evidence that the growth of industry was rapid enough during the 1920s in Eastern Europe to lead to an intensification of agricultural production, to absorb the excess labor force in agriculture, to provide agriculture with improved equipment, or to lead to the creation of agricultural industries. Although industry did grow quite rapidly in some areas, notably Warsaw, Łódź, Lwów, Kraków,

Table 6

Index of Manufacturing Production, 1920–1930

(Base: 1913 = 100)

Year	USSR	Poland	Czechoslovakia	Rumania	Hungary
1920	12.8	35.1	69.8		
1921	23.3	46.8	100.0	47.2	64.0
1922	28.9	73.9	91.8	73.2	60.0
1923	35.4	71.2	96.7	73.2	56.6
1924	47.5	56.8	129.0	89.0	66.6
1925	70.2	63.1	136.4	92.0	76.7
1926	100.3	58.9	130.4	103.7	83.4
1927	114.5	76.1	153.8	118.8	98.7
1928	143.5	86.1	166.0	131.8	108.0
1929	181.4	85.9	171.8	136.9	113.9
1930	235.5	75.8	155.5	132.5	108.1

Source: *Industrialization and Foreign Trade* (Geneva, 1945), pp. 136–37.
[a] The figures for the USSR are based on official Soviet statistics and therefore are subject to question. For an outline of the problems involved in the use of Soviet statistics of industrial production see Donald R. Hodgman, *Soviet Industrial Production 1928–1951* (Cambridge, Mass., 1954), chap. I.

---

[20] In the case of the Soviet leaders it is, of course, necessary to differentiate between immediate goals and long-range objectives. All factions in the Russian Communist Party believed that intensive industrial development was necessary, but the faction led by Bukharin believed that a prosperous peasantry would have to be developed through concessions to this class as part and parcel of industrialization or at least during its early stages. See Alexander Erlich, *The Soviet Industrialization Debate, 1924–1928* (Cambridge, Mass., 1960), pp. 8–23 and chap. IV.

the western provinces of Czechoslovakia, the Budapest region in Hungary, Zagreb and Belgrade in Yugoslavia, Ploesti in Rumania, and Sofia in Bulgaria, the results were not sufficient to change substantially the peasants' circumstances (see Table 6).

With chronic land hunger in the countryside, with a large body of dissatisfied and disillusioned peasants, Eastern Europe probably seemed easy prey to the Communists. Why shouldn't the tactics which the Bolsheviks had used so successfully in October, 1917, be applied in Eastern Europe to win peasant support for a Communist revolution? To a Marxist, an economic determinist, the differences between Eastern Europe in the 1920s and Russia in 1917 may have seemed slight, but there were significant political differences which hindered the Communists in applying the "lessons" of the Bolshevik Revolution.

SOCIAL AND POLITICAL TENSIONS

No exhaustive analysis of the social and political problems of underdeveloped countries is possible within a brief chapter. Since World War II, a number of excellent and detailed studies have been devoted to the subject.[21] Classification, terminology, and approaches have been developed and the study of peasant societies in transition is rapidly becoming a discipline in its own right.[22] Similarly, the psychological appeals of communism have been sorted out and analyzed on the basis of careful case studies.[23] These new conceptual tools have been used, at least on one occasion, to elucidate the political history of Eastern Europe during the interwar period.[24] All that I can do here is

---

[21] See the notes in John H. Kautsky's essay on the subject in his *Political Change.*

[22] See in particular Gabriel A. Almond and James S. Coleman, eds., *The Politics of Developing Areas* (Princeton, 1960).

[23] See in particular Gabriel A. Almond, *The Appeals of Communism* (Princeton, 1954). Ulam deals with the psychological appeals of communism in backward countries in a general way in *The Unfinished Revolution.*

[24] See Burks, *The Dynamics of Communism.* Burks obviously owes a great deal to the books cited in nn. 22 and 23. Hugh Seton-Watson deals with the appeals of communism in a less clinical manner in his essay "The Intellectuals and Revolution: Social Forces in Eastern Europe since 1848," in R. Pares and A. J. P. Taylor, eds., *Essays Presented to Sir Lewis Namier* (London, 1956), and in his book *Neither War nor Peace* (New York, 1960). The latter, though concerned with the appeals of communism in all underdeveloped countries, draws on the findings of sociology and political science to make some provocative judgments about East European politics.

briefly to suggest those new approaches which are most relevant to the present study.

The combined characteristics which make a society modern, and in most cases politically stable, have been described as a "comparatively high degree of urbanization, widespread literacy, a comparatively high per capita income, extensive geographic and social mobility, a relatively high degree of commercialization and industrialization of the economy, and an extensive and penetrating network of mass communication media, and, in general, widespread participation and involvement by members of society in modern social and economic processes." [25] All these factors may be present in the urban centers in a peasant society in transition, but the remainder of the country is deficient in all or some of them. It is, in fact, the increasing divergence between town and country which accounts to a large degree for the instability of a peasant society in transition. Modernization, as defined above, proceeds at such a fast pace in the cities that there is a tendency toward rural-urban polarization. Active participation in politics tends to become the special prerogative of the urbanized sector of society. Politics reflects the interests of this group and becomes its monopoly, even where peasant problems are a subject of political debate. With a growing sense of alienation from national politics the village reverts to older loyalties with a new fervor, whether they be tribal, racial, linguistic, religious, or communal. The wide gap betwen city and country tends, under a system of democratic institutions, to be reflected in the burgeoning of parties led by urban intellectuals but claiming to represent the narrow sectional interests of a small group of constituents. Politics becomes not a competition among parties which accept the primacy of the national interest but a bitter, unrestrained struggle for personal influence in which advocacy of sectional interests is only a means of power.

In a democracy the sheer weight of numbers of the peasantry is a drawback in the modernization of society. The peasants use the ballot to drag society backward, to obstruct any change which might affect their own immediate and local interests as they see them. In a traditional agrarian society, of course, the peasant is politically inert, expressing his needs in sporadic and ineffectual mass uprisings. His

25 Almond and Coleman, p. 532.

point of view is necessarily parochial because of the very nature of his life. It is because he is a peasant and not a farmer that his outlook is so constricted. A peasant may be differentiated from a farmer in the following way: "A peasant may be defined as a person for whom agriculture is a livelihood and a way of life, not a business for profit; whereas farmers carry on agriculture for re-investment and business, looking on land as capital and a commodity." [26] It is precisely because of his sentimental attachment both to the land and to a way of life, an attachment reinforced by tradition, that a peasant is essentially conservative. His social relationships remain localized and personal, and his relationships with the outer world are usually through administrative or cultural intermediaries drawn from the intelligentsia or gentry.[27] Because peasant communities are not ordinarily self-sufficient and usually exist in a state of interdependence with gentry or townspeople, anthropologists call them "part societies." [28] When peasants can vote, however, they bring their ignorance and irresponsibility into the political process, encouraging demagoguery. They tend to be a corrupting influence because they willingly throw the weight of their votes behind any party which makes extravagant verbal concessions to their private sectional interests, crowning, therefore, what may be the most extreme form of irresponsible political behavior with electoral success.

In the modernized countries of the West the pernicious influence of parochialism was leavened by the multiplicity of politically influential interest groups and by a pervasive consensus on the national interest, a consensus made possible by universal literacy and mass communication. But in the peasant societies of Eastern Europe the social structure was bottom heavy, consisting of a huge base of peasants topped by a thin crust of urbanized intellectuals and, where they survived, aristocrats. The urbanized, westernized elite was, in most cases, centuries apart from the peasants at the bottom. The intelligentsia were by far the most critical group. The intelligentsia may be defined as that narrow elite of educated men whose professions involve contact with both the village and the city. Hugh Seton-Watson

---

[26] Robert Redfield, *Peasant Society and Culture* (Chicago, 1956), p. 27.
[27] *Ibid.*, p. 61.
[28] *Ibid.*, p. 37.

suggests that the intelligentsia should not be confused with the bureaucracy and defines the intelligentsia more narrowly as those people who "received a modern secular education, but who were not government officials." [29] The gulf between the intelligentsia and the masses gave the former a feeling of acute social consciousness and frustration.[30] Caught between the opposition to change of the corrupt and inefficient bureaucracy, on the one hand, and, their own humane desire to lift the peasant out of his poverty and apparent passivity, on the other, the intelligentsia were often drawn to the most radical and doctrinaire social philosophies of East and West. Confronted with the resistance of both the government and the peasant to the radical changes which they deemed most necessary to national rejuvenation, some members of the intelligentsia were drawn to revolutionary means as well as revolutionary ends. For all these reasons this class usually provided the hard core of theorists and leaders of the radical revolutionary parties of Eastern Europe.[31]

This is not, of course, to say that the intelligentsia retain their homogeneity as the peasant society, consciously or unconsciously, begins to imitate the Western world. During this period of forced change the ranks of the intelligentsia become swollen with the type of intellectual who is most alienated from his society and most susceptible to the tendencies described above. This is the "quasi-intelligentsia," a group of "people who are not really intellectuals with a genuine interest in ideas, but who are merely seeking social status by taking on the appearance of education and intellectuality." [32] While this category

[29] Seton-Watson in Pares and Taylor, p. 398. In his earlier study of Eastern Europe printed in 1946 Seton-Watson did not stress the separate role of the intelligentsia and the bureaucracy, whereas in the essay cited here this stress is a central part of the conceptual framework. He remarks that his present definition of class includes "social groups which have a social and political significance of their own" apart from the Marxian categories which are determined by the relationship of a social group to production. *Ibid.*, p. 397, n. 1.

[30] *Ibid.*, pp. 413–14. In his more recent book, *Neither War nor Peace*, Hugh Seton-Watson described the role of the intelligentsia as a revolutionary force in all the backward countries of the world.

[31] See, for example, Burks's comments on the leading cadres of interwar Communist parties in Eastern Europe. Burks, pp. 36–37, 186, 191.

[32] Robert V. Daniels, "Intellectuals and the Russian Revolution," *American Slavic and East European Review*, XX, No. 2 (April, 1961), 271. I am indebted to Daniels for this distinction between the intelligentsia of a static

is not unknown in the West, it is a far more cohesive and influential group in peasant societies in transition, where it is more likely to produce ready recruits for militant communism than any other social category.

Increased contact with the Western world also enlarged the narrow stratum of bureaucracy at the top of the social ladder. In the absence of an informed and responsible electorate the educated bureaucracy rarely functioned in an enlightened manner, and public office was usually regarded as the proper means for achieving personal prosperity.[33] The bureaucracy also imbibed a highly chauvinistic nationalism at the universities of Eastern Europe in the 1920s. All of these factors made the bureaucracy incapable of governing in an efficient and responsible manner during this decade.[34]

The political tensions in a peasant society are probably heightened by the absence of a strong indigenous middle class.[35] The task of defeating the traditional aristocracy and breaking the bonds of custom and tradition had to be assumed by the intelligentsia, although this group lacked both the economic and the numerical strength to achieve it. Where the urban classes, in particular the middle classes and the industrial working class, were most highly developed, as in the Czech lands, the political process sems to have run more smoothly and more interest groups were taken into account.

In addition to economic grievances, which tended to alienate the peasants from the state, and political frustrations, which tended to alienate some members of the intelligentsia from the state, there was a third disruptive force, nationalism. John Kautsky warns against the dangers in using the term "nationalism" indiscriminately when referring to underdeveloped countries.[36] In countries where economic

---

society and that of a backward society coming under Western influence. For other approaches to the study of the Russian intelligentsia see Richard Pipes, ed., *The Russian Intelligentsia* (New York, 1961). Burks points out that in the East European Communist parties men born of peasant or worker origin often used the professional talents acquired in the revolutionary movement to rise into middle-class status. Burks, p. 37.

[33] As Hugh Seton-Watson put it, "In Eastern Europe the greatest fortunes are made, not in industry or banking, but in politics." Seton-Watson, *Eastern Europe*, p. 148.

[34] *Ibid.*, pp. 141–46.

[35] See "An Essay in the Politics of Development," in Kautsky, pp. 27–28.

[36] *Ibid.*, pp. 33 ff.

and political integration has been achieved as part of the modernizing process, nationalism tends to be a cohesive force inspiring most citizens to be loyal to the state. In underdeveloped countries or provinces where political and economic integration still lies in the distant future, nationalism is a divisive force threatening to create, where none existed before, new states based on older linguistic, ethnic, or tribal communities (for the natural linguistic divisions of Eastern Europe see Table 7). Relying, as it does, on familiar and obvious symbols to command local allegiances, nationalism tends to absorb all dissatisfactions in a given backward society and becomes the chief form of opposition to the state. Even the desire on the part of the intelligentsia to modernize and industrialize the state may be understood as a manifestation of virulent nationalism.[37] It is difficult, however, to measure the relative drawing power of the Comintern's anti-state nationalism compared to its agrarian program in Eastern Europe because they cannot be separated. Where the Communists won the most peasant support, as in eastern Czechoslovakia and eastern Poland, there were intense economic and minority grievances. But there is no question that among the peasants of Eastern Europe anti-state nationalism was an effective weapon in the hands of international communism, perhaps its most effective weapon.[38]

[37] This is one of the major arguments of Kautsky. *Ibid.,* pp. 46 ff.

[38] It seems to me that there has been too much easy generalizing about the impact of the Comintern's antistate nationalism. The latest orthodoxy, evident in the works of Burks and Kautsky cited above, is that antistate nationalism is the most attractive feature of communism to peasants belonging to national minorities in underdeveloped countries. This is too simple, and even Burks, who, in general, accepts this thesis, demonstrates that in Eastern Europe some alienated national minorities were not drawn to communism and some peasants belonging to the dominant or state nationalities were. Burks, pp. 54–72, 131–49. The task of isolating and measuring the appeal of the Comintern agrarian program to East European peasants by itself is made almost impossible by the fact that it was always advanced in conjunction with the Comintern program on the national question. As indicated in the text above and confirmed by Burks's figures, however, communism won its greatest victories in those areas where both a large number of peasants belonging to national minorities and conditions of economic underdevelopment prevailed. *Ibid.,* pp. 65–72, 74–78. This suggests that in backward areas inhabited by national minorities the two programs reinforced one another, while in all areas inhabited by peasants belonging to the dominant or state nationality they probably canceled one another out because most of the peasants who might be drawn to the Comintern agrarian program were probably repelled by the Comintern program on the national question. Burks suggests, on the basis of fragmentary and rather

Table 7

Distribution of Principal Languages in Eastern Europe about 1930
(approximate figures in thousands)

Languages	Bulgaria	Czecho-slovakia	Poland	Rumania	Yugoslavia
Russian	12		139	451	25
Ukrainian		569	4,442	641	31
White Russian			1,697		
Polish		100	21,993	38	18
Czechoslovakian		9,757	38	43	138
Serbo-Croatian		6		48	10,257
Slovene					1,159
Bulgarian	5,275			364	73
German	4	3,318	741	761	602
Rumanian	16	14		13,181	276
Greek	10			21	
Albanian				4	524
Gypsy	81	33		101	54
Hungarian		720		1,555	557
Turkish	622			288	180
Others [a]	58	213	2,866	561	41
Total	6,078	14,730	31,916	18,057	13,935

Source: Geza Teleki, "Industrial and Social Policies Between the Wars," in C. E. Black, ed., *Challenge in Eastern Europe* (New Brunswick, 1954), p. 144.

[a] Others include primarily Yiddish, especially in Poland.

All three of the divisive forces described above were exploited by the Bolsheviks in the Russian Revolution. But Eastern Europe in the 1920s was not prerevolutionary Russia. Were the differences great enough to thwart the Bolsheviks in their attempts to apply the "lessons" of the Bolshevik Revolution in Eastern Europe? On the surface it would seem that Imperial Russia should have had a greater resistance to Bolshevism than post World War I Eastern Europe. No East European state had the size, the variety of resources, the support of centuries of tradition which Tsarist Russia had possessed. No East European state had the established and functioning administrative

---

inconclusive statistics, that communism had little appeal for landless peasants and those with dwarf holdings, but considerable appeal for cash croppers and tobacco workers. For the two isolated and disparate cases which he presents to support his case, Bulgaria in 1923 and Slovakia in 1928, he is persuasive, but I doubt very much that these propositions would hold for other times and places in Eastern Europe. *Ibid.,* pp. 42, 54–57, 74–76. These questions are treated in greater detail in Part III below.

and military system of Tsarist Russia. It had taken a long and un-successful war to intensify and accentuate Russia's dilemma of back-wardness and make her vulnerable to Bolshevik tactics.

Fortunately for them, the new states in Eastern Europe were created as the pressures of war were receding. Precisely because these new states did not rest on long-established tradition they were strong. It was possible to have faith in them because they were as yet untried. They had not yet tested their strength against the problems of "peasant societies in transition," the problems of ethnic minorities, the prob-lems of survival in a fiercely competing world of stronger nation states. In Eastern Europe after World War I, with the possible ex-ception of Bulgaria, there was no accumulation of grievances against the established government. In fact, in most of these countries the majority of the population regarded statehood as the fulfillment of the historic destiny of their ethnic group. Party differences were tem-porarily subordinated to the joyous task of giving institutional form to the national dream. Peasant parties, having been suddenly thrust to the pinnacle of power by the new electoral laws, professed their devotion to democracy, anti-Bolshevism, and significant social and economic reforms.

Postwar agrarian reforms created, at least for the time being, the illusion that something was being done for the peasant, a conviction that was not widespread in Stolypin's Russia. Above all, in Eastern Europe after World War I there was a means of registering dissatis-faction with the policies of the new governments. These governments showed few signs at first of adopting the insufferable methods of the police state. It seemed possible in 1919 that Eastern Europe would be able to solve its problems in the parliamentary arena rather than on the barricades. In short, in each country there was a postindependence "honeymoon" in which the disruptive forces were in abeyance.[39] But, like all honeymoons, it had to end.

The strength of the new democracies in 1919 was, to a large degree, based on short-run factors. Once the enthusiasm of "liberation" and the novelty of statehood had worn off, the new democratic institu-tions would have to prove their mettle in the battle against poverty

[39] Coleman observes that the act of making a state tends to strengthen, at least temporarily, the forces of stability. Almond and Coleman, p. 550.

and ignorance, a battle which, in Eastern Europe, had to be fought against heavy odds. This battle was accompanied by a second conflict, the conflict between the agrarians, who hoped to solve these problems by existing means, and the Communists, who hoped to solve them by revolutionary means, using the "lessons" of the Bolshevik Revolution. That second conflict is the subject of this study.

CHAPTER II

The Opposing Camps

To the peasant in Eastern Europe it may have seemed that there was little real difference between the Communist and agrarian parties. Both claimed to have the best interests of the peasant at heart. Both wanted to organize the peasant in defense of his own local and immediate interests and both promised him more land. But there were some major differences between the agitational practices of the two movements. The Communists told the peasant that ultimately his needs could be satisfied only in alliance with the industrial workers in a proletarian revolution. The peasant parties, in most cases, told the peasant that his needs could be satisfied chiefly by solidarity with fellow peasants and by democratic political action. Furthermore, the East European Communist parties suffered from their own doctrinal hostility toward work among the peasantry, from a reputation as representatives of urban interests, and from a growing belief that Communists were agents of a foreign power, the Soviet Union. By way of contrast, most peasant parties were in the beginning firmly established as representatives of rural interests, all of them had a rural organization and a tradition of rural agitation behind them, and they were regarded as representatives of their own nation or nationality.

At the ideological level, of course, the two movements were far apart in their world view and ultimate objectives. Few peasants, however, were really aware of the ideological arguments of either side except where those arguments filtered into party propaganda. In the following analysis I will discuss both the ideological and the agitational aspects of the two movements. However, the tactical front of the international Communist movement was necessarily more uniform and apparent than that of the peasant movement because the former increasingly emanated from a single source, Moscow. There was far more diversity in both ideology and political practice in the peasant political movement even after the founding of the Green International in Prague because it was never centrally directed. In Part III I will deal more specifically with the strategy of individual movements and attempt to weigh the effectiveness of their political activity on the basis of electoral statistics and records of party membership.

LENIN AND COMINTERN AGRARIAN POLICY

The international Communist movement received its basic directives on the agrarian question on August 4, 1920, in the Theses on the Agrarian Question which were adopted by the Second Congress of the Communist International. The preliminary draft of the theses was written by Lenin and was edited by the Agrarian Commission of the Congress before being submitted to the whole body. The changes in the preliminary draft were, in most cases, slight and the international Communist movement was, to a large degree, directed to follow the example of the Russian movement. It is not surprising that one delegate, Serrati of Italy, should find that the agrarian theses did not reflect the needs of the revolution in the West.[1] Serrati stated that the resolutions ignored the real aspirations of the peasantry in Western Europe, which were for protection, against industrialization, and for administrative autonomy.[2] In reply, the chairman pro tempore of the commission on the agrarian question, Ernst Meyer of Germany, affirmed his belief that the directives would bring Communists victory in the social revolution of the countryside, "especially in Central and Eastern Europe."[3] Both were right. Based as they were on the Russian experience, the agrarian theses were likely to bring success, but only in Central and Eastern Europe.

Lenin's program for capturing rural revolutions undoubtedly made orthodox Marxists wince, not only because he relied so heavily on his own experience, but also because he violated some of Marx's canons. Yet Lenin made an ambitious effort to cram his theories into the orthodox mold. Marx had predicted that all societies would pass more or less through the three major social, economic, and political stages of

[1] *Vtoroi kongress Kommunisticheskogo Internatsionala—stenograficheskii otchet* (Moscow, 1921), p. 460.
[2] *Ibid.*, p. 461.
[3] *Ibid.*, p. 452.

development which he found in the history of Western Europe, the ancient, the feudal, and the bourgeois stages.[4] Thus the industrial and agricultural revolutions with all their attendant social injustices would probably have to run their course until the proper conditions were established for the last and final stage, the proletarian revolution. Toward the end of his life Marx intimated that there might be other paths to socialism, but he never fully spelled them out.[5]

While Marx had never seriously studied the peasantry in any one country,[6] he subscribed to the idea common to most agricultural economists in the nineteenth century of the innate superiority and ultimate predominance of large-scale units in agriculture as well as industry.[7] In other words, Marx states that the peasant economy would always be gradually replaced by large-scale holdings which would be socialized with the coming of the proletarian revolution. In Marx's writing there is even an emotional antipathy to the peasant as the symbol of everything he considered stupid, parochial, and inefficient in the old order.[8] In the congresses of the First International the right of the small peasants to land was stoutly defended by the Proudhonist delegations.[9] At the Third Congress of the First International at Brussels a program was adopted calling for the abolition of private property in the event of a proletarian revolution and the establishment of some form of collective ownership of agricultural land. At the Fourth Congress in Basel in 1869 this program was reaffirmed,

---

[4] Karl A. Wittfogel, in *Oriental Despotism: A Comparative Study of Total Power* (New Haven, 1957), pp. 372–77, advances the thesis that Marx also conceived a fourth category, the Asiatic mode of production. Wittfogel argues that the existence of this fourth category in Marx's writings has been systematically suppressed in the Soviet Union because of the embarrassing resemblance between this type and the Soviet political, social, and economic system.

[5] For some of the sources on this question see the bibliography, pp. 311–12.

[6] Marx did intend to study Russian forms of land tenure in detail, but this project never went beyond the collection of some statistics. *Perepiska K. Marksa i F. Engel'sa s russkimi politicheskimi deiateliami* (Moscow, 1951), p. 87.

[7] David Mitrany, *Marx Against the Peasant: A Study in Social Dogmatism* (Chapel Hill, 1951), pp. 7, 14.

[8] *Ibid.*, p. 25.

[9] *Ibid.*, p. 16. For a detailed analysis of this conflict see I. A. Bakh, "Marks i agrarnyi vopros v I Internatsionale," *Voprosy istorii*, No. 5 (May, 1958), pp. 63–82. The latter is a short survey using some unpublished material from the Central Party archives of the Institute of Marxism-Leninism.

but it was conceded that the owner of small property might continue to use it without rent during his lifetime.

When the pattern of development in agriculture which Marx predicted did not materialize, the traditional indifference of orthodox Marxists to the peasant was called into question, especially in the revisionist controversy of the 1890s. There is little doubt that this debate had a profound influence on the development of Lenin's views on the agrarian question.[10] Lenin's idol, the German Social Democratic leader, Karl Kautsky, defined his position in 1898 in a book called *The Agrarian Question.* Although he affirmed his faith in Marx's predictions, Kautsky said that Marxists could not afford to ignore the peasantry, which could be very useful in a proletarian revolution. In the short run, the rural proletariat should be strengthened through support of its immediate demands. When the revolution came peasants would certainly have to be persuaded either to fight side by side with the proletariat or to remain neutral.[11] In the long run, of course, with the victory of the proletarian revolution the peasant way of life was doomed, but agricultural production would have to be socialized by persuasion, not force. The small peasant might keep his land during his lifetime if he joined in the new partnership between industry and agriculture.

Lenin's position is not easy to ascertain because there is no internal rational consistency in Lenin's agrarian program throughout the body of his work. It is difficult to disentangle the tactical and temporary in Lenin's program from his ultimate goals. Considering Lenin's consuming absorption with the act of revolution itself, it was, perhaps, inevitable that tactical and ultimate goals would tend to merge. Although Lenin always accepted the pattern for the development of agriculture prescribed by Marx as both inevitable and desirable, Lenin's tactical position in 1917 with regard to the peasantry called for the redistribution of large estates among the surrounding peasants and ran directly counter to his avowed Marxist goals. Redistribution seemed to strengthen the small-scale unit of production and encourage the whole backward peasant way of life.

[10] On this question and the sources used in this treatment of Lenin's agrarian program see the bibliography, pp. 312–13.

[11] Peter Gay, *The Dilemma of Democratic Socialism* (New York, 1952), pp. 192–93.

In Leninism, however, the successful seizure of power is the primary task. Somehow the ultimate objectives will take care of themselves. In trying to find a role for a Marxist party in an economically backward country, Lenin was confronted with the fact that the army of the Marxist party, the industrial proletariat, was a relatively small group in Russian society. In other respects—the degree of industrial development, the persistence of semifeudal obligations, the persistence of primitive modes of cultivation—it seemed as though Russia had not yet reached that stage of economic development where a Marxist party could prepare for a socialist revolution as an immediate task. In point of fact, according to Lenin, Russia had not passed completely through the feudal stage of development; for this reason, the strategy of a Marxist party in Russia (or any backward country) was essentially different from that in the West.

It is the distinction between the bourgeois-democratic, or first, revolution and the proletarian, or second, revolution which lies at the heart of the agrarian tactics Lenin devised in his early writings. It was necessary for a Marxist party to use a different set of tactics in relation to the peasantry in the two revolutions. The task of the first revolution was also entirely different, namely, to destroy the vestiges of feudalism and clear the path for the development of capitalism. The task of the second revolution was to destroy capitalist society by wresting political power from the hands of the bourgeoisie.

Since the active role of a Marxist party could be played only after the first revolution had taken place, the Marxists must support all those movements dedicated to this revolution. Thus, not only all bourgeois revolutionary movements but also all peasant revolutionary movements deserved Marxist support. This meant also that for the time being the strategy of Russian Social Democrats would be considerably different from that of the Marxists in the West. As early as 1899 Lenin wrote:

The peasant question in Russia differs substantially from the peasant question in the West, but it differs only in that the question in the West is almost exclusively one of the peasant in capitalist bourgeois society. In Russia the question is chiefly one of peasants who suffer no less (if not more) from precapitalist institutions and relations, who suffer from vestiges of serfdom. The role of the peasantry fighting against absolutism and against the vestiges of serfdom has already been played in the West, but not yet in Russia. . . . Therefore, the Russian Social Democrat, even if he is among those who (like the writer of these lines) is decisively opposed to the preservation or support of small property or small holdings in capitalist society, that is, even if on the agrarian question he stands on the side of those Marxists who (like the writer of these lines) are cursed by the bourgeoisie and opportunists as dogmatists and purists, without changing his convictions in the slightest, but rather because of those convictions, he can and must insist that the working class party inscribe on its banner, "Support the peasantry." We must support the peasantry (not by any means as a class of small proprietors or small farmers) *in so far as the peasantry is capable of a revolutionary struggle against the vestiges of serfdom and against absolutism in particular.*[12]

Although Lenin was clearly aware of the usefulness of the peasant in the so-called bourgeois-democratic revolution, it took the revolution of 1905 to convince him that the peasant might be won over to the second, or socialist, revolution and that the two revolutions might be condensed or telescoped into one.[13]

How could Lenin find a means for winning the peasantry which was acceptable to orthodox Marxists? The desire of the peasant to enlarge his plot and receive guarantees of this property was in Marxist terms the most reactionary feature of the peasant's personality. In 1902 Lenin wrote:

Generally speaking, support of small-scale property is reactionary, for it is directed against the large-scale capitalist economy and consequently retards social development and obscures and glosses over the class struggle. In this case [the Russian], however, we want to support small-scale property, not against capitalism, but against serfdom. In this case we make this last attempt to fan the dying embers of the class (stratum) enmity of the peasants toward the serf-owning landlords. On the other hand, we clear the path for the development of bourgeois class antagonism in the country, for this antagonism is now concealed by the general and equal oppression of all peasants by the vestiges of serfdom.[14]

---

[12] V. I. Lenin, "Proekt programmy nashei partii," *Sochineniia* (4th ed.; Moscow, 1941–50), IV, 221–22.

[13] Today Soviet historians, of course, go to the opposite extreme and maintain that Lenin's agrarian program in 1917 is implicit *in toto* in his earliest writings. For example, see N. V. Alekseeva, "Ideia soiuza rabochego klassa i krest'ianstva v rannikh proizvedeniiakh V. I. Lenina," *Voprosy istorii*, No. 2 (Feb., 1959). The most balanced analysis of Lenin's agrarian program I have encountered is Alfred G. Meyer, *Leninism* (Cambridge, Mass., 1957), pp. 123–44.

[14] Lenin, "Agrarnaia programma russkoi sotsial-demokratii," *Sochineniia*, VI, 114.

Essentially this meant that the agrarian phase of the revisionist controversy, which was exclusively concerned with the struggle between the large capitalist farm and the small peasant plot, did not apply to the Russian case, where the struggle between the peasantry and the former self-owning landlord had not yet been resolved.

In the throes of the revolution of 1905 Lenin indicated that Marxist support for the peasants' struggle against vestiges of serfdom had to end before the peasant achieved his objectives.

We must help the peasant uprising in every way up to and including the confiscation of land, *but certainly not including all sorts of petty-bourgeois projects*. We will support the peasant movement as long as it is still revolutionary-democratic. We are prepared to fight against it as soon as it becomes reactionary and antiproletarian. *The whole essence of Marxism lies in this twofold task,* which can be vulgarized and compressed into a single and simple task only by those who don't understand Marxism.[15]

While Lenin warned against confusing the appropriate tactics for the different stages, he suggested that by a well-timed shift in tactics the bourgeois-democratic revolution might be transformed or "telescoped" into the proletarian.[16] While this tactical dictum was not unorthodox in itself, the pronouncement that the whole essence of Marxism lay in this course of action was. One has the uneasy feeling that there has been a radical shift in the focal point of the "ideology of the working class" when the measure of a Marxist is his policy toward the peasant.

In Lenin's preliminary draft of the agrarian theses of the Second Comintern Congress, his choice of the peasant as the chief ally of the proletariat was prescribed for all Communist parties, regardless of the level of economic development in their countries.

Industrial workers cannot fulfill their universal historical mission of liberating humanity from the yoke of capital and war if they shut themselves up within the circle of narrow craft trade union interests and limit their activities to improvement of their own fairly tolerable petty-bourgeois cir-

[15] Lenin, "Otnoshenie sotsial-demokratii k krest'ianskomu dvizheniiu," *Sochineniia*, IX, 212. The italics are mine.

[16] *Ibid.*, p. 213. Carr indicates that the idea that the Bolsheviks should complete the bourgeois-democratic revolution was first fully formulated in Lenin's *Two Tactics of Social Democracy* in the summer of 1905 and that in the article cited above Lenin for the first and last time used the phrase "uninterrupted revolution" to describe the process. E. H. Carr, *The Bolshevik Revolution, 1917–1923* (New York, 1950–53), I, 56.

cumstances. . . . The proletariat is a truly revolutionary and socialist class only when it steps forward and acts as the vanguard of all working and exploited people, as their leader in the struggle for the overthrow of their exploiters. This cannot be achieved without the introduction of the class struggle in rural areas, without the unification of the toiling masses of the countryside around the Communist party of the urban proletariat, without the training of the former by the latter.[17]

Why should the peasant support a proletarian revolution or even listen to Communist agitators? The first sentence of Lenin's preliminary draft gives the answer, and the Bolshevik land decree is undoubtedly the example intended to support the argument: "Only the urban and industrial proletariat, led by the Communist party, can save the toiling masses of the countryside from the yoke of capitalism and from the big landowners, from economic devastation and from imperialistic war, which is inevitable again and again so long as the capitalist structure survives." [18] But, of course, not all peasants would listen to this appeal to reason. Again the distinction between the bourgeois-democratic and the socialist revolution becomes vital.

According to Lenin's prerevolutionary writings, where he had Russia in mind, up to the bourgeois-democratic revolution the peasants fought as a class "not of capitalist society but of serf society, that is, a class-estate." [19] After this revolution they separated into different socioeconomic categories or strata (*sosloviia*),[20] based on the size of their holdings. This meant that at the capitalistic stage of development after the first revolution the peasantry ceased to be a class and became a composite of groups which might or might not affiliate with one or the other of the orthodox Marxist classes.[21] At the outset of the socialist revolution the interests of the poor peasant coincided with those of the proletariat, the middle peasant might be won over at

[17] Lenin, "Pervonachal'nyi nabrosok tezisov po agrarnomu voprosu," *Sochineniia*, XXXI, 129–30.

[18] *Ibid.*, p. 129.

[19] Lenin, "Agrarnaia programma russkoi sotsial-demokratii," *Sochineniia*, VI, 97.

[20] The translation of this term poses somewhat of a problem. It is usually translated "estate," but in this case, taking into account the fact that the peasant is normally considered part of the third estate, this translation seems inappropriate and misleading.

[21] This idea is not original with Lenin. Plekhanov and even Engels had used this approach on occasion. Bakh, *Voprosy istorii*, No. 5 (May, 1958), pp. 79–80.

least to neutrality by playing on his "hunger for land," while the interests of the rich or large-scale peasant would always coincide with those of the middle class opposing the second revolution.[22]

In Lenin's actual handling of events, however, he seized power during the bourgeois-democratic revolution in 1917 before it had run its course and then tried within a year (virtually combining the two revolutions) to pass to the tactics reserved for the socialist revolution.[23] At first, in order to succeed, he had to support such bourgeois measures as "nationalization" and "redistribution." Then, in November, 1918 (during War Communism), he upheld the two lower categories of the peasantry and the rural proletariat against the kulak before these bourgeois measures could wholly corrupt the lower and middle peasant. This meant bridging the gap between the two revolutions and using the tactical advantages inherent in an economically backward country which had already been affected by capitalism, in a sense, skipping the stage of bourgeois capitalism. Lenin justified this step in his famous answer to Kautsky in October, 1918.

Things have turned out just as we said they would. The course taken by our revolution has confirmed the correctness of our reasoning. First with the "whole" of the peasantry against the monarchy, the landlords, the medieval regime (and to that extent the revolution remains bourgeois, bourgeois-democratic), then with the poorer peasants, with the semiproletarians, with all the exploited against capitalism, including the rural rich, the kulaks, the profiteers, and to that extent the revolution becomes a socialist one. To attempt to raise an artificial Chinese Wall between the one and the other, to separate them by anything other than the preparedness of the proletariat and the degree of its unity with the poor peasants, means to distort Marxism monstrously, to vulgarize it, to substitute liberalism in its place.[24]

22 Lenin, "Agrarnaia programma sotsial-demokratii v pervoi russkoi revoliutsii 1905–1907," *Sochineniia*, XIII, 204–8.

23 It must, of course, be pointed out that this does not mean that Lenin believed in the possibility of "socialism in one country," least of all in an economically backward country like Russia. Although Lenin intimated here and there in his works that this might be possible in Russia, he generally accepted the Marxist axiom that the socialist revolution could not be successful in an economically backward country like Russia without a socialist revolution in the economically advanced countries of Western Europe. The Russian Revolution was intended to provide the spark for the essential revolution in the West. Carr, I, 62.

24 Lenin, "Proletarskaia revoliutsiia i renegat Kautskii," *Sochineniia*, XXVIII, 276.

This kind of approach bears within it the odd implication that the socialist revolution may occur first in the economically backward countries which have already been drawn into the Western orbit before it occurs in the most advanced countries, what might be called a "dialectics of backwardness." [25] Such a backward country may duplicate the desired modern, Western way of life without duplicating the superstructure of Western property relations, that is, it may pass from economic backwardness to socialism without passing through capitalism. There are two reasons why this might be possible. First, there is intense pressure to catch up to the West, making a backward society more receptive to radical and revolutionary programs for change, like communism, rather than modest evolutionary programs.[26] Second, there is a combined development of class antagonisms that took place separately in the West. For example, in backward countries one finds not only the peasant arrayed against the feudal landlord but also the factory worker against both the feudal landlord and the factory owner, as well as the middle class against the nobility. This gives the revolutionary leader a tremendous variety of potential allies in comparison with the situation in more advanced industrial countries and it offers him a much wider range of tactics.

Yet in his preliminary draft of the agrarian theses Lenin made no clear distinction between tactics suitable for an advanced country and those suitable for a backward country. He prescribed Bolshevik agrarian tactics for all Communist parties. In the preliminary draft Lenin spelled out the respective roles of the various peasant strata more precisely, adding two more categories—the rural proletariat and the rural semiproletariat (a peasant who combines wage labor with farming his plot)—to the small peasant (a peasant with a plot large enough to keep him at the subsistence level).[27] These three categories, argued Lenin, constituted the majority of the population in rural

[25] I have borrowed the phrase "dialectics of backwardness" from Alfred Meyer. Meyer points out that, while Lenin never explicitly converts Marxism into a dialectics of backwardness, such a conversion is increasingly implicit in Lenin's writings before 1917. Meyer, p. 264. See, for example, Lenin, "Imperializm kak vysshaia stadiia kapitalizma," *Sochineniia,* XXII, 183–84; Lenin, "Otstalaia Evropa i peredovaia Aziia," *Sochineniia,* XIX, 77–78.
[26] Meyer, p. 264.
[27] Lenin, *Sochineniia,* XXXI, 130–32. These sections were essentially unchanged in the final draft.

areas.[28] "They will stand on the side of the proletarian revolution. . . . Therefore the success of the proletarian revolution is fully ensured, not only in the city, but also in the countryside." [29] But Lenin warned that the experience of the Bolshevik Revolution demonstrated that these three categories "can give decisive support to the revolutionary proletariat only after they have settled accounts with the large scale capitalists and landlords, only after the oppressed people have seen by deeds that they have an organized leader and defender who is powerful and resolute enough to help them and lead them along the right path." [30]

With regard to the middle peasant, Lenin indicated in the preliminary draft that this group could only be neutralized during the socialist revolution, and that the "proletarian state power must bring about the transition to collectivized land only gradually and with enormous care, by force of example and without any coercion of the middle peasant." [31] The large-scale peasant was the adamant foe of socialists and the object of the class struggle in the countryside. Here, however, the proletarian state had to move cautiously: "The expropriation of even the large-scale peasants can in no way be the immediate task of the victorious proletariat because the material, in particular the technical, and therefore the social conditions for the socialization of such farms are absent." [32]

While the small and middle peasants were uncertain allies, having been tainted with the property urge, they could be used by the proletariat if the proper tactics were applied. The small peasant would be drawn to the Communists by promises of freedom from rent and mortgages, of stronger state support for the cooperative movement, and of immediate state assistance in the acquisition of agricultural machinery.[33] The middle peasant could be neutralized by the abolition of rent and debts, which would make an immediate improvement in his position.[34] Both groups would be promised the use of the land

[28] *Ibid.*, p. 132.
[29] *Ibid.*
[30] *Ibid.*, pp. 132–33.
[31] *Ibid.*, p. 134. This passage caused Stalin some difficulty during the First Five-Year Plan, when it was hurled at him by his opponents.
[32] *Ibid.*, p. 135.
[33] *Ibid.*, p. 131.
[34] *Ibid.*, p. 134.

they owned and the land they previously rented.[35] The land of the large-scale landowners would be immediately confiscated without compensation.

But for the conjuring trick to work, one had to cast the spell with the forbidden words "redistribution of land." Lenin, by his own admission, took this step in the October Revolution and won over the peasantry by adopting the Social Revolutionary agrarian program without a single change.[36] When Lenin suggested in his preliminary draft of the agrarian theses that other Communist parties might follow his example, the Comintern balked. This was the one section of Lenin's draft which was subjected to major revision in the hands of the Agrarian Commission. Lenin's version read:

> Turning to the question of the means of managing lands confiscated by the victorious proletariat from the large landowners; in Russia, owing to its economic backwardness, the prevailing method was the distribution of this land among the peasantry for their own use, and only in comparatively rare cases were so-called soviet farms preserved, that is, farms which are operated by the proletarian state itself by converting the former wage laborers into state employees and into members of the soviets which administer the state. For the leading capitalist countries the Communist International recognizes as correct the preservation of the majority of large-scale agricultural enterprises and their operation along the lines of the soviet farms in Russia.
>
> However, it would be the greatest mistake to exaggerate this rule or make it a stereotyped pattern and never to permit the free distribution of part of the expropriated land to the surrounding small and sometimes even to the middle peasantry.[37]

On the question of redistribution Lenin could combine the positive example of the Russian Revolution with the negative example of the Hungarian Revolution into a seemingly unassailable argument for

[35] *Ibid.*

[36] Lenin, "Detskaia bolezn' levizny v kommunizme," *Sochineniia,* XXXI, 53–54. The Bolshevik land decree, following the principles of the Social Revolutionary agrarian program, called for the abolition of private property in land, but not for the confiscation of the peasants' existing holdings. The land held by the large estates would be distributed among those peasants who needed it on the basis of labor or use norms. For the Social Revolutionary model see Oliver H. Radkey, *The Agrarian Foes of Bolshevism: Promise and Default of the Russian Socialist Revolutionaries, February to October, 1917* (New York, 1958), pp. 25–28.

[37] Lenin, *Sochineniia,* XXXI, 136.

the infallibility of Bolshevik agrarian tactics. The primary reason for the failure of the Hungarian Soviet Republic, according to Lenin, was the failure of that regime to follow the Bolshevik example and distribute to the peasants part of the land confiscated by the state.[38]

The Comintern, however, resisted Lenin's efforts to generalize the tactic of redistribution. It was Julian Marchlewski, the appointed secretary of the Agrarian Commission of the Second Comintern Congress, who reasserted the importance of distinguishing between backward and advanced countries. Lenin's last paragraph was deleted and Marchlewski's version was substituted in its place; Lenin's sentence referring to the correctness of the preservation of large-scale agricultural units was retained as a separate paragraph and as a general rule. Marchlewski noted that this action gave the proletariat secure control over their own food supply, an argument which Lenin had not used. Lenin's description of his own departure from this general rule in Russia was kept, but it was not recommended for emulation. Marchlewski carefully restricted the application of Lenin's tactic of redistribution to economically backward countries.

> But, on the other hand, where survivals of a medieval point of view lead to a special form of exploitation, where servitudes or a system of semisubservience is preserved, it may prove necessary to transfer part of the large landed estates to the peasants.
> In those countries and areas where there are a large number of small property owners thirsting for land, the distribution of large landlord property is the best means for drawing the peasants to the side of the revolution, since the preservation of large households has no significance in supplying the city with produce.[39]

What is most striking in Lenin's preliminary draft are the gaps in logic. The preliminary draft is the bare sketch of Lenin's agrarian program in the October Revolution without its elaborate ideological underpinnings or subtle distinctions between what is suitable in highly developed industrialized countries and what is suitable for underdeveloped and disturbed agrarian societies. In the critical resolution on the question of land distribution, the distinction between

[38] David Cattel, "Soviet Russia and the Hungarian Revolution" (unpublished Master's thesis, Department of Public Law and Government, Columbia University, 1949), p. 107. See also Lenin's comments on the Hungarian Revolution at the Second Comintern Congress, *Vtoroi kongress*, pp. 292–93.
[39] S. Bobinskii, "K istorii agrarnykh tezisov II kongressa Kommunisticheskogo Internatsionala," *Na agrarnom fronte*, No. 1 (1928), p. 67.

advanced and backward countries had to be supplied by Marchlewski. Lenin does not speak, as he had in his earlier works on the agrarian question, of the two stages of revolution, of telescoping revolutions, of the dialectics of backwardness. He does not speak of the preparatory period, the suitable tactics for a Communist party in a nonrevolutionary situation. There was no cult of Leninism in 1920 and Lenin could not assume that Comintern members would be able to fill in the omissions from their own knowledge of his writings.

The sketchy and incomplete nature of the preliminary draft, which was adopted with few changes, was probably a result of several factors. First, the preliminary draft was intended to be a description of tactics, not a theoretical document. Brevity and incisiveness were, therefore, essential. Second, the vital distinction between advanced and backward countries probably seemed academic to Lenin at the very moment when the Red Army was pushing back the Polish invaders to the gates of Warsaw and setting up a provisional Polish soviet government in its wake.[40] All that seemed important at this time was the establishment of a new and highly disciplined international which would duplicate on a world scale the organizational structure and doctrines of the Russian party and be able to exploit the victories in Poland. For the same reason it probably seemed unnecessary to devise tactics on the agrarian question for Communists to follow in a nonrevolutionary situation. The situation was revolutionary and renewed optimism swept all other considerations before it.

Serrati's suggestion that Lenin was overly impressed by his own experience in the October Revolution and that the preliminary draft did not reflect the problems of revolution in the West was ignored.[41] The new forces lending stability to Eastern Europe were mentioned, but only to be discredited. Serrati spoke of the danger of peasant political parties. Meyer suggested that "the experiment of agrarian reforms in Eastern Europe has already been rendered insignificant by events in Russia." [42]

[40] For the mood of optimism engendered in Moscow by the victories of the Red Army in Poland see Carr, III, 187–96.
[41] V. Kolarov, "Predislovie—pervonachal'nyi nabrosok tezisov po agrarnomu voprosu Kommunisticheskogo Internatsionala," *Kommunisticheskii Internatsional,* No. 9 (46) (Sept., 1925), p. 7, and *Vtoroi kongress,* p. 460.
[42] *Vtoroi kongress,* pp. 441–42.

Less than a year later the Comintern would begin to reassess its policy toward the peasantry because the agrarian theses of the Second Congress failed to bring communism any major victories in the countryside and the hope of a Communist revolution anywhere began to recede. The gaps in Lenin's preliminary draft would have to be filled, distinctions would have to be made between revolution in advanced and backward countries, nonrevolutionary tactics would have to be formulated, and account would have to be taken of the differences between postwar Europe and prewar Russia. To achieve these goals, however, the Comintern would still rely far too heavily on the Leninist scriptures and the Russian experience.

AGRARIAN IDEOLOGY

While agrarianism was not a peculiar phenomenon of East European countries, it does occupy an especially prominent place in their history in the period 1920-30. The peasant political movement achieved a position of power and prestige as a unique response to the challenges posed by the intrusion of Western capitalism into predominantly peasant societies which had just achieved some degree of political democracy. The agrarians liked to think of their movement as a third force in politics, distinct from and superior to Western liberalism and Western Marxism, though embodying some of the features of both.

It is difficult to speak authoritatively about the whole peasant political movement since it was less centralized and disciplined and consequently less uniform in its doctrines and practices than communism. The movement tended to lose some of its revolutionary characteristics and even its exclusively peasant orientation after the establishment of democratic political institutions in Eastern Europe.[43] But there are certain features of "peasantism" or "agrarianism" which all these movements shared in 1919.

Initially the popular appeal of the agrarian movement lay to a

[43] The failure to recognize that the peasant ideology did develop and change is one of the major defects of the two full-length studies in English of agrarianism in Eastern Europe: Mitrany, *Marx Against the Peasant,* and Branko M. Peselj, "Peasant Movements in Southeastern Europe, an Ideological, Economic and Political Opposition to Communist Dictatorship" (unpublished Ph.D. dissertation, Department of Political Science, Georgetown University, 1950).

large degree in the underlying assumption of the peasant mystique. — The mystique has recently been defined as "a particular aspect of mythical thought in which the idea is regarded as incarnate in the process of history." [44] It involves transforming events in history into myths which cannot be refuted by reason, but which give a meaning to history and a definition to future action.

The fundamental assumption in the peasant mystique was that the peasant had been the repository of all the virtues of man throughout the course of history, and that the Western liberals and Marxists had idealized spiritually stunted categories of society, the middle class and the industrial working class respectively. While rapturous invocations of the unique qualities of the peasant soul emanated primarily from the generation of populists before World War I,[45] the assumption that the peasant had these qualities (whether articulated or not) lies at the heart of the whole agrarian program.

To the principal theoretician of the Croatian Republican Peasant Party after World War I, Rudolf Herceg, history was an endless series of usurpations of political power by avaricious minority groups. Borrowing a leaf from Marx's book, Herceg argued that all history was the history of class struggle, but he identified the peasantry as the chosen people, the class which would triumph last and express its instincts in the creation of utopia. The emergence of the fourth estate (the workers' revolution in Russia) would usher in the successful rebellion of the fifth estate, the peasantry.[46] The reason why only the peasant could establish just and humane government was that the peasant's way of life engendered a desire for all progressive measures and the peasant class was the only class which had no interest in the exploitation of the labor of others. But victory was

[44] John T. Marcus, "The Mystique: Movement and Order," *American Journal of Economics and Sociology*, XIX, No. 3 (April, 1960), 231.

[45] The tendency of agrarians, once they leave the political arena, to see an order and consistency in the peasant movement which it did not possess in practice limits the usefulness of recent definitions of agrarianism in such works as: G. M. Dimitrov, "Agrarianism," in Felix Gross, ed., *European Ideologies* (New York, 1948), pp. 392–452, and Branko M. Peselj, "The Concept and Sources of Peasant Ideology," International Peasant Union, *Monthly Bulletin*, Sept., 1951, pp. 7–12.

[46] Rudolf Herceg, *Die Ideologie der kroatischen Bauernbewegung* (Zagreb, 1923), pp. 43–44.

not inevitable and the peasantry would have to unite, organize, and fight.[47]

While one finds little sense of vengeance in Herceg's work, the leader of the Bulgarian Agrarian Union, Alexander Stamboliiski, openly declared his hatred for the city and its inhabitants. This is the reverse side of the agrarian's faith in the peasant soul. According to Stamboliiski, the decisive fact in politics was that the virtues which the peasant possessed were wholly absent in the towns. Like Herceg, Stamboliiski borrowed from Marx and portrayed all history as a struggle betwen social groups for political power. But Stamboliiski identified these groups differently. The coming battle would be between the city and the villages—two different cultures, even two different worlds, maintained Stamboliiski.[48] The city was inhabited by parasites and leeches, men like lawyers, bankers, and brokers who could not live without exploiting the honest folk who worked with their hands. The predatory spirit generated by all this greed and corruption suffused all of urban society, tainting even the innocent industrial working class. Only the peasant, steeped in the spirit of communal cooperation, instinctively just and humane, could restore these desirable qualities to the whole society by supporting the peasant party's quest for political power.[49]

The irrational belief that the most primitive member of society was at the same time the most "natural" man and the most virtuous was not new, nor was the assertion that the peasant had a unique claim to moral superiority, though in most East European countries it was difficult to deduce the peasant's moral superiority from his primitive way of life. In their more exotic phases, almost a reversion to the fertility cults of the past, the advocates of agrarianism argued that the peasant's monopoly of virtue was due to his proximity to the soil, the mother of life. In the first issue of the official organ of the Green International at Prague, the lead article, after explaining that all virtue sprang from the mystical tie between man and the soil, and that all history could be explained in terms of man's struggle for his natural right to possess the soil he tilled, went on:

[47] *Ibid.*, p. 79.

[48] Aleksandur Stamboliiski, "Seloto i gradutu," in Nikola D. Petkov, ed., *Aleksandur Stamboliiski: Lichnost' i idei* (Sofia, 1930), p. 226.

[49] *Ibid.*, p. 232.

In order to make the most of this universal truth, in order to raise high and emphasize this idea, it is necessary to join together the desire of all nations—already strongly demonstrated, especially by the agrarian members of society—the desire to renew and preserve humanity on the basis of the natural law which reigns between man and the soil. This law is the chief motivating force in all the efforts of man to develop himself peacefully. . . . Thus the man living on the soil is and must be the creative element in the state. He is always a positivist, a creator of values, he asks nothing from society but the preservation of peace and the exercise of rights resulting from his importance and his work. In exchange he gives society bread, that is, all that it needs in order to live and breathe; he continuously creates values, thinking and profiting from them in order to fill his life with all the attainments of human progress, of science, of art, and, in general, of civilization.[50]

The special virtues of the peasant were presumed to be his individualism, his respect for his fellow human beings, his diligence, and his resistance to violent change. The Czech agrarian leader, Antonín Švehla, said:

We are convinced that the victory of agrarianism will be the victory of humanitarianism, of justice, of peace. Humanity, desiring peace, should place its future in the hands of those for whom peace is the first condition of life, that is to say, in the hands of the farmer.[51]

The agrarian image of the peasant is that of an individual with a compelling desire for sane, orderly progress within a democratic political framework. The leader of the Polish Peasant Party Piast put it this way in 1927:

The peasantry can never be the supporters of a dictator, either openly or covertly, because they need clear and stable conditions. They must be sure that the state and its administration rest, not on the caprice of one man, but on unshakable institutions. A man falls, but institutions remain.[52]

Although the peasant mystique was not the creation of the leaders of the peasant political movement, it undoubtedly flattered the peasant into supporting the movement. What was unique in the peasant movement was the program deduced from this mystique. As is so

[50] "Idée de l'agrarisme universel," *Mezinárodní Agrární Bureau, Bulletin* (hereafter cited as *MAB Bulletin*), No. 1 (1923), pp. 3–4.

[51] This is an excerpt from a speech made by Švehla at a conference of the Green International at Prague. *MAB Bulletin*, No. 5–6 (1925), p. 55.

[52] *MAB Bulletin*, No. 3 (1927), p. 171.

often the case with ideologies which claim to express the "real" instincts of a social group, the agrarians took pride in the unsystematic and often inconsistent character of their creed, pointing out, happily, that this was evidence that agrarianism was the "organic" product of the instincts of the peasants rather than of the machinations of the intelligentsia. One of the leaders of the Rumanian National Peasant Party wrote in 1927:

> It is true that the peasants have not espoused any well-defined theory. Perhaps one could even say that the movement can dispense with theories, owing to the fact that all imaginable theories are nothing without the active support of the peasant masses.
>
> The peasants see in the party a means for defending their interests against the demands of other classes. For the theoreticians the peasants are only an instrument by means of which they can establish a new social order. From the beginning there has been a deep abyss between the mentality of the peasant and the opinions of the theoreticians of the movement.[53]

In short, there was a certain scorn for the intellectual, the thinker, and an idealization of the active politician who responded to the elemental needs, desires, and instincts of the peasants.

Needless to say, this attitude toward the political process bears a marked resemblance to that of the fascist politicians, especially with their idealization of instinct and of leaders who respond to the "people's will." At first glance, the transition from leaders who respond to the "people's will" to leaders who create the "people's will" appears slight, but it is the borderline between two political worlds. Reliance on instinct and general will rather than on a systematic program and formulated theory all too easily degenerates into national or class chauvinism and demagoguery.

Two aspects of agrarianism militated against totalitarian trends in the 1920s. The first was the agrarian's own image of the peasant as an individualist and a humanitarian. The second was the fact

[53] Petre P. Suciu, "La Scission dans le Parti National Paysan Roumain," *MAB Bulletin*, No. 2 (1927), p. 71. This exaltation of an "organic" and usually unsystematic creed was also characteristic of Russian populism. As Radkey points out with regard to Russian populism, it was less an ideology than a state of mind which brought men together in the absence of concrete formulas and held them together despite divergencies over program and tactics. Radkey, p. 3.

that the peasant parties were political newcomers, upstarts and underdogs, and they had to rely on the democratic process of government in order to attain political power and perfect their own organization of the peasantry.

It is true, of course, that the agrarians' devotion to democratic methods and institutions was more apparent in the early stages of the development of their movement and that in a peasant country such methods and institutions naturally improved the political position of leaders of peasant parties. On the other hand, there were occasions when peasant leaders were willing to jeopardize their own position rather than sacrifice such institutions and methods. There seems to have been a genuine belief that the peasant, as a result of his way of life, was a shrewd, practical individualist, a "natural democrat," whose wisdom could best influence government policy through the most democratic institutions and processes.[54] In short, if peasant ideology were to be expressed in the political process, it could best be expressed through those institutional arrangements which permitted the peasants to decide on concrete issues. For this reason the radical peasant movements in Bulgaria and Croatia advocated the widest possible use of referendum, recall, and plebiscite in addition to the usual democratic procedures.

The humanitarian element had been one of the distinctive elements in Russian populism, though it had not prevented that movement from using terror as a political weapon. The East European populists after World War I maintained that their goals differed from those of other parties in that their first concern was for the well-being of the individual and his rights.[55] This avowed devotion to humanitarianism and democratic processes often conflicted with the efforts of the agrarians to achieve their social and economic program, a program which frequently required sacrifices from nonpeasant classes.

This is particularly evident when one considers the central themes of the agrarian economic program. In 1919 almost every European peasant party advocated the confiscation of large-scale property and its redistribution in such a way as to strengthen the system of small

[54] See Herceg, pp. 67–68, on the necessity of initiative, referendum, and recall and Petkov, pp. 180, 196–98. For a criticism of the idea that the peasant is a natural democrat, see n. 57.

[55] Herceg, p. 79.

peasant farms, state assistance to cooperatives in order to free the peasant from dependence on the middleman for credit and marketing, and state assistance to schools of agronomy, model farms, and agricultural stations. Aside from the enormous political obstacles to the fulfillment of such a program there were also several economic misconceptions implicit in it. The program was based on the assumption that economic development would be possible in a peasant country without social differentiation among the peasants, that the East European countries could develop a prosperous small peasantry, like that in Denmark and Switzerland. As Roberts points out in the case of Rumania, the models chosen, Denmark and Switzerland, are inappropriate since the structure of the markets and economies in those countries was entirely different from that in Eastern Europe.[56]

The whole approach of the agrarians seems utopian. The celebrated peasant virtues were the very qualities which stood in the way of the only kind of change which could solve the problems of poverty and overpopulation in the countryside. Peasant conservatism encouraged adherence to anachronistic methods of cultivation, peasant individualism was an expression of an apolitical attitude rather than of responsible political discrimination,[57] and the peasant political movement was infected with an unhealthy animosity toward urbanization, a trend which was probably irreversible.

These are, of course, only some of the general characteristics of East European agrarianism. However naïve or inconsistent their economic and political program may seem in retrospect, the agrarians were at first successful in the postwar period. The newly enfranchised peasant in most countries enthusiastically supported those parties

[56] Henry Roberts, *Rumania: Political Problems of an Agrarian State* (New Haven, 1951), p. 146.

[57] Rothschild writes: "The backward peasant, no matter how egalitarian his outlook, is not a natural democrat, and the history of peasant movements and rebellions, from Wat Tyler's in the fourteenth century through the German ones of the sixteenth, those of Razin and Pugachev in the seventeenth and eighteenth centuries, the French and the Polish *jacqueries* of 1789 and 1846, to the peasant stirrings in Russia and Eastern Europe in the twentieth century, demonstrates only that the peasant is, if anything, a natural anarchosyndicalist. He has neither respect for, nor patience with, orderly politics. He prefers burning down a manor house to casting a ballot, and looting a merchant's shop to conducting parliamentary discussions." Joseph Rothschild, *The Communist Party of Bulgaria* (New York, 1959), p. 86.

which claimed to represent his interests and which vowed to serve him exclusively. The economic program of these parties seemed reasonable to the peasant and their ideology flattered him. The agrarians' emphasis on the evils of industrialization and urban society struck a responsive chord, confirming the peasant's own instinctive reaction to forces he did not understand. But this kind of support was not enough to ensure the survival of peasantism.

One of the central problems of the peasant political movement was that the very qualities which its leaders admired most in the peasantry made it extremely difficult to organize the peasant politically, a frequent complaint of agrarian leaders. Where the movement survived in the long run, it generally did so by introducing principles not directly related to agrarianism and by attracting elements of the population that were more active and articulate than the peasant in the defense of his interests. This kind of adaptation, of course, led to the charge, frequently leveled by the Third International, that the peasant parties had abandoned the interests of the peasantry.

Felix Gross has explained the failure of the peasant movement as a failure to formulate a fully developed philosophical system or a social myth of a perfect state.[58] This explains only the absence of any real solidarity in the international agrarian movement, not the lack of any real staying power in the movement at the domestic level. Nevertheless, some agrarian leaders were apparently convinced that the absence of a "fully developed philosophical world view" was a handicap. For example, one of the leading figures in the Green International, Milan Hodža, called upon the agrarians to remedy this situation. It is significant, however, that he warned his colleagues against building such an ideology around the theme of a wholly peasant society. Hodža urged East European agrarians to end their hostility to the city and their opposition to industrialization, and then to reconstruct agrarian ideology on a scientific and systematic basis "like that of the Marxist ideology." [59]

[58] Felix Gross, "The Mechanics of European Politics," in Gross, p. 16. The Croatian Peasant Party did formulate a social myth of a perfect state. Whether it was "fully developed" is an open question.

[59] Sergei Maslov, *Novaia sila v Evrope i Milan Godzha* (Prague, 1938), pp. 102–3.

In spite of the political and economic shortcomings of the movement, it was sufficiently powerful and popular in the 1920s to encourage the Third International to formulate special tactics to combat it and to erect special institutions to compete with it.

PART II

THE CONFLICT: INTERNATIONAL

CHAPTER III

The Founding of the Red Peasant International

In the decade after World War I the competition between agrarianism and communism for the allegiance of the awakened giant, the peasantry, assumed international proportions with the advent of two rival institutions—the agrarian Green International at Prague and the Communist Red Peasant International, or Krestintern, in Moscow. Yet today, probably because of its ambiguous outcome, this ten-year conflict has become a forgotten chapter in history. The contest now seems more like a shadow boxing match than a significant historical encounter, perhaps because the visible signs of struggle appear only in the journalistic arena. But the implications of this confrontation extend far beyond the individual ink and paper scuffles of the 1920s, for behind the verbal duels was a host of party workers trying to apply the edicts and prescriptions supplied by the journals.

One can discern in the international Communist movement during the 1920s a distinct "peasantist" phase during which the peasant masses almost succeeded in replacing the industrial workers as the expected source of recruits for the regiments of the "proletarian" revolution. Many who today extroll the originality of Mao Tse-tung's peasantism forget that his ideas took shape in this decade when the role of the peasant in revolution was being exalted. In many ways the "peasantism" of the 1920s foreshadows the policies of communism in underdeveloped countries today.

For this reason the theoretical and tactical positions adopted by the international Communist movement have more than an academic interest today. Also, the development of Comintern agrarian policy should be examined as a case study of the process of decision making in the international Communist movement. One must ask the following questions: Did the agrarian policy of the Comintern reflect a real or distorted understanding of the Russian Revolution? To what degree were the Bolsheviks capable of learning from the Russian experience and to what degree did they profit from the experience of member parties in their respective countries? Were the lessons of the Russian Revolution mechanically applied to countries with a similar social and economic structure or did the Comintern draw selectively from the experience of the Bolsheviks? To what degree were the policies of the Comintern determined by the twists and turns of the power struggle in the Russian Communist Party? The answers to, or even an exploration of, these questions will reveal much about the ability of the international Communist movement to learn from experience and adapt to a variety of circumstances. And, since the Russian Revolution was not simply a Russian affair, the answers to the above questions may indicate some of the characteristics of the Russian Revolution as an event in world history. The final measure of communism's success with the peasantry, however, would be the fate of its experimental Red Peasant International.

After World War I events seemed to conspire to put the peasant in the center of the stage. The new nations which emerged in Eastern Europe out of the blood and chaos of the war sought the sanction of history in a real or imagined past. They embodied what was for that part of the world a new combination of virulent nationalism, egalitarianism, and social reformism. The peasant, as the most distinctive symbol of national identity, was to be the main beneficiary of reform legislation. Even in Bulgaria, Rumania, and Yugoslavia, where old dynasties survived in form, the new spirit threatened to sweep all before it. And the Russian Revolution served as a stimulus to political and social change, causing non-Communists to woo the poor, the unemployed, and the peasantry with reforms. The Communist revolution in Hungary was a vivid example of the consequences if one moved too slowly. However, once armed with the ballot, the peasant seemed likely to transform the political party which claimed to represent him exclusively into a third force, superior in representation and popular support to both the bourgeois liberals and the socialist wage laborers. But things were not destined to be so simple.

Events in Russia seemed to strengthen the conviction of the Bolsheviks that the future of communism lay with the peasantry and peasant societies in transition. Rationalizations about the need for a friendly peasantry which were used to justify the New Economic Policy (NEP) in Russia tended to give new vigor to earlier platitudes about Lenin's genius in combining the peasant war with the workers' revolution. For the Russian Communist and for the Comintern, developments in the Soviet Union as well as in Eastern Europe made the peasants the center of attention. From 1923 to 1926 in particular the East European peasants would be besieged by both the Communists and the populists with appeals for their votes and support.

For those years the Green International and the Krestintern served as goads to one another, but from 1926 to 1929, when the Green International reached the summit of its influence and prestige, the Comintern lost interest in the peasant as a revolutionary force and let the Krestintern flounder in its own sea of ineptitude. This strange discrepancy between the international challenge and the Comintern's response to that challenge is one of the themes treated in the following chapters.

NEP AND COMINTERN AGRARIAN POLICY

The Comintern never courted the peasant so openly and shamelessly as in 1923 and 1924. The most vivid expression of this ill-fated and rather one-sided love affair was the creation of the Red Peasant International, or Krestintern, in October, 1923. Looking back on the event, the selection of Marxist Moscow as the capital of the international peasant political movement has a paradoxical quality to it, and one is tempted to dismiss the First International Peasant Conference as a side show staged to entertain visiting dignitaries. In retrospect the Krestintern seems evanescent, the chance product of random forces, having neither the ideological sanctions nor the organizational stamina necessary for survival. But the evidence indicates that the Krestintern does not belong on that long list of organizations created by the Comintern only to provide employment for exiled Communists in Moscow.[1]

It is true that the Krestintern was a product of special temporary

---

[1] A description of the major and minor international mass organizations spawned by the Communist International is provided in Günther Nollau, *International Communism and World Revolution: History and Methods* (New York, 1961), pp. 146–48.

conditions in Eastern Europe and in the rest of the world—the New Economic Policy in Russia, the struggle for power in the Russian Communist Party, the coup d'état in Bulgaria in June, 1923, and the release from prison of a certain Polish Communist in 1923. Moreover, the waning of hope in the Comintern for new Communist revolutions and the discouraging reverses suffered by East European Communist parties when they were forced into illegal operations provided the proper mood. All these developments were necessary conditions, but they were not sufficient. In 1923 and 1924 some Soviet leaders had convinced themselves that the peasantry in certain East European countries offered the only prospect in the world for immediate revolutionary action. The care taken in organizing and justifying the Krestintern suggests that it was intended to be more than a response to temporary conditions. On more than one occasion in 1923 and 1924 the jealously guarded Marxist thesis of the hegemony of the proletariat was in jeopardy, and Moscow seemed on the verge of declaring that the peasantry was a revolutionary class equal in importance to the proletariat. The history of the Krestintern deserves attention because its experiments became part of the recognized but unspoken tradition of international communism, foreshadowing in many ways the next great victory of communism less than three decades later in another vast peasant country.

The first factor in drawing the attention of the Comintern to the peasantry was Lenin's New Economic Policy, which gave explicit recognition to the need for Communists to come to terms with the peasant. Lenin admitted that he had tried to move too fast toward socialism and had, therefore, lost the support of the peasantry.[2] Retreat was the order of the day; efforts to socialize land were slackened and a tax in kind was substituted for the forced collections of grain. The changed attitude toward the peasantry in Russia set the tone for the changed attitude of the Comintern on the agrarian question.

The diminishing expectation of revolution outside Russia made the concessions of the NEP seem even more imperative. If the Soviet Union was to be the fortress of socialism she would have to be strong

[2] Lenin, "Piat' let rossiiskoi revoliutsii i perspektivy mirovoi revoliutsii," *Sochineniia* (4th ed.; Moscow, 1941–50), XXXIII, 383–84.

at any cost, and the concessions to the peasantry under the NEP seemed to be the price. In the Commintern Lenin had already begun to adapt strategy and tactics to nonrevolutionary activity, including an increasing subordination of the Comintern to the interests of the Russian state. In the moments of doubt before the Second Comintern Congress in 1920 Lenin had written "Leftism, an Infantile Disorder," urging young Communist parties to prepare for a long struggle and to use peaceful, legal means of struggle as well as illegal means. For the first time one begins to sense in Lenin's work some doubt that there was "a close and unassailable analogy between revolutionary tactics in Russia and in countries where the proletariat had undergone a long period of indoctrination in the theory and practice of bourgeois democracy." [3]

The victories in Poland shortly thereafter, however, temporarily revived Lenin's unqualified optimism, which is reflected in his preliminary draft of the agrarian theses for the Second Comintern Congress. Still later Lenin's hopes would be dashed again by the failure of the Polish adventure. Although the Polish-Soviet government at Białystok failed to issue a land decree like that issued by the Bolsheviks in the October Revolution,[4] this mistake was never openly discussed because Lenin had come to realize that the invasion of Poland was his own error. When the leader of the Polish Peasant Party Piast, Wincenty Witos, took over direction of the young Polish state in 1920, he was less reticent about Communist failures, attributing the success of the Polish government in repelling Bolshevism to the second agrarian reform law passed at that time.[5] Witos cited the Bolshevik defeat as a great victory of agrarianism over communism and the first step toward the establishment of agrarian democracy in Poland.

By the time of the Third Congress of the Comintern in June, 1921, pessimism had again overtaken that body. The disastrous March action in Germany, the NEP, and the Anglo-Soviet Trade Agreement

[3] E. H. Carr, *The Bolshevik Revolution, 1917–1923* (New York, 1950–53), III, 179–80.
[4] Warren Lerner, "The Russian Plan to Sovietize Poland in 1920" (unpublished Master's thesis, Department of History, Columbia University, 1954), p. 82.
[5] K. Bader, "Le Paysan en Pologne," *MAB Bulletin,* No. 1 (1923), p. 36.

were all straws in the wind. As the young Communist parties in the Comintern lost confidence in their own efforts, they huddled over more expectantly around the Russian Party, which still glowed with the charisma of success.[6] Russian policy at home and in the Comintern expressed a cautious mood of concession and compromise following the ebbing of the revolutionary tide. The primary task in the international Communist movement after 1921 was to accumulate strength in preparation for the next revolutionary wave. In order to adjust to these new conditions a soft and conciliatory line toward other classes and political parties was the proper tactical front.

The united front tactic was promulgated in December, 1921, by the Executive Committee of the Comintern (ECCI). The arguments offered in support of the united front may have been quite different from those offered in support of the NEP, but it was quite clear from the outset that both were a response to the failures of revolution in the West and the Soviet Union's need for respite and reconstruction.[7] It soon became fashionable to speak of the united front as the international counterpart of the NEP and of both as a sign that the actions of the Comintern were being increasingly determined by Russian needs.[8]

But revolutionary movements thrive only in an atmosphere of enthusiasm and optimism. Somehow defeatism and pessimism had to be liquidated. A few deft strokes with the rhetorical brush were needed, and Zinoviev supplied these at the Fourth Comintern Congress in November, 1922. Those attending were told that the NEP, far from being a defeat in the development of the proletarian revolution, was a positive step forward, a newly discovered revolutionary stage through which all countries would have to pass.

We have come to the conclusion that not only our country with a predominantly peasant population but perhaps all, or almost all, countries with an enormous number of proletarians will have to pass through the same political phase in one form or another. The new economic course is

[6] Carr, pp. 197–98.
[7] *Ibid.*, p. 406. See also Jane Degras, "United Front Tactics in the Comintern, 1921–1928," in David Footman, ed., *International Communism* (Carbondale, 1961), pp. 9–22.
[8] Carr, pp. 424–25.

not only the result of our weakness, or of the weakness of the world proletariat. It is based on the actual correlation of forces between the proletariat, on the one hand, and the peasant and the petty bourgeoisie, on the other.[9]

In short, the correctness of the NEP confirmed the correctness of those Comintern policies which attracted the peasantry and the petty bourgeoisie to the Communist cause.

The united front, now sanctified by the Russian experience, became the chief weapon of the Comintern during this nonrevolutionary period. All Communist parties were ordered to try to establish the united front from below, that is, to augment their strength, first by infiltrating political reformist movements and recruiting members from those organizations, and then by trying to prove the ineffectiveness of all bourgeois reforms. Under certain specified conditions a Communist party might form a temporary alliance with the leaders of reformist political parties, or a united front from above, in order to obtain a certain amount of leverage in local politics or to create a revolutionary situation.

A variation of the united front from above was the quixotic tactic of a workers' and peasants' government. This strategem was to be applied only in those countries where the institutional structure and political alignments were still fluid. Zinoviev suggested that the slogan "workers' government" might be useful in Czechoslovakia, Germany, and Italy.[10] Radek added that the slogan "workers' and peasants' government" might be especially useful in Poland, Rumania, Yugoslavia, and Bulgaria.[11] While its precise nature was spelled out no more clearly than the slogan of the united front, the workers' and peasants' government was apparently supposed to be a temporary parliamentary government established by legal means and based on a united front from above between reformist bourgeois parties and the local Communist party. Zinoviev, insisting on the form "workers' government," maintained that such a government had to be transi-

[9] *IV vsemirnyi kongress Kommunisticheskogo Internatsionala (5 noiabria– 3 dekabria, 1922)–izbrannye doklady, rechi i rezoliutsii* (Moscow, 1923), p. 51.
[10] *Ibid.*, p. 58.
[11] *Ibid.*, p. 139.

tional, its formation only the beginning of the real struggle for the proletarian dictatorship.[12]

The final resolution of the workers' and peasants' government literally destroyed the usefulness of the slogan by imposing all sorts of impossible qualifications. For example, "Communists cannot refuse under certain conditions to negotiate with the leaders of hostile workers' parties, but the masses must be kept fully informed of the course of these negotiations." [13] The conditions for such negotiations were that the Communist party must preserve its own class purity, closely supervise negotiations, and maintain its own independence of action and propaganda. If a workers' (or workers' and peasants') government was formed in collaboration with workers' and/or peasants' political parties, the local Communist party first had to obtain the permission of the Comintern to participate in it. The government formed under such circumstances had to remain a coalition against the bourgeoisie and a vehicle for preparing a proletarian revolution. "Even a workers' government which is the outcome of a parliamentary grouping, that is, a government of purely parliamentary origin, can reinvigorate the revolutionary labor movement." [14] The resolution underscored the fact that a workers' and peasants' government was not an inevitable stage in the development of the proletarian revolution nor was it the same thing as the dictatorship of the proletariat.[15]

The agrarian theses prepared for the Fourth Comintern Congress by the Hungarian economist Eugene Varga were less up to date than the theses on the workers' and peasants' government. In spite of the need for adaptation, Varga's theses were still primarily concerned with the seizure of power. Lenin, too weak from illness to participate in the Agrarian Commission, sent a letter suggesting that these theses be clearly designated as supplementary to those of the Second Congress and not as a replacement for them.[16] Lenin suggested that the enemies of the Comintern would accuse Communists of changing

[12] *Ibid.*, pp. 58–59.
[13] Bela Kun, ed., *Kommunisticheskii Internatsional v dokumentakh, 1919–1932* (Moscow, 1933), p. 300.
[14] *Ibid.*, p. 301.
[15] *Ibid.*, p. 302.
[16] *IV vsemirnyi kongress*, p. 297.

their mind every two years unless it was made clear that the new theses were only additions to the old.

In fact, the new theses contained little that was new. There was, however, an emphasis, absent in the earlier theses, on the need to free the lower strata of the peasantry from the influence of landlords and of peasants with large holdings, both of whom were said to dominate peasant political parties.[17] Varga told Communists that they must reveal the ineffectiveness of postwar agrarian reforms.[18] Communist parties were called upon to support all movements for the improvement of the peasants' lot, in particular for the reduction of rents and for the increased allocation of land to poor farmers.[19] At the same time, Communist parties were called upon to point out to the peasants that they could not be really free until a soviet state was established, because only this kind of state could confiscate all of the land and distribute part of it free to the peasants.[20]

In defending these theses, Varga, like Meyer at the Second Comintern Congress, indicated that the postwar agrarian reforms had temporarily weakened the revolutionary movement in the countryside.[21] He called upon all Communist parties to exploit every possible shortcoming of these reforms, pointing out to the peasants that the reforms were bourgeois because they distributed land only against an indemnity.[22] Thus stood the agrarian policy of the Communist International before the Third Enlarged Plenum of its Executive Committee met in June, 1923.

BULGARIA AND ZINOVIEV'S "PEASANTIST" PHASE

The one event which, more than any other, inspired the Comintern to create the Red Peasant International was the coup d'état in Bulgaria in June, 1923. The fall of Alexander Stamboliiski, the strongest and most impressive peasant leader in Eastern Europe, seemed, at least to Zinoviev, to provide the dramatic example necessary to prove

[17] *Ibid.*, pp. 403–4.
[18] *Ibid.*, pp. 406–7.
[19] *Ibid.*, pp. 404–6.
[20] *Ibid.*, p. 407.
[21] *Ibid.*, p. 285.
[22] *Ibid.*, pp. 284–85.

to the peasants that they needed the help of local Communist parties to cope with their military and bureaucratic elite. Furthermore, the coup d'état rekindled Zinoviev's hopes for a new revolutionary wave in central and southeastern Europe. The pressure of the struggle for power in the Russian Communist Party made Zinoviev redouble his efforts to find successes which would bolster his claim to Lenin's mantle. The last ingredient, the plan for a Red Peasant International, would be provided by an obscure Polish émigré to Moscow, Tomasz Dąbal.

In Russia the event which pushed Zinoviev toward "peasantism" was Lenin's stroke in May, 1922. In the struggle for power which began immediately thereafter, Zinoviev joined with Kamenev and Stalin against the strongest contender, Leon Trotsky. One of the issues in the jousting between the triumvirate and Trotsky was the question of the proper course of Russia's future economic development. One faction in the Russian Communist Party advocated the immediate and rapid industrialization of Russia and sought the leadership of Trotsky, while another section, led by Bukharin, Zinoviev, and Stalin, agreed on the necessity of broadening the agricultural base of the Russian economy before proceeding to intensive economic development. The latter group argued that the concessions to the peasantry under the NEP should be so organized that a prosperous peasantry would be created in order to provide a wide domestic market to support the push for industrialization.[23] The first phase of this controversy began in August, 1922, and ended with a temporary victory for those supporting a continuation of concessions to the peasantry at the Twelfth Congress of the Russian Communist Party in April, 1923. At that Congress Zinoviev said:

We must not say that the serious proletarian revolutionary bows in all cases to the world proletariat and grumbles about the peasants. We must say that he who serves the proletarian class can also lead the peasants. And when they say to me, "You are guilty of a peasant deviation, you deviate toward the peasants," I answer, "Yes, we not only must deviate toward the peasantry, but we must bow and, if necessary, kneel be-

[23] For the best outline of Bukharin's theoretical justification for this position see Alexander Erlich, *The Soviet Industrialization Debate, 1924–1928* (Cambridge, Mass., 1960), pp. 9–23.

fore the economic needs of the peasants, who will follow us and give us complete victory." [24]

Although Zinoviev's stance in the debate at home made him a temporary partisan of the peasantry, it was the coup d'état in Bulgaria that converted him into a devotee of the peasant revolutionary. The French occupation of the Ruhr in January, 1923, and the accompanying disturbances in Germany had already encouraged the impressionable Zinoviev to hope for revolutionary successes to adorn his candidacy at home. Events in Bulgaria were an incredibly fortunate bonus. The government of the Bulgarian Agrarian Union was overthrown on June 9, 1923. Upon receipt of the news Zinoviev urged his Bulgarian comrades to join with the Union and form a workers' and peasants' government against the conspirators.[25] By way of analogy Zinoviev reminded the Bulgarian Communist Party of the tactical alliance between Kerensky and the Bolsheviks during the Kornilov revolt.[26]

On June 12, 1923, Zinoviev mounted the rostrum at the Third Enlarged Plenum of the ECCI and dwelt fondly on events in Bulgaria as an example of a new phenomenon, the peasant political movement.

You all know about the repeated attempts to create a so-called Green International, that is, an international of peasants. Quite recently, only a few days ago, we read a telegram about the attempt of Mr. Stamboliiski once again to create a Green International. Now, as we all know, Stamboliiski finds himself operating at a much less exalted level. Trying to struggle on two fronts, against the gross bourgeoisie and against the Communists, he lost, and has had to face bankruptcy. But, nevertheless, these attempts to form a Green International undoubtedly deserve our attention. As a matter of fact, for the first time in the political history of modern times we see several instances where a peasant party has tried to play an independent political role, not without some success. This took place in

[24] *Dvenadtsatyi s'ezd Rossiiskoi Kommunisticheskoi Partii (Bol'shevikov) 17–25 aprelia* (Moscow, 1923), p. 37. See also pp. 78–87, 116, 224 below.

[25] *Rasshirennyi plenum ispolnitel'nogo komiteta Kommunisticheskogo Internatsionala (12–32 iunia 1923 goda)* (Moscow, 1923), p. 100–102.

[26] Ironically, this analogy had already been advanced by the Bulgarian Communist Party itself one year earlier. But in June the Bulgarian Communists refused to act upon it and exploit the situation in Bulgaria. See Joseph Rothschild, *The Communist Party of Bulgaria* (New York, 1959), p. 93 and *passim*.

Czechoslovakia and in the Balkans. This was possible only after the imperialist wars, as a result of which the self-consciousness of the peasant was significantly developed. For a long time we have known full well that peasant parties cannot play an independent role. The peasant follows either the bourgeoisie or the proletariat. Our task is to ensure the second outcome. We cannot remain merely an urban party if we want to defeat the bourgeoisie. We must become a party of the urban proletariat, having at the same time a sufficient bond with the country. The Russian Communist Party was just an urban party for almost two decades. But it was able to defeat the bourgeoisie only when it established an adequate bond through the millions of soldiers and peasants with the peasants in general.[27]

Using Bulgaria as a springboard for his new peasantism, Zinoviev dropped the reticence which he had displayed at the Fourth Comintern Congress toward the slogan "workers' *and peasants'* government."

We think, therefore, that the time has come to generalize the slogan "workers' and peasants' government." At the time of the Fourth Congress we already felt that it would come to this. For some countries we have already defined their mission in this fashion. Now it has become clear that this question is of importance in almost all countries, that it has become an international question.[28]

The link between the new emphasis in the Comintern and recent Soviet experience was made explicit.

At the Fourth Congress we explained to you why we think the New Economic Policy of the Soviet Republic is an international phenomenon and not just an episode in the Russian Revolution. We showed you that almost every country will have to pass through a more or less long stage of the same policy after its revolution. We agreed that the New Economic Policy of Soviet Russia was not a purely Russian phenomenon and that the victorious proletariat of other countries, when their time came, would have to face squarely the problem of establishing the necessary coordination between the working class and the peasantry. If this is so, and it undoubtedly is, then it seems to us that the slogan "workers' and peasants' government" is a logical conclusion from this.[29]

Pravda declared that the new slogan, "workers' and peasants' govern-

[27] *Rasshirennyi plenum*, pp. 39–40.
[28] *Ibid.*, p. 42.
[29] *Ibid.*, p. 43.

ment," was the most important consequence of the meeting of the Enlarged Plenum and called on all Communists to study the lesson of the Bulgarian events, namely, that the peasant and worker had to march together.[30]

But if one strips Zinoviev's speech of its bombast, it is difficult to tell what he meant. He spoke of the new slogan as a powerful propaganda weapon, he suggested that the slogan should take its place alongside the slogan "dictatorship of the proletariat," he spoke of a workers' and peasants' government as the "way to the dictatorship of the proletariat," he spoke of winning over all peasants who did not hire labor, but he never really defined the slogan.[31]

The resolutions on the slogan were no more illuminating. They merely repeated the formulas of the Second and Fourth congresses with greater urgency. The resolutions stressed the fact that the new slogan was not supposed to replace the old slogan, "dictatorship of the proletariat," but was intended only to enlarge the possibilities for the application of the united front in rural areas. The resolutions specified two dangers which had to be avoided in the application of the slogan: one, the danger of interpreting the slogan in terms of petty-bourgeois socialism of the Russian Social Democratic variety; and two, the danger of unprincipled combinations with the leaders of peasant political parties.[32] It would appear, then, that the slogan meant exactly what it had meant at the Fourth Congress, that at a time of political instability a coalition government could be formed between Communists and peasant political parties as a prelude to the proletarian revolution. In this sense it applied specifically to the

[30] "Reshenii ispolkoma i bolgarskii opyt," *Pravda*, No. 143 (June 29, 1923), p. 1.

[31] *Rasshirennyi plenum*, pp. 36–45.

[32] *Ibid.*, pp. 281–82. The Norwegian Communist Party opposed Zinoviev's new peasantism, saying that the Russians were excessively influenced by their own experience in conducting a revolution in an agrarian country. *Ibid.*, pp. 83, 146–47. Eugene Varga expressed doubts about the slogan "workers' and peasants' government" and its implications. If implemented, said Varga, the slogan might lead Communists to ally themselves with peasants who exploited others. It would be much better, said Varga, to define one's allies more carefully and speak of "workers and toiling peasants." *Ibid.*, pp. 47–48, and E. Varga, "The Workers' and Peasants' Government," *International Press Correspondence*, III (July 5, 1923), 482–83.

events then unfolding in Bulgaria,[33] which provided a clear challenge to Zinoviev's newest and most precious tactical theme.

But, unfortunately for Zinoviev, his new slogan was not to be tested in Bulgaria. The Bulgarian Communist Party refused to join in the struggle between the Bulgarian Agrarian Union and the new Tsankov government, announcing that the conflict was "between the rural and urban bourgeoisie" and that it therefore did not concern Communists.[34] When the Comintern restored its authority over the Bulgarian Communist Party, an abortive "workers' and peasants' revolt" was staged in the second half of September, 1923. Zinoviev tried to retrieve what he could from the wreckage, arguing:

The Bulgarian events of June-September, 1923, are of profound significance, not only for Bulgaria, but for the general estimate of the importance of the peasantry. *Together* with a working class led by the Communist party, the peasant is *everything. Without* the working class and endeavoring to take up an intermediate "independent" position between the bourgeoisie and the working class, the peasantry is nothing. And every such endeavor leads to the open dictatorship of unbounded landowning reaction. Peasants of all countries, learn a lesson from the sufferings of Bulgaria. The experience gained in Bulgaria must become the property of the active sections of the peasantry of the whole world. The Communists must utilize this experience for opening the eyes of the peasants, whom the bourgeoisie and the petty-bourgeois parties make use of demagogically for their own ends.[35]

The role of Bulgarian events in crystallizing the Comintern's new orientation on the peasant question has generally been ignored or overlooked, partly as a result of the scantness and unreliability of available evidence about the mood of the Comintern during these

[33] See Zinoviev's speech of July 15, in which he explains the application of this slogan to Bulgarian circumstances. *Rasshirennyi plenum,* pp. 101–2. For a more detailed account of Bulgarian events see chap. VII below.

[34] From an appeal of the Bulgarian Communist Party on the day of the coup d'état, published in Khristo Kabakchiev, "Posle perevorota 9go iunia," *Kommunisticheskii Internatsional,* No. 28–29 (1923), p. 7691.

[35] The italicized words appeared in bold type in the original. G. Zinoviev, "The Import of Events in Bulgaria," *International Press Correspondence,* III, No. 67 (43) (Oct. 18, 1923), 752. As Rothschild points out, the September Revolt could hardly be termed a workers' and peasants' rebellion. Although the insurrectionary forces were composed primarily of peasants, it is not true that the majority of the peasantry in Bulgaria joined in the rebellion. Rothschild, p. 146.

years. Besedovskii, in his suspiciously colorful memoirs, alleges that there was an agrarian faction in the Comintern. While serving as secretary of the Ukrainian mission in Warsaw in the spring of 1923, Besedovskii testifies, he was visited by V. P. Miliutin, a prominent agronomist in the Russian Communist Party. Miliutin told Besedovskii that a minority faction in the Comintern held that the revolution in Europe should first take place in agrarian countries and that it would be a purely peasant revolution. This minority argued:

The revolution must spread from Russia to the purely agrarian countries of the Balkan peninsula, Rumania, Bulgaria, and Yugoslavia. From there the revolution would pass through Hungary to the semi-industrial countries, like Austria and Italy, transforming the purely peasant insurgent movement into the first stage of the proletarian revolution, and the revolutionary movement would spread in this way to industrialized Germany.[36]

This pattern, suggested the minority, would give the prospective German revolution a solid base, solid because the agrarian countries would be better able to withstand blockade and survive civil war than industrial Germany. But, Besedovskii reports, the minority was easily outvoted, and it was only after the defeat of the October Revolution in Germany that they gained temporary ascendancy and created the Red Peasant International.[37]

Trotsky, too, places the ascendance of the minority who favored revolutions in underdeveloped countries in 1924. In 1928 Trotsky looked back on these years and saw in the Comintern "a downright adulation of peasant demagogues."

The task for a long and stubborn struggle of the proletarian vanguard against the bourgeoisie and pseudo-peasant demagoguery for influence over the most disinherited strata of the peasant poor was being more and more displaced by the hope that the peasant would play a direct and independent revolutionary role on a national as well as an international scale.[38]

But there are some discrepancies between the evidence of these secondary sources and the facts. The Red Peasant International was

---

[36] G. S. Besedovskii, *Na putiakh k termidoru* (Paris, 1930), I, 101–2.
[37] *Ibid.*, p. 149.
[38] Leon Trotsky, *The Third International after Lenin* (New York, 1957), p. 119. Quotations used by permission of Pioneer Publishers.

created before 1924 and prior to the failure of the planned revolution in Germany. The founding congress of the Krestintern met October 10-23, 1923, and events in Germany did not reach their peak until the revolt in Hamburg, October 22-25, 1923. As early as June, 1923, the Norwegian Communist Party (at the Third Enlarged Plenum of the ECCI) complained that the Russian leaders of the Comintern were in favor of shifting the weight of Comintern activity to southeastern Europe and the East.[39] It is apparent from events leading up the the First International Peasant Conference that events in Bulgaria, not Germany, produced the inspiration and enthusiasm for the Krestintern.[40] It is reasonable to assume also that Zinoviev was the chief patron of the new organization and that he hoped through his new-found Marxist peasantism to achieve a new dramatic revolutionary successes to advertise his candidacy for Lenin's crown.

THE KRESTINTERN

The Green International at Prague, which Zinoviev mentioned in his opening remarks at the Third Enlarged Plenum of the ECCI, was to provide the point of departure for the creation of the Krestintern. The man who would weave all these strands together into a single institutional form was provided by Poland in the form of Tomasz Dąbal, a young Polish Communist who was released to Moscow in March, 1923, in exchange for some loyal Poles held by the Russians.[41] On June 19, 1923, Dąbal published an article in *Pravda* entitled "The Peasant International." [42] The article was dated June 14, 1923, two days after Zinoviev's stirring espousal of the slogan "work-

[39] *Rasshirennyi plenum,* p. 147.

[40] The Bulgarian example was cited by every major speaker at the First International Peasant Conference. *Pervaia mezhdunarodnaia krest'ianskaia konferentsiia—rechi, tezisy, vozzvaniia* (Moscow, 1924): Varga, p. 33; Kalinin, p. 7; Zinoviev, pp. 97–98; Bukharin, p. 146; Dąbal, p. 109.

[41] M. K. Dziewanowski, *The Communist Party of Poland: An Outline of History* (Cambridge, Mass., 1959), p. 326, n. 6. There are biographical articles on Dąbal in *Entsiklopedicheskii slovar' Granat,* XLVII, Prilozhenie, 31; *Malaia sovetskaia entsiklopediia,* 1st ed., II (1929), 925; *Bol'shaia Sovetskaia entsiklopediia,* 1st ed., XXIII (1931), 110–11.

[42] T. Dąbal, "Krest'ianskii internatsional," *Pravda,* No. 134 (June 19, 1923), p. 1.

ers' and peasants' government," and Dąbal was clearly taking his cue from Zinoviev's suggestions that the various attempts to form a Green International deserved the attention of all Communists.

Born in 1890, Dąbal had already enjoyed a varied career. Before World War I he had studied agronomy at Vienna and Kraków and was a member of the Polish Peasant Party Piast before the war. In November, 1918, he had returned to his home town in Tarnobrzeg, Western Galicia, a young lieutenant from Piłsudski's legions, intent on organizing the province for liberation. Assuming for a time the post of chief of the county gendarmery, Dąbal soon affiliated himself with Father Okon and his Radical Peasant Party.[43] On January 9, 1919, Dąbal began agitating for radical land reform, attempting to mobilize the peasants and returning soldiers and create an agrarian Tarnobrzeg republic. While these efforts ended in failure, Dąbal and Father Okon were elected to the newly created Polish Sejm, where Dąbal was arrested in 1922 as a confessed convert to communism and sentenced to six years in prison.

In his article for *Pravda* Dąbal drew upon his own experiences and the new developments in the Comintern to advance a strikingly novel proposal. On the negative side, Dąbal took Varga to task for trying to narrow the slogan "workers' and peasants' government" by changing it to "government of workers and toiling peasants." [44] Dąbal argued that Varga's suggestion was doctrinaire, that it would "unnecessarily narrow the base of Comintern activity," and that a similar slogan failed to justify itself in Russia. On the positive side, Dąbal proposed that a new organization be created to implement the slogan "workers' and peasants' government." Referring to Zinoviev's speech on the slogan, to the revolutionary experience of the Russians, and to the coup d'état in Bulgaria, Dąbal concluded that "it is necessary to create under the Comintern a central bureau with the name 'Peas-

[43] The only account in English of Dąbal's role in Western Galicia is Jan Slomka, *From Serfdom to Self-Government: Memoirs of a Polish Village Mayor, 1842–1927,* tr. by W. J. Rose (London, 1941), p. 245. Slomka refers to Dąbal as Chief D. There is a Communist account in *Istoriia Pol'shi,* III (Moscow, 1958), 76–77.

[44] *Pravda,* No. 134 (June 19, 1923), p. 1. For Varga's views see n. 32.

ant International.' " [45] Such an organization could be established, he argued, by an international peasant congress. Communist parties should take the initiative in preparing such a congress, inviting "representatives and leaders of the peasants of all countries." Dąbal said that the peasant problem was "the Achilles heel of capitalism" and that although "part of the demands of the peasant are undoubtedly reactionary with regard to the development of production and society itself . . . the movement does threaten the existence of the capitalist structure."

To harness this latent revolutionary force, he proposed the following:

> In practice it is necessary for each Communist party to create a section for work in the country and to send some comrades as missionaries for work among the peasants. These missionaries must enter the existing vocational and political organizations of the peasants, win the confidence of the peasant masses, and strengthen their influence. These missionaries must be primarily of peasant origin. Also, it is necessary to establish trade union organizations for the small peasants and to set these organizations against those of the rich peasants.
>
> Moreover, we must, under the leadership of those who are fully committed to us—preferably members of our own party—create peasant parties. Inside such parties it is necessary to organize party cells, and then those parties will be completely in our hands, they will cooperate with us, and a decline in the influence of rich peasants and a strengthening of our influence in the country will rapidly take place.[46]

The picture painting by Dąbal of Communists organizing peasant political parties and directing their struggles for "petty-bourgeois" interests is indeed a far cry from Marxist orthodoxy. All these efforts were to be coordinated by the new Krestintern.

A conference was scheduled for October, and Moscow apparently scoured its émigré colony for individuals who might be considered peasants. Fortunately a huge International Agricultural Exhibit had opened in August, 1923, and it was possible to draw some of the foreign delegates attending it into the proceedings. The First International Peasant Conference at Moscow opened on October 10, 1923,

[45] *Ibid.*
[46] *Ibid.*

with a standing ovation for the leading Bulgarian delegate, M. P. Gorov, who, in all likelihood, was Gavril Genov, one of the three leaders of the September Insurrection.[47] There were 158 delegates, representing forty countries, but few of the delegates qualified as authentic peasants or as representatives of peasant political organizations. Few of them appear again in subsequent Communist meetings or publications, at least under the same names. Most of the delegates used pseudonyms, but, of those who can be identified, only a few were significant political figures. These were A. P. Smirnov, Ivan Teodorovich, N. L. Meshcheriakov, all of the Soviet Union, Sen Katayama of Japan, Nguyen Ai Quoc (Ho Chi Minh) of Indo-China, Ursulo Galvan of Mexico, W. H. Green from the United States, Dąbal for Poland, M. P. Gorov for Bulgaria, and Eugene Varga for Hungary.[48] At the meetings the major speakers were Zinoviev, Bukharin, Klara Zetkin, Varga, Teodorovich, Kalinin, Dąbal, and Gorov. Eastern Europe and the Far East were most heavily represented.

With that taste for irony which Bolshevik leaders still possessed in 1923, the proceedings of the First International Peasant Conference were held in the Kremlin in the hall of St. Andrew, the former throne room of the tsars. Amid the relics of the feudal and aristocratic past the prophets of the Comintern expostulated on the coming workers' and peasants' revolution. Banners were strewn about, emblazoned with the slogans "Long live the alliance of workers and peasants of all countries," and "Long live the workers' and peasants' government." The conference ended with a gala mass meeting at the Bol'shoi theater on October 16, at six o'clock.

At the conference Zinoviev, Varga, and Kalinin gave explicit recognition to the postwar peasant political movements as stimuli to

[47] The Bulgarian delegate used the name M. P. Gorov, but Rothschild indictates that Genov became a functionary of the Krestintern. Rothschild, p. 141, n. 25. The reception given Gorov at this meeting and his continuing prominence in the Krestintern would suggest that he played an important role in the September revolt and had some status in the international Communist movement as well.

[48] From 1923 until he left with Borodin for China in 1925, Ho Chi Minh was a member of the Presidium of the Krestintern and its foremost representative for the Far East. Nguyen Ai Quoc is identified as the pseudonym of Ho Chi Minh in X. E. Eudin and R. C. North, *Soviet Russia and the East, 1920–1927* (Stanford, 1957), p. 267.

the formation of the Red Peasant International.[49] In addition to these movements, the International Agricultural Exhibit in Moscow, and the "lessons" of the June events in Bulgaria, Zinoviev cited a fourth motive for the establishment of the Krestintern, namely, the impending revolution in Germany.

> The Red Peasant International must come into being with the slogan "down with war." We must declare war on war, not when it is already a fact, but now, in the coming weeks and months while it is being prepared. We must begin to rouse the French, Italian, German, Polish, Hungarian, and Norwegian villages, in a word, the villages of the whole world. It is necessary to explain to the peasant that the bourgeoisie is preparing a new war in order to subdue the German proletarian revolution, that French, English, and Polish capitalists are preparing a new war which will be much more horrible than the war of 1914-17.[50]

Russian experience as well as the "lessons" of Stamboliiski's defeat in Bulgaria were used to support the claim that the peasant could achieve his goals only through alliance with and subordination to the Communist movement. Zinoviev went so far as to say that the revolution of 1905 needed only the alliance of peasants and workers to succeed.[51]

But it was Dąbal who was triumphant. He gave the chief address. Having found a forum and a captive audience, he proceeded to demolish all of the important distinctions Lenin had made between the peasantry and the industrial working class as revolutionary forces. In the theses he presented, he said:

> Like the working class, the peasant class is interested first and foremost in overthrowing the reign of capitalists and landowners. In most countries the majority of the population are members of the peasantry, and they are as exploited and oppressed by the bourgeoisie and the large landowners as the working class.
>
> The rule of capital is based to a large degree on the terrible distress of the peasantry.
>
> With the exception of a handful of rich farmers, the peasants and workers, on the whole, have common interests with the working class.
>
> But it is only by joining in common struggle that the peasants and

[49] *Pervaia mezhdunarodnaia krest'ianskaia konferentsiia,* pp. 7, 32–33, 50, 97.

[50] *Ibid.,* p. 99.

[51] *Ibid.,* p. 97.

workers can defeat capitalism; it is only by their collaboration that the well-being and peaceful development of all humanity can be ensured.[52]

In these theses one sees the peasant assuming an equal, if not superior, position to the worker in bringing about the so-called proletarian revolution. Dąbal naively referred to the policies of the Soviet Union toward the peasant under the NEP as proof that after the seizure of power by a Communist party the peasant would be treated as well as the worker. One might with equal justice, if parallels were to be drawn, argue that any future Communist government would also have to repeat the excesses of War Communism in rural areas. In his speech Varga steered more carefully between Lenin's theoretical strictures and underscored the fact that the use of the peasant was a temporary tactic, not an amalgamation of the peasant political movement with the Communist movement.[53] His temperance was timely, but went unheeded.

The statutes adopted at the First International Peasant Conference indicated that the purpose of the new Krestintern was to "establish and maintain firm ties with cooperatives and economic and political organizations of the peasants of all countries," and to "coordinate peasant organizations and the efforts of the peasants to realize the slogan worker's and peasants' government." [54] In particular, the Krestintern was to devote itself to the union between town and country, and to strengthening the ties between the peasantry and the working class, through mutual work and struggle against landowners and capitalists. Apparently the establishment of the Krestintern even led some Communist parties to assume that they would be called upon to create peasant political parties as well as peasant trade unions, but it was announced that this idea had been shelved for the time being.[55] Some parties ignored the ban and formed peasant political parties anyway.

The organizational structure of the Krestintern closely followed that of most Soviet administrative bodies. The permanent organization

---

[52] *Ibid.*, p. 166.
[53] *Ibid.*, pp. 26–27.
[54] *Ibid.*, p. 169.
[55] Iuz. Krasnyi, "Mezhdunarodnyi krest'ianskii sovet," *Kommunisticheskii Internatsional*, No. 3–4 (N.S.) (May–June, 1924), p. 178.

was to be located in Moscow and the five major organs were to be the International Peasant Congress, the International Peasant Council, the Plenum of the International Peasant Council, the Presidium of the International Peasant Council, and the General Secretariat. As in the Russian system of soviets, the numerically largest bodies were granted the greatest power by the organizational statutes. Also as in the soviet system, the theoretical hegemony of the mass assemblies was nullified by their unwieldy size and the infrequency of their meetings. In the Krestintern the General Secretariat was in fact supreme because only the Secretariat was continuously in session and constantly in touch with whatever organs of execution the Krestintern possessed.

The International Peasant Congress (or conference) was to be called at least once every two years; there were no fixed limits to the number of delegates sent by member organizations. The Congress elected the Presidium from among the members of the International Peasant Council, passed on major policy shifts, and had the right to choose the site of the Krestintern. The Peasant Congress, apparently, was intended to be the ultimate weapon, a truly massive demonstration of strength, reserved for the launching of major new programs or campaigns. In fact, no congresses were ever held and only two conferences, the founding conference in October, 1923, and another in November, 1927.

The International Peasant Council was intended to be the heart of the Krestintern, though not its head.[56] Delegates to the Council were to be "representatives of peasant organizations of various countries," chosen by member organizations, with the provision that there be no more than twelve delegates from each country. The first International Peasant Council had fifty-two members.[57] All policy decisions were supposed to emanate from the Council, although major policy changes were to be referred to a Peasant Congress. The frequency of the meetings of the International Peasant Council

[56] The first meeting of the Plenum of the International Peasant Council and the rules of organization which it drew up for the Krestintern are described in *Pravda*, No. 235 (Oct. 17, 1923), p. 2; the rules of organization are also included in *Pervaia mezhdunarodnaia krest'ianskaia konferentsiia*, pp. 169–71.
[57] *Pervaia mezhdunarodnaia krest'ianskaia konferentsiia*, p. 169.

was not fixed, but the Plenum of the Council was supposed to meet at least once a year. Only two plenums were ever held, the first in October, 1923, immediately after the First International Peasant Conference, and the second in April, 1925, immediately after the Fifth Enlarged Plenum of the ECCI.

Day-to-day policy decisions were to be made by the Presidium of the International Peasant Council. It had the power to admit new members, to establish new branches in other countries and define their powers, and to call special plenums or congresses. The Presidium was given the widest possible powers to fulfill the decisions of the First International Peasant Conference and build up the Krestintern. The first Presidium had eleven members, but it had the right to coopt new members as it saw fit.

The General Secretariat consisted of the secretary general and his assistant, elected by the Presidium from among its membership. Their job was to carry out the decisions of the International Peasant Council and its Presidium. The General Secretariat, as the only body in the Krestintern whose members permanently resided in Moscow, as a body in daily touch with the branches of the organization, actually ran the Krestintern and made most of the important decisions. The agents of the secretariat generally turned out to be either non-Communist political leaders with a peasant following or Communists delegated by indigenous Communist parties, although the latter group was much more common than the former. The General Secretariat was charged to create a Peasant Information Bureau, which would be used not only to gather and disseminate information but also to maintain permanent contact with peasant organizations of all countries. In order to fulfill its mission the General Secretariat was to establish a monthly journal (entitled the *Krest'ianskii Internatsional*) and to form a research auxiliary, an International Agrarian Institute. The slogan of the Krestintern was to be "Peasants and workers of all countries, unite."

The active workers in the Krestintern, as it turned out, were of disparate origins and ideological inclinations. Like many Comintern organs, it provided jobs for a few prominent "Old Bolsheviks" and émigré Communists with "rightist tendencies." The vital post of secretary general went to a prominent Russian Bolshevik functionary, Alexander Petrovich Smirnov,[58] and Dąbal was made his assistant. Smirnov was at that time an important figure in Soviet politics, a member of the Central Executive Committee of the Supreme Soviet, and the commissar of agriculture. The choice of such a prominent Communist suggests that Zinoviev expected a great deal from the Krestintern. Nine years later, A. P. Smirnov would be the last leader in the Russian Communist Party to try to revive the Right Opposition to Stalin.[59] The two other major Russian participants in the Krestintern, like Smirnov, had come to Marxism from the narodnik movement (that is, the peasant political movement), which suggests that this kind of background may have recommended them for work in the Krestintern. The first, N. L. Meshcheriakov, became organizational secretary of the Krestintern in 1924 and worked with that organization until 1927, when he left to become editor of *Malaia sovetskaia entsiklopediia*.[60] The second, Ivan Teodorovich, like Smirnov, was a member of the Commissariat of Agriculture, and in March, 1928, for a short time, he would replace Smirnov as secretary general of the Krestintern.[61]

The active participants from other Communist parties were less prominent figures. Dąbal really ran the organization as assistant

[58] Boris Voline, *12 militants russes (notices biographiques)* (Paris, 1925), pp. 39–44. There are also biographies of A. P. Smirnov in *Entsiklopedicheskii slovar' Granat*, XLI, Part III, Prilozhenie, 65–70 (autobiography); *Malaia Sovetskaia entsiklopediia*, VIII (1930), 58–59. According to Daniels, Trotsky identified A. P. Smirnov as a prominent member of the pro-peasant faction within the ruling elite of the Party in 1926. Robert Vincent Daniels, *The Conscience of the Revolution: Communist Opposition in Soviet Russia* (Cambridge, Mass., 1960), p. 323.

[59] The role of A. P. Smirnov in trying to revive the Right Opposition in 1932 is described in Abdurakhan Avtorkhanov, *Stalin and the Soviet Communist Party: A Study in the Technology of Power* (New York, 1959), pp. 192–95. Tokaev reports that A. P. Smirnov was the only prominent leader of the right to refuse to capitulate to Stalin during the great purge trials of the 1930s. G. A. Tokaev, *Betrayal of an Ideal* (Bloomington, 1955), p. 234.

[60] For autobiography see *Entsiklopedicheskii slovar' Granat*, XLI, Part II, Prilozehnie, 34–47. There is a short biographical sketch in *Malaia sovetskaia entsiklopediia*, V (1930), 193.

[61] Actually Teodorovich was Polish, but he had been educated in Russia and all his political activity had been in the Russian Party. For his autobiography see *Entsiklopedicheskii slovar' Granat*, XLI, Part III, Prilozhenie, 139–45. For biography see *Malaia sovetskaia entsiklopediia*, VIII (1930), 738–39.

to the secretary general. Both Dąbal and Smirnov were members of the Presidium, each representing his country of origin. The other countries represented in the Presidium were Germany (Richard Bürgi), France (Marius Vazei), Czechoslovakia (Otto Rydlo), the United States (W. H. Green), Bulgaria (M. P. Gorov), Scandinavia (Gerro), Mexico (Ursulo Galvan), Japan (Ken Hayashi) and Indo-China (Ho Chi Minh).[62] With the exception of Gorov, Galvan, Green, and Ho Chi Minh, few of these names appear again in Communist periodicals or records of meetings, although all of them contributed articles to the journal of the Krestintern. Ursulo Galvan of Mexico bears the unusual distinction of being the only member of the Krestintern known to have been expelled from that organization.[63]

Most of the active members of the Krestintern were drawn from Eastern Europe. In addition to Dabal and Gorov, Boshkovich (real name Filipović), former secretary of the Yugoslav Communist Party and later a member of the ECCI, was a major contributor to *Krest'ianskii Internatsional* and often spoke for the Krestintern in the Comintern.[64] Little is known about Akuzius Kheveshi and Solomon Timov, the major contributors on Hungarian and Rumanian affairs respectively.

On paper the Krestintern was impressive. Both the Comintern and the Krestintern seemed eminently suited to the task of channeling peasant discontent into the Communist movement. But what was supremely lacking in the Communist approach to the peasant question in both organizations was any real appreciation of the peasants' plight. Discussions never went beyond the stage where delegates reminded one another how important it was to have the peasant on the side of the Communist revolution. Nowhere, not even in the speeches of such trained economists as Varga, is found a detailed analysis of the agrarian problems of Eastern Europe comparable to Lenin's *The Development of Capitalism in Russia*. The atmosphere of the Comin-

---

[62] *Pervaia mezhdunarodnaia krest'ianskaia konferentsiia*, p. 142.

[63] Robert J. Alexander, *Communism in Latin America* (New Brunswick, 1957), p. 324.

[64] Filipović, as a participant in the Russian Social Democratic movement from 1899 to 1912, qualified as both an Old Bolshevik and an émigré. "Filip Filipović," *La Fédération balkanique*, No. 125 (2A) (Dec. 15, 1929), p. 2753.

tern, with the unremitting assertion by the Russian Communist Party that all Communist revolutions would follow the pattern of the Russian Revolution, seemed to stifle such analyses.

Even taking into account the orthodox doctrinal heritage of prejudice against the peasant and small holder, Comintern adherence to empty formulas is remarkable. The only real reward offered to the peasant for marriage with the Communist movement was Lenin's agrarian program, or, more specifically, confiscation of large estates and redistribution of part of this land without compensation.

At each of the four stages of development of the Comintern agrarian program the decisive influence came from Eastern Europe or Russia. At the Second Comintern Congress it was a Pole, Marchlewski, who redefined Lenin's theses on the use of land redistribution in making Communist revolutions. At the Fourth Comintern Congress it was a Hungarian, Varga, who tried to adapt Lenin's agrarian theses to the problem of Communist activity in an "era of stabilization." At the Third Enlarged Plenum of the ECCI it was Zinoviev who inaugurated a general campaign for "workers' and peasants' governments." Finally, it was a Pole, Dąbal, who launched the Comintern's most ambitious effort to capture the peasantry of the world, the Red Peasant International. This virtual monopoly by East Europeans colored the Comintern's agrarian program to a large degree, particularly in the emphasis on the power of the concept of confiscation and redistribution. Dąbal's view of the peasantry as a revolutionary class equal, if not superior, to the industrial working class was also a characteristically East European notion. Many West European Communists were offended by such un-Marxist theses and found them useless for agitational work in their own villages.

The fact that the Russian experience dominated the development of the Comintern's agrarian program is obvious from the events reviewed in this chapter. The role of external events in shaping Comintern policy cannot, however, be ignored. In 1920 the failure of the Hungarian Revolution was used by Lenin to demonstrate the correctness of his agrarian theses. At the Second Congress one speaker remarked that the agrarian reforms in Eastern Europe made the formulation of Communist agrarian policy imperative. At the Third Enlarged Plenum of the ECCI the June events in Bulgaria were displayed as a perfect example of both the extreme revolutionary potential of the peasant movement and the inability of this movement to function as a "third force" between the Communists and the bourgeoisie. Finally, at the founding of the Krestintern, Zinoviev suggested that harnessing the peasantry to the Communist movement might somehow help German Communists in their imminent effort to seize power.

These were the causes of the policy adopted, but the effect was, at least on the surface, less interesting. It was the Green International, not the Red Peasant International, that grew in succeeding years. However, the seeds of certain ideas about the peasantry had been sown, seeds which would germinate and send up strong shoots during the next two years, though the plant would never bear fruit.

CHAPTER IV

The Peasantist Phase in the Comintern, 1924–1926

Between 1923 and 1926 the subordination of the Communist International to the Soviet state, or, more accurately, to the Russian Communist Party, became increasingly obvious. Every shift in the balance of power within the ruling elite of the Russian Communist Party was ultimately followed by a corresponding shift in the leadership of the other parties belonging to the Comintern. Every controversy among the contenders for Lenin's mantle ultimately became a controversy in the international Communist movement. The policies of the Communist International and the Soviet government did not fuse completely until the victory of Stalin in his party at the end of this decade and the purges of 1929, but the history of the Comintern in the 1920s is the history of its slow strangulation by the Russian Party.

THE INDUSTRIALIZATION CONTROVERSY IN THE SOVIET UNION AND THE COMINTERN

In 1928 Trotsky looked back on the period 1923-26 and found that in these years there were two distinct phases in the history of both Soviet and Comintern policy. The first, which he called the ultra-left tendency, was the period of Zinoviev's ascendancy and ended in June, 1925, with Zinoviev's abandonment of his peasantism and the beginning of his opposition to Bukharin.[1] The second phase, which Trotsky called "the course to the right" or the "period of opportunistic down-sliding," was the period of Bukharin's ascendancy, which began to decline with the defeat of the Joint Opposition at the

[1] E. H. Carr, *Socialism in One Country, 1924–1926* (New York, 1958–), I, 61.

Fifteenth Conference of the Russian Communist Party in October, 1926.[2] As Trotsky explained it:

It is impossible to draw any rigorous ideological line of demarcation between the phase of ultra-left policy and the period of opportunistic down-sliding that followed it.

In the questions of industry and the peasantry in the U.S.S.R., of the colonial bourgeoisie, of "peasant" parties in capitalist countries, of socialism in one country, of the role of the party in the proletarian revolution, the revisionist tendencies already appeared in fullest bloom in 1924-25, cloaked with the banner of the struggle against "Trotskyism," and they found their most distinctly opportunistic expression in the resolutions of the conference of the C.P.S.U. in April 1925. . . .

For this conception [the ultra-leftism of 1924] there existed always and unalterably only the social democracy that was "disintegrating," workers who were becoming "radicalized," communist parties that were "growing," and the revolution that was "approaching." And anybody who looked around and tried to distinguish things was and is a "liquidator."

This "tendency" required a year and a half to sense something new after the break in the situation in Europe in 1923 so as then to transform itself, panic-stricken, into its opposite. The leadership oriented itself without any synthesized understanding of our epoch and its inner tendencies, only by groping (Stalin) and by supplementing the fragmentary conclusions thus obtained with scholastic schemas renovated for each occasion (Bukharin). The political line as a whole, therefore, represents a chain of zig-zags. The ideological line is a kaleidoscope of schemas tending to push to absurdity every segment of the Stalinist zig-zag.[3]

With his usual instinct for finding the pulse of history, Trotsky put his finger on the most remarkable feature of the period 1924-26, the lack of any profound policy shifts corresponding to the power shifts in the Russian Communist Party. Also, with his usual addiction to the dramatic, Trotsky did not attempt a closer and more tedious scrutiny of this apparent continuity in policy. The outward form of Communist agrarian policy did not change, but its tone and direction did.

Throughout the whole period 1923-26 in the Soviet Union and in

[2] Isaac Deutscher, *The Prophet Unarmed: Trotsky, 1921–1929* (London, 1959), p. 296.

[3] Leon Trotsky, *The Third International after Lenin* (New York, 1957), pp. 125–27.

the Comintern, the peasantry occupied the center of the stage and was the recipient of further concessions and favors. In domestic and Comintern policy the *smychka,* the alliance between the industrial workers and the peasants, became, in Stalin's words, "the cornerstone of Soviet policy." [4] This policy did not, however, go unchallenged. The proper place of the peasant in the industrialization of the Soviet Union was a persistent issue in all party debates.

In the preliminary stages of the debate in the Russian Communist Party, stretching from the scissors crisis in August, 1922, to December, 1923,[5] the central issue had been whether a domestic market, a base for industrialization, should be created under the NEP by means of further concessions to the peasantry or whether the government should industrialize immediately, financing such "forced industrialization" by imposing heavy taxes on the peasantry (the doctrine of primitive socialist accumulation). At the Twelfth Congress of the Party in April, 1923, Trotsky had refused to accept the role of spokesman for the industrial faction, although he was inclined toward its ideas. Without the prestige of Trotsky behind it, the industrial faction was forced to concede the first round to the group advocating further concessions to the peasantry, a group loosely affiliated to Stalin, Zinoviev, Kamenev, and Bukharin.[6] The decisions of the Politburo in December, 1923, involved further concessions to the peasantry. As Carr put it, they "confirmed the peasant in his commanding position as the main beneficiary of NEP and the arbiter of the Soviet economy." [7] Of course, those who had supported further concessions to the peasantry in Russia had never for a moment aban-

---

[4] Carr describes Zinoviev's exuberant support of the concessions granted to the peasantry in the Soviet Union. Carr, *Socialism in One Country,* I, 195–201; II, 60–61.

[5] This phase of the controversy is described in detail in E. H. Carr, *The Interregnum, 1923–1924* (New York, 1954), Part I. For a detailed analysis of the issues and the chronological account of the development of the whole controversy see E. H. Carr, *Socialism in One Country,* Vol. I, and Robert Vincent Daniels, *The Conscience of the Revolution: Communist Opposition in Soviet Russia* (Cambridge, Mass., 1960), pp. 154–56, 173–76, 193–214. For an analysis and evaluation of the economic theories involved see Alexander Erlich, *The Soviet Industrialization Debate, 1924–1928* (Cambridge, Mass., 1960).

[6] Carr, *The Interregnum,* pp. 26, 271–79.

[7] *Ibid.,* p. 117.

doned the ultimate goals of Marxism. But the intense struggle they had waged against peasant stubbornness and passive resistance had endowed these Russian Communists with a new respect for the peasants as a force in social change, reflected in Zinoviev's emphasis in the Comintern on the "workers' and peasants' government" and in the creation of the Krestintern.

Having won the field in the Russian Communist Party in December, 1923, the victors soon began to disagree over the meaning of that victory. Only Stalin was cautious enough to avoid extravagant exaggeration of the role of the peasantry in proletarian revolutions. Already he was adopting the proper pose for one who wanted to be known as a devout Marxist. In his lectures on Marxism at Sverdlov University in April, 1924, Stalin even argued:

> Some think that the fundamental question in Leninism is the peasant question, that the point of departure of Leninism is the question of the peasantry, its role, its position. This is absolutely wrong. The fundamental question in Leninism, its point of departure, is not the peasant question but the question of the dictatorship of the proletariat. . . .
>
> The question here is one of rendering support to those movements and those struggles which directly or indirectly help the movement for the liberation of the proletariat, those movements which play into the hands of the proletarian revolution, those movements which make it possible to transform the peasant into a reserve and an ally of the working class.[8]

Although Stalin first announced his theory of the self-sufficiency of the Russian Revolution in December, 1924—socialism in one country—it created no great stir at the time and Stalin himself was probably unaware of the importance this theory would finally assume.[9]

Bukharin, on the other hand, was moving toward a peasantism which would lead him to take up this theme where Zinoviev had left it. Bukharin became the chief press agent for "socialism in one country," interpreting it as a theory which explained the necessity for further concessions to the peasantry under the NEP. Shortly before the Fourteenth Party Conference in April, 1925, Bukharin called upon the well-to-do peasants to "enrich themselves," placing himself at the head of what might be called the "Manchester school" of Com-

[8] *Pravda,* No. 105 (May 11, 1924), p. 2.
[9] Carr, *Socialism in One Country,* II, 39–43.

munists.[10] The assumption was that the avarice of the kulak would create a domestic market upon which, ultimately and at a snail's pace, socialism could be built.[11] Among those following Bukharin in this neo-narodnik [12] or neo-populist course was A. P. Smirnov, secretary-general of the Krestintern and commissar of agriculture. [13]

Beginning in June, 1925, the old Bolsheviks, the Leningrad section of the Party, and Zinoviev and Kamenev openly opposed Bukharin's neo-narodnik trend. Stalin, with support from the Moscow sections of the Party, technicians, and the intelligentsia (old and new), lent cautious and partial support to Bukharin.[14] Zinoviev's group, which came to be known as the second opposition, was defeated on issues other than the peasant question at the Fourteenth Congress in December, 1925, and no definite policy on agriculture was adopted. To some degree Stalin blurred the whole issue by successfully contending that the second opposition wanted to destroy the alliance between the Soviet regime and the middle peasant.[15]

In a last effort to break the new diarchy of Stalin and Bukharin, Zinoviev and Kamenev, now without their Leningrad support, joined Trotsky in April, 1926. The themes of this new Joint Opposition were gradual collectivization and rapid industrialization, to be financed by heavier taxation.[16] By the time of the Fifteenth Conference

[10] There is some evidence that Stalin dissociated himself from this pro-kulak slogan at the Fourteenth Party Conference in April, 1925, but Bukharin was not forced to withdraw the slogan until November, 1925. *Ibid.*, I, 283–86, 310.

[11] Bukharin's exact words were, "We shall move forward at a snail's pace, but all the same we shall be building socialism and we shall build it." *Ibid.*, p. 352, and Erlich, p. 78.

[12] In December, 1925, Trotsky pointed to the similarity between Bukharin's arguments and those of the old Russian "narodniks." Carr, *Socialism in One Country,* II, 168.

[13] *Ibid.*, I, 246, 302.

[14] *Ibid.*, Vol. II, chap. XIII, and Deutscher, pp. 246, 252, 265, 274–75.

[15] Deutscher, pp. 282–83. At the Fourteenth Party Congress Stalin, occupying his usual safe middle position, admitted that both Bukharin's neonarodnik approach and Zinoviev's antipeasant approach were deviations but suggested that the Party was less well equipped to deal with those who underestimated the importance of the alliance with the middle peasants, and for this reason should concentrate its fire on the struggle with the second deviation. Carr, *Socialism in One Country,* II, 132.

[16] Deutscher, p. 277.

in October, 1926, the Joint Opposition was defeated. Zinoviev was deprived of his post in the Comintern and Trotsky was dropped from his post in the Politburo.[17] Presumably, the appearance of Bukharin's neo-narodnik theories in 1925 marks the beginning of what Trotsky called the right phase in the history of the Comintern and the Soviet Union.

As Zinoviev took the field in the Soviet Union against Bukharin's "wager on the kulak," he abandoned his extravagant plans for winning the peasantry of the world through the Comintern. But, while Zinoviev was becoming disenchanted with the peasant, Bukharin's love affair with the peasant was just beginning. From the spring of 1925 through 1926 it was Bukharin, not Zinoviev, who called upon the Communists of the world to bring their missionary zeal to bear on rural areas. This is not to say, as Trotsky implies, that Bukharin's policy toward the peasantry was the same as Zinoviev's. Zinoviev's peasantism was founded on the expectation of imminent revolution, while Bukharin's was based upon expectation of a long nonrevolutionary period ahead. To Zinoviev, alliance with a radical peasant party was a tactic which might be used in a politically unstable agrarian society to hasten an impending revolution and a tactic which might facilitate the creation of a proletarian dictatorship. Once communism had triumphed, such backward countries presumably could transmit the revolution to their economically more advanced neighbors. Zinoviev's peasantism was derived only tangentially from the New Economic Policy in Russia. Visions of world revolution still danced in his head. To Bukharin, the alliance with or infiltration of peasant parties was part of the slow accretion of popular support necessary in preparation for a revolutionary situation which had not yet appeared. Bukharin's peasantism was the international counterpart of his interpretation of "socialism in one country." Just as in Russia the NEP could become a means of "evolving" toward socialism, so in the international arena concessions to the peasantry and cultivation of the peasants' revolutionary instincts might bring other countries to revolution ultimately and at a snail's pace. The difference appears slight, but it is fundamental. Bukharin's approach was a product of pessimism and caution, Zinoviev's of determined optimism in the

17 *Ibid.*, p. 296.

face of adversity. The difference between the two approaches is partly a reflection of differences in temperament.[18] It became critical when the mood of Bukharin came to replace that of Zinoviev in the Comintern.

Events in Eastern Europe had already begun to turn against Zinoviev in 1923. The spectacular successes through which Zinoviev had expected to exalt his position in the Soviet hierarchy did not materialize. Although Radek bore the brunt of the responsibility for the failures of 1923, there is convincing evidence that Zinoviev's prestige was shaken as well.[19]

Zinoviev took refuge in revolutionary fantasies, and in 1924 they were fantasies. At the beginning of 1924 Zinoviev still found that Lenin's view of the peasantry, his idea of combining the workers' revolution with the peasant wars, was the "most fundamental feature of Leninism," "the most important discovery that Lenin made." [20] In keeping with this view, Zinoviev tried to diminish his own burden of guilt for Comintern failures in peasant countries in 1923 by proving that these events were not failures at all. He urged the Communist world to see in these defeats the beginning of a new tide of Communist revolution. According to Zinoviev, the events of 1923 marked the end of the "democratic-pacifist era" and the beginning of a second wave of world revolution.

Yes, the movements in Bulgaria and in Poland have been crushed for the time being. Yes, General von Seeckt triumphed in Germany. But, for all that, the events which ran high in Bulgaria, Poland, and Germany throughout September and October, 1923, are the beginning of a second wave of international proletarian revolution. True, the tempo of events is not quick enough. Our revolutionary impatience is quite natural. But, speaking objectively, everything is developing at a fairly good pace. Less than two

[18] The best analyses available in English of the personalities of these two men are available in Deutscher, pp. 77–79, 82–83; and Carr, *Socialism in One Country*, I, 152–58, 162–73.

[19] Rosmer maintains and Rothschild suggests that Zinoviev in particular was blamed for the failure in Bulgaria. Alfred Rosmer, *Moscou sous Lénine: Les origines du communisme* (Paris, 1953), p. 277, and Joseph Rothschild, *The Communist Party of Bulgaria* (New York, 1959), p. 150. Carr points out that the collapse of the German revolution could only lower the prestige of the Comintern and its president. Carr, *Socialism in One Country*, I, 156.

[20] G. Zinoviev, "V. I. Lenin—genii, uchitel', vozhd i chelovek," *Kommunisticheskii Internatsional*, No. 1 (N.S.) (1924), p. 16.

months have passed since the fierce and bloody suppression of the Bulgarian insurrection and the Bulgarian Communists are already once again on their legs. Even at the regimented elections organized by the Tsankov government, the bloc of Communists and peasants won their greatest victories. What the Russian workers and peasants demanded in the years after 1905 has only been demanded in Bulgaria in the last few weeks. Also, the workers in Germany will surely recover from the blows of reaction much more quickly than many think. One does not have to be a prophet to foresee that a new explosion of the mass revolutionary movement is inevitable this winter or next spring.[21]

The revolutionary events in Bulgaria in 1923 are only the beginning of great revolutionary shocks both in Bulgaria and in the whole Balkan peninsula. Watch both. You will see clearly that through Bulgaria the revolution will open a path for itself to all other Balkan countries.[22]

Optimism had dominated the post-mortem on the German Revolution conducted by the Presidium of the ECCI in January, 1924, in which the following resolution was adopted.

The events which took place in Germany, Poland and Bulgaria in the period from May to November 1923 marked the beginning of a new chapter in the history of the international movement.

In Germany, along with the development of the crisis in the Ruhr, the proletarian class war passed from the phase of gradual accumulation of revolutionary forces into a new phase concerning the fight for power.[23]

At the same meeting Zinoviev made it quite clear that his slogan "workers' and peasants' government" applied only to revolutionary situations.

It is essential that communists in all countries should now ponder carefully what the tactics of the United Front are and are not. They are the tactics of revolution, not of evolution, just as the Workers' (and Peasants') Government cannot be for us a marked democratic coalition nor an alliance with the Social Democrats. They are primarily a method of revolutionary agitation and mobilization. We reject all other interpretations as opportunistic.[24]

[21] G. Zinoviev, "Vtoraia volna mezhdunarodnoi revoliutsii," *Pravda,* Dec. 1, 1923, p. 1.

[22] G. Zinoviev, "Pervoe piatiletie kominterna," *Kommunisticheskii Internatsional,* No. 1 (N.S.) (Feb. 1924), p. 174.

[23] *The Lesson of the German Events* (Moscow, 1924), p. 63. According to Carr, this brief pamphlet is the only published record of these meetings, which took place January 8–21, 1924. Carr. *The Interregnum,* p. 237, n. 1.

[24] *The Lesson of the German Events,* p. 65.

Although ordinary alliances between other political parties and Communist parties were condemned, this did not apply to the Krestintern. Nevertheless, the above resolution seems to forbid the very tactics which Bukharin would soon recommend.

The year 1924 did mark the beginning of a second and new stage in the history of the Comintern, but it was not one of revolutionary optimism. The prophecies of Zinoviev were not fulfilled and the Comintern turned increasingly to Varga and Bukharin, who offered a more credible interpretation of the pattern of world events. Bukharin urged the Comintern to accept the "temporary stabilization of capitalism" as an accomplished fact and abandon all hope of quick and easy victories. The Comintern's official recognition of the absence of strong revolutionary tendencies in the West conveniently confirmed the arguments of those who said that "socialism in one country" was the only possible policy in the Soviet Union. For the Comintern it meant more intensive concentration on the use of legal means for strengthening the Communist movement, the use of more effective propaganda, the use of election campaigns, the infiltration of other parties, and the improvement of party discipline. One aspect of these new tactics was greater stress on the Krestintern and East European peasant parties.

At the Fifth Congress of the Communist International, which met from June 18 to July 8, 1924, there were already signs that Zinoviev belonged to an era that had passed. This was the first Comintern congress in which Stalin appeared as a Russian delegate, and it marked the beginning of his intervention in the international Communist movement.

At this Fifth World Congress, Stalin became known to Comintern delegates for the first time. He glided silently, almost furtively, into salons and corridors around St. Andrew's hall. Smoking his pipe, wearing the characteristic tunic and Wellington boots, he spoke softly and politely with small groups, assisted by an inconspicuous interpreter, presenting himself as the new type of Russian leader. The younger delegates were impressed by this pose as the revolutionary who despised revolutionary rhetoric, the down-to-earth organizer whose quick decisions and modernized methods would solve the problems in a changed world. The men around Zinoviev were old, fussy, outmoded.[25]

[25] Ruth Fischer, *Stalin and German Communism* (Cambridge, Mass., 1948), pp. 404–5.

Bukharin's days were also numbered. He was useful only in the struggle against Zinoviev and Trotsky.

Zinoviev, though still plotting a master stroke in the Balkans through the Krestintern and the Balkan Communist Federation,[26] assumed a defensive posture at the Fifth Comintern Congress. He halfheartedly accepted "the stabilization of capitalism," but clung tenaciously to the theory that revolution might break out in one country or another, meaning Bulgaria or Germany.[27] He denied that the slogan "workers' and peasants' government" was intended to describe a special transitional form somewhere between bourgeois democracy and the proletarian dictatorship (thus contradicting his position at the Third Enlarged Plenum of the ECCI). The slogan, said Zinoviev, was no more than a pseudonym for the proletarian dictatorship. Not surprisingly, Zinoviev was accused of inconsistency.[28] He redefined the tactic of the united front more carefully and his qualifications were incorporated in the final theses of the congress. Zinoviev indicated that the proper application of this tactic required that no alliances be made with other political parties unless at the same time there was a systematic effort on the part of the Communist party to infiltrate and subvert them.[29] Direct coalitions between workers' and peasants' parties without this kind of infiltration from below were explicitly condemned.[30] In keeping with the growing assumption of the irrefutability of the Russian experience, Zinoviev claimed that the ideal example of a united front between a workers' and a peasants' party was the alliance between the Social Revolutionaries and the Bolsheviks at the time of the Kornilov revolt.[31]

While Zinoviev was cautiously backtracking, Bukharin picked up the agrarian question where Zinoviev had dropped it at the Third Enlarged Plenum. In his report on the proposed program for the Comintern, Bukharin deduced further international lessons from the NEP in Russia, arguing that under the dictatorship of the proletariat

[26] See pp. 99–111, 251–53 below.
[27] *Piatyi vsemirnyi kongress Kommunisticheskogo Internatsionala (18 iunia— 8 iulia 1924 goda)* (Moscow, 1925), I, 91.
[28] *Ibid.,* p. 69.
[29] *Ibid.,* p. 70.
[30] *Ibid.*
[31] *Ibid.*

agricultural cooperatives and syndicates could become instruments for the creation of socialism in the countryside.[32] This meant that the distribution of part of the confiscated land to the peasantry in the October Revolution was not a step backwards. The distribution of land, said Bukharin, won the peasant over to the task of creating socialism after the revolution. Bukharin concluded by saying:

To recapitulate my main ideas: I think that the reports presented at the Fourth Congress must be the basis of our new attitude toward this question. What is actually new is the declaration of our philosophy and the more comprehensive treatment of the New Economic Policy of the proletariat.[33]

This was an indication that the Russian experience would continue to provide the model for the agrarian policy of the Communist International.

Vasil Kolarov, the Bulgarian Communist leader, fresh from his failures in Bulgaria, gave the major address on the agrarian question. Since he, Dimitrov, and Genov had outdone themselves in following Comintern orders, their prestige was enhanced, rather than diminished, by the ill-fated putsch of September, 1923.[34] Kolarov announced that "the Fifth Congress is concerned with peasant movements and the evaluation of the peasant masses." [35] He pointed out that "up till now we have paid almost no attention to peasant organizations, we still have not defined our tactics in relation to these organizations." [36]

Fully accepting Zinoviev's new definition of the tactic of the united front, Kolarov indicated that the best examples of the proper application of the united front from above were the events in Bulgaria in September, 1923, in Croatia and the United States in 1924.[37] But Kolarov was careful to point out that no single rule for peasant political parties everywhere could be devised and that Communist parties should decide their policies on the basis of local conditions.

Kolarov also had extravagant praise for the Krestintern, saying that it had "enormous political and revolutionary significance."

[32] *Ibid.*, pp. 497–506.
[33] *Ibid.*, p. 505.
[34] Rothschild, p. 108, n. 4.
[35] *Piatyi vsemirnyi kongress*, I, 744.
[36] *Ibid.*, p. 753.
[37] *Ibid.*, p. 755.

In order to strengthen this [International Peasant Council] we must attract all the organizations of toilers in the countryside, we must provide guidance to all the dissident elements which arose in all countries as a result of the war and the economic crisis. The Communist International and Communist parties must unconditionally and energetically support the peasant movement.

We must look upon this newborn organization as an ally and an assistant to all Communist parties in their revolutionary work of decisively winning over the peasant masses to alliance with the working class and for social revolution.[38]

The relationship between the Comintern and the Krestintern was defined in the resolutions of the Fifth Congress. Resolution One stated in part:

It [the Comintern] states that between the theses adopted by the First International Peasant Conference and the theses of the Second and Fourth congresses of the Comintern there is no divergence. In view of this it [the Comintern] directs all sections of the Comintern to support the work of the International Peasant Council and its sections in separate countries in organizing toilers, the equally oppressed workers and peasants, for struggle against the existing social structure.[39]

And Resolution Nine stated in part:

As a general rule, Communist parties must maintain constant ties with sections and organizations of the International Peasant Council in separate countries and energetically bend peasant organizations toward it.[40]

From the proceedings it is clear, however, that few of the delegates demonstrated a great deal of enthusiasm for the agrarian question. By the time Varga rose to speak on this question most of the delegates had left the hall.[41] Few delegates offered new or practical suggestions. A Polish delegate, Gordon, indicated that the agrarian theses were too abstract and vague, but offered no suggestions of his own.[42] The most pointed comments came from a Swiss delegate, Bringolf, who indicated that the Communists could learn a great deal from the study of successful peasant political movements like that of Dr. Laur in his

[38] Ibid.
[39] Ibid., II, 132.
[40] Ibid., p. 134.
[41] Ibid., I, 763.
[42] Ibid., pp. 764–66.

own country.[43] In particular, Bringolf maintained, workers who were sent into rural areas should receive special training so that they would know how to speak "the language of the peasants" and woo the peasantry on the basis of its concrete needs.[44] Bringolf concluded with the observation that some of the peasants of Western Europe were not ready for revolt, and that in this area the primary task of the Krestintern would have to be the dissemination of propaganda.[45]

As was usually the case, the delegates from Eastern Europe dominated the discussion of the agrarian question, four of the seven speakers on this question (including Kolarov) being from that area. The final resolutions on the question strongly stressed the need for infiltrating peasant organizations and winning the peasants away from the "landowners and kulaks" who, according to the Comintern, usually controlled peasant political parties.[46] Also, as usual, the complaints of dissenting delegates went unanswered.

Between the Fifth Comintern Congress in the summer of 1924 and the Fifth Plenum of the ECCI in March, 1925, it became apparent that the Krestintern was losing ground. Early in March that organization began to apologize for its deficiencies. First of all, the Krestintern pointed out that, unlike the Comintern, it did not have any existing sympathetic party organizations on which it could build.[47] Secondly, terroristic methods were being applied against members of the International Peasant Council.[48] Lastly, the Krestintern asserted that its own program was too general and abstract; what was needed was the formulation of tactics and methods of organization suited to the special needs of each individual country.[49]

Presumably, the Fifth Plenum would remedy the situation. This plenum met on the eve of Zinoviev's open opposition to Bukharin's pro-kulak policy at home. Bukharin was still flushed with his recent victories over Preobrazhensky, and "socialism in one country" would

[43] Ibid., p. 767.
[44] Ibid., pp. 767–68.
[45] Ibid., p. 768.
[46] Ibid., II, 133.
[47] "K plenumu Mezhdunarodnogo Krest'ianskogo Soveta," Krest'ianskii Internatsional, No. 1–2 (Jan.–Feb., 1925), p. 4.
[48] Ibid., p. 5.
[49] Ibid., p. 6.

be officially accepted as a guiding precept by the Fourteenth Conference of the Russian Communist Party at the end of the month.[50] One of the major themes of the Fifth Plenum was the "Bolshevization of Communist parties," which means essentially bringing the conflict within the Russian Party into the international arena and weeding Trotsky's supporters out of member parties. A second theme was the "stabilization of capitalism," a phrase which would soon replace Zinoviev's phrase "the democratic-pacifist era" to describe the absence of revolutionary tendencies in Europe between 1923 and 1927.

Within this context Bukharin gave a report to the plenum on "The Peasant Question and the World Proletarian Revolution," explaining sixty-three lengthy new theses on this subject which he had composed for the occasion. Bukharin referred pointedly to the conflict within the Russian Party.

The last crisis, for example, in the Russian Communist Party was by no means superficial. We needed a new orientation on the peasant question. This was the objective significance of our discussion. I will turn to this in my report on Trotskyism. We tried to grope our way toward the correct line and we succeeded. Now we are putting into practice the correct tactic in the peasant question. Here is the chief reason for our struggle against Trotskyism, and other Communist parties will have to follow our example as soon as they declare themselves against Trotskyism. Their first problem will be to formulate the correct point of view on the peasant question and, what is even more important, conduct themselves according to the new political line. As long as comrades do not hew to the correct line on the peasant question, they do not have the right to call themselves Leninists.[51]

It could be argued that Bukharin's theses were completely in accord with the synthesis of the writings of Marx and Lenin in vogue at that time. In Bukharin's new resolutions the importance of maintaining Communist control of every phase of the revolution was repeated,[52] the technical superiority of large-scale agriculture was reaffirmed,[53] and the twin dangers of Social Democratic and narodnik deviations were recognized.

[50] Carr, *Socialism in One Country*, II, 45–51.
[51] *Rasshirennyi plenum ispolkoma Kommunisticheskogo Internatsionala—protokoly zasedanii (21 marta–6 aprelia, 1925)* (Moscow, 1925), p. 317.
[52] Resolution 31, *ibid.*, p. 536.
[53] Resolution 14, *ibid.*, p. 532; Resolution 33, *ibid.*, 537.

In all their work among the peasantry, Communists must, on the one hand, avoid the Social Democratic deviation (passivity in the peasant question) and, on the other, avoid unprincipled pandering to the peasant, surrendering all Marxist positions. A Communist must also avoid the narodnik deviation (rubbing away the distinction between the proletariat and the peasantry, slurring over the question of differentiation among the peasantry, ignoring the idea of proletarian hegemony).[54]

Bukharin also gave proper deference to the agrarian theses of the Second and Fourth congresses of the Comintern, pointing out that his own theses merely elaborated the general line established at these congresses.[55] Bukharin repeated Lenin's classification of the peasantry and the two basic "lessons" in the agrarian question—the Hungarian lesson on redistribution and the Bulgarian lesson on the impossibility of the peasant playing the role of the third force in politics.[56]

What is different about Bukharin's theses is the image of the proletarian revolution which he describes as an example and a definitive pattern for all Communist parties. It was in this way that the industrialization controversy was to affect the agrarian policy of the Comintern, altering the whole tone of Comintern directives on this question. While admitting that concessions to the peasantry strengthened the peasant's desire for property, Bukharin held that if such concessions were made by a proletarian dictatorship they would lead to socialism.

These new conditions [the proletarian dictatorship] make possible the noncapitalist evolution of the peasant economy. In its development it can now pass through cooperation to socialism, though in contradictory forms. While under conditions of capitalism cooperatives established by the unification of peasant households inevitably are converted into capitalist enterprises as soon as they show signs of vitality (because they are dependent on capitalist banks and the capitalistic economic milieu), in general, under the dictatorship of the proletariat they develop in a different direction because they are dependent on proletarian industry, proletarian banks, etc. In other words, if under capitalism they grow into a system of capitalistic economic organizations, under the new conditions, given the correct policy on the part of the proletarian state, they will grow into a system of socialist economic relationships.[57]

[54] Resolution 58, *ibid.,* pp. 542–43.
[55] Resolution 1, *ibid.,* p. 528.
[56] *Ibid.,* p. 320; Resolution 58, *ibid.,* pp. 542–43.
[57] Resolution 25, *ibid.,* p. 535.

For this reason, maintained Bukharin in his theses, colonial or semicolonial countries could "jump over" the capitalistic stage, passing from feudalism or semifeudalism directly into socialism.[58] This meant that in economically backward countries the study of the peasantry, work among the peasantry, and, above all, winning the peasants over to the Communist cause acquired special significance.[59]

In addition to the "lessons" of the NEP, Bukharin used two arguments which brought him to the brink of deviation from orthodoxy. First, there was the implication that the peasantry was becoming a self-conscious social group.

The war and the course of events after the war were accompanied by a fall in productive capacity and, in general, a disruption of the old relationship between town and country in a number of countries. The economic power of the village as a producer of goods providing immediate nourishment grew greatly. Simultaneously the specific gravity of all rural classes rose, but in the first place that of the peasantry.

On the other hand, the shock to the whole economic system, the great widening of the ideological horizons of the peasantry, brought on by the war and the postwar revolutionary ferment, has greatly heightened the activities of the peasantry, of the poor and middle peasants as well as of rural bourgeois circles. Finally, the blows suffered by imperialistic forces have to the highest degree intensified the colonial liberation movement in which the peasants play a huge role.[60]

Second, Bukharin raised the old populist argument that the peasants were important simply because there were so many of them.

As long as the huge majority of the population of this world is peasants, the question of the struggle of the peasantry stands as one of the central questions of policy both from the point of view of the struggle of the proletariat for power and from the point of view of strengthening its power and its economic base.[61]

For Bukharin it was clear that in the great majority of countries the proletarian dictatorship could not be established "without the direct assistance of the petty peasantry and the neutrality of the middle peasantry." [62] He departed wholly from orthodoxy by insisting

---

[58] Resolution 27, *ibid.*, pp. 535–36.
[59] Resolution 42, *ibid.*, p. 539; Resolution 48, *ibid.*, p. 540.
[60] Resolutions 34–35, *ibid.*, p. 537–38.
[61] Resolution 2, *ibid.*, p. 528.
[62] Resolution 21, *ibid.*, p. 534.

that the middle peasantry need not be condemned to neutrality in the proletarian revolution; it might under certain conditions in both capitalist and semifeudal countries become an active ally of the proletariat.[63]

To attract peasants before the revolution, Communist parties were supposed to use three lines of attack, a campaign against taxes, a campaign against the high prices of manufactured goods, and a campaign against war.[64] Parties were ordered not to be content with slogans like "dictatorship of the proletariat" or "workers' and peasants' government." Peasants, said Bukharin, would be won only by supporting their concrete and immediate demands.[65]

Where peasant parties did not exist, Communists could form peasant trade unions on the same basis as industrial trade unions, but Communist parties were explicitly forbidden to form peasant political parties.[66] Communist parties were told to form blocs with peasant political parties where they existed and, if they could not dominate these peasant political organizations, they were to split them until a faction had been created which the Communists could dominate.[67]

This, then, was Bukharin's peasantism in the Comintern. While sufficiently pale in comparison to the real article, it was so unorthodox in Marxist terms that it provided first Zinoviev and then Stalin with a "straw man" to knock down in the struggle for political power. While Stalin supported Bukharin against the opposition from 1925 to 1927, he remained sufficiently aloof from this side of "Bukharinism" to turn it against Bukharin in the long run.

The debate which followed Bukharin's report was conducted primarily by the East European members of the Plenum. It centered largely on the question of suitable forms of organization for peasants converted to the alliance between the peasants and the workers. Boshkovich and Dąbal argued in favor of Communist-sponsored peasant political parties, perhaps on the basis of the disappointing experiences they had in the Krestintern in trying to

---

[63] Resolutions 9 and 13, *ibid.*, pp. 531–32.
[64] Resolution 43, *ibid;* p. 540.
[65] Resolution 44, *ibid.*
[66] Resolutions 50–53; *ibid.*, pp. 541–42.
[67] *Ibid.*

organize the peasantry without being able to deal with sympathetic, organized political parties.

Meshcheriakov suggested that the resolutions be altered in order to delegate to the Krestintern all responsibility for work among peasants in colonial countries.[68] Varga argued that, while he personally did not favor Communist-sponsored peasant political parties, a peasant union could seek redress only from the state (unlike industrial trade unions, which could seek redress from the factory owner). A peasant trade union, said Varga, would therefore tend to become a political party, no matter what it was called.[69] Dąbal raised the eternal question of the indifference of Communist parties to work among the peasants. He pointed out that in France, as soon as the International Peasant Union established a branch there, the French Communist Party turned all work in rural areas over to this section, as if to rid itself of an undesirable burden.[70] Dąbal, like Varga, raised the question whether one could draw a sharp line between peasant unions and peasant parties, indicating that Stamboliiski's party was both an economic and a political organization.[71] Boshkovich proposed that the work of all agrarian sections of Communist parties be strengthened by appointing to each a member of the party's central committe.[72] None of these suggestions was accepted.

There was a certain schoolmarm quality about Bukharin's rebuttal to these criticisms which contrasts sharply with the earlier revolutionary bombast of Zinoviev and the subsequent ponderous canonical quality of Stalin's pronouncements. Bukharin sounded less like a revolutionary and more like a philosophy professor carefully building a case against a school of thought he personally disliked.

Bukharin dismissed Meshcheriakov's proposal as a move which would undermine the hegemony of the Communist parties in revolutions in colonial areas.[73] His reply to those who stated that peasant

[68] *Ibid.*, pp. 342–43.
[69] *Ibid.*, pp. 340–41.
[70] *Ibid.*, p. 534.
[71] *Ibid.*, p. 355.
[72] *Ibid.*, p. 337.
[73] *Ibid.*, pp. 359–60. Carr erroneously asserts that the founding of the Krestintern "helped to kindle in Bukharin fresh hopes of the revolutionary potentialities of the peasant." Carr, *Socialism in One Country*, I, 170. Bukharin

unions would inevitably become peasant parties was that "from the point of view of strictly formal logic, this, perhaps, is true, but from the dialectical point of view it is untrue and does not correspond to actuality." [74] Bukharin agreed that, just as the peasant soviets were politically oriented in 1917, so peasant unions would be politically oriented in 1925, but he advanced two reasons why the union form of organization was preferable to the political party.

> Why do we prefer an organization of this type? Because it has the widest appeal. In a political party only those people can be members who accept its program and who are willing to conduct themselves as prescribed by the party. Here is why we prefer the form of the peasant union. Such unions would give us great freedom of movement. Given the amorphous condition of the peasantry, our comrades can enter into such a broad union and create the proper environment for winning new adherents. This is why this form, at present, is more correct, more suitable, not to mention the problem peasant parties would pose after the seizure of power. Among other things it is necessary to take this latter factor into account.[75]

So, in effect, Bukharin believed that through the instrument of peasant unions a wider variety of peasants might be won over to the Communist cause and the task of Communist infiltrators would be considerably easier. Also, the peasant union would be easier to deal with than a peasant political party after the seizure of power. There is implicit in the latter point a genuine fear of the vitality of the peasant political movement.

Bukharin's theses were never really rescinded and the agrarian question was not discussed again in any detail until the Sixth Comintern Congress in 1928. Bukharin would replace Zinoviev as the chief of the Comintern in the fall of 1926. The theses represented part of the cumulative trend toward the formulation of Comintern policy without reference to conditions outside the Soviet Union or to the experience of member parties. As a result the program was excessively general and theoretical, and too strongly influenced by conditions prevailing in Russia. Although in the short run the new program led to more intensive Communist efforts in rural areas, in the long run

---

never expressed much enthusiasm for the Krestintern, and his "fresh hopes" must be explained in some other way.

[74] *Rasshirennyi planum*, 1925, p. 356.

[75] *Ibid.*, p. 358.

it brought the Comintern no great victories in the villages of Eastern Europe.

The Red Peasant International did profit from the new emphasis placed on the peasantry in the Russian Communist Party. For a short time in 1924 it acutally seemed as though the Krestintern might become a major arm of the Comintern. However, with the exception of a few sensational, but historically insignificant, incidents in the 1920s, the Krestintern never won a place among the chief organs of the international Communist movement, though it seems to have lingered on in the shadow of the Comintern until 1939.[76]

The goals of the Krestintern were clearly defined, but the means for achieving those goals were not. According to the organizational statutes, the Krestintern was supposed to support itself by contributions from its members, but there is no doubt that it had to be heavily subsidized by the Soviet state.[77] Although local Communist parties

[76] The statement of Carr that "immediately after the congress [the founding congress of the Krestintern in October, 1923] the International Peasant Council held its first, and apparently its only, session," is not correct. Later meetings were held. The dissolution of the Krestintern is attested by a biography of Kolarov in which the following passage appears: "From 1928 up to the dissolution of the Peasant International in 1939, Kolarov was chairman of its executive committee." *Bol'shaia sovetskaia entsiklopediia*, 2d ed., XXI, 580. Actually, its dissolution may have occurred earlier. In *Malaia sovetskaia entsiklopedia*, 2d ed., Vol. V (Nov. 1936), under the heading *Krest'ianskii Internatsional,* the reader is referred to the heading *Mezhdunarodnyi krest'-ianskii sovet.* Turning to the section of *Malaia sovetskaia entsiklopediia,* 2d ed., Vol. VI (Oct. 1937), where this heading should appear, one finds nothing. Presumably this organization's existence as a phase in the history of the Comintern ended some time early in 1937 when many of the Krestintern's original leaders fell victim to the Great Purges. Dąbal was executed in 1935 for "having associated with bourgeois circles (his wife was from that milieu) and with the Polish police." M. K. Dziewanowski, *The Communist Party of Poland: An Outline of History* (Cambridge, Mass., 1959), p. 338, n. 25.

[77] The organizational statutes of the Krestintern are not very explicit about its financial base. Article 12 says that "the necessary means for the conduct of affairs will be drawn from the dues of peasant organizations which have joined the International Peasant Council." *Pravda,* No. 235 (Oct. 17, 1923), p. 2, and *Pervaia mezhdunarodnaia krest'ianskaia konferentsiia—rechi, tezisy, vozzvaniia* (Moscow, 1924), p. 171. Since most of the "several million" members claimed by the Krestintern were supplied by official Soviet peasant organizations (see below, p. 99), it seems likely that the Soviet government provided most of the financial support for the Krestintern in the guise of dues.

apparently assigned some of their members to work with the Krestintern, there seems to have been a chronic shortage of personnel. Some radical East European peasant leaders were enticed into the Krestintern, at least temporarily, notably Ivan Bodnar (Lokat) in Czechoslovakia, Stjepan Radić in Yugoslavia, and Wojewódzki and Tarashkevich in Poland. But, on the whole, such alliances were ephemeral. The Krestintern seems to have used two approaches, sometimes simultaneously, in dealing with peasant political parties: direct negotiation in order to achieve a united front from above; propaganda, infiltration, and especially indoctrination in order to achieve a united front from below. In trying to establish a united front from above the Krestintern was able to add to its own talents the combined resources of the Soviet diplomatic corps and the regional bureaus of the Comintern (especially the Central European Bureau of the Comintern at Vienna).[78]

In countries where a peasant political party had a solid and effective national organization, the attempt to establish a united front from above was the most common method. In trying to establish a united front from below the Krestintern, through appeals and telegrams, tried to advertise its cause and draw genuine peasant political parties into its activities, exposing party members to the Communist point of view. This method was used in all countries, but was most effective where there was a tendency for the peasant movement to split into factions, as in Bulgaria and Poland. The Krestintern had one advantage over the Comintern in applying both versions of the united front. One could join the Krestintern and support the idea of joint Communist-agrarian activity without embracing the whole Communist program and accepting the stigma of Comintern membership. A third approach, never officially sanctioned by the Comintern, was the creation of peasant political parties by local Communist parties. This tactic seems to have been successfully applied in Poland. Where peasant political parties had not yet developed and Communist

[78] There were four major regional branches or permanent bureaus of the Comintern in the early 1920s, the South American Bureau in Buenos Aires, the West European Bureau in Berlin, the South Eastern Bureau in Vienna, and the Far Eastern Bureau in Vladivostok. Günther Nollau, *International Communism and World Revolution: History and Methods* (New York, 1961), pp. 139–42.

parties could operate legally, as in Sub-Carpathian Ruthenia in Czechoslovakia, Communists tried to garner the peasant vote for their own party. What was most amazing in all these efforts was the almost negligible role played by Comintern agrarian policy, so painstakingly worked out in Moscow. Alliances were forged and peasant support was won generally as a result of Comintern policy on the national question.

The Krestintern never seemed closer to its goals than in the summer of 1924. Trotsky described the Krestintern's year of triumph as follows:

During 1924, *i.e.*, in the course of the basic year of "stabilization," the communist press was filled with absolutely fantastic data on the strength of the Peasant International. Dąbal, its representative, reported that the Peasant International, six months after its formation, already embraced several million members.[79]

These hordes of loyal peasants, however, bear closer scrutiny. Four million of the supposed members were from official Soviet organizations.[80] The remainder belonged to peasant organizations with which the Krestintern had established precarious alliances.

In July, 1924, two pro-Communist peasant political parties were formed in Poland, probably with the connivance of the Krestintern: the Independent Peasant Party of Wojewódzki and the Belorussian Workers' and Peasants' Hramada of Tarashkevich. In March, the Czechoslovak Communist Party won an impressive victory in the special elections in Sub-Carpathian Ruthenia with the help of a peasant Communist, Ivan Bodnar (real name Lokat). These triumphs are treated in more detail in later chapters. The main thrust of the Comintern, involving neither the creation of peasant political parties nor electoral victories, was in the Balkans. Here the joint efforts of the Krestintern and the Balkan Communist Federation threatened to unite all the revolutionary forces on the peninsula and drown the established governments of Bulgaria, Rumania, and Yugoslavia in revolution. This was to be accomplished, however, almost exclusively by a united front from above, an alliance between the

[79] Trotsky, p. 119.
[80] "Pervaia godovshchina," *Krest'ianskii Internatsional*, No. 1–2 (Jan.–Feb. 1925), pp. 6–7.

leaders of the Communist parties and the largest radical peasant
political movements in these three countries. At the end of April,
an alliance was concluded in Vienna between the militant Internal
Macedonian Revolutionary Organization (IMRO) and Communist
delegates in which the former agreed essentially to lend its support
to the revolutionary efforts of the Balkan Communist Federation.[81]
IMRO agreed to support all revolutionary federalist movements in
the Balkans, including the Croatian Republican Peasant Party.[82]
On July 1, 1924, the leader of this party, Stjepan Radić, was accepted
as a member of the Krestintern at his own request. In August, Nedelko
Atanasov and Khristo Stoianov, two leaders of the Bulgarian Agrarian
Union, met in Prague with George Dimitrov and agreed on behalf of
their party to join Communist efforts to establish a workers' and
peasants' government in Bulgaria.[83] The missing link in the chain of
alliances was Rumania. In October, ten days after Radić had returned
to Yugoslavia, a prominent leader of the Rumanian Peasant Party,
Dr. Lupu, attended the congress of the Croatian Republican Peasant
Party at Radić's request, and the rumor was widespread that the former party would join the Krestintern,[84] a rumor the Krestintern did
little to suppress. Dąbal later indicated that Lupu had strong sympathy
for the Krestintern and its goals.[85] At the end of October the Krestintern sent a secret letter to the leaders of the Rumanian Peasant

[81] Joseph Swire, *Bulgarian Conspiracy* (London, 1939), pp. 182–90. The
manifesto released by IMRO spelling out the terms of the alliance is available in Elizabeth Barker, *Macedonia: Its Place in Balkan Power Politics*
(London, 1950), pp. 55–57. For a full and annotated treatment see Rothschild, chap. IX.

[82] Rothschild, p. 186. Rothschild reports that the Bulgarian government
claimed to have documents proving that a "Communist-Federalist revolt was
planned to be launched in Petrich on September 15, 1924." *Ibid.*, p. 188, n.
65. The confidence of the Communists that civil war in Bulgaria and
Yugoslavia was imminent was reflected in the Seventh Conference of the
Balkan Communist Federation in July, 1924. *Ibid.*, p. 232.

[83] Kosta Todorov, *Balkan Firebrand: The Autobiography of a Rebel, Soldier
and Statesman* (New York, 1943), pp. 218–22. For an account of these events
by the participants see the documents collected by the Tsankov government,
La Conspiration bolchéviste contre la Bulgarie (Sofia, 1925), pp. 65–75. For
an analysis see Rothschild, pp. 165–68.

[84] A. Badulescu, "K IV Rumynskoi Krest'ianskoi Partii," *Krest'ianskii
Internatsional*, No. 10–12 (Nov.–Dec. 1924), p. 30.

[85] T. Dąbal, "Zadachi i dostizheniia Krestinterna na Zapade," *Krest'ianskii
Internatsional*, No. 3–5 (March–May, 1925), p. 36.

Party on the occasion of their Fourth Congress, inviting them to a conference of all peasant and Communist parties of Balkan and Danubian countries. The purpose of the conference would be to arrive at some agreement through which they could all unite their efforts to create a "single great union of workers' and peasants' republics in the Balkans." [86]

The Rumanian Peasant Party refused the invitation. The other alliances subsequently proved to be very fragile indeed. The publication of the agreement between the Communists and IMRO led to its repudiation by those IMRO leaders who had signed it. Their role in negotiating the pact was one motive in their assassination later in the year. The agreement with the Bulgarian Agrarian Union was not recognized by those agrarian leaders who controlled the party. Stjepan Radić renounced the Krestintern in March, 1925, and entered the Yugoslav government a few months later. The Bulgarian and Yugoslav cases deserve closer examination here because they reveal the miscalculations of the Krestintern.

The attempt of the Krestintern to draw in the Bulgarian Agrarian Union was entrusted to the three heroes of the September uprising in Bulgaria, Dimitrov, Genov, and Kolarov. It seems likely that Genov (or Gorov) was already serving as the chief delegate of the Krestintern in the whole affair. After unsuccessful negotiations in Vienna in January, 1924, a prominent leader of the Bulgarian Agrarian Union, Todorov, was invited to Moscow later in the month to continue these talks. According to Todorov, Kolarov offered to give the Bulgarian Agrarian Union arms from Odessa if the Communists were promised four ministerial posts in any future Bulgarian revolutionary government (specifying that the Communists wanted the key posts of war, the interior, and communications).[87] Todorov countered with a proposal that the two parties cooperate in the revolutionary struggle in Bulgaria, but that any future government in Bulgaria would be a provisional peasant government which would restore civil liberties,

[86] S. Timov, *Agrarnyi vopros i krest'ianskoe dvizhenie v Rumynii: Antineoiobăgia (Kritika neokrepostnicheskoi teorii K. Dobrodzhanu-Geriia)* (Moscow, 1929), p. 249; Badulescu, *Krest'ianskii Internatsional,* No. 10–12 (Nov.–Dec. 1924), p. 38.

[87] Todorov, p. 200. The most authoritative account of these negotiations is Rothschild, pp. 161–69.

legalize the Communist party, and hold new elections to determine what the future government would be.[88] Kolarov turned down this proposal, but Dimitrov finally offered to give Todorov the ministry of either war or the interior, appoint Gavril Genov as his assistant, and contribute twenty million French francs to the revolutionary cause if the Bulgarian Agrarian Union would join the Krestintern.[89] Dimitrov explained that all the progressive peasant parties of Europe, including the Croatian Peasant Party, were joining the Krestintern to work with the International Peasant Council for the creation of workers' and peasants' governments.

The outcome of these negotiations is not clear. According to Todorov, he flatly rejected these last proposals.[90] There was certainly no public announcement that the Bulgarian Agrarian Union had entered the Krestintern. Another account indicates that a general and unspecific agreement was reached on the principles of revolutionary struggle, according to which the two parties conceded little more than their joint devotion to the overthrow of the Tsankov government.[91] But, it is evident that Todorov was somewhat of an opportunist and probably received money and arms from the Communists.[92] In August, 1924, it would appear that Dimitrov persuaded two other leaders of the Bulgarian Agrarian Union to accept his terms, but the agreement had little effect owing to Todorov's opposition.[93] The last open approach to the leaders of the Bulgarian Agrarian Union was made on January 7, 1925, when the Krestintern invited them to prepare an article for *Krest'ianskii Internatsional* and exchange information on events in the Balkans.[94] The invitation was declined.

In the Bulgarian case the Krestintern had simply tried to barter with an exiled political party which had strong peasant support at

[88] Todorov, pp. 203–4.

[89] *Ibid.*, p. 204.

[90] *Ibid.*, p. 205.

[91] Rothschild, p. 164, indicates that this latter account is probably the correct one.

[92] *Ibid.*, pp. 164–67.

[93] Todorov, pp. 218–22. The rival accounts of these negotiations by participants was published by the Tsankov government in *La Conspiration bolcheviste*, pp. 67–75.

[94] The reply was published in *La Bulgarie sous le régime de l'assassinat* (Paris, 1925), pp. 473–76.

home, offering Soviet money and arms in exchange for support of the Krestintern and a share for the Communists in any future workers' and peasants' government in Bulgaria. Undaunted by the frustrating negotiations with the Bulgarian Agrarian Union, the Comintern tried to win adherents for the Krestintern elsewhere. Apparently the only prerequisite for admission to the Krestintern was that a peasant party be in opposition to the policies of its own government. In 1924 the Polish Peasant Party Wyzwolenie received a rather casual invitation to enter the Krestintern,[95] and at the same time the Krestintern began to court the Croatian Peasant Party.

The Krestintern was interested in the latter party because it was an opposition party, strong in membership and electoral support in a country where the indigenous Communist party was weak and declining.[96] Under Stjepan Radić's leadership the Croatian Peasant Party had refused to recognize the new Yugoslav government formed after the March elections in 1923 or to send its elected delegates to the national legislative assembly, the Skupština. But the Party was not very radical in its social program nor very revolutionary in its choice of political methods. It is difficult to see how it qualified as a prospective member of the Krestintern.

Radić opposed the Vidovdan Constitution, demanding greater autonomy for Croatia than was provided for in this document. Specifically he demanded that Croatia be permitted to govern herself from Zagreb, though she would accept a royal governor from Belgrade.[97] On July 14, 1923, the friction between Radić and Pašić's coalition government in Belgrade reached the breaking point when Radić made a speech strongly critical of the king and the government. Radić left the country in order to avoid arrest and went to London, where he hoped to obtain diplomatic support for his program.[98] Finding none, he returned to Vienna in February, 1924, where he

[95] *Krest'ianskii Internatsional,* No. 1 (April, 1924), pp. 184–88.

[96] Between 1920 and 1923 the proportion of the total popular vote won by Radić rose from 14 percent to 21 percent, while the proportion of total votes won by the Communist Party of Yugoslavia or its legal front party declined from 12 percent to 1 percent. B. Boshkovich, "Radich i khorvatskoe krest'ianstvo," *Krest'ianskii Internatsional,* No. 8–9 (Aug.–Sept. 1925), pp. 59–60. The figures for the Yugoslav Communist Party are from Branko Lazić, *Les Partis communistes d'Europe, 1919–1955* (Paris, 1956), p. 150.

[97] Vladko Maček, *In the Struggle for Freedom* (New York, 1957), p. 96.

[98] *Ibid.,* p. 97.

decided on a two-front campaign. His lieutenant, Maček, was sent to feel out Davidović's Democratic Party (an opposition party) for a possible compromise agreement, while Radić "took a hop" to Moscow to see what support he could obtain there.[99]

Radić had reason to hope that he would find the atmosphere congenial in Moscow. Dr. Goldenstein, secretary to the Soviet ambassador to Austria, and a ubiquitous agent of the Vienna Bureau of the Comintern, visited Radić on February 9 and March 26, 1924, to arrange the trip.[100] Like many Croatian Catholic leaders, Radić was possessed by a warm Pan-Slav sentiment for Mother Russia.[101] In spite of his close personal ties to Prague, Radić was repelled by the International Agrarian Bureau there, considering it an instrument of Czechoslovak foreign policy and too closely tied to that government.[102] He resented, in particular, the lack of support from the Green International for the Croatian cause,[103] and may have felt that he could best obtain this kind of support from the enemy of the Green International, the Krestintern, in Moscow. The Presidium of the Krestintern had sent Radić, through Goldenstein, a copy of its program and agenda, so he did not enter these negotiations in complete ignorance.[104]

Radić's guide in Moscow was the chief of the Balkan section of the Commissariat of Foreign Affairs, Sandomirskii, but Dąbal was assigned the task of persuading Radić to enlist in the Krestintern.[105] In an article written for the official organ of the Krestintern, Radić said very little about this organization and made it clear that his flirtation with Moscow was predicated upon the nationalities policy promulgated at the Fifth Comintern Congress and the Thirteenth Congress of the Russian Communist Party.[106] While having nothing

[99] *Ibid.*, p. 98.

[100] G. S. Besedovskii, *Na putiakh k termidoru* (Paris, 1930), I, 72; Robert G. Livingstone, "Stjepan Radić and the Croatian Peasant Party, 1904–1929" (unpublished Ph.D. dissertation, Department of History, Harvard University, 1959), p. 462.

[101] Livingstone, p. 464.

[102] *Ibid.*, p. 481.

[103] *Ibid.*

[104] *Ibid.*, p. 463.

[105] *Ibid.*, p. 468; B. Boshkovich, *Krest'ianskoe dvizhenie i natsional'nyi vopros v Iugoslavii* (Moscow, 1929), p. 91.

[106] Radić wrote: "The Thirteenth Congress of the Russian Communist Party and the Fifth Congress of the Comintern speak quite definitely and

but praise for the nationalities policy of the Russian Communist Party and the Comintern, Radić strongly criticized the Yugoslav Communist Party.

> The worker-Communists are, unfortunately, organized under the command of Serb Communists, centralists, who stand for the same point of view as the Serb militarists, especially on national and administrative questions.
>
> The Serb Communists recognize only the official nationality of the realm [Yugoslavia], which completely ignores the rights of the Croats and all other non-Serb nationalities.
>
> With reference to the political administration, it is the Serb Communists who are the most violent and severe centralists, refusing to agree to the slightest political autonomy for Croatia, barely agreeing to give it any sort of administrative autonomy. All these ideas on the national question and state structure stand in sharp opposition to the principles and practices of the Russian Communist Party, whereas they fully correspond to the principles of the Serb imperialistic bourgeoisie.
>
> Under such conditions it is only natural that the Croatian workers and the majority of the members of the Yugoslav Communist Party came over and entered the organization of the peasant party, where they remain to this very day.[107]

This is a completely inaccurate description of the position of the Yugoslav Communist Party, which had not just one, but two positions on the national question. A large so-called rightist Serbian faction in the Yugoslav Party denied that the national question was important, and urged the Party to concentrate its energies on the proletarian revolution rather than on bourgeois nationalistic dreams. But even this faction believed in the ultimate desirability of federal autonomy for national minorities, like that offered in the Soviet Union. A second, so-called leftist faction, consisting chiefly of members from the national minorities, gave wholehearted support for national self-determination up to and including secession, but had serious doubts about Radić and his "bourgeois" party as allies. The attitude of neither corresponded to the interests of Radić and the Comintern in 1924,

---

clearly on the national question in relation to the Balkans and the Croatian people. They recognize their full right to self-determination up to secession." Stjepan Radić, "Sovremennaia Khorvatiia kak novyi tip gosudarstvennogo stroitel'stva," *Krest'ianskii Internatsional*, No. 3–5 (June–July, 1924), pp. 53–54.

[107] *Ibid.*, p. 53.

and the Yugoslav Communist Party had already been seriously criticized for its "deviations" by the Comintern.[108] A considerable amount
of time was devoted to the national question in Yugoslavia at the
Fifth Comintern Congress, and a number of specific resolutions were
adopted on the question, resolutions which were not, apparently,
heeded by the Yugoslav Communist Party.

On June 27, 1924, Radić sent a letter to the Krestintern in which
he informed them that the plenum of his party, in its meeting of
May 1, 1924, authorized him to affiliate with the Krestintern in the
name of the Croatian Peasant Party.[109] He requested some decision on
the part of the Krestintern with regard to his application, since he
planned to leave Moscow in a matter of days. However, Radić's adherence was so qualified as to render it practically meaningless.
Radić offered to bring his party into the Krestintern on the following
basis:

First of all, it stands to reason that the Croatian Republican Peasant Party
will continue to pursue its own program using its own tactics, more or less,
and that in all other respects it fully agrees with the chief goal of the
Peasant International, which is an alliance of peasants, workers, and other
forces to end imperialistic wars for all time. Each side will join with the
other, and in the spirit of social justice they will take power in their hands
in all countries for the improvement of the lot of all toilers and for the
construction of a new peasants' and workers' state.[110]

The alliance was not without its humorous side, since Radić went
on to explain that an alliance between peasants and workers could
easily be achieved in Croatia if everyone joined the Croatian Peasant
Party, a party which already represented the interests of the Croatian
workers. Radić argued that the Communist Party of Yugoslavia need
play no role in the establishment or consolidation of a workers' and
peasants' government in Croatia since the accession of the Croatian

[108] See pp. 221–24 below.

[109] The letter is reprinted in full in *Krest'ianskii Internatsional*, No. 3–5
(June–July, 1924), pp. 144–46, along with the Krestintern's letter of
acceptance. Livingstone indicates that in May Radić had been granted "full
powers" by a meeting of the leaders of his party on the specific question of
adherence to the Krestintern. The Central Committee of the Croatian Peasant
Party did approve Radić's actions *ex post facto* on the basis of the power
granted to him in May. Livingstone, pp. 487, 489.

[110] *Krest'ianskii Internatsional*, No. 3–5 (June–July, 1924), pp. 144.

Peasant Party to power would be the same thing as the establishment of such a government.[111]

Radić insisted that there be no representatives in the Krestintern for Yugoslavia as a whole, since his party did not recognize Yugoslavia as a national unit.[112] Finally, there was one condition demanded by Radić which leads one to suspect that this entire farce was no more than an attempt to use the Communist bogey to frighten the Yugoslav government into a compromise with Radić. Radić stipulated that the Croatian Peasant Party, which had used only peaceful means of struggle up to this point, would move toward revolution "only in extremity." [113]

Extraordinary as it seems, the Krestintern accepted all these conditions, justifying its acceptance in a rather strange fashion. First, the Krestintern pointed out that the type of state sought by the Croatian Peasant Party was "nearest of all democratic republics to our type of workers' and peasants' republic." [114] This statement was sheer fantasy, as Sandomirskii inadvertently admitted when he described Radić's concept of the mission of the peasantry as being very close to that of the Russian narodniks.[115] Perhaps more relevant was this statement:

111 Radić wrote: "Among other things the Croatian Peasant Party has from its very inception fully recognized all the demands of the workers to nationalize all means of production of factory industry, so that the creation of a peasant republic in Croatia is really the same thing as the creation of a worker's republic and the fulfillment of all the strivings of the working class." *Ibid.*

112 Presumably Radić meant by this that he would accept the adherence of other Yugoslav peasant parties to the Krestintern if they claimed to represent only one of the other national groups in Yugoslavia.

113 This is apparently the closest Radić ever came to bringing his program to the point where his party would qualify in Moscow's terms as a "revolutionary" party. Besedovskii indicates that, in Vienna, Goldenstein had tried without success to convince Radić that the Croatian Peasant Party could achieve its program only by revolutionary struggle. Radić was said to have replied that he was more interested in the economic side of the peasant question than the political and that he believed that King Alexander was well disposed toward the peasantry and understood its interests. Besedovskii, I, 73.

114 The Krestintern's letter of acceptance is dated July 1, 1924, *Krest'ianskii Internatsional*, No. 3–5 (June–July, 1924), p. 145. The Krestintern's acceptance of these conditions is suggested by Sandomirskii's explanation of Radić's eligibility. G. Sandomirskii, "Stjepan Radić i ego partiia," *Krest'ianskii Internatsional*, No. 3–5 (June–July, 1924), pp. 44–46.

115 Sandomirskii, *Krest'ianskii Internatsional*, No. 3–5 (June–July, 1924), p. 45.

His party [the Croatian Peasant Party] is one of the largest organizations in the Balkans. It can, under the leadership of the Peasant International, play a huge historical role, not only in Yugoslavia and the Balkans, but also in international politics in general. Comrade Radić is in the most immediate sense familiar with methods of revolutionary struggle and the revolutionary achievements of the USSR, with the international peasant movement and the work of the Peasant International. He will not hesitate to use this experience in the task of liberating the peasants in alliance with the proletariat, not only in his country, but also at the international level.[116]

This passage suggests that in the eyes of the Krestintern Radić was destined for a larger role than he bargained for. Besedovskii reports that the Politburo wanted Radić to accept the post of secretary general in the Krestintern because as a genuine peasant politician he would give that organization sufficient stature to attract peasant political movements throughout the world.[117] This also fits with a suggestion made by one member of the Krestintern that in 1924 this organization was to be the instrument through which the joint forces of communism and peasantism would conquer the Balkans.[118] After several unsuccessful delaying actions designed to force him to accept a larger role, the Russians permitted Radić to leave Moscow on August 4, 1924. Livingstone, in his careful study of Radić's career, indicates that Radić "appears to have truly believed that the Peasant International was a genuinely independent organization representing the interests of the world's peasantry." [119] If so, this was indeed a tribute to Dąbal's powers of persuasion.

Radić's party was the only real peasant political party that ever formally entered the Krestintern. The event did serve temporarily to dramatize the significance of Zinoviev's new peasantism in the Krestintern, though no lasting alliance had been consummated. Zinoviev, himself, could scarcely conceal his elation. At the end of July, when he had become convinced that Radić would join the Krestintern, Zinoviev told a group of Leningrad party workers how Lenin, lying on his deathbed, had followed the First International Peasant Con-

---

[116] *Ibid.*, p. 46.
[117] Besedovskii, I, 73.
[118] Timov, p. 249.
[119] Livingstone, p. 471.

ference with intense interest, attaching great significance to it. Now, with the accession of Radić imminent, said Zinoviev, it was clear that Lenin's intuition was vindicated.

After the war the peasantry of the whole world became different. The war struck the peasant hard and he was a peasant no more. Now we have acquired a great helping, clumsy giant, the peasantry. The workers in Europe can be victorious only where they have an auxiliary force and the Peasant International is becoming this force. If the Croatian Party enters it fully, it means that the Krestintern will grow.

. . . Observing the development of the Peasant International, I am convinced that the fundamental idea of Bolshevism, the alliance of the working class and the peasantry, has begun to develop on an international scale. We say: here is the beginning of the triumph of Leninism on a world scale.[120]

Maček, Radić's second in command, met Radić when the latter returned to Vienna and asked him what he had achieved in Moscow. Radić replied, "Nothing, the Communists do not want allies, only servants." [121]

In Yugoslavia the three largest parties were Pašić's Radical Party, the Croatian Peasant Party, and Davidović's Democratic Party, in that order. An alliance between any two of these parties would have led to a strong coalition government, but they were unable to come to terms with one another between 1923 and 1925. After the elections of 1923 Pašić, as the leader of the largest party, formed a coalition government, but by 1924 it was apparent that he could not muster enough votes in the Skupština to remain in control. Since the Croatian Peasant Party refused to take its rightful place in the Skupština, the leader of the third largest party, Davidović, was asked to form a new cabinet in June, 1924. While Radić had been dallying with the Krestintern, his party had tried unsuccessfully to form an alliance with Davidović. The negotiations continued when Radić returned from Russia, but Radić's terms were unacceptable. When the projected alliance did not materialize, Radić resumed making inflammatory

[120] G. Zinoviev, "Osnovnye itogi V kongressa Kominterna," *Pravda,* No. 164 (July 22, 1924), p. 4.
[121] Maček, p. 100. Besedovskii reports that Radić was singularly unimpressed with all Soviet officials except Chicherin, and that the peasant leader found Stalin "sly but quite limited politically." Besedovskii, I, 72.

speeches. This intemperate behavior contributed to the fall of Davidović's cabinet and in November, 1924, Radić's old adversary, Pašić, returned to power.

In order to strengthen his Radical Party's position in the forthcoming elections, Pašić ordered the arrest of the leaders of the Croatian Peasant Party in December, 1924, on charges of treasonable relations with subversive Communist organizations (the Krestintern and IMRO).[122] They were seized on Christmas eve, but continued to receive salaries as representatives to the legislative assembly. Pašić's tactics would seem to have improved, rather than weakened, the position of the Croatian Peasant Party, for it won a resounding victory at the polls in February, 1925. Since his frontal attack had failed, Pašić decided to come to terms with the Croatian agrarians. On March 27, 1925, the Croatian Peasant Party renounced all ties to Moscow, accepted the Vidovdan Constitution, entered the Skupština, and, on July 18, joined a coalition government with Pašić's Radicals, accepting four ministerial posts.[123]

During this entire interval the Krestintern continued to display the Croatian Peasant Party as the most brilliant jewel in its diadem, even though Radić apparently did not send the stipulated representative of his party to Moscow.[124] Boshkovich, a former secretary of the Yugoslav Communist Party, found himself writing a grudging eulogy in the fall of 1924. While maintaining that Radić was in error when he stated that the Yugoslav Communist Party was losing all its members to the Croatian Peasant Party, Boshkovich welcomed Radić's party into the ranks of those fighting fascism (the existing government) in Yugoslavia.[125] In the December issue of the official organ of the Krestintern, the editors contributed an article commiserating with Radić on his imprisonment.

Finally in July, 1925, after Radić entered the Yugoslav government

[122] Gilbert In der Maur, *Der Weg zur Nation: Jugoslawiens Innenpolitik 1918–1938,* Vol. III of his *Die Jugoslawen einst und jetzt* (Berlin, 1936–38), pp. 144–46.

[123] *Ibid.,* pp. 160–70, and Maček, pp. 105–6.

[124] This can be ascertained from the fact that no member of the Croatian Peasant Party signed any of the appeals or correspondence appearing in *Krest'ianskii Internatsional.*

[125] B. Boshkovich, "Natsional'nyi vopros i raboche-krest'ianskii soiuz v Iugoslavii," *Krest'ianskii Internatsional,* No. 7–9 (Sept.–Oct., 1924), p. 50.

Boshkovich was able to revert to a more normal attitude toward the Croatian Peasant Party.

Stjepan Radić and other cowardly fellow travelers of the Croatian liberation movement have left the Krestintern. But the Croatian peasantry will not follow the path of these pitiful traitors. They will remain in the ranks of the Krestintern in order to continue their heroic struggle. Under the banner of the Krestintern they will fight until they have defeated the enemies of the toiling masses.[126]

In his endeavor to portray Radić in the most unfavorable light possible, Boshkovich revealed that Radić claimed to be unaware of any direct connection between the Comintern and the Krestintern. While Boshkovich put this forward as evidence of Radić's duplicity, it is likely that Dąbal tried to give Radić this impression in June, 1924. Boshkovich quoted the statement made by Pavel Radić, Stjepan's nephew, on March 27, 1925:

With reference to the Krestintern, all the available information about it supports our point of view, that is, that the Krestintern has nothing in common with the Comintern. The Croatian Republican Peasant Party has not yet entered into the affairs of the Comintern and we have no obligations toward it. This will be confirmed at the earliest opportunity.[127]

In October, 1925, Dąbal, in a somewhat franker mood than Boshkovich, explained the alliance with Radić as follows:

In the first place we [the Krestintern] had to establish a firm tie with the peasantry of many countries. Since we did not have at our disposal the means, neither proper apparatus in the center nor peasant organizations conforming to the program of the Krestintern, and because of inadequate resources to guide us toward proper organization and to indicate the proper path and direction of work, we had to establish all sorts of alliances with the most diverse persons. Sometimes, as in the case of Mr. Radić, we were forced to establish ties with persons completely alien to us, in order to use this temporary bond to get close to the peasant masses.[128]

By October, 1925, then, Dąbal maintained that there was no similarity between the goals of the Krestintern and those of Radić, and

[126] B. Boshkovich, "Radich i khorvatskoe krest'ianstvo," *Krest'ianskii Internatsional*, No. 8–9 (Sept., 1925), p. 71.
[127] *Ibid.*, p. 66.
[128] T. Dąbal, "1923–1925: dva goda sushchestvovaniia Krestinterna," *Krest'ianskii Internatsional*, No. 10 (1925), p. 4.

that the alliance had been merely an instrument for the infiltration of the Croatian Peasant Party. He did not, however, explain how an alliance which required Radić to do no more than send a representative of his party to Moscow could serve as an instrument of infiltration. It is more likely that the snaring of Radić served two other functions. First, it temporarily bolstered Zinoviev's sagging prestige by confirming the usefulness of the new international organization he had sponsored. Second, it made the future prospects of the Krestintern seem even brighter. If the Krestintern actually had won over the Croatian Peasant Party or had persuaded Radić to become titular chief of the Krestintern, the Peasant International would undoubtedly have seemed to be a genuine peasant organization and hence more attractive to other radical peasant parties.

The year 1925 was one of disappointment and decline for the Krestintern. Its work demonstrated that even by exploiting the virulent nationalism of minorities in Eastern Europe the Krestintern could obtain no firm foothold in the peasant political movement. On April 9, 1925, three days after the Fifth Plenum of the ECCI, the Second Plenum of the International Peasant Council met to take stock of Bukharin's new theses on the peasant question.[129] It was a rather tedious session, which is not surprising, since all the agrarian theses of the preceding two years had proved to be of little avail. Dąbal announced at the plenum that from that moment all Krestintern work would be conducted in area committees, taking due account of local differences, and that this was a sign "that the Krestintern was leaving the preliminary stage of organization and becoming a body which would plan its work on the basis of a detailed analysis of the conditions of the peasantry in each country." [130] But the Krestintern's failures were not confined to Eastern Europe. The vision of a world-wide workers' and peasants' revolution was also slipping away. In July, 1924, the projected Communist alliance with the Progressive and Farmer-Labor Party movements in the United States had

[129] This meeting of the plenum of the Peasant International was called the Second Plenum. The First Plenum had been called immediately after the First International Peasant Council. Most of *Krest'ianskii Internatsional,* No. 3–5 (March–May, 1925), is devoted to the Second Plenum.

[130] Dąbal, *Krest'ianskii Internatsional,* No. 3–5 (March–May, 1925), p. 10.

dissolved and W. H. Green resigned from the Krestintern. The last spectacular demonstration of the Krestintern's desperation and inadequacy was the election of a member of the Central Committee of the Kuomintang, the versatile Hu Han-min, to the Presidium of the International Peasant Council on February 15, 1926.[131] By no stretch of the imagination could Hu Han-min be described as a Communist, a peasant, or a peasant political leader, and within a few months he would join Chiang Kai-shek in purging Chinese Communists from key posts in the Kuomintang.[132]

One can hardly blame the Krestintern or its leaders. It is little wonder that the Krestintern, provided with directives which were increasingly removed from reality and based almost exclusively on Russian experience and the twists and turns of politics in the Russian Communist Party, experienced one failure after another. In October, 1925, on the occasion of the second anniversary of its founding, Dąbal drew a dreary picture of past failures. The only achievements which the Krestintern could claim were the telegrams which it had sent to peasant political parties in Eastern Europe.[133]

The Krestintern's chief assets were at the same time its chief liabilities. While Marxism itself often attracted some members of the intelligentsia in Eastern Europe, Dąbal's synthesis of Marxism and agrarianism did not. Dąbal's program lacked the logical consistency and determinism of either Marxism or agrarianism. While the Krestintern could temporarily attract peasant or nationalistic political leaders because behind it stood the awesome Comintern and the money and arms of the Soviet Union, such alliances were found to be temporary and inherently distasteful expediencies on the part of peasant politicians. The promise of Comintern backing or of Soviet money and arms could be powerful motives for joining the Krestintern, but only as long as the peasant movement needed this support and the efforts of the Krestintern to dominate the movement could be resisted. As for mobilizing the individual peasant, the Krestintern

---

[131] *Krest'ianskii Internatsional*, No. 1–2 (Jan.–Feb., 1926), pp. 122–23.
[132] M. N. Roy, *Revolution and Counter-Revolution in China* (Calcutta, 1946), pp. 394, 402.
[133] Dąbal, *Krest'ianskii Internatsional*, No. 10 (Oct., 1925), pp. 4–6.

proved completely incapable of this kind of activity. Dąbal mournfully stressed this fact at the Second Plenum of the International Peasant Council:

If the Krestintern were a workers' organization its work would be simpler. Workers unite in the very process of production and easily pass on to the formation of unions and other groups. Many years of practice in the workers' movement have created an intricate network of political, cooperative, cultural, and other types of organizations, which become more and more highly developed and through which the mass of proletarians become accustomed to the creation of their own class organizations. The peasants, on the other hand, are divided, dispersed, separated from one another in the process of production. This cultivates and strengthens in them an individualistic psyche. The peasants are, therefore, not accustomed to construct their own class organizations.[134]

Even if the Krestintern had mustered and deployed its feeble forces for mass recruitment in rural areas, it probably would not have attracted much of a following. The International Peasant Council made no secret of its connections with Moscow and the Bolshevik Revolution. At the very least, peasants were aware that movements emanating from Moscow favored the interests of the industrial workers over those of the peasant. At the most they were aware that even under the New Economic Policy Moscow remained committed to the nationalization of land, large-scale agricultural undertakings, and the elimination of the peasant small-property holder. The peasants' own political parties took pains to make them fully aware of the reality behind the Krestintern's mask, as illustrated by the following excerpt from a letter written and widely published by the Bulgarian Agrarian Union in response to an invitation in January, 1925, to contribute to *Krest'ianskii Internatsional*.

Messrs. Dąbal, Gorov, and Orlov, representing the Peasant International, cannot be ignorant of the fact that our organization participates in the International Agrarian Bureau, an organization of four Slav nations, Czechoslovakia, Poland, Yugoslavia, and Bulgaria, or that the Peasant International wages a merciless battle against this bureau. We would like to point out to the Communist International that we consider it to be the greatest enemy of the Bulgarian Agrarian Union, that when the Stamboliiski government was in power it sent arms to the Communists to be

[134] T. Dąbal, "K plenumu Mezhdunarodnogo Krest'ianskogo Soveta," *Krest'ianskii Internatsional*, No. 1–2 (Jan.–Feb., 1925), p. 4.

used against us. We reject with indignation any idea of collaboration with the Peasant International, behind which is the Communist International and the Russian Bolshevik Party, a party which has viciously oppressed the Russian peasant in a most outrageous manner, a party which has drawn up a constitution making one worker's vote equal to five peasant votes, a party which has suppressed all peasant movements against the Bolshevik dictatorship with the same cruelty as the military dictatorship in Bulgaria.[135]

By the middle of 1926 the great hopes which some Communist leaders had nurtured for the Red Peasant International had begun to fade. The number of copies published of each issue of the official journal of the Krestintern, and the frequency of its appearance, provide a rough fever chart of Comintern enthusiasm for the project. In 1926 *Krest'ianskii Internatsional* became a thin bimonthly, rather than a monthly, and with issue No. 3-4 for March-April it ceased publication altogether. This was one outward sign of the organization's decline. But events in Russia rather than failure abroad finally brought the whole Krestintern experiment to an end.

[135] *La Bulgarie sous le régime de l'assassinat,* pp. 474–75. On the development of the International Agrarian Bureau to which the Bulgarian peasant leaders refer see pp. 138–50 below.

CHAPTER V

The Decline of Peasantism in the Comintern and the Rise of the Green International

The third phase of the struggle for power in the Russian Communist Party led ultimately not only to an abandonment of concessions to the peasantry in Russia, but also to a deemphasis of the role of the peasant in international revolution and an outright hostility to peasant political movements. Just as Stalin had used Zinoviev's former peasantism in the struggle against him in 1926,[1] so Stalin would ultimately turn Bukharin's peasantism against him in 1928 and 1929,[2] and thus bring to an end the Comintern's courtship of the peasant throughout the world. In order to appreciate the parallel between Soviet agricultural policy and the agrarian program of international communism it is necessary to sketch briefly the stages in the development of the former.

THE SECOND SOVIET AGRARIAN CRISIS
AND THE STRUGGLE FOR POWER

By December, 1927, the Joint Opposition of Trotsky and Zinoviev had reached a point similar to that of the first opposition in De-

[1] As early as the Fourteenth Congress of the Russian Communist Party in December, 1925, Stalin reminded delegates that Zinoviev had once "confessed" to deviations toward the peasant. As evidence Stalin quoted (out of context) Zinoviev's statement to this effect (see above, p. 61) to prove that Zinoviev had veered from peasantism in 1923 to antipeasantism in 1925, and that Zinoviev was, therefore, an altogether unstable and inconsistent extremist. I. V. Stalin, "XIV s'ezd V.K.P. (b.) 18–31 dekabria 1925 g." in I. V. Stalin, *Sochineniia* (Moscow, 1946–51), VII, 377–78.

[2] For example, in a speech delivered in April, 1929, Stalin ridiculed Bukharin's thesis that the kulak could "grow into socialism." I. V. Stalin, "O pravom uklone v V.K.P. (b.)," *Sochineniia,* XII, 39.

cember, 1923.[3] At the Fifteenth Congress of the Russian Communist Party a new domestic crisis tended to drive the victors in opposite directions. What had seemed to be a victory of those advocating further concessions to the peasantry became in fact a victory for those within the Party who desired immediate and rapid industrialization at the peasants' expense.

To some degree the Russian peasants themselves seem to have discredited the conciliatory policies of the Soviet government by demanding too much. Starting in the autumn of 1927, peasants began to resist the collections of grain, grain collectors were driven out of the villages, and there were riots in rural areas where collectors appeared. The peasants claimed that official prices for grain were too low in relation to the prices of manufactured goods.[4] One effect of this crisis was to hasten the banishment of Trotsky to Alma-Ata.[5] This was the first crisis Stalin had to cope with as undisputed leader of party and state, and he could no longer fall back on the foggy platitudes he had used in the past to put defeated factions in their place.

While Stalin had a ready stock of explanations for the crisis,[6] he moved toward a conclusion which was instrumental in provoking a break with Bukharin. At a meeting of the Russian Communist Party, on July 9, 1928, Stalin announced that the grain crisis was aggravated by increased peasant earnings and that it could be resolved only by collectivization.[7] This measure, said Stalin, would give the state the power to extract from the peasantry the capital needed to industrialize.

Bukharin argued, on the contrary, that greater concessions should be made to the peasantry. For the last time the approach of Bukharin's group prevailed [8] and the opposing factions signed a statement of unity, agreeing not to bring their disagreements out into the

[3] Isaac Deutscher, *The Prophet Unarmed: Trotsky, 1921–1929* (London, 1959), p. 308.

[4] *Ibid.*, p. 403.

[5] *Ibid.*, p. 404.

[6] These are explained in detail in Alexander Erlich, "Stalin's Views on Economic Development," in E. J. Simmons ed., *Continuity and Change in Russian and Soviet Thought* (Cambridge, Mass., 1955), pp. 91–94.

[7] Stalin, *Sochineniia,* XI, 163.

[8] Deutscher, pp. 426–27.

open.[9] But Bukharin suddenly became aware of the precariousness of his position and started negotiations with the defeated opposition on July 11, 1928, after the plenum of the Central Committee of the Russian Communist Party.[10] Bukharin reported that Stalin's recent retreat on the peasant question was simply a tactic designed to lull the fears of the Central Committee and weaken the Bukharinites. Now, said Bukharin, Stalin had won over Voroshilov and Kalinin in the Politburo and was ready for the final offensive against private farming.[11] Bukharin claimed that Stalin had decided that in Russia, because of the absence of colonies and the impossibility of obtaining foreign loans, socialism could only be achieved by "primitive socialist accumulation," a method which would increase peasant resistance. Therefore, Stalin felt he would have to build a monolithic "police state" in order to achieve his goals.

One reason for Bukharin's new sense of insecurity was that Stalin's course had certain political advantages over his own. Bukharin's original position had been that Russia could grow into socialism "at a snail's pace" through the slow development of an internal market by means of concessions to the peasantry. While in late 1927 and early 1928 Bukharin had moved further toward a program of rapid industrial development, his position was still more moderate than Stalin's, particularly on the peasant question, and therefore more attractive to the engineers, economists, and technicians who had survived the civil war.[12] But Stalin's course, combining more rapid industrial development with large-scale collectivization, had great appeal among the rank and file of Communists and it seemed to put an end to the peasants' opportunities to resist. Stalin's course was therefore more attractive to many party members because collectivization would end the ambiguity in the relationship between the proletarian state and the petty-bourgeois peasant. By the same token, Bukharin's plan was unattractive to many party members because

[9] I. V. Stalin, "Gruppa Bukharina i pravyi uklon v nashei partii," *Sochineniia*, XI, 320.
[10] Deutscher, p. 440, n. 1.
[11] *Ibid.*, p. 443.
[12] Ruth Fischer, *Stalin and German Communism* (Cambridge, Mass., 1948), p. 473.

it meant another retreat and more concessions to capitalistic elements. On the one hand, Stalin's plan differed from that of the defeated Joint Opposition in its emphasis on large-scale collectivization; in a sense, Stalin had supplied the missing equation. On the other hand, Stalin's new program was close enough to that of the defeated opposition to enable him to recruit support against Bukharin from their ranks.[13] Finally, Stalin's course seemed a more positive response to the threat of attack from the capitalist world, which was believed to be imminent,[14] and to the failure to create a socialist revolution anywhere outside of Russia.

On January 22, 1929, Trotsky was forced into foreign exile, and at approximately the same time Stalin renewed the attack on Bukharin inside the Party at a joint meeting of the Politburo and the Presidium of the Central Committee of the Party.[15] The collectivization drive began in the summer of 1929, and in July Bukharin was removed from the post in the Comintern which he had inherited from Zinoviev. The dismissal of Bukharin was expressly linked to his attitude toward economic policy, which, it was said, he had tried to expand into an "international system." [16]

Once adopted, the methods of the First Five-Year Plan came to be accepted as the only, the inevitable, and the ideal mode of organizing a national economy in preparation for socialism. Since Bukharin's peasantist approach to economic development had its counterpart in the political tactics formulated for the Comintern, one might reasonably expect that the fall of Bukharin and the initiation of the First Five-Year Plan would be accompanied by a change in Comintern agrarian tactics. But, in fact, no abrupt shift took place.

It would be, of course, a great oversimplification to argue that the

[13] Throughout July and August Stalin dropped broad hints about the possible recall of the Left Opposition to administer his new course. Deutscher, pp. 443–45.

[14] There is, of course, some reason to suppose that this belief was not widespread, in spite of official propaganda.

[15] Stalin, of course, claimed that Bukharin had already broken the truce in his article of November, 1928, published under the title "Notes of an Economist." Stalin, *Sochineniia,* XI, 320.

[16] "Teoreticheskie vyvody tov. Bukharina i politicheskii vyvod Kommunisticheskogo Internatsionala," *Kommunisticheskii Internatsional,* No. 34–35 (Aug. 31, 1929), p. 9.

leaders of the Comintern were responsive only to these internal Russian developments. They were aware of the international situation, but there is no question that even the non-Russian leaders of the Comintern tended to see the world through the tinted glasses provided by Soviet leaders. In the preceding chapter I pointed out how, during the period of the New Economic Policy, first Zinoviev and then Bukharin had projected the policy of concessions and compromise at home into the international arena.

At the time of the Fifth Plenum Stalin seemed very close to Bukharin, except for Bukharin's theories about "evolving into socialism." Before this plenum Stalin agreed that in most of the world the period of revolution had come to an end, and he urged Communists to concentrate on the national revolutionary movement in colonial countries and "winning over the small peasantry." (He was careful to confine his recommendation to the "small peasantry.") [17] But even at this early date Stalin deduced another important lesson for the Comintern from the doctrine of socialism in one country. It was now the duty of the Comintern members, said Stalin,

to support the Soviet regime and to frustrate the interventionist machinations of imperialism against the Soviet Union, bearing in mind that the Soviet Union is the bulwark of the revolutionary movement in all countries, and that to preserve and strengthen the Soviet Union means to accelerate the victory of the working class over the world bourgeoisie.[18]

For the Comintern the doctrine of socialism in one country, as Stalin saw it, would mean the final stitch in that garment which international communism had assumed with the twenty-one conditions of admission. Once the fate of the Comintern was completely bound to that of the Soviet Union, any change in Soviet policy would necessarily be followed by a change in Comintern policy, the two policies being now part of the same cloth.

The beginning of a new "general line" in the Comintern was announced, characteristically, at the Fifteenth Congress of the Russian Communist Party in December, 1927. There were external pressures which demanded a new line. The diplomatic rupture between Mos-

---

[17] I. V. Stalin, "K mezhdunarodnomu polozheniiu i zadachi kompartii," *Sochineniia*, VII, 57–58.
[18] *Ibid.*

cow and London created a real war scare in the fall of 1927.[19] The failure of the Canton uprising in December signaled the bankruptcy of the Comintern's policy in China.[20] On the face of it, these defeats seemed to confirm Stalin's thesis that Russia must move forward as rapidly as possible toward socialism at home to counter failures abroad. But, although these failures called for some dramatic response, they did not predetermine the pattern of that response. Once adopted, however, the Stalinist course was portrayed as the only possible course of action, and once again it was the Russian domestic policy that provided a model for Comintern policy.

At the Fifteenth Congress of the Russian Communist Party Stalin announced *ex cathedra* that the "era of stabilization" had come to an end and that capitalism was entering a new and third period in its development since 1917.

A year or two ago one could and one had to talk about a period of relative balance between the Soviets and the capitalist countries and about their "peaceful coexistence." Now we have every reason to say that the period of "peaceful coexistence" recedes into the past, giving place to a period of imperialist attacks and of preparation for intervention against the USSR.[21]

The Comintern would therefore adopt a new and militant face to the world, it was implied, and abandon the united front. It is generally accepted that the turn to the left was less a response to external events, which offered little promise of revolutionary success and few tangible threats to the Soviet Union, than a tactic geared to Stalin's intended domestic policies. Stalin stimulated and used this fear of the outside world. It provided a rationale both for the extreme measures subsequently employed in the Russian economy and for the elimination of the chief architect of Comintern policy in the "period of stabilization," Nikolai Bukharin.

Throughout 1928 the pressure on Bukharin mounted. The Ninth Plenum of the ECCI in February formalized the new "left turn." In keeping with the concept of a "third period in the development of

---

[19] Franz Borkenau, *World Communism: A History of the Communist International* (New York, 1939), p. 337.

[20] Deutscher, p. 422.

[21] *XV s'ezd Vsesoiuznoi Kommunisticheskoi Partii (b.)—stenograficheskii otchet* (Moscow, 1928), p. 47.

capitalism since the war," this meeting focused its attention on fascism, which was treated as a concrete manifestation of this third period.[22] The new tactics of the Comintern were to be devised on the assumption that "socialism in one country" could best be served by revolutionary struggle against fascism abroad and by revolutionary struggle against war on the USSR.

The approved tactics toward other political parties in this period also changed. Just as the truce in the Soviet Union with the peasants was rapidly coming to an end, so the truce between non-Communist political groups and Communist parties abroad had ended.[23] All the signs indicated, according to the new "line," that the Great Powers were preparing war on the Soviet Union and that the reformist left parties were the secret allies of the imperialists. The same economic dislocations which had turned the political leaders in the west toward thoughts of war on the Soviet Union had, however, also created the basis for a new revolutionary period, a period, paradoxically, in which Communist parties would have to exploit the situation without allies in the form of other political parties.

The process of weeding out potential opponents in the international Communist movement had already been initiated by Stalin before 1928.[24] Between 1928 and 1934 all remaining independence of thought was eliminated.[25] For all intents and purposes the Comin-

[22] Bennet, "Uroki pervogo desiatiletiia Kominterna," the preface to Khristo Kabakchiev, *Kak voznik i razvivalsia Kommunisticheskii Internatsional* (Moscow, 1929), p. 27.

[23] Aldo Garosci writes: "But as a result of the decisions of the Sixth Congress of the International in the summer of 1928, the attack against non-Communist democratic parties increased in violence. According to the International, the world, after the revolutionary period of 1917–21 and the subsequent period of stabilization had now entered a third period of violent revolutionary crisis. In this period who was not with the Communist International was against it and was fascist." Aldo Garosci, "The Italian Communist Party," in Mario Einaudi, ed., *Communism in Western Europe* (Ithaca, 1951), p. 170. Borkenau indicates that after the Sixth Comintern Congress ordinary political activity in parliaments and trade union work was considered secondary to the problem of preparing for revolution. Borkenau, p. 338.

[24] The best description, on the basis of personal experience, of the kind of intimidation and indoctrination used by Stalin to win control of foreign Communist parties is found in Fischer, Part V.

[25] Borkenau's comments would seem to indicate that before the elimination of Bukharin there was still room for independence of thought. Borkenau, pp. 384–85.

tern became an arm of the Soviet power and an additional tool for the construction of "socialism in one country." In refuting those who maintained in 1928 that the new Comintern program was "too Russian," Stalin again insisted on the primacy of the revolution in the Soviet Union.

There is no doubt that the international character of our revolution imposes on the proletarian dictatorship of the USSR certain obligations with regard to the proletarian and oppressed masses of the whole world. Lenin was thinking in these terms when he said that the meaning of the existence of the proletarian dictatorship in the USSR consists in the fact that it would do everything it could to develop the proletarian revolution and bring about its victory in other countries. But what follows from this? From this it follows, at the very least, that our revolution is part of the world revolution, the base and the instrument of the world revolutionary movement.

It is indisputable also that not only does the revolution in the USSR have duties toward the proletariat of all countries, duties which it is discharging, but also that the proletariat of all countries have certain rather important duties toward the proletarian dictatorship in the USSR in its struggle against internal and external enemies, in war against any war designed to strangle the proletarian dictatorship in the USSR in its struggle against internal and external enemies, in advocating that imperialist armies should directly go over to the side of the proletarian dictatorship in the USSR in the event of attack on the USSR. But doesn't it follow from this that revolution in the USSR is inseparable from the revolutionary movements in other countries, that the triumph of the revolution in the USSR is a triumph for revolution throughout the world.[26]

Deutscher maintains that this shift to the left was a sign of disillusionment with the Comintern and its potentialities, and that Stalin did not seriously expect any concrete results abroad from the new tactics.[27] While it is probably true that Stalin did not have much faith in the efficacy of international communism, he may very well have feared foreign intervention and hoped that the Comintern might be

[26] I. V. Stalin, "O programme Komintera," *Sochineniia,* XI, 151–52. This is part of a speech given by Stalin on July 8, 1928, to the Plenum of the Central Committee of the Russian Communist Party.

[27] Deutscher describes the new "leftism" in the Comintern as the initiation of a mock fight, saying, "Its [the Comintern's] ultra radicalism was so unreal that Stalin, in all probability, countenanced it only because he attributed very little practical significance to what the Comintern did in those years." Isaac Deutscher, *Stalin: A Political Biography* (New York, 1949), p. 405.

of some use in averting it. Perhaps more to the point was the fact that the new Comintern program undermined the prestige that Bukharin had acquired as the advocate of tactics of compromise and concession in the international Communist movement.[28]

The critical decisions of the Sixth Comintern Congress in June, 1928, were all made before the congress, and the delegates were treated to a burlesque of unanimity by Bukharin and Stalin in the speeches and theses.[29] Prior to the congress, according to Stalin, Bukharin had tried to obtain international support for his point of view by distributing his theses on the international question before those theses had been approved by the Russian Communist Party.[30] This put Stalin in the embarrassing position of issuing countertheses on the international situation through the Russian Party, rather crudely revealing the deciding voice of that party. The differences between the two sets of theses are revealing. According to Stalin, Bukharin did not take much stock in Stalin's theory of the "third period" in the development of western capitalism since World War I, a period in which economic crises provided the basis for renewed revolutionary agitation.[31] Bukharin was said to have omitted Stalin's new doctrine of the need for "struggle with left Social Democracy." [32] Stalin also considered Bukharin's theses too mild, since they did not include a proscription against those who tried to find a middle ground between the "rightists" in any Communist party and the bulk of party members.[33] Finally, Stalin felt that Bukharin's theses gave insufficient stress

[28] Speaking of the replacement of Bukharin by Manuilsky, Kuusinen, and Molotov in 1929, Borkenau wrote: "The choice of this personnel was a clear implication that international communism was no longer regarded as important in itself, but as a minor dependency of the Russian state, directed not even so much along the lines of Russian raison d'etat, as according to the necessities of Stalin's fight with his factional adversaries in Russia." Borkenau, p. 339.

[29] Deutscher cites the testimony of many participants in the Sixth Comintern Congress to the effect that in the congress there was a general atmosphere of uncertainty, owing to the attempt to conceal the conflict between Stalin and Bukharin. Deutscher, *The Prophet Unarmed*, p. 44.

[30] Stalin, *Sochineniia*, XII, 20. This was a speech delivered at a joint meeting of the Plenum of the Central Committee of the CPSU (b.) and of the Central Control Commission of the CPSU (b.) in April, 1929.

[31] *Ibid.*, p. 21.

[32] *Ibid.*

[33] *Ibid.*, p. 22.

to the problem of "iron discipline" and "unconditional subordination of party members to this discipline." [34]

The link between Bukharin's views on the tactics of the Comintern and his views on economic policy in the Soviet state is provided in an article which, although it was not published until after Bukharin had been removed from the Comintern in 1929, refers back to Bukharin's actions at the Sixth Comintern Congress.

Up to this point [the Sixth Comintern Congress] Comrade Bukharin had referred to the CPSU and the question of socialist construction. But in defending his opportunistic views, these opportunistic errors inevitably blossomed into an international system, especially since those views, as we have seen above, were already concealed in embryonic form at the Sixth Congress of the Comintern. This development also follows from the deep international significance of the problems of socialist construction in the USSR. The man who underestimates the growth of socialist construction in the USSR, the man who does not see here the powerful creative enthusiasm of the masses, must inevitably underestimate the growth of the revolutionary initiative of the working masses in capitalist countries and the beginning of a new revolutionary wave. The man who approaches the kulaks in the USSR with timidity and caution and who overestimates the capitalist elements here must inevitably overestimate the stabilization of world capitalism and the power and organization of monopoly capitalism. The one follows from the other, the one *explains* the other.[35]

What is implied, of course, is that Bukharin opposed the turn to the left in the Comintern not because he failed to appreciate the danger of external threats to the Soviet Union but because he had an entirely different conception of the historical role of the prosperous peasant in the proletarian revolution *both* at home and abroad.

One would assume that, if Bukharin's whole theoretical position was endangered by Stalin's, Bukharin's theses on the peasant question in the Comintern would be rescinded and an entirely new tactical position adopted. But such was not the case. Along with the attempt to preserve an outward appearance of solidarity in the Russian Communist Party, there were no startling changes or innovations in Comintern agrarian policy in spite of the reorientation on the question of the imminence of revolution and the question of

---

[34] *Ibid.*
[35] *Kommunisticheskii Internatsional,* No. 34–35 (Aug. 31, 1929), p. 13.

alliances with peasant political parties. This reticence may be another example of Stalin's customary tactic of absorbing some features of his opponent's program in order to capture part of his opponent's support. In explaining those sections in the new general program for the Comintern which pertained to the agrarian question, Stalin adhered to old and familiar phrases. He insisted that a great deal of attention had to be paid to the peasantry and that all countries would have to pass through a stage of economic development similar to the New Economic Policy.[36]

With regard to Eastern Europe, Stalin, like Bukharin before him, rejected Zinoviev's formula at the Fifth Congress that the "dictatorship of the proletariat and the peasantry" was simply a synonym for the dictatorship of the proletariat. One finds a foreshadowing of the notion of "people's democracies" in Stalin's explanation of the course of socialist revolution in various countries. There were, maintained Stalin, three types of revolution: revolution in colonial countries, revolution in underdeveloped countries, and revolution in developed capitalist countries.

Besides developed capitalist countries, where the victory of the revolution will lead at once to the proletarian dictatorship, there are also countries which are only slightly developed capitalistically, with vestiges of feudalism and a special agrarian problem of the antifeudal type (Poland, Rumania, etc.), countries where the petty bourgeoisie, especially the peasantry, is sure to have a weighty word to say in the event of a revolutionary upheaval, and where the victory of the revolution, in order to lead to a proletarian dictatorship, can and will certainly require some intermediate stages in the form, say, of a dictatorship of the proletariat and the peasantry.[37]

In conclusion Stalin specified: "There is scarcely reason to doubt that Poland and Rumania belong to the category of countries which will have to pass, more or less rapidly, through certain intermediate stages on the way to the dictatorship of the proletariat." [38] Stalin also indicated that there had been considerable debate in the preparatory commission on the question of the renewed emphasis in Comintern

[36] Stalin, *Sochineniia*, XI, 145.
[37] *Ibid.*, p. 155.
[38] *Ibid.*, p. 156.

propaganda on "neutralization of the middle peasant" and "the nationalization of land " as revolutionary slogans.[39] The renewed emphasis on these slogans was a sign of the return to leftist direct revolutionary activity and to a more rigid adherence to orthodox doctrine on the peasant question.

But, however successful Stalin may have been in plastering over the theoretical differences between himself and Bukharin, the nature of Comintern activity was drastically changed. The radical transformation in the whole atmosphere of the Comintern produced a different attitude toward work among the peasantry and peasant political parties. The gradual replacement of the existing leaders of the Comintern with pro-Stalinist leftists accentuated the trend toward putschist attempts to seize power. At the same time, the new leftists were more dependent on Stalin than former leaders had been and made more of an effort to fulfill and overfulfill primary tasks as designated by the Comintern. The primary task of Communist parties in the "third period" was the struggle in defense of the Soviet Union and against war. The new theses on the international situation were quite explicit on this score:

The problems of struggle against imminent imperialist war, the defense of the Soviet Union, the struggle against intervention in China and its partition, the defense of the Chinese revolution and colonial rebellion, these are the primary, chief international tasks of the Communist movement at the present moment. The efforts to perform these tasks must be integrated with the daily struggle of the working class against the offensive of capital and must be part of the struggle for the dictatorship of the proletariat.[40]

According to these theses, because the peasant was the "raw material of imperialist armies, member parties were asked to reinvigorate

[39] Although these slogans were not new, the renewed emphasis on them was. The real objection to them was not that they were incorrect in terms of inherited doctrine but that they were impractical in terms of actually winning the peasant over to the Communist cause. For a summary of the debate in the Agrarian Commission of the Preparatory Committee for the Sixth Comintern Congress, see Martynov, "Vopros o natsionalizatsii zemel v proekte programmy Kominterna," *Kommunisticheskii Internatsional*, No. 27–28 (July 13, 1928), p. 31–34, and Mad'iar, "Agrarnyi vopros v programme Kominterna," *Na agrarnom fronte*, No. 9 (Sept., 1928), pp. 20–30.

[40] Bela Kun, ed., *Kommunisticheskii Internatsional v dokumentakh, 1919– 1932* (Moscow, 1933), p. 780.

their work among the peasants and to cooperate with the Peasant International.[41] But vigorous prosecution of the primary tasks tended to stifle the efforts of Communists in the countryside.

This is most evident in the reports delivered at the Tenth Plenum of the ECCI, which met in July, 1929. Bukharin was replaced by Stalin's trusted cohorts, Molotov, the Finn Kuusinen, and the Ukrainian Manuilsky. A. P. Smirnov, a supporter of Bukharin, had already been replaced as director of the Krestintern by the more malleable Teodorovich. Dąbal, who had always spoken for the Krestintern in the past when there was a discussion of the agrarian problem, was conspicuous by his absence.

This meeting adopted the theme of "intensification of the new revolutionary upsurge." [42] Peasant parties, instead of being treated as allies or at least as recruiting ground, were lumped together with other fascist organizations. Kolarov proposed:

I would like to mention another form of fascism—so-called agrarian fascism. There exists not only social fascism but also agrarian fascism. In agrarian countries we run up against attempts to form peasant regiments having a fascist character. In Czechoslovakia and Rumania we already have new forms of agrarian fascism winning over the peasant masses by such demagogic devices as the appeal for the need of defending private property in order to defeat the proletarian revolution.[43]

The *Communist International,* official organ of the ECCI, had already indicated in June, 1929, that the correct interpretation of the theses of the Sixth Congress referring to the agrarian question (which were scant and unspecific) was that the peasant political parties and their international organizations should be considered as allies of the fascists.[44] At the Tenth Plenum the correct tactic with regard to other political parties was the "united front from below only," meaning that Communist parties could recruit from other political parties but could not form alliances with the leaders of other parties.[45]

[41] *Ibid.,* pp. 784, 802.
[42] *Desiatyi plenum ispolkoma Kominterna* (Moscow, 1929), I, 277, 459.
[43] *Ibid.,* pp. 185–86.
[44] Manner-Rusticus, "Mobilizatsiia trudovogo krest'ianstva na bor'by protiv imperialisticheskoi voiny," *Kommunisticheskii Internatsional,* No. 23–24 (June 20, 1929), pp. 33–34.
[45] *Desiatyi plenum ispolkoma Kominterna,* I, 279.

The essential task among the peasants then was to "intensify the class struggle in the country " and mobilize the peasants against war or against war on the USSR.[46] The new directives administered the coup de grâce to the Krestintern. Its only successes had been won through direct negotiations with the leaders of peasant political movements and national minority movements. Essentially it had remained primarily a propaganda organization, relying on local Communist parties and the sections and bureaus of the Comintern to provide its agents. In 1928 and 1929 it was asked to go to individual peasants with a message which could only fall on deaf ears.

THE DECLINE OF THE KRESTINTERN

From 1925 to the Sixth Comintern Congress in 1928 the Krestintern survived as an enclave for Dąbal and his faithful coterie. From time to time valuable men like N. L. Meshcheriakov and Ho Chi Minh were retrieved for more useful work elsewhere, but Dąbal, Boshkovich, Timov, and Kheveshi continued to write articles extolling the radical peasant political movement and prophesying its imminent conversion to communism. Except for the rise of pro-Communist peasant political parties among the national minorities in the eastern borderlands of Poland, however, the Krestintern seems to have achieved very little. Even the Polish successes seem to have been the work of local Communist parties with little more than inspiration provided by the Krestintern.

At the Sixth Plenum of the ECCI in February, 1926, there were no representatives of the Krestintern present and the organization received only passing reference in Zinoviev's speech.

Finally, I would like to stress the fact that in my opinion this organization [the Krestintern], though still a young organization, has achieved in the past year its first, though in fact, small successes. In several countries the Krestintern has succeeded in really establishing contact with peasant movements. In this connection I would like to point out that important parties, in their number the German, Czech, Swedish, Norwegian, Polish, etc., have finally begun work among the peasantry, and, one must say, not without some success.[47]

[46] Manner-Rusticus, *Kommunisticheskii Internatsional,* No. 23–24 (June 20, 1929), p. 36.

[47] *Shestoi rasshirennyi plenum ispolkoma Kominterna (17 fevralia–15 marta, 1926)–stenograficheskii otchet* (Moscow, 1927), p. 3.

One misses the ebullient optimism of the earlier Zinoviev and senses something of his fatigue and indecisiveness in this halting endorsement. This was, however, the kind of highly qualified praise which the Krestintern received at all Comintern meetings until the Sixth Comintern Congress in 1928. After 1929 the Krestintern was not mentioned at all in Comintern meetings.

At the Seventh Plenum of the ECCI in November, 1926, Zinoviev sent a brief but touching note, begging to be released from his post as president of that body.[48] Bukharin took his place, reading the usual keynote address on the international situation and the tasks of the Comintern. This plenum marked the final phase of the struggle betwen Trotsky and Stalin at the international level, and Stalin made one of his rare appearances before the full plenum to deliver a long report on this struggle. In spite of all this, the Krestintern figured prominently in the proceedings. Boshkovich, an ardent adherent of the Krestintern, was elected to the ECCI.[49] Dąbal and the Soviet agronomist Dubrovskii were asked to work out some changes in the Comintern agrarian program.[50] The leaders of the Krestintern never seemed more influential in the Comintern.

In the reports on the peasant question at the Seventh Plenum, Dąbal indicated that the agrarian and national programs of the Comintern were together proving extremely successful in Central Europe and implied that the Krestintern would wean most of the peasantry away from the peasant political parties there.[51] Boshkovich went even further, indicating that the experience of the Polish Communist Party in its work among the peasantry provided an example for all sections of the Comintern.

The experience of the Communist Party of Poland among the peasants proves that the slogan of peasant unity with the worker was enormously popular and that the use of this slogan along with the revolutionary slogans of "struggle for land without compensation" and "struggle against the bourgeoisie" not only resulted in a significant shift of the peasantry to the left but also united revolutionary elements of the peasantry in the strug-

[48] Puti mirovoi revoliutsii—sed'moi rasshirennyi plenum ispolnitel'nogo komiteta Kommunisticheskogo Internatsionala (22 noiabria–16 dekabria) (Moscow, 1927), I, 14.

[49] Ibid., p. 8.

[50] International Press Correspondence, VII, No. 9 (Jan. 27, 1927), 176.

[51] Puti mirovoi revoliutsii, I, 194.

gle to fulfill them. We should take note of the unification of peasants according to their respective nationalities, and of the creation of special left peasant organizations, including the Ukrainian Peasant Union Selrob, the Belorussian Workers' and Peasants' Hramada, and the Independent Peasant Party.[52]

Although Bukharin stated that the leader of the Polish party, Warski, expected too much from these peasant organizations, he recommended the establishment of such federations of left peasant organizations everywhere.

The chief error of many parties is that they hurry to create many small revolutionary peasant organizations instead of using existing peasant organizations for shifting the peasant masses to the left. . . .

We must bring together the dispersed peasant movements in multinational states like Yugoslavia, Czechoslovakia, Rumania, Poland, etc., and also in groups of states where the struggle of the peasantry is interconnected. I do not support the notion of creating special centralized peasant parties which can only unite certain peasant strata, and also I do not consider it necessary to strengthen in the peasant the illusion that he can play an independent role, an illusion disseminated by petty-bourgeois politicians. It seems to me that the path followed in Poland (unification of left peasant organizations on a federal basis) is the most suitable method for solving this problem.[53]

Boshkovich pointed out that the greatest weakness of Comintern work among the peasants was that party members paid little attention to the concrete and immediate problems of the peasant, to peasant prejudices, or to the general backwardness of the peasant.[54]

Conflict broke out in the Agrarian Commission of the Seventh Plenum, however, and no new resolutions were submitted.[55] The question of the agrarian program of the Comintern was deferred until the Sixth Comintern Congress in 1928.

From 1928 to 1931 the weight of Comintern activity centered in Berlin, where Dimitrov, as chief of the Comintern's West European Bureau, drew all the threads into his hands.[56] As early as January,

[52] *Ibid.,* p. 198.
[53] *Ibid.,* p. 201.
[54] *Ibid.*
[55] *International Press Correspondence,* VII, No. 9 (Jan. 27, 1927), 176.
[56] Günther Nollau, *International Communism and World Revolution: History and Methods* (New York, 1961), pp. 142–46.

1927, when it began to publish in Berlin, a newsletter for the peasantry, the *Internationaler Bauern Korrespondent*,[57] the Krestintern seems to have shifted its base of operations to that city. The declining fortunes of the Krestintern were apparent in the make-up of the new monthly. In comparison with the defunct *Krest'ianskii Internatsional,* the new periodical was a feeble effort indeed. Badly edited and poorly printed, the newsletter consisted of a few pages of articles, generally written by Krestintern veterans. It claimed to be a nonpartisan farmers' and peasants' journal, the cloak of nonpartisanship often being assumed by weak united front organizations in their journals, such as, for example, the Balkan Communist Federation in *Fédération balkanique.*

When the Comintern next met, the new conflict in the Russian Party had not yet emerged, but signs of disagreement between Stalin and Bukharin were already evident. The three major themes of the ECCI in May, 1927, were the danger of war, the Chinese Revolution, and the problem of the Communist Party of Great Britain. At this plenum Bukharin continued to assert (contrary to Stalin's expressed opinion) that the economy of Poland and all of Central Europe was becoming more, not less, stable, thereby justifying Comintern tactics of "persuasion" among the peasants as opposed to revolutionary agitation.

There is, therefore, no possibility of throwing doubt on the regrouping of forces in the direction of the stabilization of capitalism and a consolidation and a firm establishment of its political position in Central Europe, and there is little doubt that Zinoviev was in error when he recently stated that stabilization had already disappeared.[58]

At the same time, Bukharin attributed the failures of the Chinese Communists to their neglect of Comintern warnings on the "necessity of a thorough change of tactics in the present higher stage of revolution, because, as a result of the defection of the national bourgeoisie to the camp of the counter-revolution, the agrarian revo-

---

[57] Published from 1927 through 1929 in German and English. The English edition was called *Farmers' and Peasants' International Correspondent.*
[58] N. Bukharin, "The Results of the Plenary Session of the E.C.C.I.," *International Press Correspondence,* VII, No. 37 (June 20, 1927), 707.

lution had become the major theme in the anti-imperialist struggle." [59]

If anything, the momentous events in China seemed temporarily to strengthen the existing agrarian line in the Comintern. Even Lenin's wife, the venerable Krupskaia, admitted that, although she had sympathized with the opposition in 1925, in 1927 she felt that the peasantry held the key to the revolution in China.[60] On the surface it would seem that external events should have strengthened the existing course in Comintern agrarian policy.

An international peasant conference was hastily called by the Krestintern in November, 1927, to impress a group of so-called peasant delegates visiting Russia on the occasion of the tenth anniversary of the October Revolution.[61] There were forty-six delegates (twenty-two of whom were already Communists) representing only nine countries. The sole East European country represented was Czechoslovakia. The peasant delegation was given a tour of the Soviet Union and then, according to the Comintern account, the delegates all joined the Krestintern. The conference was undistinguished, as evidenced by its four themes:

(1) Unconditional confiscation of all large-scale estates and the transfer of portions of this land to the peasantry.

(2) The right of national self-determination up to secession.

(3) The struggle against the danger of war.

(4) The necessity of creating workers' and peasants' governments.[62]

Dąbal expounded these hackneyed themes and also remarked:

The Black and Green Internationals are enemies and betrayers of the peasantry, whom they wish to prevent from fighting along with their class

[59] N. Bukharin, "The Results of the Plenary Session of the E.C.C.I.," *International Press Correspondence,* VII, No. 37 (June 30, 1927), 707.

[60] Krupskaia pointedly referred to the well-known article by Mao Tse-tung on the peasant movement in Hunan province. *International Press Correspondence,* VII, No. 46 (Aug. 11, 1927), 1030.

[61] N. I. Meshcheriakov, "Krest'ianskaia delegatsiia v. SSSR," *Kommunisticheskii Internatsional,* No. 51 (Dec. 23, 1927), pp. 24–28. An extremely abbreviated record of the conference was published under the title *Stenogram und Beschlüsse–Internationale Bauernberatung* (Berlin, 1928). Most of *Internationaler Bauern-Korrespondent,* No. 5 (Dec., 1927), is devoted to the conference.

[62] Meshcheriakov, *Kommunisticheskii Internatsional,* No. 51 (Dec. 23, 1927), pp. 27–28.

comrades in independent organizations for their own interests. Intensive work of enlightenment must therefore be undertaken concerning the national and international activity of these enemies of peasant organizations everywhere. The broad masses of the peasantry must feel that only the Peasant International is carrying on an earnest and energetic struggle for the interests of the working peasants, no matter what views the latter may hold. . . . In order to carry on effectively and successfully the struggle for the interests of the toiling peasantry, a close bond must be established with all real peasant organizations and groups.[63]

By 1928, however, with the increasing shift to the left, the very survival of the Krestintern became an issue. Even Trotsky, far away in Alma-Ata, called for a housecleaning.

The Sixth Comintern Congress must seriously review the work of the Peasants' "International" from the standpoint of proletarian internationalism. It is high time to draw a Marxian balance to this long drawn-out experiment. In one form or another the balance must be included in the program of the Comintern. The present draft does not breathe a single syllable either about the "millions" in the Peasants' International, or for that matter, about its very existence.[64]

Trotsky's hopes were fulfilled. Bukharin was frank about the Krestintern's defects, but blamed the Comintern.

We must pay more attention to the peasant question, and in this connection we must help the Peasant International to transform itself into a real and vigorous organization. I cannot present you with a report on the activity of this organization, but I must say that its work has been more or less of a propagandistic character and has consisted chiefly in the publication of assorted materials. Its organizational work has been completely insignificant. The organization is very weak in terms of the number of adherents, although it has had a few haphazard successes. I think that it is not only the fault of the Peasant International but also the fault of the Communist International, our collective fault. We did not provide this organization with enough strength, we have not devoted enough attention to its work. The events in Rumania and the results of the elections in France and Germany are obvious proof of this. We must deal with this question in the immediate future and do all we can to improve the situation.[65]

[63] A. I., "The International Peasant Conference," *International Press Correspondence*, VIII, No. 23 (April 19, 1928), 446–47.

[64] Leon Trotsky, *The Third International after Lenin* (New York, 1957), p. 227.

[65] *VI kongress Kominterna—stenograficheskii otchet* (Moscow, 1929), I, 56.

But it was Kolarov, the chief spokesman on agrarian problems in the 1930s, who gave the peasant question a new slant by stressing the radicalization of the poor peasants in Western Europe, indicating that this process was providing the basis for a new revolutionary situation there.[66] On the Krestintern, Kolarov said:

I must say quite plainly that we are not satisfied with the work of the Peasant International. And because the Krestintern is an independent organization this means that we are not satisfied with the work of the Communists in it. The question is not entirely one of personal responsibility. There is no doubt that the Comintern must accept a significant share of the responsibility for the inadequacies of its work. Nevertheless, Communists must fully understand that the Krestintern cannot, and must not, be a second, though, of course, inferior edition of the Comintern. The Krestintern must be a special organization, it must work out its own special approach to the peasant masses and not copy that of the Comintern. It must devise its own language different from the language of the Communist parties, a language with which it speaks to the peasant masses. These are things which the Krestintern has not yet achieved. It must be converted into a special mass organization of the poor and middle peasants in the capitalist and colonial countries, which I have already mentioned, and in this work it must conduct its agitation and propaganda in the name of the slogan "workers' and peasants' alliance" under the leadership of the proletariat. In this lies its *raison d'etre,* in this lies its specific problem, and it must solve this problem.[67]

Kolarov, who considered himself thoroughly in tune with the new orientation of the Comintern, maintained that the Krestintern was primarily an organization for work with the peasants themselves, rather than with their political parties. He implied that up to this time the efforts of the Krestintern had been unnecessarily concentrated in those "states bordering Russia," that is, Eastern Europe. Finally, Kolarov maintained that the "danger of war" was one of the most potent themes in propaganda work among the peasants. After the congress this theme, in fact, replaced the emphasis on more immediate local grievances in propaganda work among the peasants.

The most vitriolic attack on the Peasant International came from Ruggiero Grieco, who was then on his way up in the Comintern apparatus. Grieco had participated in the work of the Presidium of

[66] *Ibid.,* pp. 164–65.
[67] *Ibid.,* p. 165.

the Krestintern in 1925 and he spoke at the Sixth Comintern Congress under the pseudonym of Garlandi.[68] Grieco, who was personally familiar with the work of the Peasant International, did not mince words.

Comrades, do we have an agrarian policy? I say we do not. We have only agrarian theses. The political outlook of all our sections are still too narrow. To work out an agrarian policy for all our parties, we will have to recognize the popular and national character of the victorious proletarian revolution.[69]

Grieco pointed out that member parties formulated agrarian theses in conformance with Comintern directives and then filed them away without applying them. However, he blamed the ECCI explicitly, and Bukharin implicitly, for not pressing the issue. Grieco reminded the congress that, among other things, the recently appointed Agrarian Commission of the Comintern had presented no report on its activities and goals.[70] Like Bringolf at the Fifth Comintern Congress, Grieco called for campaigns in the countryside based on a specialized knowledge of rural problems. Grieco's chief target, however, was the Krestintern itself:

I would like to turn to an old question, a question to which I have still received no answer. Getting down to brass tacks, what is the Peasant International? Is it a directing center for Communist peasant factions or for mass peasant organizations? We have always believed that the Krestintern ought to be a mass organization and that it should work toward that goal. What does this mean? It means that the Krestintern must organize its work among the revolutionary peasantry in terms of the peasant's struggle for his own partial demands, and these partial demands must be linked to the general demands which are at the base of the workers' and peasants' bloc.

In Europe the peasantry has never heard of the Krestintern. The Krestintern does not have any concrete or precise program of work, it has not studied the actual problems encountered in various countries. For example, has the Krestintern studied the problem of share cropping in various countries? Does it know what to say to tenant farmers who are struggling to improve their condition? What does a Communist say to this small

[68] Branko Lazić, *Les Partis communistes d'Europe, 1919–1955* (Paris, 1956), p. 226.
[69] *VI kongress kominterna*, I, 314.
[70] *Ibid.*, pp. 315–16.

renter, fighting for his immediate needs? One cannot simply repeat over and over again that it is necessary to overthrow the capitalist structure. One must tell them something else or these village proletarians will find some other way to defend their interests and they will remain in the camp of our adversaries. The peasants are not going to come over to the Krestintern just to please us.[71]

Grieco stated that the Peasant International needed to be placed under the direct control of the Comintern if these deficiencies were to be corrected.

The burden of defending the Krestintern fell on Dąbal's shoulders. Although he didn't realize it, this was the last time he would speak in the name of the organization he had fostered in the Comintern. Dąbal followed the customary line of defense: the lack of clear Comintern directives and the lack of existing organizations in rural areas on which the Krestintern could build.[72]

By 1929 both Smirnov and Dąbal had been removed from the Krestintern and the organization itself disappears from the public record. Although it was not dissolved until 1939, it was relegated to whatever unknown limbo the Comintern reserved for unsuccessful united front experiments. A last feeble attempt was made by the Krestintern to rise from its own ashes by organizing an active subdivision called the European Peasant Committee, which was essentially all that the Krestintern had been from the beginning. The new project claimed to have several distinguished sponsors, such as Dr. Mitrany of Oxford, Dr. Miglioli of Rome, and Dr. Fehr, the Bavarian minister of agriculture.[73] The Czechoslavak agrarian party warned its members against attending this new peasant assembly, at least as delegates of their party.[74] The European Peasant

[71] *Ibid.*
[72] *Ibid.*, pp. 438–47.
[73] Karel Mečíř, "La Soi-disant Union Paysanne Européene et la soi-disant Congrés Europeen," *MAB Bulletin*, No. 4 (1929), p. 295. Other accounts of the first congress of this new organization are available in "Le Premier Congrés Europeen Paysan à Berlin," *La Fédération balkanique*, No. 132–133 (9–10A) (April 15, 1930), pp. 2878–84; "Pervyi evropeiskii kongress trudniashchegosia krest'ianstva," *Kommunisticheskii Internatsional*, No. 10 (April 10, 1930), pp. 28–33; "Evropeiskii Kongress trudniashchegosia krest'ianstva," *Agrarnye problemy*, No. 4–5 (April–May, 1930), pp. 161–78.
[74] Mečíř, *MAB Bulletin*, No. 4 (1929), p. 298.

Committee held its first congress in November, 1929, and two more in 1930 and 1932, but it was, like its mother organization, no more than a pale shadow of the Comintern.[75]

Essentially the Krestintern, and the international and national peasant movements as well, belonged to a special era in which internal developments in the Soviet Union encouraged Communists to woo the peasants and in which the political potentialities of the peasantry seemed exciting and important. While events in Bulgaria, Poland, Yugoslavia, and Rumania betwen 1923 and 1930 might seem to indicate that the peasant political movement had succumbed to nationalistic and nondemocratic forces, the Comintern's declining interest in peasantism was due more to Russian political circumstances than to a careful analysis of developments in Eastern Europe. Actually the Comintern stopped courting the peasant political movement at a time when international agrarianism was moving toward one of its greatest triumphs.

THE COMPETITION OF THE GREEN INTERNATIONAL

In May, 1928, Prague seemed to be realizing the very ambition which Moscow was then abandoning, the dream of becoming the international capital of the peasant political movement. In many ways Prague was better suited to the role. It was the capital of a small country and therefore few peasant political parties feared that Czechoslovakia would use its military and economic strength to dominate the international agrarian movement. The agrarian party in Czechoslovakia in some ways set an enviable example for kindred parties in neighboring East European countries by remaining politically powerful in its own country during the entire interwar period. Czechoslovakia was also a natural bridge between developed Western Europe and underdeveloped Eastern Europe because the republic harbored within its borders both advanced Bohemia and Moravia and backward Slovakia and Ruthenia.

Of course, Prague could not hope to become the capital of agrarianism as Moscow was the capital of communism. In Czecho-

[75] The second congress was in December, 1930, and the third in April, 1932. A. Kheveshi, "Evropeiskii Krest'ianskii Komitet i krest'ianskoe dvizhenie," in V. Kolarov, ed., *Shest' let bor'by za Krest'ianstvo,* Vol. II of *Agrarnyi vopros i sovremennoe krest'ianskoe dvizhenie* (Moscow, 1935), pp. 18–34.

slovakia the agrarian party was one of many parties; a strong party, but one which stayed in power by compromise with other parties. The Czech party did not have the prestige of capturing political power and transforming society according to the principles of agrarianism. For this reason it could not, either by its traditions or its achievements, hope to exact the kind of obedience from agrarian parties which Moscow exacted from Communist parties.

On the other hand, Prague had distinct advantages over Moscow as the capital of *agrarianism*. Even under the New Economic Policy Moscow could not pose as the bastion of peasantism as long as the nationalization of land and belief in the superiority of large-scale agriculture remained fundamental tenets of Marxism, however weakened these tenets might be by Bukharin's theoretical gyrations. Even Radić's token accession to the Krestintern was founded on political expediency and attraction to Moscow's nationality policy rather than Comintern agrarian policy. The latter policy was one of Moscow's greatest handicaps. In the heat of the struggle for power in the Russian Communist Party, the Comintern's agrarian policy became more and more a series of abstract formulas with little reference to realities outside the Soviet Union. This may explain the persistent indifference of member parties to the agrarian question. Boshkovich and Dąbal tried to find some way out of this impasse by requesting permission to form peasant political parties. In practical work it was not easy to persuade the peasantry to join Communist parties or to form rural trade unions, as was required by Bukharin's theses at the Fifth Plenum of the ECCI.

For all of these reasons the Krestintern feared the International Agrarian Bureau, better known as the Green International, at Prague. The Green International could do something the Krestintern could not do, namely, command the loyalty of existing peasant political parties. As early as 1926 Dąbal warned of the Krestintern's competition at the Seventh Plenum of the ECCI.

The rise of the pomeshchik-kulak, black-green international this year under the International Institute of Agriculture at Rome; the participation in its creation of the kulak Green International; the agrarian orientation of the Second International and its separate sections; the agrarian reformism of Lloyd George, etc.—all these things prove that the struggle for the peasantry takes on organizational forms even on an international scale.

It is necessary to emphasize the fact that the black-green international is closely connected through the International Institute of Agriculture at Rome with the League of Nations and is its instrument in the enslavement of the toiling peasantry to finance capital. From this fact we see the necessity for the toiling peasantry to link its struggle with the struggle of the world proletariat, developing and strengthening the solidarity of the toiling strata of the peasantry.[76]

The kulak Green International to which Dąbal refers was the same organization which, according to Zinoviev in October, 1923, "faded before it ever bloomed." [77]

In the passage quoted above Dąbal had succeeded in confusing several similar movements with one another. In 1926 and 1927, partly in response to the danger of the Red Peasant International, there were three new efforts to establish an international coordinating center for the peasant organizations. However, they were almost as hostile to one another as they were to the Krestintern in Moscow. This rivalry did have one salutary effect. It compelled the self-styled leaders of the international agrarian movement to translate their rhetoric into deeds.

The prime mover was Dr. Ernst Laur, general secretary of the Swiss Peasant Union. In 1924, at the International Institute of Agriculture in Rome, and in June, 1925, at the Twelfth International Agricultural Congress in Warsaw, Laur proposed an international confederation of agricultural organizations to unite the respective efforts of national peasant and farmer organizations at the International Labor Office in Geneva and at the League of Nations and also to establish closer liaison between the International Institute of Agriculture and the International Commission of Agriculture.[78] The Twelfth International Congress of Agriculture decided

[76] Puti mirovoi revoliutsii, I, 196.

[77] Pervaia mezhdunarodnaia krest'ianskaia konferentsiia—rechi, tezisy, vozzvaniia (Moscow, 1924), p. 99.

[78] For a description of Laur's proposals see "Projet de M. Laur de créer une union internationale des associations agricoles," MAB Bulletin, No. 5–6 (1925), pp. 60–61, and "La Conférence internationale des associations agricoles à Berne," MAB Bulletin, No. 8–9 (1925), pp. 41–46. For the Communist reaction to Laur's proposals see A. Kheveshi, "Chernyi internatsional—agent finansogo kapitala," in Dąbal et al., Bor'ba za krest'ianstvo (Moscow, 1925). This article was also published in Krest'ianskii Internatsional, No. 12 (Dec., 1925), pp. 5–19.

that Laur's proposal was premature.[79] The Krestintern promptly labeled Laur's project the Black International of Agrarians because, it said, the new body was to be an instrument of black reactionary landlords and rich peasants.[80]

The two organizations which Laur hoped to bring closer together were located in two of the most important capitals in Europe, the International Commission of Agriculture in Paris, and the International Institute of Agriculture in Rome. The former had been organized in 1889 at the First International Congress of Agriculture on the initiative of Jules Melin (the French minister of agriculture).[81] Its purpose was to prepare for periodic international congresses on the technical problems of world agriculture. The International Institute of Agriculture was inspired by the American David Lubin.[82] It had been founded in 1905 to bring together the efforts of various governments in the area of agricultural statistics and agricultural research.

In September, 1925, in Berne, Laur worked out his proposals in greater detail and formed a provisional organization of the sort he had proposed, calling it the International Conference of Agricultural Associations. Such an organization, he pointed out, was needed to oppose the Communist threat.

An international peasant conference was held in Moscow October 10-16, 1923, in which some 120 delegates from 100 countries participated. The International Peasant Council, which was created by this conference, serves as an arm of the Soviet power for the destruction of the present system of world agriculture by general revolution.[83]

The Krestintern in Moscow interpreted Laur's plans as a dark enterprise directed toward the creation of an "agrarian Locarno." [84]

[79] MAB Bulletin, No. 2 (1927), p. 84; Le Musée social, No. 7 (July, 1927), pp. 220–21.

[80] See Kheveshi in Dąbal, Bor'ba za krest'ianstvo.

[81] Vladislav Brdlík, "International Organization of Agriculture," International Peasant Union, Monthly Bulletin (June–July, 1955), p. 23.

[82] Ibid.

[83] Laur, as quoted in B. Boshkovich, ed., Zelenyi Internatsional i ego kulatskoe litso (Moscow, 1933), p. 16.

[84] Kheveshi, "Chernyi Internatsional," in Dąbal, p. 52. See also Sigismund Gargas, Die Grüne Internationale (Halberstadt, 1927), pp. 37, 52. Gargas confirms the fact that Laur's efforts were in part motivated by a desire to establish a bulwark against Bolshevism. Communist allegations seemed borne out when the Green International was listed as a branch of Laur's organization,

The Italian delegates to Berne resisted Laur's proposals and insisted that any international organization of agricultural associations be under the complete control of the Institute of Agriculture at Rome. A month after the Berne meeting the Institute at Rome established its own international organization in competition with Laur's, to be founded on the principles advanced by the Italian delegation. The organization at Rome, called the International Association of Agricultural Associations,[85] was a regional secretariat providing agricultural organizations with the opportunity to render advice to the Institute and receive professional advice in return. In 1927 Laur's International Conference on Agricultural Organizations was absorbed by the International Commission of Agriculture in Paris, which transformed itself "from a general agricultural welfare organization to an international body, supported and controlled by national farm organizations." [86] Paris threatened to become the chief coordinating center for all political and professional agricultural organizations and to absorb its competitors elsewhere.

Laur's own orientation on the agrarian question, however, alienated the East European agrarian parties. Laur believed in limiting the influence of the state on agriculture, in increasing the number of independent farmers and peasants, and in retaining large estates except in those countries where conditions were ripe for intensive farming and an active cooperative movement.[87] As Mitrany points out, the third point was anathema to East European peasant parties, "for whom a radical land reform was as much a political as social necessity." [88]

Prague was stirred by all this competition. Faced with rival international agricultural organizations in Rome, Paris, and Moscow, she

---

but the Green International promptly denied that it had joined or even supported Laur's project. "La Réunion de la Commission internationale d'agriculture à Vienne," *MAB Bulletin,* No. 2 (1928), p. 136.

[85] "La Réorganisation de la Commission d'agriculture," *MAB Bulletin,* No. 1 (1926), p. 49, and Asher Hobson, *The International Institute of Agriculture* (Berkeley, 1931), pp. 216–18.

[86] Hobson, p. 221. See also *Le Musée social,* No. 7 (July, 1927), pp. 220–21, and Brdlík, International Peasant Union, *Monthly Bulletin* (June–July, 1955), p. 24.

[87] Gargas, pp. 39–40.

[88] David Mitrany, *Marx Against the Peasant: A Study in Social Dogmatism* (Chapel Hill, 1951), p. 251.

decided that bold counteraction was the order of the day. From 1921 to 1925 the International Agrarian Bureau at Prague had been an extremely loose and inactive federation of four East European peasant parties, the Czechoslovak Republican Party of Small Farmers and Peasants, the Serbian Peasant's Union, the Bulgarian National Agrarian Union, and the Polish Peasant Party Piast. Although the International Agrarian Bureau had been created on the initiative of the Bulgarian agrarian leader, Stamboliiski, one source suggests that the Czech leaders were anxious to

put to profit these attempts at creating a Green International and turn it into a Slav democratic movement on which Czechslovakia might rest her policy in Central and Eastern Europe. Thus the movement in favor of the Green International is becoming a movement of democratic Pan-Slavism inspired by the Czechoslovaks.[89]

While this conclusion is not positively confirmed by the material published by the Green International, there is little doubt that the organization favored democratic forms of government, that it was dominated by the Czechoslovak agrarian leaders, especially Švehla and his lieutenant, Hodža, and that until the end of 1925 the organization had a Pan-Slav orientation. It is difficult to visualize, however, a means by which the International Agrarian Bureau could influence the policy of other countries or parties since it had no formal organizational ties with its four members, no one of which was strong enough to assume power in its own country except in coalition with other parties. The only activities of the International Agrarian Bureau were its annual congresses and the publication of a trilingual quarterly, *Mezinárodní Agrární Bureau, Bulletin*.

The challenge posed by Laur seemed to force the Green International into a more aggressive and less parochial posture. At its

[89] Petco-Stainov, as quoted *Ibid.*, p. 250, n. 96. There is abundant evidence of Pan-Slavism in the speeches of the leader of the Czech agrarian party, Antonín Švehla, at the annual May Conference of the International Agrarian Bureau in 1925. *MAB Bulletin*, No. 5–6 (1925), p. 55. But this conference would mark a retreat from virulent Pan-Slavism to a more catholic approach to the peasants and farmers of the world. The new tendency was manifest in the appeal formulated by the May Conference and elaborated in an article by Švehla's lieutenant, Milan Hodža, later in the year. M. Hodža, "La Politique étrangère et l'organisation internationale agriculteure," *MAB Bulletin*, No. 8–9 (1925), pp. 20–25.

annual May meeting in 1925 the International Agrarian Bureau ran up its new flags with an appeal to the farmers of the world, and the word "Slav" was conspicuous by its absence.

> After an epoch when false social and political doctrines have brought men to demoralization, famine, and defeat, humanity ought to draw upon the moral and material force, the spirit of hard work of the farmer, for the regeneration of society. Here is precisely the meaning of agrarianism, to bring together the farmers of all countries for the common task. They must be awakened and made aware of their force and exact their just share of domestic and international political power.[90]

The editors of the official organ of the Green International also attacked Laur's proposals directly. Apart from the fact that Laur was stealing their thunder, the editors opposed Laur's proposal because he had no consistent criteria for admission to his organization and proposed to mix leaders of peasant political parties with professional agronomists and members of agricultural ministries. "What is lacking is precisely unification on the basis of an idea, the agrarian idea, which would tend to give such an organization an influence over domestic and international social, economic, and political policy."[91]

A new personality was brought in to command the International Agrarian Bureau in its campaign, Karel Mečíř. A close friend of the agrarian premier, Antonín Švehla, Mečíř had been recently removed from his post as Czechoslovak ambassador to Athens with some hint of scandal. In June, 1925, he was dispatched to the Twelfth International Congress of Agriculture in Warsaw as a delegate of the International Agrarian Bureau to parry Laur's thrusts.[92] He apparently performed with distinction because in July he was appointed Secretary of the Bureau and editor-in-chief of its official organ.[93] Mečíř began a campaign in 1926 which would ultimately bring twelve more peasant

---

[90] *MAB Bulletin*, No. 5–6 (1925), p. 58.

[91] *Ibid.*, p. 60.

[92] For Mečíř's own account of his experience see K. Mečíř, "Le Congrès international d'agriculture et l'agrarisme," *MAB Bulletin*, No. 7 (1925), pp. 16–21.

[93] *MAB Bulletin*, No. 8–9 (1925), inside back cover. The former general secretary and editor of the *Bulletin* was George Fiedler. According to the Krestintern, Fiedler was fired for embezzling funds. A. Kheveshi, "Perspektivy rimskogo mezhdunarodnogo kongressa agrariev," *Krest'ianskii Internatsional*, No. 3–5 (March–May, 1926), p. 13. I have not discovered any information which confirms this allegation.

parties into the Bureau within the next two years. The first targets were France, Rumania, and Finland.

Mečíř outlined his new program at the end of 1926. He recognized that peasants could not be brought into international organizations as individuals, but he pointed out to all European peasant parties that membership in the International Agrarian Bureau would enable member parties to perform more effectively because they could renovate and invigorate their programs by profiting from the examples of other parties, by supporting their own demands with the successes of agrarian parties of other countries, and by avoiding the mistakes made by other peasant parties.[94] The Bureau was defined as a center of information whose purpose was to disseminate and "deepen" the idea of agrarianism.[95] This, of course, did not square with all the other goals Mečíř projected for the organization. He admitted that in time the Bureau would have to do more than publish a quarterly and hold annual meetings. The informational function was only a preliminary stage.

The more we are helped in informational activity, the sooner we will reach our goal. The day when agrarian parties, represented by their delegates, can gather together to form a similar program of action, to proclaim the establishment of international bonds, the world will learn that a new force has appeared in the field of social reform, an enormous but powerful force, desiring only the peaceful development of peoples, strengthening the foundations of society—the agricultural population.[96]

In 1927 Karel Mečíř, as secretary general of the Green International, was asked to approve Laur's new plan in the name of the Prague organization and to become a member of the preparatory committee for the first plenary conference of the new Paris organization in the fall of that year.[97] In a reply dated September 1, Mečíř

[94] K. Mečíř, "Le Bureau international agraire," *MAB Bulletin*, No. 4 (1926), p. 27. Thinking perhaps of Dąbal and Laur, Mečíř defended Prague as the center for an International Agrarian Bureau. He argued that, like the Second Socialist International, the Green International chose the capital of a minor power in Europe as its seat in order to escape the preponderant influence a larger state might exert if its capital were chosen.

[95] *Ibid.*, p. 28.

[96] *Ibid.*, p. 29.

[97] "Le Project d'une union parlementaire internationale agricole," *MAB Bulletin*, No. 3 (1927), pp. 133–37.

objected strongly to the phrasing of the statutes of the new organization, pointing out that it was to consist of "national agricultural groups." He argued that, unless some definite political criteria were adopted, members of any political organizations, including the Communists, could participate.[98]

But he was most concerned about the question whether the term "national agricultural groups" was intended to include peasant political parties, Mečíř was indignant:

We would like to point out that it is the unique function of the International Agrarian Bureau at Prague to organize peasant political parties on an international scale, and the International Agrarian Bureau has already enjoyed some success in this field of activity.[99]

For these reasons Mečíř refused to participate in the new organization as then constituted. He implied that if the term "national agricultural groups" was defined more precisely in order to exclude peasant political parties, and if the organization clearly stated its intention to confine its activities to technical and social problems, then the International Agrarian Bureau might join it.[100]

In November, 1927, at the same time that the Paris organization was holding its first plenary meeting, the International Agrarian Bureau sent a letter to all peasant political parties in Europe,[101] calling attention to the various efforts to create international agricultural organizations. The Bureau pointed out that none of these new organizations were devoted exclusively to the establishment of an international organization of peasant political parties except the unit in Prague.[102]

The letter indicated that the only effective method for improving the lot of the peasantry was the creation of such political parties, and yet the peasant had been relatively backward in this kind of activity.[103]

According to the International Agrarian Bureau, the peasant political movement could best be strengthened by the establishment

[98] *Ibid.*, p. 139.
[99] *Ibid.*, p. 140.
[100] *Ibid.*
[101] The letter was said to have been composed by Švehla and Mečíř. *MAB Bulletin*, No. 1 (1934), p. 2.
[102] "Vers la création d'une internationale politique agraire," *MAB Bulletin*, No. 1 (1928), p. 3.
[103] *Ibid.*, pp. 4–5.

of a real international organization of peasant political parties which would reinforce the peasant political movement in three ways.[104]

(1) It would provide moral reinforcement to peasants everywhere by contact between the stronger and the weaker peasant political movements and by thus creating a feeling of international solidarity.

(2) It would enable peasant political parties everywhere to profit from the successes and achievements of each other.

(3) Solidarity and unity would give added force and prestige to local peasant political movements.

The International Agrarian Bureau indicated that if it were to perform these services for member parties it would need strong moral support from peasant political parties everywhere.[105] The letter was signed by Mečíř and Švehla and included the proposed constitution for the new Bureau.

This constitution began with a statement of fundamental principles, of which the first was an affirmation of the necessity of preserving the institution of private property.[106] The other principles followed very closely the agrarian precepts already described—the desirability of low tariffs, the value of cooperative organization of agricultural enterprises, the need for social insurance, the need for technical education, and the necessity for thorough agrarian reforms.[107]

The vital question, of course, was the relationship between member parties and the International Agrarian Bureau. The new organic statutes stated first of all that "only peasant political parties can be regular members of the International Agrarian Bureau." [108] Provisions were made for those parties which represented a nationality rather than an entire state. The Bureau was to continue to serve as a medium for the exchange of information about the activities of member parties. The informational function, however, was now to serve as a means for exerting some influence in international politics. "By its admission to the International Agrarian Bureau the peasant political party acquires the right . . . in case of events of exceptional gravity, to appeal to the International Agrarian Bureau for transmission of this news as quickly as possible to the journals of all peasant political

---

[104] *Ibid.*
[105] *Ibid.*, p. 5.
[106] *Ibid.*, p. 6.
[107] *Ibid.*, p. 7.
[108] *Ibid.*

parties, initiating, in effect, an international action." [109] Members were required to pay dues to the International Agrarian Bureau according to their numerical strength and to assign a permanent representative to the center at Prague. Two major additions were made to the draft constitution. The first (Article III) provided for the exclusion of any member party that failed to live up to its obligations (abiding by the fundamental principles of the organization, paying dues, sending a permanent representative, and supplying information).[110] A second clause provided that the International Agrarian Bureau should offer its good offices where inter- or intra-party conflicts broke out.[111]

Thus there were no real teeth in the organization, such as, for example, the twenty-one conditions in the Comintern. The International Agrarian Bureau would give the international peasant movement reinforcement through the creation of a sense of solidarity, the exchange of information, and the sharing of experience. But it would not direct or influence member parties except in the most indirect sense, through moral suasion, intervention in party quarrels, and the opportunity to publicize injustices imposed on the peasantry.

Nevertheless, one should not underestimate the importance of the program. It was broad enough to win the support of eleven European peasant parties, including the formerly hostile Rumanian National Peasant Party and the Croatian Peasant Party.[112] By the time of its first General Assembly in May, 1929, the Green International had an impressive array of seventeen members, representing peasant parties from most of the countries in East Central Europe.[113]

[109] Ibid.

[110] MAB Bulletin, No. 2 (1929), p. 101.

[111] Ibid., p. 102.

[112] Between November, 1927, and February, 1928, the following peasant parties adhered to the newly organized International Agrarian Bureau: the Bulgarian National Agrarian Union, the Estonian Farmer's Party, the Peasant Agrarian Union of Finland, the Platterlandersbond of the Netherlands, the Peasant Party of the Canton of Argovie (Switzerland), the Rumanian National Peasant Party, the Czechoslovak Republican Party of Small Farmers and Peasants, the Bund der Landwirte (Sudeten German), the Serbian Agrarian Union, the Croatian Peasant Party, and the Slovenian Small Peasant's Party. MAB Bulletin, No. 1 (1928), pp. 11–12.

[113] The new parties were the Lettish Peasant Party, the Agrarian Party of France, the Lithuanian Peasant Party, the Polish Peasant Party Piast, the Peasant Party of the Canton of Bern (Switzerland), and the Austrian Landbund für Österreich. MAB Bulletin, No. 2 (1929), p. 109.

In a preparatory conference in May, 1928, Milan Hodža, the successor to Švehla as leader of the Czech agrarian party, triumphantly declared that all of Central Europe was the home of "agrarianism," —a considerable change from his former Pan-Slav point of view—because in this area the industrial tradition was still young and weak, while the agrarian tradition was old and strong.[114] This, said Hodža, was why it was the International Agrarian Bureau at Prague that first established cordial relations among the farmers of northern, western, and southern Europe. Hodža stressed the role of peasant political movements as a bulwark against communism and as the mainstay of democracy.[115] He exulted a bit in the alleged achievements of the peasants, falling back, perhaps inadvertently, on the use of the word "Slav."[116]

Mečíř spoke also, significantly omitting Hodža's stress on Central Europe as the true home of agrarianism with its implication of Slavic superiority. For Mečíř, the International Agrarian Bureau had already become an all-European institution. "The International Agrarian Bureau exists from the Atlantic Ocean to the Black Sea, from the Arctic Ocean to the Aegean."[117] Apparently Mežiř's approach won out. When the first General Assembly of the new Bureau met on May 23-25, 1929, there was little evidence of Hodža's earlier parochial Pan-Slav orientation in his speech before that body.[118] At this assembly the Bureau decided to enlarge the scope of its activity by campaigning for the creation of peasant parties in countries which did not yet have them.[119]

The difficulty with the organization created in Prague was that, while its program of moral reinforcement was broad enough to draw existing peasant parties into the fold, such a program relied for its success on the individual successes of its members, rather than on the discipline, guidance, and direction provided by the central international organization. This, of course, was in striking contrast to the methods of the Communist International, which by 1929 had perceptibly weakened its member parties in order to

114 *MAB Bulletin,* No. 2 (1928), p. 103.
115 *Ibid.,* p. 108–11.
116 *Ibid.,* p. 111.
117 *Ibid.,* p. 118.
118 *MAB Bulletin,* No. 2 (1929), pp. 120–22.
119 *Ibid.,* p. 99.

strengthen the authority and stature of the central international organization. The difference is critical, however, because the discipline and cohesiveness of the Comintern remained intact until its limited but loyal followers could be used again.

Apparently the Comintern feared the potentialities of the Green International in 1929, since the latter organization was selected, along with other international agricultural organizations, for special mention as a fascist body.

In opposition to these points of view [the points of view of the International Commission of Agriculture at Paris and the International Institute of Agriculture at Rome] the Prague Agrarian Bureau advances the point of view of "peasant democracy" and tries to create a union of peasant political parties. Both these organizations [the International Commission of Agriculture and the International Agrarian Bureau] are similar in that they unconditionally support the policies of the League of Nations in questions of peace and disarmament. In this respect their position on the danger of war is fully defined. The undisguised fascist war machines of the national organizations of the agrarian bourgeoisie are thus complemented by international organizations using "other means" of pacifist mass deceit and disarming fraud.[120]

On the whole, the years 1921-29 were years of promise for the East European peasant political movement. The leaders of this movement seemed to have discovered a new and dynamic political program admirably adapted to the special needs of economically backward countries. It appeared for a time in 1929 that the necessary cohesion and cooperation had at last been provided to erect a solid barrier to the penetration of communism and, through emphasis on democratic methods and institutions, the development of fascism. This illusion would be swept away by the economic crisis of 1929-30 and by the continuing failures of individual peasant parties in Eastern Europe. But the leaders of the Comintern did not have second sight. The Comintern made its decisions before the world economic crisis and without the benefit of soothsayers; it chose to abandon its efforts to harness the peasant political movement at the very moment when that movement seemed to have shown its greatest strength and international solidarity.

[120] Manner-Rusticus, *Kommunisticheskii Internatsional,* No. 23–24 (June 20, 1929), p. 34.

PART III

THE CONFLICT: NATIONAL

CHAPTER VI

From Theory to Practice

The only conclusive test of the efficiency of revolutionary theory is revolutionary practice. Part III, therefore, examines Comintern agrarian policy in five East European countries at critical junctures in their history. But in passing from the policy-making organs of the Comintern to the local organs of execution one adds another dimension to the study of the international Communist movement. In tracing the development of Comintern agrarian policy it was possible to bring a variety of sources to bear on a single city, revolutionary Moscow, and conjure up the tone and mood of decision making there. But the pursuit of those decisions to their final destination brings a whole new series of considerations into play. In order to test the wisdom and judgment of Moscow one has to fathom the mood and tone in the cities and villages where Comintern policy was applied and, above all, to comprehend, not only the distinctive characteristics of the local Communist party but its pre-Communist traditions and habits of mind as well. It would be easier if one could ignore the idiosyncrasies of indigenous parties and simply pit Comintern agrarian theory against the political and economic realities of Eastern Europe in the 1920s. But such a study would be no more than an academic exercise because Comintern agrarian policy was never applied in its undiluted original form. It was first filtered through the local party. Sometimes Comintern directives were changed because of the local party's prejudices and inhibitions and sometimes because the local party was on the scene and had a better understanding of what was possible and desirable.

Unfortunately, the writing of local Communist party histories has become ritualized. In both the Soviet and the non-Soviet world, historians have treated the decade after World War I as the era of Bolshevization, signifying subjection to and imitation of the Russian

Party. The story of Bolshevization becomes a modern-day morality play in which the victim rises through the stages of purgatory to redemption. In the beginning the indigenous Communist party is covered with sins which are ambiguously labeled right and left (and occasionally even center) deviations, Social Democratic survivals, or some such opprobrious term. These sins are systematically washed away until the party is redeemed and has become pure and shining and indistinguishable from its Russian model.

The orthodox Communist scheme for party histories is apparently so persuasive that a number of Western scholars, even unsympathetic ones, have adopted it. Like their Communist counterparts, they dutifully record the "stages of Bolshevization," scoff at vestiges of Social Democratic illusions, sneer at ebbing militancy wherever it appears, and exult in the final redemption which, we are told, has produced a new and perfect conspiratorial organization. Like their Communist counterparts, they often seem to forget that communism ultimately triumphed in most of East Europe because of the Russian occupation rather than because of any special qualities imparted to the Communist parties by the Comintern. Although Western scholars clearly regard Russian communism as inhumane and reprehensible, at the same time they betray a marked tendency to measure all things with the yardsticks provided by their subject. In both Soviet and non-Soviet studies the disturbing fact that Bolshevizing a party always resulted in a decline in its membership and influence is dismissed as irrelevant. The temporary losses, one is told, are inconsequential because a Bolshevized party, however small, is a truly disciplined fighting machine. The vital question whether the aims of communism might best be achieved without fighting or, at the very least, without a party that was a fighting machine, is rarely discussed.

But Western scholars must reexamine the orthodox histories of Communist parties and the qualitative judgments which they have so uncritically borrowed from them. A Marxist party, even by its own standards, was not obligated by its ideology to make itself a replica of the Russian party or even to make a Bolshevik Revolution. Each Communist party had its own traditions growing out of its immediate awareness of the special problems of its country. Its own individual programs and methods were often much better suited to the task of winning popular support and political power than were Comintern recipes for Bolshevization. The so-called deviations of the 1920s, which even in Western studies are often treated as manifestations of naïveté or doctrinaire irascibility, may have represented a more realistic adjustment to local political and economic circumstances than is generally recognized.

The distinctive character of local Communist parties was less apparent in the formative period of the Comintern when such parties often outdid themselves in adopting the outward image of the successful Russian Party. From 1921 to 1925 the Comintern compelled every party to adopt the Russian-inspired theses of the Comintern on all questions from organizational structure to agrarian policy. But it was a token conformity. Actually, most Communist parties during this period began to revert to their former traditions. Where Comintern theses were applied, it was to capture electoral support, not to make or even prepare for revolutions.

During Bukharin's ascendancy from 1925 to 1928, the leadership in East European Communist parties was generally placed in the hands of rightists, that is, those who, like Bukharin, saw a long period of stabilization ahead. When the Comintern occasionally beat the revolutionary drum, such leaders turned a deaf ear, arguing that in their country there were "special conditions" which the Comintern did not understand. A recurrent theme in the local party's defense of its position was "agrarianization, " the theory that its country was a semicolony being denuded and deindustrialized by the great imperialistic countries of the world. Every East European Communist party advanced the theory at one time or another and in one form or another in the 1920s. The agrarianization thesis acted as an ideological smoke screen behind which local parties could evade embarrassing Comintern demands and appeal to their constituents as they had done under another label before the October Revolution. It was argued that an agrarianized country was moving away from the proletarian revolution and back toward a bourgeois-democratic war of national liberation. The primary task of a Communist party was, then, not to call for revolution against the national government but to ally itself to the radical reformist parties of the petty-bourgeois left, to become a leader in the battle against the external imperialistic threat, and, incidentally, to win elections. To put it more bluntly, after the excitement of 1917-21, most Communist leaders in Eastern Europe yearned to return to legal political operations, which they understood best, and fight for ballots, which was a struggle they knew how to wage. Since there was no immediate hope for revolution, legal activity seemed the only practical way to recruit members. On the other hand, those East European Communists who were still hypnotized by the events of 1917-21 and by Comintern theses conducted a continuous battle against the "blindness" of their rightist leaders, so most parties also suffered from enervating factionalism.

Two forces propelled East European parties toward an adoption of Comintern agrarian tactics. The first was the constant pressure from the Comintern for conformity to an agrarian program advanced as a lesson of the October Revolution. The second was the growing disillusionment in all East European parties when they were forced against their will to operate illegally. The Hungarian Communist Party and the Polish Communist Party had to go underground in 1919, the Yugoslav in 1920, the Bulgarian in 1923, and the Rumanian in 1924. Only the Czechoslovak Communist Party remained legal during the entire interwar period. All of them suffered a striking decline in membership and found it difficult and frustrating to adapt to the conditions of illegal operations. To many, the prospect of augmenting their depleted ranks from the hordes of peasants in their economically underdeveloped countries must have seemed very attractive indeed. Even in those areas where the Communist party could operate legally, as in Bulgaria before 1923 and Czechoslovakia during the entire period, the prospect of capturing the peasant vote was attractive.

There were, however, major impediments to complete acceptance of the Comintern agrarian program. Among the older Communist leaders there was a strong strain of Marxist orthodoxy which militated against rural agitation and alliances with "petty-bourgeois" peasant political leaders. In addition, there was the dread of absorption. In a country where the majority of the population were peasants, the class purity of the proletarian party had become almost an obsession for fear of drowning in a peasant sea. Alliances with numerically superior peasant parties were even more suspect for the same reason.

Another impediment was the closely related national question. In many cases in Eastern Europe the Comintern agrarian program had to be advanced in conjunction with the Comintern program on the national question. Many provinces which seemed likely to respond to the Comintern's agrarian program, because they had a high proportion of peasants to the total population and were suffering the usual problems of peasant societies in transition, were at the same time provinces in which ethnic or linguistic minorities were predominant. In such provinces neither the peasants nor their parties were willing to listen to the messages of those who did not support national self-determination up to and including secession. Stalin seemed aware of this when he argued that the national question was at the same time a peasant question (see Chapter IX), and it is difficult to tell, especially in Poland and Czechoslovakia, which was more important in explaining Communist successes, need or nationality. But, whereas the Comintern program on the agrarian question and the Comintern program on the national question tended to reinforce one another in areas inhabited by national minorities, they were likely to cancel one another out in areas inhabited by the dominant or state nationality. When member parties reluctantly bowed to Comintern pressure on the national question, their fears were borne out as their parties were swamped with recruits from the ethnic minorities. In much of Eastern Europe this meant that, although an obedient Communist party gained support among the peasants from the national minorities, it also tended to lose its appeal among all social classes in the areas inhabited by the dominant nationality and became less representative of the nation as a whole. In many cases it even ran the risk of becoming less representative of the industrial working class.

These were some of the major obstacles which the Comintern faced in trying to persuade member parties to comply with its agrarian program. The tension between the Comintern and member parties diminished only after the Comintern, for purely Russian reasons, made its abrupt turn to the left late in 1928, abandoned united front tactics in general, and imposed Moscow-trained leftist leaders on most East European Communist parties. This change marked the last stage of Bolshevization, according to the official Communist histories, and the end, for the time being, of any serious Comintern efforts to win the peasantry and peasant political parties.

CHAPTER VII

Bulgaria: Communism and the Peasant Paradise, 1919–1923

Bulgaria was the first testing ground for the slogan "workers' and peasants' government. " On the surface it seemed ideally suited to the purpose. It was economically underdeveloped, a country in which the political situation was still fluid, and in which the peasantry had exhibited an unprecedented degree of political consciousness since World War I. The Bulgarian Communist Party was, in the words of Radek, "one of the mass parties of the Comintern," and "among the first to accept unconditionally the principles of communism." [1] Yet when the opportunity came to exploit all these assets and lead a workers' and peasants' revolt, the Party balked and actually refused to obey Comintern orders. This insubordination demonstrates in several ways the deficiencies of the Comintern agrarian program.

STAMBOLIISKI, AGRARIAN MESSIAH

In 1919 Bulgaria, like prewar Russia, was an economically backward country drawn into the Western orbit, primarily Greek Orthodox, and ruled by a monarch. Unlike Tsarist Russia, however, most of Bulgaria's land was already divided into small peasant holdings and the old serf relationship had largely disappeared. Unlike Russia, Bulgaria suffered a decline in economic development between 1878 and 1900, a decline from which she was just beginning to recover after the turn of the century.[2]

After World War I certain kinds of industry grew rapidly in

[1] *Rasshirennyi plenum ispolnitel'nogo komiteta Kommunisticheskogo Internatsionala (12–23 iunia 1923 goda)* (Moscow, 1923), p. 261.
[2] Joseph Rothschild, *The Communist Party of Bulgaria* (New York, 1959), p. 8.

Bulgaria,[3] although this growth was accompanied by an increasing monopolization of commercial and industrial credit by four foreign banks.[4] State aid to Bulgarian industry was rather modest,[5] and other sources of investment capital were lacking. In spite of the few promising developments in industry, emigration to the city was not proceeding at a high enough rate to drain off the increase in rural population.[6]

In the years immediately after 1919 a special burden that inhibited the growth of the economy as a whole was the heavy weight of reparations payments.[7] The combined pressure of these payments and an inherited national debt contributed to the postwar inflation. By 1922 Bulgarian currency had depreciated to one-thirtieth of its 1919 value.[8] As in the case of most East European states, financial instability led to political instability.

The failure to resolve the agrarian question was another source of political unrest. The influx of refugees after the war only increased the problem of rural overpopulation. As late as 1934, 63 percent of the farms in Bulgaria were less than five hectares in size and 27 percent were dwarf farms (two hectares or less in size).[9] In 1937, according to one careful estimate, 28 percent of the agricultural population were surplus.[10] The problem was apparently a persistent

[3] In his essay, "Some Aspects of Industrialization in Bulgaria, 1878–1939," Gerschenkron points out that the only industries to show significant gains in the productivity of labor and an increase in relative importance in relation to other areas of industrial production were pottery manufacturing and the production of energy. Alexander Gerschenkron, *Economic Backwardness in Historical Perspective* (Cambridge, Mass., 1963), p. 213.

[4] Leo Pasvolsky, *Bulgaria's Economic Position* (Washington, D.C., 1930), pp. 214, 284. Gerschenkron argues that neither domestic nor foreign banks in Bulgaria possessed much entrepreneurial vigor or financial broadmindedness. Gerschenkron, p. 231.

[5] Gerschenkron, p. 229.

[6] Janiki S. Mollov, ed., *Die Sozialökonomische Struktur der bulgarischen Landwirtschaft* (Berlin, 1936), pp. 48–49.

[7] Pasvolsky, p. 116.

[8] *Ibid.*, p. 115.

[9] S. D. Zagorov, Jenö Végh, and Alexander D. Bilimovich, *The Agricultural Economy of the Danubian Countries, 1935–45* (Stanford, 1955), pp. 48–49. These data refer only to privately owned farms and include forest land if operated within the agricultural farms.

[10] Nicholas Spulber, *The Economics of Communist Eastern Europe* (New York, 1957). For comment on the method used see note to Table 5. Alternative figures, based on somewhat more arbitrary standards, are those of Tomase-

òne throughout the entire interwar period. The Agrarian Reform Act of May 21, 1920, had provided in general for confiscation and redistribution of all cultivated land held in properties over thirty hectares in size, but Bulgaria was already a land of small farms. By the end of 1923, 81,652 hectares had been confiscated under this law, while there were 79,527 eligible peasant families petitioning for a portion of this land.[11] One author calculates that even with the strictest application of the law it would only have been possible to bring the average size of a recipient's plot up to three hectares, while at least five hectares was deemed necessary to support a family without outside work.[12]

Under these circumstances it is not surprising that after World War I the peasantry turned for help to the one party which claimed to represent its interests, Alexander Stamboliiski's Bulgarian Agrarian Union. In the first postwar elections Stamboliiski won 85 of the possible 245 seats in the Subranie; he formed a cabinet in which five out of nine portfolios were held by the agrarians.[13] In the elections of March, 1920, at the peak of a "Red scare" and amidst the fears and insecurity induced by the country's financial instability, Stamboliiski gained again. The number of seats held by the agrarians rose to 110 and Stamboliiski formed a one-party cabinet.[14] In April, 1923, with the help of a new electoral law imposed on the country by the Bulgarian Agrarian Union, Stamboliiski won 212 out of the 245 seats and threatened to establish a peasant dictatorship.[15]

Developments in Bulgaria were followed with breathless fasci-

---

vich, who calculates that the surplus population increased from 27 percent to 30 percent in Bulgaria from 1921 to 1931. Jozo Tomasevich, *Peasants, Politics and Economic Change in Yugoslavia* (Stanford, 1955), p. 316. Moore estimates a 35.5 percent surplus population for 1930. Wilbert E. Moore, *Economic Demography of Eastern and Southern Europe* (Geneva, 1945), p. 71. All three sources agree that the degree of overpopulation in Eastern Europe was greatest in Yugoslavia and that Bulgaria ranked next.

[11] M. Tz. Bouroff, *La Réforme agraire en Bulgarie, 1921–1924* (Paris, 1925), p. 89.

[12] *Ibid.*, p. 106.

[13] Max Lazard, *Compulsory Labour Service in Bulgaria*, Series B, No. 12, Studies and Reports (Geneva, 1922), p. 25.

[14] *Istoriia Bolgarii* (Moscow, 1954–55), II, 64.

[15] *Ibid.*, p. 95; Rothschild, pp. 114–15.

nation by the leaders of peasant political parties in the rest of Eastern Europe. If Stamboliiski succeeded in establishing a peasant republic in Bulgaria, it would be an example and an inspiration to the whole agrarian movement, but especially to its left wing, an influence comparable in some respects to the reinforcing effect of the Russian Revolution on the development of radical Marxism.

One of Stamboliiski's greatest assets was his appearance and manner. He was a big lumbering man with bushy hair, a bristling moustache, and a ready stock of peasant aphorisms. At the same time, he was a living demonstration that a peasant could achieve his secret ambition and graduate to the ranks of the very class he claimed to despise, the intelligentsia.[16] In spite of the fact that Stamboliiski was regarded by the Bulgarian peasants as a kind of agrarian messiah, he was notably deficient in many of the qualities necessary to a practical politician. One of his most devoted lieutenants, Alexander Dimitrov, said of him: "He is a prophet. He leads us to Canaan, but we have to clear the way ourselves." [17] To some degree Stamboliiski was also a prisoner of the traditions of Bulgarian politics. In Bulgaria, as in most East European countries, politics had always been a struggle between extremely narrow interest groups for the spoils, a struggle somehow divorced from the real and fundamental problems which plagued the nation.[18] Stamboliiski seems to have been as susceptible to the temptations of political power as his predecessors,[19] and he united the other political parties against him by threatening to keep all the spoils for himself.

The great appeal of Stamboliiski's program lay not only in its provisions for the preservation and strengthening of the peasant class but also in its exploitation of the antagonism between town and village. The Bulgarian Agrarian Union, he maintained, was a

[16] Though born of peasant stock, Stamboliiski had studied at the universities of Halle and Munich, where he had come into contact with the ideas of German socialism. Nikola D. Petkov, ed., *Aleksandur Stamboliiski: Lichnost' i idei* (Sofia, 1930), p. 7.

[17] Kosta Todorov, *Balkan Firebrand: The Autobiography of a Rebel, Soldier and Statesman* (New York, 1943), p. 155.

[18] Rothschild, pp. 8–9.

[19] *Ibid.*, p. 85, n. 11.

class or estate (*suslovie*) organization, representing the interests of the largest and most important class in Bulgaria.[20] With the exception of the enslaved urban working class, who were to be pitied, all other city dwellers were categorized as social parasites and were to be so treated by a peasant government.[21] Apart from this definition of attitude one looks in vain in Stamboliiski's program for a policy dealing rationally with the question of the relationship between the industrial and agricultural sectors of the economy.

Stamboliiski's answer to the problem of overpopulation was to attempt to enlarge the average size of a plot through the agrarian reform law, to improve the techniques of cultivation and marketing, and to extend the development of the cooperative system. Stamboliiski believed that the institution of private property was firmly based on a desire innate in human nature and that it was the root of individual and social development.[22] Observing that middle holdings were the predominant type in France, Italy, Spain, and the United States, he stated that their effectiveness in these countries demonstrated that they were the type best suited to reach the highest levels of agricultural production and efficiency.[23] At the same time, Stamboliiski berated the socialist theorists, saying that "mechanization" or the conversion of agriculture into an industry was not the most rational means of organizing agricultural production.[24]

However, the failure of the Stamboliiski government was a political failure, not an economic one. His arrogance, self-righteousness, and extralegal methods antagonized all political parties, but he gave both the left and right wing parties special reasons for desiring his elimination. The right wing parties saw in him a dangerous demagogue who might destroy the very fabric of custom and tradition upon which the Bulgarian state was based and their own profitable privileges with it. The Bulgarian Communist Party carefully watched every move of the Bulgarian Agrarian Union, confident that the agrarians would soon provide them with the "opening" which they

[20] Petkov, p. 182.
[21] *Ibid.*, pp. 226–27, 299–300.
[22] *Ibid.*, p. 184.
[23] *Ibid.*, p. 188.
[24] Bouroff, p. 106.

could exploit, as the Bolsheviks had exploited Kerensky, to establish a soviet republic in Bulgaria.[25]

Until 1923 Stamboliiski's attitude toward the Bulgarian Communist Party was somewhat ambivalent. On the one hand, he saw little danger in a class party whose bitterest enemy was its own amputated tail, the Bulgarian Social Democratic Party (the Broads).[26] Also, he seems to have felt some sympathy and tolerance for a party which represented another downtrodden class:

We do not raise the question of destroying the proletariat, it is one of the social strata, a necessary one. . . . At this time, when the people are fighting reactionaries who want a pogrom and a war between the agrarian stratum and the proletarian, we will have, instead of struggle, competition.[27]

At the same time, Stamboliiski was driven by his own antiurbanism to despise a political program based in part on the need to transform agricultural production in the image of the urban factory. While, on the one hand, he seemed to feel that there were only two real social experiments in Europe, his and Lenin's, on the other, he portrayed his peasantism as the chief bulwark against communism in Europe.[28]

Stamboliiski maintained that the Communist solution to the agrarian problem would be infinitely more horrible than serfdom.[29] In particular, he rejected all Communist schemes because, he said, they required the overthrow of democratic institutions.

How can anyone be so blind as not to see the fundamental differences between communism and our program? One means dictatorship and the other means democracy. Our social system is like an old tree. The Bolsheviks say that it has lived too long and would cut it down and plant a sapling in its place. We peasants say that it should not be cut down, for it has taken a long, long time to grow. We merely believe in pruning it and letting in a little more light.[30]

[25] Rothschild, p. 93. The idea that Stamboliiski's party represented a third force in politics fighting both the left and the right, a concept prevalent in all agrarian parties, is developed in A. Panov, *Stamboliiski v politicheskiia zhivot' na Bulgariia* (Sofia, 1921), p. 41.

[26] Petkov, p. 296.

[27] *Ibid.*

[28] Rothschild, p. 112.

[29] Petkov, p. 73.

[30] As quoted in "Bulgarian Backgrounds," *The Living Age,* CCCXIX (1922), 504.

In 1923 Stamboliiski began a major attack on the Bulgarian Communist Party, which was then the second largest party in the country. Apparently the success of the Communists in the January elections convinced Stamboliiski that the Party would have to be destroyed, and he initiated a campaign of terror and persecution.[31] Although the Communist Party received approximately the same proportion of votes in the 1923 general elections as in 1920, under the new agrarian electoral law and with Stamboliiski's arbitrary cancellation of a number of seats, the Communists lost thirty-four seats in all.[32] By the end of May the number of beatings and arrests of Communist leaders reached its peak, and Stamboliiski announced that the Bulgarian Agrarian Union would rule Bulgaria alone for forty years.[33] This was, however, only one aspect of Stamboliiski's increasingly arbitrary attitude toward established political institutions.

The colossal political blunders by which Stamboliiski destroyed himself began earlier, in June, 1922, when his own unruly paramilitary group, the Orange Guard, arrested and mauled a number of leaders of the opposition parties who were on their way to an anti-Stamboliiski rally.[34] Between June, 1922, and July, 1923, Stamboliiski succeeded in alienating influential factions in his own party, as well as in every other political party including the powerful Internal Macedonian Revolutionary Organization (IMRO).

The other political parties were most disturbed by the fact that they no longer had any control over the course of events. In the fall of 1922, four of the "bourgeois" opposition parties began negotiating with the dissatisfied Reserve Officer's League in order to plan a course of action which would forestall the establishment of a peasant dictatorship.[35] Stamboliiski's agreement with Yugoslavia in 1923 to curb the activities of IMRO encouraged that organization to join the conspiracy already in the making.

Stamboliiski's own strength lay entirely in his popularity with the

[31] Rothschild, pp. 113–14.
[32] *Ibid.*, p. 114.
[33] G. Tsonev [Gavril Genov] and A. Vladimirov, *Sentiabr'skoe vosstanie v Bolgarii 1923 goda* (Moscow, 1934), p. 70.
[34] A. B——off [Aleksander Baschmakoff], *Mémoire sur le mouvement communiste en Bulgarie durant les années 1921 et 1922* (no publishing data), pp. 81–85; an anti-agrarian and anti-Communist account.
[35] *Istoriia Bolgarii*, II, 118–19.

peasants and in his rather badly trained Orange Guard. Even in his own party he had weakened his position. In August, 1919, one of the founders of the Bulgarian Agrarian Union, Dragiev, was excluded from the party for refusing to accept Stamboliiski's uncompromising "peasantist" course.[36] Dragiev took most of the large party organization of Stara Zagora district with him when he left, and this organization remained relatively passive when Stamboliiski was overthrown.[37] In February, 1923, three agrarian ministers, Tomov, Manolov, and Turlakov, representing another moderate faction, were expelled.[38] They founded a third agrarian party.

It is one index of Stamboliiski's blindness that on the eve of the insurrection the police were in the hands of General Mustakov, a man Stamboliiski knew to be involved in the conspiracy against him.[39] On June 9, 1923, the cities in Bulgaria were seized by the army and IMRO and the Tsankov government replaced Stamboliiski's agrarian government. Stamboliiski was left to the pleasure of the Macedonian savages, who ultimately beheaded him. The end of the "peasantist phase" in Bulgarian politics, however, precipitated a crisis in the Bulgarian Communist Party.

THE RELUCTANT REBELS

There were striking but deceptive similarities between the Russian Communist Party and the Bulgarian Communist Party (BCP). The founder of the latter, Dimitur Blagoev, had imbibed his Marxism at the Russian fountainhead while studying at St. Petersburg.[40] Although Blagoev had not followed Lenin's lead in the wartime conferences of the Zimmerwald movement without major qualifications, Blagoev's party was one of the first large parties to join the Comintern and adopt the name Communist. Perhaps because of close cultural ties between the two countries and their Communist move-

---

[36] Petkov, pp. 287–90.
[37] Rothschild, p. 118, n. 3.
[38] *Istoriia Bolgarii,* II, 92.
[39] *Ibid.,* p. 85.
[40] Rothschild, pp. 11–13. Although I don't always agree with Rothschild's conclusions, I found this detailed study of the development of the BCP from 1883 to 1936 extremely valuable. For the official account of the origin of the Party see *Istoriia Bolgarskoi Kommunisticheskoi Partii,* trans. from the Bulgarian by A. Kirshevsko and A. Nikol'skii (Moscow, 1960), chaps. I–VIII.

ments, or perhaps because of the impressive size of the Bulgarian Party, its members enjoyed an influence in the Comintern quite disproportionate to the size and importance of their country.

The Bulgarian Marxist movement, like the Russian, split into two factions in 1903, and, like its Russian counterpart, the Bulgarian left faction was primarily concerned about the discipline and devotion of party members.[41] Blagoev, however, claimed that the centralism and discipline upon which he insisted for his party was not an effort to make it a conspiratorial organization and "had nothing in common with the Blanquist-Bonapartist centralism of Lenin." [42] Although Blagoev demanded that his party be a narrow (hence the sobriquet Tesniaki) elite of dedicated Marxists bound together by their common devotion to the cause and the discipline of a centralized party, he did not regard preparation for the proletarian revolution as the immediate task of the party. In a small, poor, and semicolonial country like Bulgaria, argued Blagoev, the proletarian revolution depended for its success three quarters on the success of proletarian revolutions in the larger industralized West European countries and one quarter on the efforts of the local Marxist party.[43] Lenin, in Blagoev's opinion, underestimated the need for a long preparatory stage to revolution (in backward countries) and the Bolsheviks only diminished their effectiveness by concentrating on the development of an illegal conspiratorial organization.[44] The immediate task of the Tesniaki, according to Blagoev, was to strengthen the party, win greater influence over industrial workers, and win elections.

To tear the People's Subranie from the hands of that class [the bourgeoisie] means to tear power from their hands. This in essence is the meaning of the electoral struggle being waged in all countries for the right to vote. This in essence is the historical problem of the present.[45]

Consistent with this view, the Tesniaki, though opposing Bulgarian

[41] Rothschild, p. 32.
[42] L. Bazhenov, "Sentiabr'skoe vosstanie v Bolgarii, *Istorik Marksist,* No. 3–4 (1932), p. 256.
[43] *Ibid.,* p. 263, and Tsonev and Vladimirov, p. 17.
[44] Tsonev and Vladimirov, p. 13. The differences between Lenin and Blagoev are somewhat muted in the latest official history of the BCP, though the anti-Bolshevik features of the Tesniaki movement are duly noted. *Istoriia Bolgarskoi Kommunisticheskoi Partii,* pp. 78–99.
[45] Tsonev and Vladimirov, p. 8.

participation in World War I, did not adopt Lenin's thesis about transforming the imperialistic war into a class war.[46]

More critical, from the Comintern's point of view, was Blagoev's hostility not only toward the peasant political movement but also toward agitation and recruitment in rural areas. One of the issues in Blagoev's departure from the Bulgarian Social Democratic Party in 1903 was his implacable opposition to an electoral alliance with the peasant movement.[47] The Tesniaki rejected the peasant as an ally, claiming that, while the peasant should be told what to expect under capitalism, a Marxist party could not be expected to defend the interests of the petty bourgeoisie.[48] Blagoev took pride in the class purity of the party and in 1907 wrote:

Social Democracy in Bulgaria was from the very first steps in its struggle isolated, alone, surrounded by solid reactionary masses. On the one side stood the petty-bourgeois and agrarian masses, reactionary to the core, on the other, the bourgeoisie, crudely reactionary toward the proletarian class, with all its paid and unpaid defenders. . . . Therefore the isolation of the party as a representative of the proletariat is an inevitable consequence of its tasks and its ideals. These are the conditions under which the Social Democrats fight and develop.[49]

The Tesniaki advanced no candidates in the countryside and guarded the virginal purity of the party against rude nonproletarian intruders.

Yet when the Tesniaki adopted the name "Bulgarian Communist Party" and entered the Comintern, it proudly puffed itself up as the only prewar mass party of a truly "Russian complexion to enter as a unit." [50] It is true that the BCP adopted the twenty-one conditions and the agrarian theses of the Comintern and accepted the need for an underground conspiratorial section.[51] But a leading member of the Party later declared that it only gave lip service to Comintern directives.[52] This judgment may be too harsh. The Party did continue to regard the electoral struggle as its primary task and failed to

---

[46] *Ibid.*, p. 21. Bazhenov, *Istorik Marksist*, No. 3–4 (1932), p. 259.
[47] Rothschild, p. 22.
[48] Tsonev and Vladimirov, pp. 14, 16. Bazhenov, *Istorik Marksist*, No. 3–4 (1932), p. 266.
[49] *Istoriia Bolgarskoi Kommunisticheskoi Partii*, p. 99.
[50] Rothschild, p. 82.
[51] *Istoriia Bolgarskoi Kommunisticheskoi Partii*, p. 187.
[52] Tsonev and Vladimirov, pp. 14, 56.

establish an underground fighting organization, but in other respects the Party leaders were impressed by the Russian Revolution and, in spite of Blagoev, emulated the Russian example. The Party still went to rural areas with the message that the peasantry was doomed as a class and refused to defend the peasants' demands for more land, but it did defend the peasants' immediate interests in other ways and began publishing a peasant newspaper, *Selski vestnik*.

The BCP, along with the Bulgarian Agrarian Union, had profited from Bulgaria's war weariness.[53] By 1919 the nation had already begun to turn to the two parties which had most consistently opposed Bulgaria's entry into the war. In 1918 and 1919 the Bulgarian Tesniaki actively supported the Bulgarian Agrarian Union in the movement for amnesty for the Bulgarian soldiers who participated in the mutiny at Radomir.[54] Without calling for revolution, the Tesniaki held mass meetings throughout the country in which it demanded bread, housing, and work for all Bulgarians.[55] Bulgarian war prisoners suffused with enthusiasm for the Bolshevik Revolution returned to their homeland to join in the agitation.[56] In May, 1919, the Twelfth Congress of the Bulgarian Social Democratic Party (Tesniaki) adopted the name Bulgarian Communist Party.

Of the 38,036 members claimed in 1922, only 9,139 were listed as members of urban Party organizations.[57] The most rapid growth in Party membership had been from 1915 to the end of 1919, an increase from 3,031 to 35,478.[58] The bulk of these new members were peasants.[59] However, available sources are not adequate for a precise determination of the number of peasants in the Party, and the attempts by Rothschild and Burks to arrive at some breakdown are inaccurate and misleading.[60] Burks is much more persuasive in

[53] M. A. Birman, *Revoliutsionnaia situatsiia v Bolgarii v 1918–1919 gg.* (Moscow, 1957), p. 39.

[54] *Ibid.*, pp. 176–83.

[55] *Ibid.*, p. 185.

[56] *Ibid.*, p. 187.

[57] Raichko K. Karakolov, ed., *Bulgarskata Komunisticheska Partiia v rezoliutsii i resheniia* (Sofia, 1951), II, 93, 165.

[58] *Ibid.*, p. 92.

[59] Tsonev and Vladimirov, p. 37.

[60] Burks's figures for class composition of the Party in 1919 bear little, if any, relation to reality. If he had consulted the source cited by Rothschild, he

demonstrating statistically that, although the Party made impressive gains in votes and members between 1919 and 1923, it was not getting the votes of dwarf holders or landless peasants, as expected.[61] There is also evidence that Party recruiters were not very successful in winning the peasantry as a whole. Genov writes: "The Tesniaki [the Bulgarian Communist Party] went to the country regarding the peasants as tomorrow's proletariat, convinced of the

would have saved himself from both Rothschild's errors and his own. Burks has accepted only industrial workers as "workers," a definition which no Communist would have accepted in 1919. He has then borrowed Rothschild's figure for the number of middle-class members of the Party, a figure which happens to be wrong. Then he has subtracted these two figures from 100 percent on the wholly unwarranted assumption that all those who were not workers or members of the middle-class were peasants. R. V. Burks, *The Dynamics of Communism*, p. 35. Unfortunately, Burks's statistical sleight of hand was performed without even the benefit of reliable known facts. Rothschild's figures for the percentage of industrial workers in the Party was accurate, but not his figures for the percentage of middle-class members. Rothschild wrote that in May, 1919, of 21,577 members of the Party, "as many as 9,421 were of the bourgeoisie." Rothschild, pp. 95, 106. A judicious choice of words, but still very misleading. The category beside which this figure appears in Karakolov, whom Rothschild cites as his primary source, is "petty landowners in town and country," a category which undoubtedly includes all peasants with property. Karakolov, II, 1. This comedy of errors is summarized below. Remember, both Burks and Rothschild supposedly base their information on Karakolov.

	KARAKOLOV			
Major occupational categories	Percentage	Rothschild	Burks	Category
Industrial workers	10.5	10.2	10.2	workers
Artisans	17.9			
Agricultural workers	15.0			
State and municipal employees	8.0		46.2	peasants
Free professions	4.5			
Small property owners of town and country	43.6	43.6	43.6	middle class

Amateur statistics, like amateur etymology, is fraught with hazards. The plain fact is that one cannot tell from Karakolov's figures how many members were peasants. In view of the above and Genov's comment below, the actual percentage may have been higher than Burks's estimate of 46.2 percent.

[61] Burks, p. 44. Burks uses a technique known as multiple correlation analysis to demonstrate that the Communist vote was not increasing in those districts where the number of peasants with dwarf holdings and the number of agricultural laborers were increasing. Unfortunately his calculations for the table in note 60 are not fully documented.

inevitability of their proletarianization, and taking this to signify the peasant's future interests." [62]

The trends in membership from 1921 to 1922 offer some clues to the appeal of the Party in the countryside. In the fifteen districts into which Bulgaria was divided, Party membership increased most rapidly between May, 1921, and June, 1922, in the south-central tobacco-growing district of Plovdiv, in the highly nationalistic Macedonian district of Petrich (which is also a tobacco-growing district), in the grain-producing Vratsa district in the Danubian lowlands, and in Sofia district where the capital was located. [63] This would seem to confirm Burks's assumption that only certain categories of peasants were being drawn into the Communist movement, categories which do not readily fit into the Leninist typology. In rural areas it was the tobacco workers, the cash cropper, and the national minorities who were being attracted. [64] Each group had its own special brand of grievance, but these groups by no means included the poorest peasants in Bulgaria or those necessarily most wanting in land. In the postwar years these three were desperate groups in Bulgarian society, but in the case of the first two it was a desperation born of their dependence on the market rather than their relative status within the peasant class. It seems likely under these circumstances that they were drawn to communism because it was the strongest voice of protest against the inhumane, impersonal whims of the market, not because it had an attractive agrarian program. In fact, the Comintern agrarian program was not tailored to the interest of any of these three groups.

In contrast to the 120,000 members of the Bulgarian Agrarian Union in 1922, the BCP had less than 40,000 members at its disposal, excluding attached organizations in both cases. [65] In practice the Party continued to be guided by many of its old prejudices. It

[62] Tsonev and Vladimirov, p. 14.

[63] Karakolov, II, 93. The cultivation of tobacco had a more important place in the district of Plovdiv than in any of the other fifteen districts in Bulgaria. Edouard Fernandez-Diaz, *Le Tabac en Bulgarie* (Paris, 1926), p. 125.

[64] Burks, pp. 54–57, 78.

[65] Stoian Petrov, *Septemvriiskoto vustanie 1923 godina i bolshevizatsiia na BKP* (Sofia, 1960), p. 60. According to this source, which can hardly be accused of favoritism toward the Bulgarian Agrarian Union, over 100,000 of its members were small and landless peasants.

still viewed the peasant political movement as a party of the rural bourgeoisie with which it could not apply the united front from above and denied that those parts of Comintern theses which called for a united front from above were applicable to Bulgaria.[66]

At the same time, the Bulgarians repeatedly urged on the Comintern the theory that Stamboliiski was "but a more stupid version of Kerensky, who could be shouldered aside at will." [67] At the end of World War I the Tesniaki had rejected an alliance with the Bulgarian Agrarian Union in a revolution against the established government. When some regiments of the Bulgarian army rebelled in September, 1918, Stamboliiski decided to lead them and asked the Tesniaki to join him. It refused, declaring that any quarrel between the Bulgarian Union and other bourgeois parties was a bourgeois quarrel and that the Tesniaki could not support the "reactionary, propertied, peasant masses." [68] This characterization of the agrarians became the accepted one among the Bulgarian Communists and was reaffirmed several times between 1919 and 1923.

In January, 1923, the Party resolved that a united front between Stamboliiski and the Communists was unthinkable and could not lead to a peasants' and workers' government.[69] This stand did not become insubordination until the Party was actually ordered by the Comintern to form such a coalition.[70] When Stamboliiski was overthrown, the Central Committee of the BCP ordered its members to remain neutral and passive. "The working class and the toiling peasant must not interfere in the armed struggle between the rural and urban bourgeoisie, because this would mean pulling the chestnuts out of the fire for your own exploiters." [71]

[66] See, for example, Khristo Kabakchiev, "Pered perevorotom v Bolgarii," *Kommunisticheskii Internatsional*, No. 26–27 (1923), pp. 7296–7328.

[67] Rothschild, p. 93.

[68] *Ibid.*, p. 81. For the current Communist interpretation see Birman, chap III.

[69] Kabakchiev, *Kommunisticheskii Internatsional*, No. 26–27 (1923), p. 7324.

[70] The article cited above was originally published in *Internationale Press-Korrespondenz*, No. 57 (April 3, 1923), pp. 459–64, without critical comments.

[71] Bazhenov, *Istorik Marksist*, No. 3–4 (1932), p. 271. This appeal was published on June 10, 1923, the day after the insurrection. The first declaration of Party neutrality was reprinted in Khristo Kabakchiev, "Posle perevorota 9go iunia," *Kommunisticheskii Internatsional*, No. 28–29 (1923), p. 7691,

On June 12, 1923, Zinoviev, still ignorant of this position of the Party, urged it to remember how the Bolsheviks had acted when Kerensky was attacked by Kornilov.[72] But the analogy was not convincing, even though the Party had originally suggested it. Throughout 1922 and 1923 the BCP had specifically repudiated several features of the Comintern's agrarian theses, including the suggestion that a workers' and peasants' government could be formed in Bulgaria by an alliance between the Communists and the agrarians. The Bulgarian Communists cogently argued that Bolshevik agrarian policy, as it appeared in Comintern theses, could not be applied indiscriminately to the special conditions prevailing in Bulgaria. There were profound differences between prewar Russia and postwar Bulgaria which made Zinoviev's Kerensky analogy inappropriate. In the first place, in Bulgaria in 1923, unlike Russia in 1917, the peasants were less likely to be responsive to promises of land. There were no large estates which could be promised to the peasantry and no landlord class to be overthrown. Secondly, the political situation in Bulgaria in 1923 did not bear out Zinoviev's analogy. As one Bulgarian Communist later pointed out, Kerensky's government was created by revolution, and in defending him the Bolsheviks were also defending the revolution and workers' and peasants' soviets.[73] In Russia the revolutionary situation antedated the Kornilov threat and there was spontaneous opposition to the threatened coup d'état. Neither of these conditions was present in Bulgaria in 1923. In addition, the Bulgarian Communists had long regarded the entrenched agrarian government as the chief obstacle in Bulgaria to a Communist victory by electoral means. They could only welcome Stamboliiski's downfall. Finally, there was also the tradition of "legalism" in the BCP, an unwillingness to risk a solid organization in a chancy adventure. Stamboliiski's strong-arm tactics against the Communist Party had not won him friends in the party. Along with the voiced belief that the defeat of the Bulgarian Agrarian Union might make things

---

along with the resolution of the plenum of the Central Committee of the Party on that day. *Ibid.*, pp. 7701–4.

[72] *Rasshirennyi plenum, 1923*, p. 101.

[73] Khristo Kabakchiev, "Posle perevorota 9go iunia," *Kommunisticheskii Internatsional*, No. 28–29 (1923), pp. 7709–10.

easier for the Party, there was the unspoken, but justifiable, fear that in any alliance with Stamboliiski's organization the Communist Party might be absorbed.

At the last session of the Third Enlarged Plenum of the ECCI on June 23, 1923, Radek delivered a blistering attack on the BCP. He made it clear that it was the duty of the Party to ally itself with the Agrarian Union or at least with its left wing. Radek accused the Party of completely misunderstanding the revolutionary role of the peasantry and the proper Leninist approach to this class.[74] He seized upon the disgrace of the Bulgarian Party as an example for the whole Comintern, saying:

The duty of a Communist party when a struggle occurs between the great capitalist strata, on the one hand, and the petty-bourgeois peasant stratum, which seems on the basis of its own past record to represent the interests of capital, on the other, is not to limit itself to the role of simple onlooker but to try, even if it is impossible, to take power in its own hands, to enter into coalition with the petty-bourgeois stratum of the population.[75]

Radek also used the event to justify Comintern intervention in the affairs of member parties.

We hope not only that the Communist parties will elicit a common tactical lesson from the present situation in Bulgaria but also that on the basis of this experience, which may cost the Bulgarian Party hundreds and thousands of lives and delay the victory of the revolution in the Balkans for a long time, others will understand why we [the Comintern] cannot adopt a policy of nonintervention.[76]

Radek interpreted the coup d'état in Bulgaria as a threat to the Soviet Union, that is, as part of a concerted international effort to encircle Russia.[77]

For the Comintern this was the first real test of its new slogan "workers' and peasants' government." It is not surprising, therefore, that one senses a tinge of personal resentment in Zinoviev and Radek's criticism of the Bulgarian Party. *Pravda* declared that the new slogan was the most important consequence of the meeting of the Enlarged

[74] *Rasshirennyi plenum, 1923,* pp. 257, 259–61.
[75] *Ibid.,* p. 260.
[76] *Ibid.,* p. 262.
[77] *Ibid.,* p. 255.

Plenum and called upon all Communists to study the lesson of the Bulgarian events, namely, that the peasant and worker had to march together if they wanted to avoid the fate of Bulgaria.[78]

When the BCP refused to alter its position in July, the conflict between the Comintern and the Party ripened into a real debate, one which involved not only the events in Bulgaria but the prestige of Zinoviev and Radek and the authority of the Communist International. The Bulgarian Party was bitterly divided on Comintern demands, and one of its oldest and most respected members, Kabakchiev, stoutly defended the insubordination of the party in the pages of the official organ of the Communist International.[79] But the pressure exerted by the parent organization was inexorable. Kolarov returned to Sofia from Moscow on August 5, and in the next two days he compelled the unwilling Central Committee of the BCP to reverse its stand and prepare for an armed insurrection to establish a workers' and peasants' government in Bulgaria.[80]

The passivity of the BCP in June had been prudent, and it is no wonder that the preparations for an insurrection in August and September seemed suicidal to a number of Party leaders. It looked as though the Party was expected to give itself as a burnt offering to placate the gods at Moscow. While the September revolt may have been necessary to reassert the authority of the Comintern and was undoubtedly connected with events in Germany,[81] a realistic ap-

[78] "Reshenii ispolkoma i bolgarskii opyt," *Pravda,* No. 143 (June 29, 1923), p. 1.

[79] Kabakchiev's articles appeared side by side with Radek's denunciation at the Enlarged Plenum and an open letter to the BCP composed by Zinoviev on June 28. Khristo Kabakchiev, *Kommunisticheskii Internatsional,* No. 26–27 (1923), pp. 7295–7326; Khristo Kabakchiev, "Kriticheskie zametki," *Kommunisticheskii Internatsional,* No. 28–29 (1923), pp. 7741–54; K. Radek, "Perevorot v Bolgarii i Kommunisticheskaia Partiia," *Kommunisticheskii Internatsional,* No. 26–27 (1923), pp. 7327–40; G. Zinoviev, "Uroki bolgarskogo perevorota," *Kommunisticheskii Internatsional,* No. 26–27 (1923), pp. 7341–54.

[80] Rothschild, p. 133.

[81] The exact motives of the Comintern in ordering this insurrection are not clear. Souvarine indicates that there was a close connection between the revolts planned in Germany and Bulgaria, and that as soon as Zinoviev heard that the Germans and the French were negotiating on the Ruhr crisis he ordered the uprising in Bulgaria to be pushed forward, hoping that it would be a stimulus to the German uprising. Boris Souvarine, *Stalin: A Critical*

praisal on the part of the Comintern would have revealed that a Communist revolt had little prospect of success in any sense of the word. It was not only unlikely to restore the BCP to its former position; it was unlikely to have even a nuisance value in international politics. The Party had already squandered whatever good faith it may have had with other radical parties by its policy of neutrality in June and they refused to respond to Communist plans in August for an insurrection. The Communists had few arms and no conspiratorial organization prepared. Although there had been some popular opposition to the coup d'état in June, the country was largely reconciled to the new regime by September. The new government in Bulgaria had already consolidated its control over the political and military machinery and on September 12 it arrested a large number of key Communist Party functionaries.[82]

One is not surprised that the Communist revolt in September, therefore, was a classic study in ineptitude. The date had originally been set for October or November in order to precede or coincide with the revolution planned in Germany, but the date was advanced as a result of the actions of the Tsankov government against the Communist Party.[83] The rebellion began prematurely in three small villages in Central Bulgaria on September 17 and spluttered about in this area through September 19 and 20; it finally fizzled out in

---

Survey of Bolshevism (New York, 1939), pp. 335–36. Ruth Fischer indicates that Radek, in opposition to Zinoviev, adopted the position that the Bulgarian uprising was not the beginning of a new revolutionary wave in Europe, but a prop to Russian influence in the Balkans, and that the revolution should result in the restoration of the agrarians to power. Ruth Fischer, *Stalin and German Communism* (Cambridge, Mass., 1948), p. 311. Rosmer, on the hand, indicates that, far from being secondary to events in Germany, the events in Bulgaria reduced the importance of the German revolution to second place and that the Bulgarian effort was a major one. Alfred Rosmer, *Moscou sous Lénine,* p. 277. This would, however, contradict Besedovskii's assertion that those favoring concentration upon revolution in economically advanced countries were ascendant in the Comintern until after the German revolution. G. S. Besedovskii, *Na putiakh k termidoru* (Paris, 1930), I, 102, 149. Finally, there is the possibility suggested by Rothschild that Zinoviev sought glory wherever he could find it, misread the situation in Bulgaria, and assumed that there was a real possibility for a successful revolution there. Rothschild, p. 150.

[82] Rothschild, pp. 137–39.

[83] Tsonev and Vladimirov, p. 107. Tsonev is the pseudonym of Genov, one of the leaders of the insurrection.

the northwestern districts of Vratsa and Vidin by September 28. One indication that it was primarily a peasant uprising was the fact that no major urban centers were taken, only two minor market towns in Vratsa district, the towns of Ferdinand and Berkovitsa.[84] The two areas in which the September revolt was most successful were the tobacco-growing areas of south-central Bulgaria and the fertile Danubian lowlands in the district of Vratsa. The latter contained the most intensively cultivated grain-producing area and the most productive cattle district in Bulgaria.[85] The location of the revolt is thus significant in seeming further to confirm Burks's thesis that the tobacco worker and the cash cropper were particularly susceptible to Communist persuasion.

The key role of the district of Vratsa deserves some explanation. The town of Ferdinand (now Mikhailovgrad) was chosen as the headquarters of the insurrection. While Rothschild's assumption that the BCP "had probably chosen to establish their headquarters here because it afforded the quickest route of retreat into Yugoslavia" [86] is probably sound, there were other considerations as well. Rothschild correctly points out that Genov's assertion that the capital, Sofia, could be dominated strategically from the Vratsa district was nonsense,[87] but Genov also maintained that there was a government cache of 180 machine guns and 100,000 rifles in the city of Vratsa.[88] Perhaps even more to the point was the fact that between 1921 and 1922 the Party organization in the Vratsa district had increased

[84] *Ibid.*, p. 125. The fact that no major urban centers were taken may, however, also be accounted for by the fact that the arrest of the leading cadres of the Party on September 12, 1923, had critically weakened the city organizations. Also, in two districts, Russe and Burgas, the local Party leaders refused to sacrifice themselves and gave no order for an uprising. Rothschild, p. 142.

[85] In describing the northwestern districts of Bulgaria, one study points out: "In the whole region there is a surplus of foodstuffs; in the first place, grain. The people of this region are first in the country in the production of grain, meat, dairy products, and eggs per capita. Industry is insignificant here. There are no large-scale industries. Small enterprises are primarily engaged in the processing of local agricultural goods." E. V. Valev, *Bolgarii: ekonomiko-geograficheskoe opisanie* (Moscow, 1949), p. 261. See Burks's arguments, pp. 56–57.

[86] Rothschild, p. 142.

[87] This is a point which the Soviet scholar Bazhenov also makes, Bazhenov, *Istorik Marksist*, No. 3–4 (1932), p. 286.

[88] Tsonev and Vladimirov, p. 121.

in numbers, moving up from the fourth to the second strongest district organization by June, 1922.[89] It seems reasonable to suppose under these circumstances that the leaders of the BCP believed that, if all else failed, a Communist-dominated peasant republic could be established in the inaccessible district of Vratsa which might then be supplied from outside and used as a base of operations against the rest of the country.[90]

By the end of September the revolt was over and the dejected leaders, George Dimitrov, Gavril Genov, and Vasil Kolarov, led the ragged band of peasants across the Yugoslav frontier. Ironically, it was one of the leaders of the Bulgarian Agrarian Union who provided them with passports and money at the border, while at the same time gently taunting them for leading a rebellion of a few petty-bourgeois peasants.[91] The revolt revealed the innocence of the BCP when confronted with conspiratorial tasks, and the absence of any close bonds between the peasantry as a whole and the Communists. Rothschild points out: "While most of the rebels were peasants, it is not true that the majority of the peasant population joined in the uprising." [92]

The splendid self-immolation of the BCP did win certain advantages for the survivors. The leaders who had obediently followed Comintern orders, and destroyed their organization in a foolhardy escapade, arose phoenixlike from the ashes of their party to join the exalted ranks of the high functionaries of the Comintern. They were told that their blind submission to Comintern decrees and their baptism in revolutionary fire had Bolshevized their party, or what was left of it.

For the Comintern, the significance of events in Bulgaria was less clear cut than Zinoviev would have us believe. The act of revolution

[89] Karakolov, II, 93, 165.

[90] Rothschild suggests that there was a plan to draw off the government forces by scattered uprisings on the perimeter so that urban organizations could take over the cities with ease. Rothschild, p. 141. This may have been the initial strategy, but it made little sense after the arrests of September 12, which critically weakened the urban Party organizations.

[91] Todorov, p. 197.

[92] Rothschild, p. 146.

against the Tsankov government, quite apart from the Communist program on the agrarian or any other question, did bolster the popularity of the BCP in its own country, making it temporarily the leader of the opposition forces.[93] While in the long run this would prove useful to the Communist movement in Bulgaria, in the short run it crystallized "bourgeois" support behind the Tsankov regime at home and gave it considerable support abroad as well.[94] For these reasons the revolt was not a success for Zinoviev. He needed and expected quick and decisive victories, not long-run advantages, and it was probably the hope of quick successes which prompted him to gamble in Bulgaria. In this sense it was a gamble that failed, both for Zinoviev and for his brand of "peasantism."

The Comintern agrarian program was not applied successfully in Bulgaria. Zinoviev may have been blinded by his own conviction of the universality of the "lessons" of the October Revolution. But Bulgaria in 1923 was not Russia in 1917. In Bulgaria there were no large estates to be confiscated, no Communist support in the army, and the pressures imposed by an unsuccessful war had already receded. Stamboliiski was not a Kerensky and Tsankov was not a Kornilov, but the BCP was ordered to act as though they were. Under Stamboliiski's tutelage the peasant and the peasant's political organization had come to regard communism as an urban ideology and to believe that the next battle was to be waged between city and country, rather than between peasant and landlord.[95] The small number of peasants that did rally under the banner of the Comintern had special grievances and were probably drawn to the Comintern for reasons other than the Comintern's agrarian program.

While Zinoviev could maintain publicly that "the September defeat is one of those defeats bearing within it the inevitability of coming

[93] *Ibid.*, p. 148. Rothschild points out that the successes of the BCP in the November, 1923, elections are one demonstration of this fact.

[94] For a detailed analysis of the effects of the September insurrection on the development of the BCP, see *ibid.*, chaps. XII and XIII.

[95] As late as 1937 Irwin Sanders, in studying one Bulgarian village intensively, discovered that the majority of the peasants there still regarded communism as an urban movement and the worker as a servile class below the peasant. Irwin Sanders, *Balkan Village* (Lexington, Ky., 1949), pp. 22, 217.

victory," [96] falling back on its long-run effects, it was evident to all but the most obtuse that he had tried to use the "lessons" of the Russian Revolution where they were not applicable. Stamboliiski's failure in June had temporarily dramatized the vulnerabilities of the peasant political movement, apparently highlighting the potential usefulness of the tactic of a workers' and peasants' government, but the revolt in September did little to confirm its universal validity.

However, by means of the mysterious alchemy performed in the inner chambers of the Comintern, the futile action of the Bulgarian Communist Party in September became the badge of its Bolshevization and the occasion for development and elaboration of the very agrarian tactics that had produced no significant immediate results in Bulgaria.

[96] Zinoviev, *International Press Correspondence*, III, No. 67 (Oct. 18, 1923), 252.

CHAPTER VIII

The Comintern and the Polish Peasant Movement, 1923–1927

In Poland the Comintern won and lost its last major campaign for the allegiance of peasant political leaders. The exact role played by the Krestintern and its staff in the founding and development of the three radical peasant parties in Poland's eastern border regions from 1924 to 1927 will probably never be known. After Radić's arrest at the beginning of 1925 for his widely publicized enlistment in the Krestintern, that organization became more secretive about its recruiting activities. But in the charges levied by the Polish state against the peasant political movement in eastern Poland the Krestintern was identified as one of the sources of conspiracy. At the Second Plenum of the Krestintern in 1925 Dąbal himself claimed that the spectacular growth of the radical peasant movement in Poland was a result of Krestintern activities.[1] Boshkovich went even further at the Seventh Plenum of the ECCI in November, 1926, and held up the Polish workers' and peasants' front as a model for all the members of the Comintern to follow.[2] Like Bulgaria in 1923, Poland in 1926 provided a "lesson" for the whole Communist movement.

THE AGRARIAN PROBLEM BEFORE THE PIŁSUDSKI COUP D'ÉTAT

Poland seemed a logical choice for a new experiment with Comintern agrarian policy. It was a country of contradictions, including within its borders some highly developed industrial centers along with some of the most backward and underdeveloped regions

[1] Dąbal, "Zadachi i dostizhenie Krestinterna na Zapade," *Krest'ianshii International*, No. 3–5 (March–May, 1925), p. 32.

[2] *Puti mirovoi revoliutsii—sed'moi rasshirennyi plenum ispolnitel'nogo komiteta Kommunicheskogo Internatsionala (22 noiabria–16 dekabria)* (Moscow, 1927), I, 198.

in Eastern Europe. The non-Polish peasantry of the eastern border regions suffered, not only from the usual maladies of peasant societies in transition but also from a feeling of resentment toward the new Polish state, which was widely regarded as a vehicle for Polish domination. The land reforms, the new political system, and, finally, the Piłsudski coup d'état in 1926 did little to allay these fears. But the Comintern found in trying to exploit Belorussian and Ukrainian resentments and apprehensions that nationalistic passion was a political weapon that could backfire.

While the three major sections of the new Polish state all shared a common language and a great and dramatic historical and cultural tradition, they were quite different in economic structure and political tradition. Each of these areas, the former Austrian, Prussian, and Russian parts of Poland, had experienced more than a hundred years of tutelage under their previous masters. This diversity may help in accounting for the dangerous proliferation of political parties. If one examines a few of the available indices, the differences in economic structure are apparent (see Table 8).

The postwar land reforms removed the last vestiges of servile obligations, but Poland, like Rumania, remained a country in which large estates survived up to World War II though the large-estate system was not as prevalent in either country as it was in Hungary.[3] In this sense it would seem as though Poland would be fertile ground for Communist propaganda. The high density of population, the high rate of natural increase, the fairly high proportion of population engaged in agriculture, and the low level of productivity indicate the probable existence of a "land hunger" which could be directed against those who owned large estates.

However, there were important differences among the provinces in Poland. Only in the eastern provinces, for example, does one find the pattern of production characteristic of much of prerevolutionary Russia: low levels of productivity, a high rate of natural increase, a high proportion of the population engaged in agriculture, but extensive cultivation and a low density of population per kilometer.[4] The low density of population made this area a possible

[3] See Table 2, p. 9.
[4] *Pologne, 1919–1939* (Neuchatel, 1946), II, 134; and Werner Markert, *Polen* (Cologne, 1959), p. 74.

Table 8

Some Demographic Features of Poland around 1930

Region	Increase per 1,000 inhabitants 1921–25[a]	Density of population per sq. km.[a]	Percent of population dependent on agriculture[b]	Per capita production (in agricultural crop units)[b]	Surplus population[b] (percent)
Poland		83	60	21	29.4
Central	15.4	97	55	21	28.6
East	20.7	45	79	19	18.4
West	16.5	95	38	41	– 10.0
South	14.4	107	69	16	50.1

[a] "Vie économique," Vol. II of *Pologne, 1919–1939* (3 vols.; Neuchatel, 1946–47), pp. 102, 131. As the author of the article on demography points out, the rate of natural increase in Poland between 1919 and 1938 was higher than in any of the West European states. *Ibid.*, p. 104.

[b] Derived from Wilbert E. Moore, *Economic Demography of Eastern and Southern Europe* (Geneva, 1945), pp. 72, 203. These figures for the year 1930 are estimates based on highly controversial statistical devices and are therefore useful only for purposes of general illustrations. Crop units, for example, are a statistical device designed to take into account quantities of different kinds of agricultural products by applying a series of weights to the amounts produced based on their unit value. *Ibid.*, pp. 30–31. For a standard of comparison, Moore estimates that per capita production in crop units for France in 1930 was 75. For the rest of Eastern Europe, per capita production in crop units was estimated as follows: Bulgaria, 20; Czechoslovakia, 45; Hungary, 33; Rumania, 21; Yugoslavia, 17. *Ibid.*, p. 36. It is impossible to arrive at an exact determination for the areas in question in Poland, since the census of 1931 was reported on the basis of new administrative units.

location for the transfer of peasants from the more densely populated regions in ethnic Poland, though the soil in the eastern regions was of low quality.[5] The difficulty was that the bulk of the peasantry in most of the eastern regions, as in Eastern Galicia, was not Polish, but the landowners and new colonists were.[6] In this area, then, the Communists could, presumably, apply Comintern tactics on both the agrarian question and the national question.

The section most critically affected by rural overpopulation was obviously south Poland, including most of the former Austrian provinces. According to Moore, this area had the highest proportion of surplus population in Poland. The national problem was less intense here, however, since the Ukrainian peasants were concen-

[5] *Pologne*, II, 60–61.
[6] *Ibid.*, pp. 114–17; Markert, pp. 37–42.

trated only in Eastern Galicia (or the Western Ukraine, if you prefer) east of the San River. The Communists had to compete in south Poland with the powerful Peasant Party Piast.

Central Poland occupied an intermediate position between western Poland, whose economic structure more closely resembled that of Prussia, and the more primitive regions. Here although the Comintern's agrarian policy would seem most applicable, the Peasant Party Wyzwolenie offered strong competition. However, Wyzwolenie was schooled in the Russian revolutionary tradition and it seemed possible that it might therefore be vulnerable to the Krestintern's Russian-inspired tactics.

Land distribution alone was certainly not the answer to Poland's problems of rural overpopulation. In fact, the persistence of part of the large-estate system diminished the danger of large-scale unemployment by providing jobs for agricultural workers.[7] It has been estimated that, if the arable land (excluding forests) in excess of fifty hectares had been confiscated, it would have only satisfied the immediate needs of two thirds of the dwarf holders and landless peasants, without taking into account the effects of natural increase in the population.[8]

During the interwar years the hope that the surplus rural population would somehow be absorbed by the growing towns was disappointed.[9] But in the early 1920s the general feeling was that something would come of the agrarian reforms, and much was expected from the creation of political machinery through which the peasant parties could advance the peasant's interests. This feeling of optimism hampered the efforts of the Polish Communist Party to fulfill Comintern directives by convincing the peasant that rural conditions could only be improved by supporting the proletarian revolution.

The failure of peasant parties to use the new political machinery to institute dramatic and sweeping agricultural reforms, however, led gradually to a decline of public confidence in both the new institutional system and the established peasant parties.

[7] Wilbert E. Moore, *Economic Demography of Eastern and Southern Europe* (Geneva, 1945), p. 224.

[8] *Pologne*, II, 202.

[9] *Ibid.*, p. 143.

In many respects the problems of the two largest agrarian parties in Poland, Piast and Wyzwolenie, exemplify the dilemma of agrarianism in Eastern Europe in general. One party, Piast, regarding politics as the art of the possible, tried to achieve its goals by using the strategy of barter and compromise with the strongest Polish parties. The other, Wyzwolenie, used unrelenting pressure for its maximum program. Neither succeeded. Although these failures are often cited as causes of the failure of democracy in Poland, they are probably only symptoms of the maladies which plagued Polish democratic institutions from the beginning.

The Polish Peasant Party Piast had evolved from the Polish Peasant Party founded by an émigré aristocrat from Russia, Bolesław Wysłouch, in Western Galicia in 1895.[10] From the beginning the party's primary goal had been to awaken the peasantry by means of political education and the fight for full social, political, and economic rights. It lacked both the doctrinaire reformism and the antiurban flavor of the Bulgarian peasant political movement. The Party also failed to identify itself very strongly with either Polish nationalism or the Catholic church. Having passed through the hard school of Austrian politics, first in the Galician Diet and then in the Reichsrat, as a minor party claiming to represent what was an oppressed and despised social class, the Polish Peasant Party learned to perfection the art of political compromise. Thugutt, a leader of the Polish Peasant Party Wyzwolenie, which evolved in the Russian portion of Poland, described the differences between the Russian school of politics and the Austrian.

Nowhere as much as in politics is the question so vital as to whether someone began his political activities under the Russians or under the Austrians, that is to say, whether in the tradition of the insurrectionary struggles and underground conspiratorial work or in an atmosphere of petty skirmishes for the attainment of very secondary ends. [11]

On December 14, 1913, there was a split in the Polish Peasant

10 On the founding and early history of the Party see Peter Brock, "Bolesław Wysłouch, Founder of the Polish Peasant Party," *Slavonic and East European Review,* No. 74 (Dec., 1951), pp. 139–63, and Peter Brock, "The Early Years of the Polish Peasant Party," *Journal of Central European Affairs,* No. 4 (Oct., 1954), pp. 219–35.

11 As quoted in Peter Brock, "The Politics of the Polish Peasant," *International Review of Social History,* I (1956), Part I, 215.

Party. Wincenty Witos organized a large section along more conservative lines under the name Polish Peasant Party Piast. Witos was a true son of the soil, who worked on the two-acre plot of his father and as a woodcutter in the forests of a local nobleman until he was twenty years old. But in 1906, at the age of thirty-four, he was elected to the Home Parliament in Lwów and in 1912 to the Vienna Parliament.[12] It was Wincenty Witos who became premier of Poland in August, 1920, rallying the country at home against the Soviet counteroffensive of that summer while Piłsudski, as chief of state and commander in chief of the armed forces, led the Polish army in the field.

While Piast drew most of its support as late as 1930 from the former Austrian regions,[13] the second major peasant political party, the Polish Peasant Party Wyzwolenie, was founded on December 15, 1915, in the Polish territories then occupied by Russia. Unlike their Galician counterpart, the members of Wyzwolenie had no parliamentary experience. Wyzwolenie represented the radical left wing of the agrarian movement in Poland, refusing to participate in coalition governments and opposing compensation to landlords whose lands had been confiscated. Even after Piłsudski's coup d'état in May, 1926, the two peasant parties continued to feud.[14] It was not until April, 1931, that they merged to form a united agrarian party.[15] Factionalism was the rule in Polish politics, even in movements with very similar aims.

In the elections of November 5, 1922, for the Sejm, Piast won seventy of the 444 seats in the powerful lower house. This gave Witos more seats than any other party leader, and he had to decide how to dispose of his new strength. Up to this point Witos had tried to reach his objectives by occupying a central position between the forces of the right and those of the left. He decided to change his tactics in 1923 and on May 15 made the "Pact of Lanckorona" with some of the major Polish parties of the right and center (the National Democrats or Endeks, the Christian Democrats, the Cath-

[12] Stanislaw Kot, "Wincenty Witos," International Peasant Union, *Monthly Bulletin*, Sept., 1955, p. 14.

[13] Brock, *International Review of Social History*, I (1956), 215.

[14] See the speech of Witos at the Piast Party Conference in 1927, *MAB Bulletin*, No. 3 (1927), p. 172.

[15] *MAB Bulletin*, No. 2 (1931), pp. 153–56.

olic People's Party, and the Christian Nationalists). By his decision Witos became premier of a coalition government and helped to establish the pattern of Polish politics for the next three years.

A coalition of right and center parties representing ethnically Polish interest groups though occasionally yielding power to non-Parliamentary cabinets, effectively excluded the parties of the left and the parties of national minorities from power.[16] Losing all hope of influence over the course of events, the leftist leaders, especially among the Slavic national minorities, increasingly split off from their original organizations and formed new splinter parties with schismatic deputies from the established parties of the left and center that were less committed to democratic procedures. If the right-center coalition had solved some of the economic, social, and national problems besetting the new Polish state, its monopoly of political power might have been tolerable and perhaps even beneficial. But Witos was a prisoner of his compromises, and the failure of the coalition to take decisive action on any question only intensified the frustration of those who were denied political power. Probably a country in which the dominant tradition was revolutionary rather than parliamentary and in which there were so many different interest groups was likely to produce more than its share of political factions. But those who deserted their own parties from 1923 to 1926 were also deserting the Polish democratic system because it made possible the domination of right and center. Factionalism and the increasing intransigence of the left ultimately led to parliamentary paralysis, while the legacy of unsolved problems testified daily to the failure of the democratic system.

Yet Witos had considered himself a realist. He had argued, much in the manner of the Czech agrarian leader Švehla, that, because of the multiplicity of political groupings, only compromise legislation would be successful. He said that he entered the coalition in order to hammer out an agrarian reform which would be enforceable because, he implied, it would be accepted by the influential as well as the needy.[17] In the Lanckorona Pact Witos had agreed

[16] Markert, pp. 37–42.

[17] *Ibid.,* p. 74; *Pologne,* II, 200. The financial crisis had stifled every effort between 1920 and 1923 to realize the ambitious goals formulated in the 1920 law.

to consult with the other parties of the right in the formulation of any comprehensive land reform bill.[18] The project which he finally worked out was acceptable to them because it was moderate. It established relatively high maximum limits for the size of holdings and called for gradual confiscation of lands exceeding those limits, with partial compensation to the original owner. Moreover, confiscation would be highest among non-Polish landlords.[19] He argued for compensation by saying: "I do not want stealing, but lawful acquisition of land. . . . That is the principle on which to create a free citizenry with a respect for law." [20] Witos was forced to resign in December, 1923, before he had won approval for his reform. There were many factors leading to the failure of "moderate agrarianism" at that time. First, the financial crisis and the inflation were unresolved; second, there was a general strike in November, 1923; third, Piast began splitting as individual members rejected Witos' compromises on the agrarian question.[21] At first Wyzwolenie was the beneficiary of this dissatisfaction, as when Jan Dąbski and Wysłouch, with thirteen other Piast deputies, moved over to that party.[22] In December, thirteen more Piast deputies under Bryl left to form the Peasant Association.

It is legitimate to question Witos' motives. Perhaps he was driven by ambition and his espousal of fiscal responsibility for the peasant and cooperation and compromise with Polish parties of the right was mere subterfuge. But, whatever his motives, his arguments would have been sound only in a country which had a firm parliamentary tradition. What the young Polish republic needed before 1925 was

18 Markert, p. 35.

19 Cechlin, "Pol'sha," in M. Zering [Max Sering], ed., *Agrarnaia revoliutsiia v Evrope* (Berlin, 1925), pp. 261–64. While this project did not pass in 1923, the conservative agrarian law passed at the end of 1925 embodied many of the features of the Witos' project, although the latter called for full compensation to affected landowners. Ferdynand Zweig, *Poland Between Two Wars* (London, 1944), pp. 131–33.

20 Quoted in Brock, *International Review of Social History*, I (1956), 217.

21 Malbone T. Graham, *New Governments of Eastern Europe* (New York, 1927), p. 505.

22 Brock, *Slavonic and East European Review*, No. 74 (Dec., 1951), p. 162; Jan.–Dec., "Les Partis agraires en Pologne," *MAB Bulletin*, No. 5–6 (1925), p. 37; Alexander J. Groth, "Parliament and the Electoral System in Poland, 1918–1935" (unpublished Ph.D. dissertation, Faculty of Political Science, Columbia University, 1960), p. 147.

showmanship not craftsmanship. To capitalize on the optimism and patriotic fervor which made Polish rebirth possible, the government neded bold and dramatic reforms which would at least create the impression that it was working in the interests of the whole nation, and therefore deserved the support and confidence even of those who disagreed with it. As it turned out, the nation did not have the patience to endure Witos' disappointing cautious bargains or his pious rationalizations.

Wyzwolenie was equally ineffective, but in a different way. Given the strength of the right-center coalition and the growing irreconcilability of the parties of the extreme left, the members of Wyzwolenie were condemned from 1922 to 1926 to a career of sterile opposition to all governments. A party frozen in hostile impotence is no more attractive than one which dilutes its program and, like Piast, Wyzwolenie suffered a number of defections.

This dilemma is particularly evident in the career of Stanisłas Thugutt, leader of Wyzwolenie. When Władisław Grabski formed a nonparliamentary cabinet of "experts" or "personalities" at the end of 1924, Thugutt was offered a post as minister without portfolio. His party denied him the right to accept, since Wyzwolenie was in opposition to the Grabski government, and participation in it would be a betrayal of party discipline. Thugutt resigned from his party in disgust, pointing out that the Grabski government was a government of experts grappling with a financial crisis which might destroy the young Polish republic and that nothing would be gained in opposition for its own sake.[23] He accepted the post of vice-premier in the Grabski government.

As vice-premier, Thugutt tried to push through a rapid extension of agrarian reforms which would be fair to the national minorities. Without any real power over the machinery of government, without a strong political party in back of him, and against the stubborn opposition of the brother of the premier, the minister of interior, Stanisłas Grabski, there was little Thugutt could do and he soon resigned.[24]

[23] Robert Machray, *Poland, 1919–1930* (London, 1932), p. 280.
[24] Thugutt took five deputies with him and formed a new reform party, the Labor Club. Graham, p. 522.

The polarization and multiplication of Polish political parties between 1922 and 1926 defeated all constructive political efforts. The country was ruled during this period by an alternating succession of cabinets of experts and cabinets formed by coalitions of the parties of the right and center. Under the pressure for long-delayed completion of the agrarian reforms, the crisis of mounting inflation, and impatience with the declining rate of accomplishment under the existing institutional structure, the parties of the left continued to grow, generally at the expense of the parties of the center, while the strength of the parties of the right remained fairly constant.[25] In particular, the big peasant parties, Piast and Wyzwolenie, continued to split into factions which advocated more rapid and more radical social reforms and a firmer defense of the rights of national minorities. By 1925 there were at least twenty-two major political parties as compared with seventeen in 1922.

Naturally one of the chief beneficiaries was the Communist Party of Poland (CPP). By 1923 this party had jurisdiction over two subparties, the Communist Party of Western Belorussia and the Communist Party of the Western Ukraine,[26] both of which also retained ties to their counterparts in the Soviet Union. Along with its subdivisions and front organizations, the CPP seemed to the unwary to have adopted by 1923 the political position formerly occupied by the peasant parties. It called not only for national self-determination up to and including secession (and reunification of Belorussia and Ukrainian lands with their Soviet counterparts) but also for a land reform program which included confiscation without compensation of all large-and medium-sized estates and redistribution of such lands to the needy by elective committees of the poor and landless peasants.[27]

[25] Groth provides detailed information on the shifts which took place between the elections of 1922 and the Piłsudski coup d'état, but, by grouping all the national minority parties together in his tables, he fails to demonstrate the gains made by the left in the formation of new and more radical national minority parties. Groth, pp. 141, 147–48, 149, 151. One really has to count the pro-Communist national minority parties in a separate category with the Communist parties.

[26] M. K. Dziewanowski, *The Communist Party of Poland: An Outline of History* (Cambridge, Mass., 1959), p. 105.

[27] *Ibid.*, p. 104.

On July 6, 1924, after a Ukrainian delegate was expelled from the Sejm for trying to speak Ukrainian, several deputies from the national minorities and Wyzwolenie joined the Communist faction and left the hall, each group singing its own song.[28] In November four Ukrainian Social-Democrats joined the Communists as a protest against the trial of several Ukrainian and Belorussian revolutionaries.[29]

In July, 1924, four deputies under the leadership of Sylwester Wojewódzki left Wyzwolenie to form a new Independent Peasant Party.[30] This party called for cooperation with the parties of the left, for confiscation of land without compensation, and for conciliation of national minorities.[31] In June, 1925, four deputies under the leadership of Boris Tarashkevich left the Belorussian National Club to form the Belorussian Workers' and Peasants' Hramada, a peasant party whose national and agrarian program strongly resembled that of the Communist Party.[32] The Hramada, like the Independent Peasant Party, later pledged joint action with the CPP.[33]

On June 26, 1925, the CPP, the Independent Peasant Party, and the Belorussian Hramada presented their program for agrarian reform. Following the Comintern line, this project called for the confiscation without compensation of all church and estate land over thirty hectares in size and the redistribution of this land among peasants and agricultural workers.[34] The land was to be distributed by elected peasant committees without cost. The committees in the

---

[28] *Istoriia Pol'shi*, ed. A. Ia. Manusevich, I. A. Khrenov, and F. G. Zuev (Moscow, 1954–55), III, 228.

[29] *Ibid.*, p. 229. Their names were A. Pashchuk, F. Pristup, I. Skrip, and Ia. Voitiuk.

[30] *Ibid.*, p. 230. In addition to Wojewódzki, there was Alfred Fideriewicz, Feliks Hołowacz, and Stanislas Ballin. They were later joined by Wlodzimiers Szakun, Adolf Bon, and Antoni Szapiel.

[31] *Ibid.*

[32] *Ibid.*, p. 232. In addition to Tarashekevich, there was S. Rak-Mikhailouski, P. Miatla, and P. Valoshyn.

[33] Dziewanowski contradicts himself in discussing the origins of the parallel Ukrainian organization, Selrob. On one page he states that it was organized in the summer of 1924; on another, in 1927. Dziewanowski, pp. 112, 332, n. 22. Communist sources state that Selrob was organized in October 1926. *Istoriia Pol'shi*, III, 274.

[34] The whole proposal is available in *Bor'ba trudiashchikhsia Zapadnoi Belorussii za sotsial'noe i natsional'noe osvobozhenie i vossoedinenie s BSSR* (Minsk, 1962), Vol. I, Doc. No. 210.

Western Ukraine (or Eastern Galicia) and Western Belorussia (Eastern Poland) were to have their own separate administration for the agrarian reform. This project was defeated on July 15, with both Piast and Wyzwolenie voting against it.[35] On December 28, 1925, an extremely conservative agrarian reform bill was passed calling for gradual confiscation (with full compensation) and distribution of land on a basis which permitted the retention of relatively large farms in the eastern regions. While there were many reasonable arguments for moving slowly and not destroying large estates which were effectively using their land, the small landholders were disappointed.[36]

One indication of the crisis in Polish politics was the fact that even Witos, an ardent advocate of democratic institutions, had come to the conclusion that the Polish parliamentary system could not work without a stronger executive, though he was not thinking of Piłsudski for the job. One month before the Piłsudski coup d'état Witos belatedly published a program for the revision of the constitution which would strengthen the powers of the Senate, eliminate the formation of small political groups, and provide a framework for a strong and durable government and a workable Sejm.[37]

Witos wrote:

In the event of the Sejm failing to carry out this program Poland will be compelled to seek another way out, in order to be able to carry on its work, which may change present conditions utterly, but which may become disastrous for its future.[38]

On May 12, 1926, Piłsudski marched on Warsaw, and shortly thereafter, with the tacit support of the left, including the Communist and pro-Communist factions, he formed a non-parliamentary government of his own choosing and pledged to restore law, order, and financial stability and to begin a "moral renaissance." [39] It was widely believed that Piłsudski's action would mean constitu-

[35] *Ibid.*
[36] For a brief summary of the arguments for and against the law see Raymond Leslie Buell, *Poland: Key to Europe* (New York, 1939), pp. 211–16.
[37] Zweig, pp. 47–48.
[38] *Ibid.*, p. 48.
[39] Machray, p. 320.

tional revisions to hasten the enactment of all needed reforms, an end to the domination of the right and center parties, and new responsibilities for the leaders of the parties of the left who had for so long been deprived of power.[40] The powers of the president of the Polish Republic were enlarged and needed reforms were instituted in short order, but the leaders of the left had a rude shock when Piłsudski began to court the conservative aristocracy and rule through nonparliamentary cabinets.[41] Piłsudski's victory proved to be a victory of personality rather than a victory of faction.

There were several reasons for Piłsudski's success. First, the parties of the left, which overtly or otherwise gave him support, misjudged him. The Communists in particular, in regarding Piłsudski as another Kerensky, another representative of "petty-bourgeois democracy" who might serve as a tool in their hands, failed to appreciate his real strength. While there is no question that the timing of the Piłsudski coup d'état was directly related to the immobilization of parliament and the mounting financial crisis and that Piłsudski's appeal lay partly in his stature as the strongest leader of the left, Piłsudski was also widely popular simply as a national hero and as the symbol of the heroism, individualism, and militancy which had enabled the Polish nation to survive one hundred years of partition.[42] It was natural that after seven years of apparently inept and rather undramatic democracy the Polish people should welcome a strong and flamboyant national hero who would (they hoped) cut the Gordian knot of domestic politics.

Perhaps the image of Piłsudski as a popular hero might not have been so persuasive if splintering political parties and a succession of coalition governments had proved equal to the task of economic reconstruction. But the combination of Piłsudski's personal appeal, the miscalculation of the left, the mounting pressure of inflation, and the ineffectiveness of the Polish Parliamentary system proved decisive. To compensate for its misjudgment the

[40] For a brief, but succinct, analysis of the political and economic factors favoring Piłsudski see Zweig, p. 43.

[41] Markert, p. 46.

[42] For a detailed and, in my opinion, illuminating analysis of Polish national character in these terms see Alicja Iwanska, ed., *Contemporary Poland: Society, Politics, Economy* (Chicago, 1955).

Comintern tried to mobilize the radical peasant political movement against Piłsudski after May, 1926.

Two factors which favored the Comintern in this effort were Piłsudski's attitudes toward land reform and national minorities after the coup d'état. Piłsudski faithfully implemented the agrarian law of 1925 but, probably because of pressure from his conservative aristocratic allies, made no effort to go beyond its inadequate and inequitable provisions.[43] Although the national minorities expected much of Piłsudski, they were misled by his former espousal of a multinational federal Poland.[44] His policies on the national question proved to be no more palatable than those of the National Democrats before him. Once in power he displayed his new rightist orientation with a policy of centralization, Polonization, and, as a last resort, "pacification" of the minorities in the East by force.[45] Piłsudski's seizure of power was not followed by any substantial change in the government's policy on the national question except perhaps a tougher attitude toward autonomists. The anxiety of the political representatives of national minorities was unrelieved, and the minorities remained in opposition.

THE COMINTERN, PIŁSUDSKI, AND THE POLISH PEASANT

The CPP was the second Communist party to be created in Eastern Europe.[46] It was organized in December, 1918, at a joint conference of the Social Democratic Party of the Kingdom of Poland

[43] Buell says the aristocrats persuaded Piłsudski to slow down the agrarian reform. Buell, pp. 208–9. But the statistics do not bear him out. See *Pologne,* II, 198, and Markert, p. 76. However, the law was inequitable, allowing as a maximum size 180 hectares in the Polish provinces and up to 300 hectares in the eastern provinces, while exempting the vast forests of the aristocracy from all its provisions. It was also inadequate and, although, as pointed out elsewhere, land reform alone could not solve the agrarian problems of Poland, the peasants blamed the land reform.

[44] It is generally agreed that Piłsudski's advocacy of a federal Polish state was simply a cloak for his ambitions for a Great Poland in Eastern Europe. Naturally a federation of Polish, Ukrainian, Belorussian, and Lithuanian states would be subject to Polish hegemony. S. L. Sharp, *Poland: White Eagle on a Red Field* (Cambridge, Mass., 1953), pp. 116–17.

[45] Groth, p. 211, and Markert, p. 50.

[46] The Hungarian Communist Party was the first. It was founded in November, 1918.

and Lithuania and the Polish Socialist Party–Left.[47] Like its agrarian counterpart, Wyzwolenie, the CPP (or the Communist Workers' Party of Poland, as it was first called) had its deepest roots in those parts of Poland which were formerly part of the Russian Empire. The CPP was outlawed by the new Polish Republic at the beginning of 1919. By 1922, profiting from the despair and confusion of postwar reconstruction and dissatisfaction with the form of Poland's rebirth, the Communists had acquired 10,000 members.[48] They would not enjoy this level of strength again for more than a decade.

In ethnic Poland, perhaps even more than in any East European country except Rumania, the identification of communism with Soviet Russia was a political liability, since Russia had always been a menace to Polish nationalism. When the CPP adopted the Comintern's program on the national question in 1923, with its support of national self-determination up to and including secession and calling for the return of Belorussian and Ukrainian lands, the Russian threat seemed to have been resurrected in Communist form. After 1923 in native Poland the poor and needy peasants turned increasingly to other leftist parties and to faith in Piłsudski for solace, but rarely to communism. But the Communist party had an unexploited source of strength. Whereas in native Poland the Russian connection was a liability, in the eastern border regions it was an asset. Among Western Belorussians and Western Ukrainians the impression was widespread that their brethren in the Soviet Union were better off.[49] Invidious comparisons were made between the privileges of national minorities in the Soviet Union and those in Poland. Although the Grabski government had introduced some moderate legislation in 1924 to protect national minorities, it did not satisfy the groups for whom it was intended because it maintained Polish primary schools.[50] In the eastern border regions the

[47] Dziewanowski, pp. 76–77.

[48] Ibid., pp. 97–99; Branko Lazić, Les Partis communistes d'Europe, 1919–1955 (Paris, 1956), p. 95.

[49] The exact number of Ukrainians and Belorussians in the eastern border regions is a matter for debate. Horak indicates why there is reason to doubt official Polish statistics. Stephen Horak, Poland and Her National Minorities (New York, 1961), pp. 88 ff.

[50] Graham, pp. 510–11.

Communist Party, as the one political party with the least interest in the preservation of the Polish state, seemed to many the natural leader of the struggle for minority rights.

As early as June, 1926, Stalin urged the Party to seize this role. He condemned the passivity of the CPP during the Piłsudski coup d'état, branding it the "May error." Piłsudski was not, as the Comintern and the Party had asserted, a representative of the petty bourgeoisie (like Kerensky or Stamboliiski). He was an agent of Anglo-American imperialism whose assignment was to make Poland a firm base for the imminent military attack on the Soviet Union.[51] But all was not yet lost. Piłsudski, said Stalin, was vulnerable.[52] He could not solve the problems of labor because the only adequate solutions would bring him into conflict with the capitalists at home and abroad upon whom he depended. He could not solve the agrarian question because the only effective reforms would bring him into conflict with the landed aristocracy, which provided him with his highest officers. He could not solve the national question without alienating the Polish nationalists and fascists who gave him strong moral support. According to Stalin, even though Piłsudski's policies might appear to stabilize the Polish economy it was a "rotten stabilization" and would soon dissolve in proletarian revolution. In short, Stalin predicted that Piłsudski's efforts to transform Poland into an anti-Soviet armed camp would fail because his policies would only antagonize labor, the peasantry, and national minorities. By implication the task of the CPP and its branches was to maximize the growing dissatisfaction of these three social categories and guide them toward revolutionary action.

For more than a year after the Piłsudski coup d'état the Comintern treated Poland as the chief advance post of the capitalist world in the forthcoming attack on the Soviet Union, but the efforts of the

[51] Dziewanowski, p. 123. Stalin's reinterpretation of Polish events was soon taken up in the organ of the Communist International in "Fashistskoi perevorot v Pol'she i Kommunisticheskaia Partiia Pol'shi," *Kommunisticheskii Internatsional*, No. 8 (Aug., 1926), pp. 6–18. See I. A. Khrenov, ed., *Kommunisticheskaia Partiia Pol'shi v Bor'be za nezavisimost' svoei strany* (Moscow, 1955), pp. 79–81.

[52] Stalin, "Ob angliiskoi zabastovke i sobytiiakh v Pol'she," *Sochineniia* (Moscow, 1946–51), VIII, 170–71.

CPP to forestall this attack were hampered by inner factionalism. From 1926 to 1929 the schism acted as a contact mine, finally exploding when the party was subjected to its first severe shocks at the hands of the Piłsudski government. The two factions were bitterly divided on the question of the "May error" and Stalin's interpretation of it. Both factions agreed on the tactics suggested by Stalin, but they differed on his conclusions. The majority, led by Warski, dominated the Central Committee from 1926 to 1928 and were closely tied to Bukharin. They argued quite accurately that Piłsudski's coup d'état was in several respects a revolt of the radical intellectuals and petty bourgeoisie with the support of the broad masses of the workers and peasants against the great landowners and capitalists.[53] The majority held that the Piłsudski regime was merely a military dictatorship evolving into fascism. They did not accept Stalin's notion of "rotten stabilization" and saw a long period of stability and prosperity, rather than revolution, in the immediate future. While Piłsudski was helping Poland to complete the capitalist stage of development, it was the task of the CPP to consolidate its strength by working with and infiltrating the petty bourgeoisie and their parties, which represented a third force between fascism and democracy. One member of the right, Henryk Brand, even advanced the "agrarianization" theory commonly used by rightist Communist leaders in Eastern Europe to justify concentration upon parliamentary activity and recruitment of mass support.[54] Their approach made the majority ideally suited to the task of implementing Comintern agrarian policy.

The minority, led by Julian Leński (real name Leszczyński), followed Stalin literally. For them the Piłsudski government was already fascist and incapable of stabilizing the economy or the country. For the left, the belief that Poland had to wait for the completion

[53] Dziewanowski, p. 124. Dziewanowski gives an excellent description of the issues dividing the two factions, but I would take issue with his statement, "Roughly speaking, the viewpoint of the majority coincided with that formulated by Trotsky, while the minority followed Stalin." As he correctly points out elsewhere, the majority echo the views of Bukharin, not Trotsky. For Communist accounts see *Istoriia Pol'shi,* III, 270–71, 283–84, 296.

[54] Dziewanowski, p. 331, n. 12.

of the capitalistic stage of development was an obsolete Marxist notion. Piłsudski had created, they argued, the objective conditions for a proletarian revolution, which the Party could win without any compromising alliances with petty-bourgeois political parties. The left would not be ascendant, however, until Bukharin was deposed in the Comintern.

The beginning of the CPP's successes in the countryside coincided with Warski's return to power in December, 1925, before the Piłsudski coup d'état. At the Fourth Party Conference in that month it was announced:

The Communist Party of Poland pledges itself to persevere in seeking a rapprochement with the workers and peasants from radical and petty-bourgeois parties on the basis of the struggle for independence, explaining patiently and tirelessly with the help of all the latest facts that, just as in the eighteenth century the rule of the gentry increased the slavery and oppression of the people and lost Poland her independence, so also now, each day, the rule of the gentry and bourgeoisie hastens disintegration, deepens and sharpens the danger threatening its independence.[55]

The first of the "petty-bourgeois" parties to benefit from Communist support was the Independent Peasant Party. Its leader, Sylwester Wojewódzki, is still something of an enigma. He was a Polish delegate from Lida in Western Belorussia, an aristocrat, and a former intelligence officer of the Polish general staff.[56] At one point he was suspected of being an *agent provocateur* of the Polish police. Investigation by a Polish judge disclosed that, far from being a Polish police agent, he was under close surveillance by the Polish police as a suspected Comintern agent.[57] He was later executed in Russia, however, as a Polish secret agent. Some of the leaders of the Independent Peasant Party were Belorussians or Poles living in Belorussia, and it is impossible to determine from available evidence the exact national composition of its membership or its

55 Khrenov, p. 75.
56 Dziewanowski, p. 329, n. 34.
57 *Ibid.*, pp. 147–48. Wojewódzki did contribute an article to the Krestintern's Berlin organ in 1929, when it no longer made any difference what the Polish police thought of him. S. Wojewodski, "Die faschist. Kriegsvorbereitungen und die Bauern in Polen," *Internationale Bauern Nachrichten* No. 6–8 (1929), pp. 76–78.

leadership.[58] At the time of its dissolution in 1927 it claimed to have 75,000 members.[59]

In theory it was supposed to be the Polish arm of the worker-peasant front. As one member of the Belorussian Hramada testified:

The difference between the Independent Peasant Party and ourselves is that the Independent Peasant Party is a Polish party and the Hramada is Belorussian. Both parties have identical programs and try to achieve their goals by the same means. The parties are territorial—they work in Poland and we in Belorussia. There are no differences between us.[60]

In practice, the work of the Independent Peasant Party seems to have been largely confined to the Poles in the eastern border regions and the heavily populated Lublin and Kielce provinces.[61]

Although the relationship between Wojewódzki and the Krestintern can only be a matter for speculation, Dąbal hailed him as a kindred soul in 1924.

From an interview granted by the delegate, Wojewódzki, the present leader of the Independent Peasant Party, and on the basis of an appeal which that party addressed to the peasant masses of Poland, it is evident that its program differs hardly at all from the fundamental theses of the Peasant International, which are extremely popular among the peasant masses of Poland.[62]

[58] One example is deputy Feliks Hołowacz, a Belorussian deputy for the Independent Peasant Party who was arrested along with the Hramada deputies in 1927. *Zapadnaia Belorussia na skam'e podsudimykh protsess Belorusskoi Krest'iansko-Rabochei Gromady 23 fevralia–22 maia, 1928* (Minsk, 1929), p. 44. One official Communist account acknowledges that the "Independent Peasant Party received support not only from Polish but also from Belorussian peasants." V. Poluian and I. Poluian, *Revoliutsionnoe i natsional'no-osvoboditel'noe dvizhenie v Zapadnoi Belorusii v 1920–1939* (Minsk, 1962), p. 56. Burks, however, is mistaken when he identifies the Independent Peasant Party as a Belorussian party, a mistake which colors his whole analysis of Polish Communist and Communist-front movements. R. V. Burks, *The Dynamics of Communism in Eastern Europe* (Princeton, 1961), p. 82. In the 1928 elections in Poland the acknowledged successor of the Independent Peasant Party, the Self-Help Party, received all of its electoral support from primarily Polish regions. *Concise Statistical Yearbook of Poland* (Warsaw, 1930), p. 37.

[59] *U surovyia podpollia i uspaminy bylykh chlenau KPZB* (Minsk, 1958), p. 74.

[60] *Zapadnaia Belorussia na skam'e*, p. 213.

[61] Dziewanowski, p. 127.

[62] T. Dąbal, "A Change in the Peasants' Movement in Poland," *International Press Correspondence*, IV, No. 83 (Dec. 11, 1924), 952.

In January, 1925, Dąbal treated the emergence of the Independent Peasant Party as a turning point in communism's campaign to win the Polish peasantry.

After the liquidation of its right wing, the Communist Party of Poland has been able to achieve significant influence in the country and to inoculate the peasant masses with their slogans, chiefly the slogan "workers' and peasants' alliance" and the slogan of seizure of church and landlord land without compensation. Proof of this, among other things, is the appearance of the Independent Peasant Party, which includes these two slogans in its political platform.[63]

At the Fifth Plenum of the ECCI in March, 1925, Dąbal spoke of the rise of the Independent Peasant Party in Poland as a spontaneous movement which called for some concrete policy statement from the Comintern on the relationship between Communist parties and friendly peasant parties.[64] But at the Second Plenum of the Krestintern immediately thereafter Dąbal referred to those "left radical peasant groups in Poland which have adopted the Krestintern's program of action." [65] It is not possible to discern beneath Dąbal's oratory the exact role which the Krestintern played in the creation or support of radical peasant parties in his own state. It would appear that it played a negligible role and that Dąbal was simply grasping at straws in order to glorify the organization he had created.

The second and most effective party to benefit from Communist support was the Belorussian Hramada, which claimed to have 150,000 members at the time of its dissolution in 1927, and the third was Selrob. Selrob, or the Ukrainian Peasant-Workers' Socialist Union, was founded in October by the amalgamation of two older parties, the Galician People's Will Party and the Volhynian Village Alliance.[66] Although there do not seem to be any figures for the membership of Selrob, it was probably as successful as its counterparts in other regions of Poland. There were two other parties which later Communist historians claim as their own—the new

---

[63] T. Dąbal, "Bor'ba za krest'ianstvo v Pol'she," *Krest'ianskii Internatsional,* No. 1–2 (Jan.,–Feb., 1925), p. 10.

[64] *Rasshirennyi plenum ispolkoma Kommunisticheskogo Internatsionala—protokoly zasedanii (21 marta–6 aprelia, 1925)* (Moscow, 1925), pp. 354–55.

[65] Dąbal, *Krest'ianskii Internatsional,* No. 3–5 (March–May, 1925), p. 32.

[66] Ie. F. Hirchak, *Shumskiizm i rozlam v KPZU* (Kharkhov, 1928), p. 95.

Polish Socialist Party—Left and the Ukrainian Party of Labor—but there is little solid evidence that they were part of the Communist faction before the elections of 1928. In July, 1926, there was a schism in the Ukrainian section of the Polish Socialist Party and a new Polish Socialist Party—Left was formed under Andrzej Czume and Jozef Rosenzweig-Rozycki.[67] On May 15, 1927, six deputies left the Ukrainian National Democratic Union and founded the Ukrainian Party of Labor.[68] On the eve of the election at the beginning of 1928 the pro-Communist bloc in the Sejm consisted of approximately twenty deputies, not counting the last two parties mentioned above.[69] At the Seventh Plenum of the ECCI in November, 1926, Boshkovich called the attention of the whole Comintern to the successes of the CPP, urging that its methods of close cooperation with the radical peasant political movement be used as a model by all Communist parties.

But there were serious limitations to the united front campaign among the peasants in Poland. For one thing, the successful policies of the CPP were identified with Warski's rightist leadership; after the fall of Bukharin in 1929 the rightist majority would be purged in April at the Sixth Plenum of the Party and the leadership

---

[67] Jan Reguła, *Historia Komunistycznej Partii Polski* (Warsaw, 1934), p. 177.

[68] M. Felinski, "Les Ukraniens à parlement de la Pologne restaurée," *Questions minoritaires*, No. 4 (Oct., 1930), p. 137.

[69] Reguła, p. 144., Reguła indicates that at the end of 1926 the Communist faction in the Sejm consisted of six deputies from the Polish Communist Party, seven from the Independent Peasant Party, six from Hramada, four from Selrob. Four Hramada deputies and one deputy from the Independent Peasant Party were arrested and three members of the Independent Peasant Party defected in 1927. It is not clear whether the deputies of the Ukrainian Labor Party and the Polish Socialist Party—Left should be counted as members of the Communist faction in 1927. Therefore the Communist faction in the Sejm consisted of at least twenty deputies at the beginning of 1928, of which five were in jail. This alignment is confirmed in "Vybori v Pol'she," *Mezhdunarodnaia zhizn'*, No. 2 (1928), p. 19; see also Groth, p. 153. As usual, Burks makes some mistakes in his evaluation of the situation. Burks, pp. 82–83. First, he leaves the reader with the erroneous impression that the alliance of Communist and front deputies in the Sejm did not change between 1926 and the beginning of 1928. Second, although the Communist bloc voted together, they did not join in a single parliamentary club, as Burks suggests. Third, although he correctly points out that "three fourths of the communist faction came from minority stocks" before the elections of 1928, he fails to point out that over half of the Communist deputies came from Polish stock after the elections of 1928. (See n. 106 below.)

would pass to the doctrinaire left minority under Leński. For purely extraneous reasons, therefore, a faction which viewed peasant parties with hostility and suspicion, which overestimated the possibility of proletarian revolution in Poland, and which minimized the importance of parliamentary activity would be given control of the Polish Party.

Even more ominous, perhaps, were the weaknesses inherent in the nature of the worker-peasant front itself. These weaknesses can best be brought out by a closer look at one of the worker-peasant parties, the Belorussian Hramada.

Although the exact relationship between Moscow and the Hramada may never be known,[70] it is reasonably well established that the Communist Party of Western Belorussia had a hand in the founding of the Hramada and supplied it with funds and cadres of Communist agitators for organizing the masses. With or without the foreknowledge of the leaders of the Hramada, that organization provided the CPP with machinery for legal operations in and out of the Sejm.[71]

When the leaders of the Hramada were tried by the Polish government on charges of treasonable activity, the prosecution traced the origins of the Hramada back to the founding of the Krestintern and the Fifth Comintern Congress.[72] At the trial the tale unfolded as turncoats and double agents followed one another to the witness stand. According to the deposition of a former member of the Central Committee of the Communist Party of Western Belorussia, Mikhas Guryn (known in the Party as Ian or Stakh), the Comintern decided in July, 1925, to support the Belorussian Workers' and Peasants'

[70] It is known that at least one of the peasant front organizations was subject to discipline by the Comintern and the Krestintern. The leaders of the Self-Help Party, which replaced the Independent Peasant Party in 1928, were brought before both the Comintern and the Krestintern for disciplinary action. Oskar Chervets, "Kompartii Pol'shi v bor'be za Krest'ianskie massy," *Kommunisticheskii Internatsional*, No. 25 (1929), p. 33.

[71] In a recent study one author gravely misleads his readers by categorically denying any Communist influence or sympathies in the Hramada: "This liberal party was never considered to be communist or pro-Soviet. . . . Its political orientation was equally directed against Poland and Soviet Russia." Horak, p. 172.

[72] *Zapadnaia Belorussiia na skam'e* pp. 59–60, 234–40.

Hramada, using Sylwester Wojewódzki, leader of the Independent Party, as intermediary.[73] According to Guryn, Wojewódzki invited Tarashkevich to a conference with delegates of the Comintern (including a Russian) at Danzig in August. A recent Communist account indicates that such a meeting did take place, though it only mentions Tarashkevich, one member of the CPP, and several delegates from the Communist Party of Western Belorussia as participants.[74] This account also asserts that before the Danzig meeting Pavel Korchyk (political secretary of the Communist Party of Western Belorussia) and other leading workers of the Belorussian Party met with Tarashkevich and Rak-Mikhailouski to discuss the question of the future development of the national liberation movement in Belorussia.[75] According to Guryn, it was decided that the Hramada would receive 30,000 gold rubles for its publishing activity, to be placed on deposit with the Belorussian Cooperative Bank in Vilna.[76] Guryn said that the Comintern hoped through the Hramada to provide military training to Belorussians who could serve as pro-Soviet partisans in the event of war.[77]

The basis for transforming the Hramada from a parliamentary faction into a mass political party was not laid until the beginning of 1926. Following the Fourth Conference of the CPP in December, 1925, which restored Warski's rightist majority to power, the Third Conference of the Communist Party of Western Belorussia was called in January, 1926, to bring Party strategy into line with that of the new Polish leadership. This latter conference decided to abandon the Party's bankrupt policy of military resistance, partisan warfare, and sabotage [78] and turn to Warski's tactics of infiltration and support for legal mass organizations. Shortly thereafter, all sections of the Communist Party of Western Belorussia were given special directives ordering them to designate part of their membership for work organizing and extending the influence of

[73] *Ibid.*, pp. 110, 119–21, 145, 245.
[74] Poluian and Poluian, p. 82.
[75] *Ibid.*, p. 80.
[76] *Zapadnaia Belorussiia na skam'e,* pp. 81–83.
[77] *Ibid.*, p. 245.
[78] Poluian and Poluian, p. 86.

the Hramada. In the first half of 1926 over two hundred Communists were so assigned.[79]

The Polish state alleged later at the trial of the leaders of the Belorussian Hramada in 1928 that the Hramada was no more than a parliamentary faction until after the Piłsudski coup d'état, when it launched a tremendous publishing and propaganda campaign in the West Belorussian countryside.[80] This assumption is probably correct. Although the Communist Party of Western Belorussia had provided agents to step up the Hramada's recruiting campaign in the first half of 1926, it was not until June, after Piłsudski's coup and most likely because of it, that the Communists decided to make the Hramada a truly massive operation.[81] Bursevich, the general secretary of the Hramada, reported a phenomenal increase in membership for the last four months of 1926 and the beginning of 1927 (see Table 9).

Table 9
Membership in the Belorussian Hramada

Month	Year	Membership
June	1926	950
September	1926	45,000
December	1926	68,000
January	1927	100,000
February	1927	117,000
March	1927	150,000

Source: *Bor'ba trudiashchikhsia Zapadnoi Belorussii za sotsial'noe i natsional'noe osvobozhdenie i vossoedinenie s BSSR* (Minsk, 1962), I, 554.

Riding on the coattails of the Hramada, the Communist Party of Western Belorussia grew and, with the Communist Party of the Western Ukraine probably began to dwarf its mother party, the CPP (see Table 10).

Why was the Hramada so successful? Certainly the Comintern had exploited not only the poverty and land hunger of the peasants

[79] *Ibid.*, p. 88. These authors indicate that most of the local Hramada leaders were Communists.

[80] *Zapadnaia Belorusiia na skam'e*, pp. 200, 203–5. Poluian and Poluian, pp. 97–98, describe the publishing operations of the Hramada.

[81] Poluian and Poluian, pp. 96, 117–18.

Table 10
Membership in the Communist Party of Poland

	1922	1924	1925	1926	1927	1930
CPP	10,000 [a]	3,000			2,500	3,300
CPWB		1,000 [b]	2,100 [c]	3,000 [c]	1,000	2,000
CPWU		1,000 [d]			3,400	1,300
Total	10,000	5,000			6,900	6,600

Source: S. Vlodavskii, "Pol'sha," in *Shest' let bor'by za Krest'ianstvo*, ed. V. Kolarov, Vol. II of *Agrarnyi vopros i sovremennoe krest'ianskoe dvizhenie* (Moscow, 1935), p. 64.

[a] B. Lazić, *Les Partis communistes d'Europe, 1919–1955* (Paris, 1956), p. 95. Figures for 1922 are for the period before the affiliation between the CPP and those parties of the eastern border regions.

[b] *U surovyia gody podpollia i uspaminy bylykh chlenau KPZB* (Minsk, 1958), p. 6.

[c] *Bor'ba trudiashchikhsia Zapadnoi Belorussii za sotsial'noe i natsional'noe osvobozhdenie i vossoedinenie s BSSR* (Minsk, 1962), I, 432, and V. Poluian and I. Poluian, *Revoliutsionnoe i natsional'no-osvoboditel'noe dvizhenie v Zapadnoi Belorussii v 1920–1939* (Minsk, 1962), p. 129.

[d] M. P. Gerasymenko and B. K. Dudykevich, *Borot'ba trudiashchykh Zakhidnoi Ukrainy za vozziednannia z Radianskoiu Ukrainoiu* (Kiev, 1955), p. 6.

of the eastern border regions but also, and perhaps primarily, the illusion of national minorities in Poland about the amount of land and freedom accorded to their brethren in Soviet Belorussia.[82] Outraged by Polish treatment of the eastern regions as conquered territories and Polish efforts to Polonize their government and schools, the Belorussians were eager to believe that things were better on the Russian side of the border. Also, disappointed by the failures of Wyzwolenie and the Polish Socialist Party, peasants and members of the intelligentsia turned to the Hramada as a new and as yet untarnished activist nationalistic movement.[83] At the trial of the Hramada a Belorussian senator, who was not a member of the Hramada, testified:

That the Belorussian masses are attracted to the East, where there is a Belorussian Soviet Republic, is a fact which cannot be denied. In the East the Belorussians are building a home of their own. There are Belorussian schools, a Belorussian press. The policy of the USSR toward the Belo-

[82] Dzienwanowski, pp. 111–12.

[83] Poluian and Poluian, pp. 101–2, indicate that many Hramada recruits were from Wyzwolenie and the Polish Socialist Party.

russian is much wiser than the policy of Poland and it is necessary to take this into account.[84]

Tarashkevich, leader of the Hramada, echoed the above sentiments, pointing out that he himself was skeptical about Soviet Belorussia until he heard glowing reports from impartial visitors.[85] He denied, however, that either the devil or the Comintern inspired him to create the Hramada, only, he said, a growing sense of outrage at the Polish state's persecution of Belorussians. Significantly, the agrarian question was mentioned far less often as a motive and weapon of the Hramada.

In its program the Hramada was clearly revolutionary, though not especially Communist.[86] The first and major plank was the right of national self-determination up to and including secession, to be achieved by close cooperation among workers, peasants, and intelligentsia.[87] The secondary planks were:

(1) Confiscation of landlord and church land without compensation and its distribution without cost to peasant committees composed of local peasants and agricultural laborers.

(2) Elimination of state and military colonization and the distribution of land in the hand of colonization commissions among local peasants and agricultural laborers.

(3) Nationalization of forests and waterways owned by the church and landlords.

(4) Liquidation of remaining servitudes.

(5) Transferal of taxes which oppress the people by their severity to

[84] *Zapadnaia Belorussia na skam'e*, p. 52.

[85] *Ibid.*, p. 184.

[86] As Poluian and Poluian point out, pp. 92–94, the Hramada included several planks in its program which were unacceptable to the Communists. The Party was in favor of small peasant property, and its program called for the unification of all Belorussian lands and the creation of an independent state, rather than the Communist plan for the absorption of West Belorussia by the Belorussian Soviet Socialist Republic. The authors also find the wording of the plank on the need for establishing "a close socialist union of European people" too vague. The program was inadequate in that it didn't call for the nationalization of any key branch of industry. The program was devoid of Marxist clichés, such as the need for a "dictatorship of the proletariat" and the construction of a socialist society. The authors also admit that the Hramada was poorly organized even for carrying out the tasks in its program.

[87] *Bor'ba trudiashchikhsia Zapadnoi Belorussii*, Vol. I, Doc. No. 266. This is a fairly complete copy of the program of the Hramada published in April, 1926.

the shoulders of the rich and complete liberation of the poor, landless, small-landed, and middle peasants from taxation.

(6) Elimination of all duties in kind.

(7) Diminution of terms of military service and a considerable diminution of army, police, and administrators.

(8) Elimination of political police and the system of beatings and spying.

(9) Transformation of the standing army into people's militia.

(10) Full freedom of assembly.

(11) Amnesty for all political prisoners.

(12) The right to free counsel for political crimes.

(13) Abolition of the death penalty.

(14) The creation of people's courts elected by the people.

(15) Separation of church and state.[88]

Although the Hramada's program specifically bound the party to legal methods of struggle,[89] it is apparent that the rest of the program could only be achieved by revolution. This was a program which fully justified the fears of the Polish state,[90] but not the brutal and arbitrary methods which the state adopted to suppress the Hramada.[91]

On January 18, 1927, the Polish government launched its campaign against the Hramada and the Independent Peasant Party. Five deputies of the former were arrested and one deputy of the latter, along with some 800 members of both parties.[92] Those arrested were brought to trial more than a year later (February 23 to May 22, 1928) for conspiring with the CPP, the Comintern, and the Krestintern to overthrow the legal Polish government. Both the Hramada and the Independent Peasant Party were declared illegal before the parliamentary elections in March, 1928. Many of the leaders of the two parties, following their trial and conviction were later exchanged for Polish political prisoners held in the Soviet Union.[93]

The "front" peasant parties proved to be extremely vulnerable to direct attack. The Hramada was destroyed by Piłsudski's campaign

---

[88] *Zapadnaia Belorussiia na skam'e,* pp. 200–201.

[89] *Bor'ba trudiashchikhsia Zapadnoi Belorussii,* Vol. I, Doc. No. 266.

[90] For examples of the attitudes of the state see *ibid.,* Docs. 271 and 348.

[91] Nicholas P. Vakar, *Belorussia: The Making of a Nation; a Case Study* (Cambridge, Mass., 1956), pp. 127–28.

[92] *Zapadnaia Belorussiia no skam'e,* p. 44.

[93] Vakar indicates that the leaders of the Hramada were all purged in one way or another in the Soviet Union in the early 1930s. Vakar, pp. 145–47, 257, n. 18.

208 THE CONFLICT: NATIONAL

against it. Its work was taken over in the Sejm from 1927 to 1930 by a small faction of deputies calling themselves the Zmahanne,[94] but even Communist sources agree that the Zmahanne never acquired a significant mass following.[95] Mass agitation among the Belorussians was also continued through the Association of Belorussian Schools, but the revelations at the trial of the Hramada led to major defections from that organization.[96] It never had more than 20,000 members. The Hramada trials also inspired defections from the Independent Peasant Party, three of whose deputies expressed shock at the discovery of Communist infiltration, though they were probably more shocked at the prospect of arrest, and broke away to form their own peasant party, which they called "Unity." [97] The work of the Independent Peasant Party was taken up by the Polish Self-Help Party, a more dependent front group and a less successful one.[98] The division in the CPP between the majority and the minority became more

[94] Actually the work of the Hramada was carried on by two organizations between 1927 and 1930, of which the first was a Belorussian parliamentary faction called Zmahanne, consisting of deputies I. Dvarchanin, O. Haurylik, F. Valynets, I. Gretski, and P. Krinchik. (Gretski was elected on the Selrob-Left list in the Brest region and Valynets was a defector from the Belorussian Christian Democratic Party of Ia. Staganovich.) Poluian and Poluian, p. 124. Poluian and Poluian refer to Zmahanne as "the leading center of legal political work of the Communist Party of Belorussia among the masses." *Ibid.*, pp. 122–27. Mass agitation was conducted by the cultural organization, the Association of Belorussian Schools, which, at its height, claimed 20,000 members. *Bor'ba trudiashchikhsia Zapadnoi Belorussii*, I, 17, 591, n. 126; *Istoriia Belorusskoi SSSR* (Minsk, 1961), II, 364–65; Poluian and Poluian, pp. 138–46. The work of the Independent Peasant Party was continued by the Peasant Self-Help Party. Dziewanowski, p. 127. The work of Selrob was carried on by Selrob-Left and later by the Selrob Unity Party.

[95] Poluian and Poluian, p. 148, frankly testify: "However, as a whole, the peasant movement in this period, beginning with April, 1927, was considerably weaker than in the period from 1926 to the beginning of 1927.

[96] Astrouski and Lutskevich left the Association of Belorussian Schools and formed a rival Society for Belorussian Education, which, they said, would seek cultural privileges for Belorussia under the Piłsudski government, instead of trying to overthrow that government. *Istoriia Belorusskoi SSSR*, II, 370, and Poluian and Poluian, p. 141.

[97] Deputies Bon, Szakun, and Szapiel, the last deputies to join the Independent Peasant Party, were the first to break away from it. They argued that they had never intended to solve the social and economic problems of the eastern borderlands by destroying the Polish state. *Bor'ba trudiashchikhsia Zapadnoi Belorussii*, I, 465–66, 499–500.

[98] See n. 58 above.

critical, and a parallel split took place at the Fourth Congress of the Communist Party of Western Belorussia in September, 1927, accounting for the sharp drop in the membership of that organization.[99] Certainly the divided leadership in the mother party made all sorts of factionalism in the subparties and front organizations that much easier.

Piłsudski's attacks on Communist-front peasant nationalist organizations revealed the fragility of such entities. Not only did they crumble under persecution, but arrests seemed to have terrorized many of their leaders enough for them to end their dallying with Communists and defect from front organizations altogether. Perhaps if the Comintern's policy on the national question had not alienated the Poles there might have been more solid resistance to Piłsudski's attack on the Hramada. But the Polish membership in the CPP was probably declining between 1924 and 1927 at the same time that Belorussian and Ukrainian membership was increasing (see Table 10). By 1927 almost two-thirds of the members of the Polish Party were from the national minorities. As early as November, 1926, Boshkovich warned the Party that this imbalance was dangerous and that the Party had to strengthen its work in native Poland.[100] But it was not until the suppression of the Hramada that Boshkovich's assumptions were confirmed. The Fourth Congress of the CPP in September, 1927, resolved:

Until now the Party has not learned how to create in practice a workers' and peasants' bloc between native Poland and the peasants of Western Belorussia and the Western Ukraine. Thus, for example, the campaign of the Party against the attacks by the fascist government on the Belorussian Hramada did not evoke enough response from the Polish masses and, on the other hand, there is the fact that the Łódz strike was not supported by the Ukrainian and Belorussian masses.[101]

Although the central organization of two of the major pro-Communist peasant parties was shattered by the Piłsudski regime, the third, the Ukrainian Peasant-Workers' Socialist Union (Selrob),

[99] Poluian and Poulian, p. 137. Table 10 above.
[100] *Puti mirovoi revoliutsii*, I, 198.
[101] *Bor'ba trudiashchikhsia Zapadnoi Belorussii*, I, 485.

was shattered by a schism in the Ukrainian Communist movement on the national question. Events in the Soviet Ukraine were destroying Ukrainian illusions about Communist policies on the national question. In July, 1927, both the Communist Party of the Western Ukraine and Selrob split down the middle over the question of national deviationism or Shumskiism.[102] In the opinion of one study of Ukrainian communism:

In a word the Western Ukraine, by virtue of its linguistic racial and cultural ties with the U.S.S.R., and also thanks to its peculiar geographical location, became, in the strategy of world revolution, a starting point—a *Platzdarm*—for Communist expansion into the central Danube region and into Central Europe. Thanks to Shumskiism and the subsequent split in the K.P.Z.U., this grand scheme collapsed like a house of cards, forcing a complete revision of the Comintern's strategy and turning the Western Ukraine from a springboard of World Revolution into a *Platzdarm* "from which world imperialism concentrates the preparation of war against the U.S.S.R." [103]

The germ of anti-Soviet nationalism and the pressure of Piłsudski's police tended to produce a whole series of splits in all of the Belorussian and Ukrainian Communist and front organizations in 1927 and 1928.[104]

The last opportunity of the CPP to capitalize on its appeal before all of these forces led to its paralysis and disintegration was in the relatively free elections of March 4, 1928 (see Table 11). As many as thirty-nine electoral lists appeared in some provinces. There is considerable difference of opinion among scholars about the success of the Party at the polls in 1928.[105] The actual size of the

[102] For an analysis of the impact of the so-called Shumskii controversy on Selrob see Hirchak, pp. 44–61, 143–66, 241–43. The controversy is treated in Basil Dmytryshyn, *Moscow and the Ukraine, 1918–1953* (New York, 1956), chap. IV. The split of 1927 was only the first of many. In Septemeber, 1927, Selrob split into Selrob and Selrob-Left (the pro-Soviet faction). In December, 1928, the original Selrob was destroyed by the formation of a new and completely pro-Soviet Selrob. M. Felinski, *The Ukrainians in Poland* (London, 1931), pp. 91–93.

[103] Dmytryshyn, p. 114.

[104] For a list of the condemned schismatic factions see Chervets, *Kommunisticheskii Internatsional,* No. 25 (1929), p. 33.

[105] A remarkable plague of credulity seems to have struck some of those who have studied East European communism. Dziewanowski accepts without

Communist and Communist-front party votes cannot be accurately
determined, but it was probably somewhere between 800,000
and 900,000 votes out of 11,800,000 votes cast, or approximately
7 percent of the total.[106] In validated votes the Party and its front

question a figure of 940,000 votes (validated and invalidated) for Communists
in 1928, or 7.9 percent of the total vote cast, a figure which Burks dutifully
echoes without question. Dziewanowski, p. 127. Burks, p. 83. Dziewanowski
cites a former Polish police officer as his source. One Communist source also
gives a figure this high, citing the Lwów oblast archives, but this may be a
report of the same Polish police officer. M. P. Gerasymenko and B. K. Dudykevich, *Borot'ba trudiashchykh Zakhidnoi Ukrainy za vozziednannia z Radianskoiu Ukrainoiu* (Kiev, 1955), p. 96. Far more frequently cited in Communist and non-Communist sources is the figure 830,000 votes cast (including
validated and invalidated ballots). Vakar, p. 153, n. 25. Reguła, p. 205. E.
Brand, "The Communist Election Victory in Poland," *International Press
Correspondence*, VIII (March 15, 1928), 326. *Kommunisticheskii internatsional pered shestym vsemirnym kongressom* (Moscow, 1928), p. 239. Inter-
estingly enough, Vakar cites not only Reguła as his source but also the same
Polish police officer as Dziewanowski. Both Vakar and Reguła insist on a
rather inconvenient exact figure of 829,416, while the Communist sources
round it off to 830,000. In view of the fact that only 543,000 validated
Communist votes can be discovered (see n. 106 below), and considering that
only 324,000 votes were invalidated for all parties, the figure of 830,000 seems
more reasonable.

[106] The validated votes won by the Communist and Communist front groups
are listed below.

VOTES IN THOUSANDS

No.	National list	Total	Center	East	West	South	Deputies
13	Workers' and Peasants' Unity	217	201	13		3	5
19	Selrob-Left	143		69		74	3
26	Ukrainian Party of Labor	45				45	1
	Local list						
37	Self-Help (Łódź)	49	49				2
37	Self-Help (Lublin)	18	18				1
38	Zmahanne	71		71			3
		543	268	153		122	15

Source: *Concise Statistical Yearbook of Poland* (Warsaw, 1930), p. 137. The
front parties are identified with the help of Brand, *International Press Correspondence*, VIII (March 15, 1928), 325–26, and B. Borovski, "Pol'sha posle
vyborov," *Mezhdunarodnaia zhizn'*, No. 3 (1928), pp. 37–47.

The pattern of invalidation in 1928 was unusual and would indicate that groups showed as much strength in strictly Polish regions as in the eastern border regions, electing eight deputies to the Sejm in the former area and seven in the latter.[107]

To summarize: On the surface it seemed from 1926 to 1927 that Comintern agrarian policy in conjunction with its policy on the national question was being applied with great success in Poland. The Comintern had clearly miscalculated in underestimating Piłsudski and giving orders that could be interpreted by the CPP as scriptural support for its passive reaction to Piłsudski's coup d'état. But, following Stalin's specific directives, the Party was able to recover some of its former prestige by exploiting Piłsudski's inaction on the agrarian and national minorities questions even though Piłsudski had ended the financial crisis. Large pro-Communist radical peasant parties were appearing in Poland, particularly in the east and southeast. It seems likely that in these areas the Comintern programs on the national question and the agrarian question reinforced one another, in making Communist and front parties attractive to the peasantry, whereas in the purely Polish regions they seem to have

---

the East, where the Communists had made their greatest gains since 1926, suffered the most from invalidation.

INVALIDATED BALLOTS IN THOUSANDS

Date	Total	Center	East	West	South
1922	59	26	14	6	13
1928	320	55	196	32	37
1930	484	299	64	9	112

Source: *Concise Statistical Yearbook of Poland* (Warsaw: 1931), p. 133.

Groth says that in the 1928 elections invalidated ballots constituted a potentially significant factor in at least six of the nine districts in the East. Groth, p. 241. Elections were not even held in two electoral districts in Lwów and in upper Silesia. *Annuaire statistique de la Republique Polonaise* (Warsaw, 1930), pp. 458–59. The Communists claim 328, 832 votes in the East (of which 153,000 were validated) or 26 percent of the total vote cast in that area. Poluian i Poluian, p. 124, and *Bor'ba trudiashchikhsia Zapadnoi Belorussii*, I, 513. Adding together each individual Communist claim of invalidated ballots in the above sources to the validated ballots, one gets about 803,000 votes.

[107] As usual, Burks and Dziewanowski mislead. Dziewanowski gives the Communists nineteen deputies instead of fifteen. Dziewanowski, p. 27. Burks misquotes Dziewanowski and gives the Communists twenty deputies instead of fifteen, including eight Ukrainians instead of three. Burks, p. 83.

canceled one another out, for the Communist and front vote in the east was wholly from rural areas, while in the west and center it was almost wholly from urban areas.[108] For this reason it seemed possible that the experience of the Polish Party in eastern and southern Poland might become a "lesson" for the whole Comintern, a lesson demonstrating the effectiveness of Comintern agrarian and national minority policies when applied properly.

Table 11
Polish Elections of 1928

Party		Seats in Sejm
Government bloc		125
National Democrats		38
Peasant Party		25
Peasant Union		3
Wyzwolenie		41
Christian Democrats ⎫ Piast ⎭		34
Polish Socialist Party		64
Communist bloc [a]		15
Polish Communist Party	7	
Polish Self-Help Party	1	
Ukrainian Labor Party	1	
Belorussian Zmahanne	3	
Ukrainian Selrob—Left	3	
National Minority Parties		80
Other		19
	Total	444

Source: *Concise Statistical Yearbook of Poland* (Warsaw, 1930), pp. 137–38.
[a] The front groups are identified on the basis of E. Brand, "The Communist Election Victory in Poland," *International Press Correspondence,* VIII (March 15, 1928), 325, and "Der polnische Fascismus macht Wahlen," *Internationaler Bauern-Korrespondent,* No. 3 (March, 1928), p. 21. The latter is the Berlin organ of the Krestintern. After the elections Zmahanne acquired two more delegates, one from Selrob—Left and one from the Belorussian Christian Democrats. The single Ukrainian Labor Party delegate joined Selrob—Left, giving the Communist faction in the Sejm sixteen deputies in all. V. Poluian and I. Poluian, *Revoliutsionnoe i natsional'no-osvoboditel'noe dvizehnie v Zapadnoi Belorusii v 1920–1939* (Minsk, 1962), p. 124.

[108] Using only the validated ballots cited in n. 106, one discovers that almost two thirds of the electoral support from Communist and front groups in the elections of 1928 came from rural areas. But in central Poland 80 percent of their support came from urban areas, while in eastern and southern Poland 91 percent came from rural areas. They received no validated votes in the economically more advanced western provinces where there was a strong German minority. *Annuaire statistique de la Republique Polonaise,* pp. 448–49.

But three factors intruded to prevent the Polish "lesson" from becoming a significant one. First, the Independent Peasant Party and the Belorussian Hramada were apparently unable to withstand the attacks of the newly strengthened Polish government. This bared some of the inherent weaknesses in the Comintern's policy toward peasant political parties. The tactics recommended by the Comintern could only be effective when Communist propaganda was tolerated or in an atmosphere of crisis. Perhaps if Dąbal's request at the Fifth Plenum of the ECCI in 1925 for an authoritative definition of the proper relation between Communist parties and sympathetic peasant political parties had been answered, there would have been greater solidarity and strength among the various pro-Communist movements. But Bukharin had answered Dąbal with a proposal for the formation of agrarian unions, a proposal based on inappropriate invocations of Russian revolutionary experience.[109]

Secondly, in the Western Ukraine the Comintern apparently misjudged the intensity of national feeling and found when it threatened to take precedent over Communist goals that it was necessary to split and therefore weaken both the Communist Party of the Western Ukraine and Selrob. Last of all, the increasingly close tie between Comintern policy and the struggle in the Russian Communist Party only intensified the normally schismatic tendencies in the CPP, finally imposed unrealistic leadership upon it in 1929, and weakened the emphasis on capturing the thriving peasant political movement.

For all these reasons the temporary successes of the CPP were soon frittered away and never became an enduring "lesson" for the Comintern as a whole in the same sense as the Hungarian and Bulgarian experiences.

[109] See pp. 95–96.

CHAPTER IX

The Effete Party: Comintern Policy in Yugoslavia, 1924–1929

Yugoslavia in the 1920s would seem to have been an ideal target for Comintern propaganda on the agrarian question. Most Yugoslav provinces suffered from rural overpopulation and there was widespread poverty, land hunger, and dissatisfaction with the postwar agrarian reforms. The country was poor, it had only begun to industrialize, and the majority of the population were peasants. Like Bulgaria, Yugoslavia had a strong peasant political movement, the Croatian Peasant Party. Like Poland, Yugoslavia suffered from bitter rivalry among the nationalities which had been joined together in the new state. But the Communist Party of Yugoslavia (CPY) was one of the declining parties in the Comintern from 1919 to 1930. It accepted Comintern directives with reluctance and resentment, and a large faction in the Party argued that collaboration with the Croatian Peasant Party and the adoption of Comintern directives on the national and agrarian questions could only weaken the Communist Party. Caught between the persecution of the Yugoslav government and the growing pressure from Moscow, the CPY was torn by factional disputes, which were brought to an end only when a largely non-Yugoslav party leadership was appointed by the Comintern. As many Yugoslav Communists saw it, Bolshevization was a catastrophe for their own interests.

THE CROATIAN PEASANT PARTY
IN YUGOSLAV POLITICS

After the Bulgarian Agrarian Union, the second major peasant political party to draw the attention of the Comintern had been the Croatian Peasant Party. It was especially galling to the Comintern that Radić had used his flirtation with it only as a means for forcing compromise at home. Members of the Croatian Peasant Party participated in every coalition government from July 18, 1925, to February 1, 1927, but Stjepan Radić and the majority of the Party passed back to their more customary role of opposition with the formation of the Užonović cabinet on April 8, 1926.[1] Because of Radić's "betrayal" in 1925, the Comintern no longer considered him or his party a suitable ally, but it still hoped to cultivate the seeds of dissension which Radić sowed in his wake.

On the face of it, the weaknesses of the new Yugoslav state which were most useful to the Communist cause were not economic but political and social. While most Yugoslavs were akin in language, the separate historic provinces had quite different political, social, and economic traditions. In particular, Croatia provided one of the most striking examples of regional nationalism in Eastern Europe.[2] As a Catholic province which claimed a thousand years of proud history, as well as privileged position in the former Austro-Hungarian Empire, Croatia, or her intelligentsia, resisted absorption by the crude and orthodox Serbian state.

In 1919 there were also pronounced differences among the historic provinces in economic structure. With the exception of a few urban enclaves, Yugoslavia was barely touched by industrialization as late as 1931. A little more than 10 percent of the population were employed or supported by industry.[3] In the "northern areas," Slovenia, the Vojvodina, and Croatia and Slavonia, economic development had begun earlier and had proceeded at a somewhat faster rate than in the other provinces.[4] South of the Sava and Danube rivers economic development was very slow and peasant subsistence agriculture was the rule.[5] Even in agriculture Yugoslavia was extremely backward. Bosnia, Herzegovina, and Macedonia were still in the

[1] The composition of these cabinets is listed in Gilbert In der Maur, *Der Weg zur Nation*, Vol. III of his *Die Jugoslawien einst und jetzt* (Berlin, 1936–38), pp. 186, 226, 248, 259.

[2] Hugh Seton-Watson, *Eastern Europe Between the Wars* (Cambridge, 1946), p. 153.

[3] Jozo Tomasevich, *Peasants, Politics, and Economic Change in Yugoslavia* (Stanford, 1955), p. 172.

[4] *Ibid.*, pp. 171–72.

[5] *Ibid.*, p. 212.

grip of a semifeudal form of land tenure in 1918.[6] The former provinces of Montenegro, Herzegovina, Dalmatia, and southern Croatia and Slavonia were acutely afflicted with rural overpopulation and were described as "passive regions," that is, areas which were unable to feed their population because of an inadequacy of land and capital resources.[7] The situation was only somewhat less desperate in the other provinces with the striking exception of the Vojvodina, which produced an agricultural surplus.[8] Throughout Yugoslavia the techniques of cultivation remained extraordinarily primitive.[9]

As in most of Eastern Europe, the agrarian reform proved to be only a temporary palliative.[10] Of all the Balkan states, Yugoslavia remained the one most afflicted with rural overpopulation in the interwar period (see Table 12).

In spite of these pressing problems in agriculture, the Croatian Peasant Party paid little attention to the question of land reform or the peasants' economic interests.[11] This may have been because after 1919 the Party became the refuge and home of the Croatian intellectuals, who were far more concerned with national self-determination for Croatia.[12] The primary goal of the Party after World War I was the establishment of a Croatian state within a Yugoslav federation, a state which would "embrace all the lands to which the Croatians were entitled" and which would be "less of a state and more of a homeland or alliance of peasant households." [13]

[6] Ibid., p. 160.
[7] Ibid., pp. 322–23.
[8] Ibid., pp. 321, 324.
[9] Ibid., pp. 211, 335.
[10] Ibid., pp. 381–82.
[11] Robert G. Livingstone, "Stjepan Radić and the Croatian Peasant Party, 1904–1929" (unpublished Ph.D. dissertation Department of History, Harvard University, 1959), p. 208.
[12] Maček writes: "Relatively few educated professionals belonged to the Croatian Peasant Party before the war. Now after the war many young men who had just finished their academic studies joined us." Vladko Maček, In the Struggle for Freedom (New York, 1957), pp. 80–81. This seems to have been a cumulative process, for Livingstone wrote: "By 1927 the HSS [Croatian Peasant Party] was more or less a nationalistic party run by the urban bourgeoisie. But its prestige in the Croatian villages was still as great as ever." Livingstone, p. 558.
[13] Livingstone, pp. 347–59.

Table 12
Surplus Population in Yugoslavia

Country	1921 [a]	1931 [a]	1930 [b]	1937 [c]
Yugoslavia	41	43	38.8	35
Bulgaria	27	31	35.7	28
Rumania	25	15	23.1	20

[a] Jozo Tomasevich, *Peasants, Politics, and Economic Change in Yugoslavia* (Stanford, 1955), p. 316. Tomasevich calculates surplus agricultural population by simply relating rural population to land resources.

[b] Wilbert E. Moore, *Economic Demography of Eastern and Southern Europe* (Geneva, 1945), pp. 71–72.

[c] Rosenstein-Rodan as quoted in Nicholas Spulber, *The Economics of Communist Eastern Europe* (New York, 1957), pp. 275–76. For a comparison of the methods used by Rosenstein-Rodan and Moore see Table 6, note *a*.

Once in a position of political power, Radić apparently did very little for the peasant and would appear to have indulged in graft and to have concentrated on the expansion of his party organization into other parts of Yugoslavia.[14] At the same time, Radić drifted toward violent and irresponsible attacks on the political parties. Livingstone in his authoritative study of Radić writes: "His career of opposition had not prepared him for the sacrifice and compromise required to put through the social program to which he was dedicated." [15]

Yugoslav democracy, with the help of Radić, soon began to suffer from the same malady as Polish democracy, a succession of weak, coalition cabinets and interminable parliamentary debates on irrelevant issues. By March, 1928 the parliamentary machinery had come to a complete standstill, and the assassination of Radić in the Skupština in June only served to dramatize the failure of democracy to function successfully in Yugoslavia.[16] A last and unsuccessful attempt was made by the king to win Croatian support for parlia-

[14] *Ibid.*, pp. 541, 543, 554.

[15] *Ibid.*, p. 556. On the other hand, Radić's wild attacks on other political leaders earned him the reputation of a tribune of the people. Even the Montenegrin Communist, Milovan Djilas, wrote: "To ordinary people, who were not infected with partisan passions, Radić, though only the leader of the Croatian peasantry, appeared as the vigilant conscience of the entire country." Milovan Djilas, *Land Without Justice* (New York, 1958), p. 317.

[16] As Djilas put it: "The shooting in Parliament turned Radić into a martyr for liberty in the eyes of all honest people. But it also buried Parliament morally." Djilas, p. 317.

mentary government,[17] and on January 6, 1929, the royal dictatorship was announced. True to its traditions, the Croatian Peasant Party refused to condone revolutionary methods of opposition to the new dictator.

On the surface it would seem, under these circumstances, that the CPY would experience little difficulty in successfully applying the agrarian theses of the Comintern and taking over the role the Croatian Peasant Party had relinquished. Although Lenin's typology of the strata within the peasantry and his special tactics with regard to countries with "vestiges" of serfdom did not apply, there was a place in Yugoslavia for a party which would support the social and economic demands of the peasants and lead them out of a subsistence economy. The CPY might have taken that place if it had agreed with the Comintern that Communists should give unqualified support to the demands of national minorities and the poor peasants. But it did not.

THE COMINTERN, RADIĆ, AND THE YUGOSLAV COMMUNIST PARTY

In 1920 the CPY claimed to have as many as 80,000 members, and in the election of that year it garnered 12.4 percent of the popular vote and won fifty-eight seats in the Skupština.[18] The electoral statistics reveal that the Communists received very strong support among the national minorities in underdeveloped Macedonia and Montenegro and much more modest support in their home territory, Serbia, and the most industrialized province in Yugoslavia, Slovenia. The Party received very few votes in Radić's province, Croatia, or in Moslem Bosnia and Herzegovina. In August, 1921, the Party was declared illegal. By 1926 membership in the Party was down to 2,300 and the pro-Communist list received only 1.8 percent of the popular votes in elections of the following year.[19] By 1932 membership had dropped to 200. The Party had proved unable

[17] On January 4 and 5 King Alexander called Maček and Pribičević to the palace, but Maček demanded something similar to dominion status for Croatia before he would bring his party back into the Skupština. Maček, pp. 121–23.

[18] Branko Lazić, *Les Partis communistes d'Europe, 1919–1955* (Paris, 1956), pp. 149–50. For a detailed analysis of the voting in the 1920 elections see R. V. Burks, *The Dynamics of Communism*, pp. 78–79, 102, 226.

[19] The figure for Party members in 1926 is from *Istoriia Iugoslavii*, ed. by L. B. Valev, G. M. Slavin, and I. I. Udal'tsov (Moscow, 1963), II, 96. The other figures are from Lazić, pp. 149–50.

to exploit its initial popularity, so clearly revealed in the elections of 1920.

Even taking into account the handicaps that illegality imposed, it is difficult to understand how a political party could be so unsuccessful. In 1948 Josip Broz Tito, describing the history of the Party, gave several reasons for its weakness during these years.

[As a result of the] erroneous stand of the CPY leadership of that time (1920-1928) as regards the national and peasant question, the working class remained isolated from the strong peasant movement, not only in Croatia, that is from the masses in Croatia, but in other regions as well. The leaders of the CPY of that time had a completely negative Social Democratic attitude towards the peasant movement which at the same time represented the struggle of the Croatian and other peoples for equality. They even ridiculed this movement which would have been a powerful ally of the working class in its struggle against the bourgeoisie, if they had the correct line at that time regarding this question as well as the others.[20]

Tito also listed other shortcomings: the weaknesses of the Party leaders, the inability to adapt to illegal activities, and the absence of a genuine revolutionary ideology. But Tito neglected to point out that supporting Radić was a hazardous venture and that in many respects the specific directives of the Comintern to the CPY often served to weaken that party and made it extremely difficult for it to apply Comintern agrarian tactics successfully.

The difficulties were twofold. On the one hand, the CPY was formed out of the Social Democratic parties of all the separate provinces, but the former members of the Serbian Social Democratic Party were the dominant element, and that party had a strong tradition against alliance with any part of the peasantry or its parties, a tradition which militated against Comintern decrees.[21] The first Politburo was composed exclusively of Serbs,[22] who were unlikely to support peasant parties at all, let alone one like Radić's which called for greater Croatian autonomy. In the second place, as

[20] Josip Broz Tito, *Political Report of the Central Committee of the Communist Party of Yugoslavia* (Belgrade, 1948), pp. 23–24.

[21] *Istoriia mezhdunarodnogo rabochego i natsional'no osvoboditel'nogo dvizhenia* (Moscow, 1958–62), I, 400. Burks points out that the Serbs from Serbia were reinforced by the *prečani,* or Serbs from the provinces. Burks, p. 107.

[22] Branko Lazič, *Tito et la révolution yougoslave* (Paris, 1957), p. 10.

Burks points out, when the CPY was driven underground it tended to divide into two factions, the right wing, composed mainly of Serbs from Serbia, and the left wing, composed mainly of the other nationalities.[23] Moscow strove to heal the breach between the left and the right, but at the same time demanded conformity to the Comintern program on the national and agrarian questions, which were two of the major issues dividing the Party.

The Comintern criticized the position of the CPY after the poor showing of its legal front party, the Independent Worker's Party, in the elections of March, 1923.[24] At the Third National Party Conference in December, 1923, the left wing in the CPY gained control and adopted a program on the agrarian question close to that of the Comintern,[25] calling for the expropriation of large estates and state lands and the redistribution of part of these lands to the poor peasants, for the administration of food and credit programs by committees of poor peasants, for state aid to the "passive" agricultural regions, and for the elimination of taxes and rents paid by the peasants.[26] Also, for the first time in its history the CPY formally acknowledged that Yugoslavia was a multinational state. The newly dominant position of the left faction in the party did not bring stability, however.[27] It was only the beginning of a "factionalism"

[23] Burks, p. 109. Burks's informant is a former member of the left wing in the Central Committee of the CPY, Anton Ciliga.

[24] For legal work the CPY organized the Independent Workers' Party of Yugoslavia in January, 1923. *Istoriia Iugoslavii*, II, 72. It was declared illegal in July, 1924. *Istoriia mezhdunarodnogo rabochego*, II, 272.

[25] Suzanne Sommes Williams, "The Communist Party of Yugoslavia and the Nationality Problem" (unpublished Master's thesis, Department of Public Law and Government, Columbia University, 1955), pp. 27–28.

[26] Herzegovina, Southern Bosnia, and Dalmatia were specifically named as passive regions. Williams, p. 27, n. 4.

[27] The CPY began its schismatic syndrome in the spring and summer of 1921 when the Party went underground. The left opposition took shape at the first illegal plenum of the Central Committee, which met in April, 1921. At the First National Party Conference in Vienna in July, 1922, the Comintern demanded that ten members of the left be coopted into the Central Committee in order to prevent a complete split. The most Prominent leaders of the left were Živko Jovanović, Triša Kaclerović, Kosta Novaković, Moša Pijade, and Raiko Jovanović. At an illegal plenum in Belgrade in December, 1922, it was decided to establish a legal front party, which proved to be dominated by the right. At the Second National Party Conference in Vienna in May, 1923, however, the left took over the regular Party leadership and elected Kaclerović secretary of the Central Committee. This was really a

which would prove to be the Party's most dangerous weakness between 1923 and 1929.

The right faction, like its counterparts in the rest of Eastern Europe, saw its future in terms of a return to legality, electoral struggle, and a slow accumulation of strength while the bourgeois-democratic revolution was brought to completion. There was more than a trace of Serbian nationalism in the reluctance of the right to support the "national-liberation" struggles of the minorities in Yugoslavia. The right only grudgingly admitted that there were national minorities in Yugoslavia, and it regarded the creation of the Yugoslav state as a positive achievement. In 1924 there was a right faction led by Života Milojković, who had a strong following among the workers of Belgrade. Milojković believed that cooperation with Radić would be a betrayal of Marxism since Radić's party represented the Croatian bourgeoisie, and that the first task of the CPY was to recover legal status.[28] A somewhat different stand was adopted by Dr. Sima Marković, the acknowledged leader of the right and a professor of mathematics in Belgrade. Marković maintained that alliance with Radić was desirable, but at some time in the distant future.[29] In the first place, Marković doubted that the national question could be solved by separate workers' and peasants' governments, if only because the CPY was too weak to create them. It was the duty of the Party to return to legal work and recruit a mass following while the other political parties completed the bourgeois revolution, in the course of which the national question would be solved by "constitutional revision on the basis of full democracy and far reaching regional autonomy." [30] In other words, first things must come first and a bourgeois revolution had to precede the workers' and peasants' revolution.[31]

Pyrrhic victory. It was possible only because of the arrest and imprisonment of most of the prominent Party members, who also happened to be members of the right faction. At the Third National Party Conference in December, 1923, the left again awarded themselves most of the top Party posts, but factionalism continued unabated. Jovan Marjanović, *Potsetnik iz istorije Kommunističke Partije Jugoslavije, 1919–1941* (Belgrade, 1953), pp. 21–33.

[28] Williams, p. 36.
[29] *Ibid.*, p. 49.
[30] *Ibid.*, pp. 39, 42.
[31] *Ibid.*, p. 79.

Marković recognized the legitimacy only of Croat and Slovene aspirations for federal autonomy. But he argued that even here the bourgeois parties representing the Serbs, Croats, and Slovenes would be able to hammer out a satisfactory compromise.[32] Because the national question was the concern of those trying to complete the bourgeois revolution, it was therefore a bourgeois question and of little importance to a Communist party. Marković was impatient with those who would put the national question in the foreground. The problem would no longer exist, he said, when Yugoslavia was ready for a proletarian revolution, and excessive preoccupation with it before then only diverted Communists from their real tasks of preparing for the proletarian revolution. Marković's attitude toward the national question led him to the conclusion that alliance with Radić's party would be desirable and possible only after the bourgeois revolution, when, providing all the demands of the Croatian Peasant Party were not satisfied, the CPY could use him without the danger of being itself absorbed.[33] In effect this meant that for the time being Marković opposed both Comintern policy on the national question and alliance with Radić because such a course would endanger the Communist Party's popularity with Serbs and all others who supported the new Yugoslav state.

One of the difficulties was that, in spite of its avowed indifference to large membership lists, the Comintern was more impressed with the Croatian Peasant Party as a potential revolutionary force than it was with the CPY. As early as the Fourth Congress in November, 1922, the Comintern had designated Yugoslavia as one of those countries in which a workers' and peasants' government was possible.[34] After Zinoviev's rebuke of the Yugoslav Party at the Third Enlarged Plenum of the ECCI in June, 1923,[35] and the victory of the left in December, one would assume complete con-

---

[32] *Ibid.*, p. 7.

[33] *Ibid.*, p. 49.

[34] See Radek's speech at the Fourth Comintern Congress, *IV vsemirnyi kongress Kommunisticheskogo Internatsionala—5 noiabria–3 dekabria, 1922—izbrannye doklady, rechi i rezoliutsii* (Moscow, 1923), p. 137; and the resolutions on "workers' and peasants' government," Bela Kun, ed., *Kommunisticheskii Internatsional v dokumentakh, 1919–1932* (Moscow, 1933), p. 302.

[35] *Rasshirennyi plenum ispolnitel'nogo komiteta Kommunisticheskogo Internatsionala (12–23 iunia 1923 goda)* (Moscow, 1923), p. 33.

formity to Comintern decrees. Although Yugoslavia received no attention at the First International Peasant Conference in October, 1923, at which the Yugoslavs were not even represented, by the time of the Fifth Comintern Congress in June, 1924, Zinoviev's schemes for a Balkan revolution were maturing and the negotiations with Radić were in the center of the stage. Kolarov, giving the major report on the agrarian question at the Fifth Comintern Congress, referred pointedly to the Croatian Peasant Party.

For example, the united front is possible and necessary with the Bulgarian Agrarian Union, in which the masses, to a large degree, are already revolutionary. They want to go with the workers against the bourgeoisie and to fight for the seizure of power by revolutionary means.

The same solution to the question is possible with regard to the Croatian Republican Peasant Party, the Farmer Labor Party in the United States, and others.[36]

The resolutions of the Fifth Comintern Congress on the nationality question signaled the beginning of a major campaign to win over both the peasant political parties and the national liberation movements everywhere in Eastern Europe.

The importance of the struggle against national oppression is still further increased by the fact that the oppressed nationalities in Poland, Czechoslovakia, Yugoslavia, Rumania, and Greece are largely peasants in their social composition, and the struggle for national liberation is at the same time the struggle of the peasant masses against foreign landlords and capitalists.

In view of these facts, the Communist parties of Central Europe and the Balkans are confronted with the task of lending full support to the national revolutionary movements of the oppressed nationalities.[37]

In the resolutions, Czechoslovakia, Poland, and the Balkan countries are specifically mentioned as countries where a workers' and peasants' revolution was still possible in spite of the stabilization which had set in elsewhere.

Although the new leftist leadership in the Yugoslav Party under the direction of Triša Kaclerović anticipated Comintern decrees in its resolutions in December, 1923, it did not succeed in translating

[36] Piatyi vsemirnyi kongress Kommunisticheskogo Internatsionala—(18 iunia–8 iulia 1924 goda)—stenograficheskii otchet (Moscow, 1925), I, 755.
[37] Ibid., II, 123.

these resolutions into action. The debate between the right and the left continued in the Party journals. The chief subject of debate was the imperfect coalition with Radić. The right faction in the Party, in a statement of its position in October, 1924, said, "The Marxist proletariat will support only that peasant party which has an exclusively anticapitalist character and which exhibits revolutionary and progressive tendencies." [38] Radić did little to endear himself to his would-be allies among the left faction in the Party. He consistently ignored the Communists in spite of his membership in the Krestintern.

When the share of the popular vote won by the CPY remained minute in the elections of 1925 and when factionalism appeared to be as strong as ever in the Central Committee of the Party, the Comintern decided to bring all the problems of the Party before the Fifth Enlarged Plenum of its Executive Committee.[39] In his keynote address before that body, Zinoviev still clung to his faith in the possibility of revolution in the Balkans, pointing out three factors making revolution possible—the peasant movement, the national liberation movement, and the workers' movement.[40] Boshkovich attributed the failures of the CPY in the elections of 1925 to the machinations of the deposed "right deviation."

Until now the Communist Party of Yugoslavia has been equivocal in its position on the peasant question. Thus, recently the right opposition [Milojković's group] left the Party, explaining their departure by the fact that the Party turned to Radić with a proposal for a united front. Because in the Balkans the industrial proletariat forms only a narrow stratum, the chief reserves of the revolution are the peasants and oppressed nationalities. The right deviation was fatal. The bourgeoisie exploited our errors in the elections of February 8, 1925, and attracted most of the peasants to their side.[41]

Kolarov, in his report on the findings of the special Commission

[38] B. Boshkovich, "Polozhenie v Kompartii Iugoslavii," *Kommunisticheskii Internatsional*, No. 4 (1925), p. 58.

[39] The share of the popular vote obtained by the CPY and its front parties declined from 12.4 percent in 1920 to .7 percent in 1925 and rose to 1.8 percent in 1927. Lazić, *Les Partis communistes*, p. 150.

[40] *Rasshirennyi plenum ispolkoma Kommunisticheskogo Internatsionala—protokoly zasedanii (21 marta—6 aprelia, 1925)* (Moscow, 1925), p. 48.

[41] *Ibid.*, p. 335.

on the Question of the Yugoslav Party, indicted the right but accused the whole Party of a failure to reject its Social Democratic heritage and accept the new techniques and goals of the Communist movement.[42] The right was wrong in its unwillingness to support the peasant and national liberation movements and the left was wrong in not trying to draw the right back into the Party. Kolarov pointed out that the Balkans were the one area in Europe where stabilization had not yet set in, explaining that this was because the agrarian and national questions had not been resolved there.[43] On the position of the right on the agrarian question, Kolarov commented:

In the third place, there are deviations in the peasant question. Here we have already observed the lack of comprehension of the role and significance of the peasant movement in the revolutionary epoch, for example, in the assertion that existing peasant organizations are none other than bourgeois organizations with which we should have no relations. When the question of a workers' and peasants' bloc was posed at the last election, those comrades of an oppositional state of mind advanced against this slogan. It is clear that we are dealing here with Social Democratic survivals. Such also is the assertion that the slogan "workers' and peasants' government" has only a propagandistic, and not a political, character, that is, the assertion that the slogan does not have as its object the mobilization of the masses. Finally, the refusal of the Party to conduct a policy of a workers' and peasants' bloc with the Peasant Union of Serbia under the presupposition that this union is monarchistic belongs in the same category. All this shows to what degree the character and role of peasant movements is not yet clear to the Yugoslav Party.[44]

Characteristically, Stalin did not speak at the Fifth Plenum, but he played an active role in the committee on the Yugoslav question, where an acrimonious debate broke out between him and Marković. Marković slyly based his arguments on Stalin's famous article on the national question in 1912. Stalin accused Marković of misunderstanding the article and took issue with Marković's assertion that the national question was only a constitutional problem which could be solved by a bourgeois government.[45] While maintaining that the na-

[42] Ibid., pp. 473–75.
[43] Ibid., p. 475.
[44] Ibid., pp. 475–76.
[45] This speech was delivered at the Committee on the Yugoslav Question of the ECCI on March 30, 1925. It was first published in Bol'shevik on April

tional question and the agrarian question were not identical, Stalin asserted that the national question was essentially a peasant question and that underestimation of the former led to underestimation of the role of the peasant in revolution.[46]

But it is also beyond doubt that, after all, the peasant question is the basis, the quintessence, of the national question. This can be seen precisely in the fact that the peasant provides the main army of the national movement; there is no powerful national movement without the peasant army nor can there be. This is exactly what they have in mind when they say that the national question is a peasant question. I think that in Semich's [Marković's] rejection of this formula is manifest an underestimation of the strength of the national movement and a lack of understanding of the deeply popular, deeply revolutionary character of the national movement. This lack of understanding and this underestimation of the internal potential strength of the Croatian movement for national liberation is pregnant with serious complications for the whole Yugoslav Communist Party.[47]

Stalin concluded that "the point of departure for a program on the national question must be the creation of a Soviet revolution in Yugoslavia. Without this, the overthrow of the bourgeoisie and the victory of the revolution, the national question cannot in any way be solved satisfactorily." [48]

The argument between Stalin and Marković continued after the plenum. Marković attempted a compromise with Stalin's point of view and Stalin provided a ponderous rejection of the proferred olive branch. The exchange was published in the June issue of *Bol'shevik* in 1925. Marković's line of reasoning and Stalin's reply were based primarily on doctrinal analyses of the writings of Lenin and Marx, rather than on a concrete analysis of conditions in Yugoslavia. Naturally it was Stalin's updated views of 1925 (not his views of 1912) on the national and peasant questions which finally prevailed.

The Fifth Plenum warned the CPY that it could not be victorious unless it "attracted the broad masses of the peasantry to the active

15, 1925. I have used I. V. Stalin, "K natsional'nomu voprosu v Iugoslavii," *Sochineniia* (Moscow, 1946–51), VII, 69–70.

[46] *Ibid.*, p. 71.
[47] *Ibid.*, p. 73.
[48] *Ibid.*, p. 74.

struggle against the monarchy, against Serb imperialism and capitalism." [49] The Party was warned to make the union of the proletariat and peasantry the basic goal of its activity. In concrete terms the Party was told to concentrate on the real needs of the peasants, to join in the struggle against the vestiges of feudalism, to support agrarian reforms and the lowering of taxes.[50] The resolution pointedly referred to the Party's indifference to the national question, indicating that this was why the peasants flocked to the "petty-bourgeois national parties" at the expense of the Party.[51]

The Comintern resolutions clearly called for the formaton of a bloc with the Croatian Peasant Party and, under certain conditions (particularly during election campaigns), with the Serbian Peasant Party.

> The slogan "workers' and peasants' government" is not purely a propagandistic slogan, it is a slogan of mass agitation and political mobilization. It is especially applicable in this sense to the Balkan states, in particular to Yugoslavia. The struggle of the Communist Party under this slogan under certain conditions can lead to the formation of a workers' and peasants' bloc.
>
> This bloc must always be a real bloc of struggle which has as its goal not only cooperation at the top but also mutual mass action on one or several questions on the basis of a general program of action. Thus this kind of bloc can be concluded only with those peasant organizations or groups that are ready to struggle actively for definite and substantial goals common to proletariat and peasantry. This by no means signifies that our comrades from the opposition may demand as a fixed condition that such a peasant party must in all cases without exception bear an anticapitalist character.[52]

The resolutions expressly condemned the view that because the leaders of the Croatian Peasant Party were members of the "bourgeois intelligentsia" this automatically excluded the possibility of a united front from above with them. The decisive fact, according to the resolutions, was that the radical peasant parties, at least partially and implicitly, represented a movement against landowners and capitalists.[53] The resolutions stated that "in so far as

[49] *Rasshirennyi plenum, 1925,* p. 597.
[50] *Ibid.,* p. 598.
[51] *Ibid.,* p. 599.
[52] *Ibid.,* p. 600.
[53] *Ibid.,* p. 599.

the Croatian Peasant Party actually tries to fulfill its primary platform, its work moves fundamentally in a progressive direction." [54] The Comintern indicated, however, that the CPY might experience some difficulty in keeping the Serbian Peasant Party moving in a "progressive direction." It might even be necessary to split the Serbian Peasant Party and form a new left peasant union which would then unite with the CPY to form a workers' and peasants' bloc "like that formed with the Croatian Peasant Party." [55]

One small concession was made to Marković's point of view. The Comintern admitted that "under certain conditions it might prove to be difficult for the Yugoslav Communist Party to preserve its political and organizational independence in a bloc with its strong peasant allies." [56] The Comintern, however, offered no real solution to this problem other than the statement that the Communist Party must "try" to "take into its own hands the leadership of any workers' and peasants' bloc." On the surface the resolution appears to be a masterpiece of inconsistency. It asserts on the one hand that "a policy of dependence or hanging on the coattails of the workers' and peasants' bloc will lead the Party to destruction," while on the other hand it maintains that "it would be too much to go to the primitive conclusion that inasmuch as we have not acquired direct and decisive leadership we will not cooperate with the workers' and peasants' bloc." [57] What is meant is that the CPY should lie in wait for the opportunity to seize control of the workers' and peasants bloc.

While an alliance with the peasant parties was virtually decreed by the Comintern, the resolutions called upon the CPY to subject the ideology of its allies, the peasant parties, to constant criticism. "In this respect one should subject to criticism, not so much the features of the program which reflect the petty-bourgeois ideology of a given peasant organization, as its wavering and halfheartedness in the cause or struggle." [58] To be more concrete, the resolutions referred to Radić's acceptance of the Vidovdan Constitution on

54 *Ibid.*
55 *Ibid.*, p. 600.
56 *Ibid.*, p. 601.
57 *Ibid.*
58 *Ibid.*, p. 602.

March 27, 1925, as a betrayal of the ideals of his party, a betrayal, however, which apparently did not at once alter the attitude of the Comintern toward the Croatian Peasant Party. In short, the Comintern wanted all sorts of mutually incompatible things, an alliance in which the CPY, though the weaker partner, controlled policy, retained its autonomy, and could criticize its allies without weakening the alliance itself. This was asking for quite a bit of tolerance from the peasant ally.

Comintern resolutions apparently did not evoke an immediate response from the CPY. In April, 1926, the Presidium of the ECCI adopted a resolution stating that the Yugoslav Party had taken no steps toward the fulfillment of the resolutions of a year before.[59] At the proposal of the Comintern, and as a means of achieving unity, Marković was appointed secretary of the Party at the Third Party Congress in May in Vienna and all of the Comintern's resolutions from the Fifth Plenum were adopted unanimously.[60] Apparently the whole Party, including Marković, accepted the criticism of the Comintern. The elevation of Marković was, on the one hand, a sign that he had recanted and, on the other, a sign that the Comintern was vitally interested in strengthening the CPY and reuniting its factions.

With reference to the peasant question, the Congress can state that the Party has finally adopted a Leninist course in its relations with the peasant movement. The leaders of the opposition were liberated from their deviations in the peasant question. Thus the CPY has surmounted the chief barrier between it and Bolshevism.[61]

Presumably the CPY was now ready to cope with peasantism in Yugoslav politics. At the elections in September, 1927, while

[59] Lazić, *Tito et la révolution yougoslave,* p. 14. Although Yugoslavia was clearly a peasant country, by 1925 the CPY, was still primarily urban. Sixty-eight percent of its members were workers and 24 percent were peasants. V. Ognianovich, "Chastichnaia stabilizatsiia v Iugoslavii i zadachi Kommunisticheskoi Partii," *Kommunisticheskii Internatsional,* No. 5 (April, 1926), p. 142. But the Comintern letter dispatched in April, 1926, indicated that most members of the CPY were connected with small-scale production and that this was the foundation of "individualistic deviations." Boshkovich, *Kommunisticheskii Internatsional,* No. 17 (April 27, 1928), p. 45.

[60] Marjanović, p. 35.

[61] B. Boshkovich, "III s'ezd K. P. Iu.," *Kommunisticheskii Internatsional,* No. 1 (Sept. 15, 1926), p. 40.

the Croatian Peasant Party lost almost one third of the popular vote it had received in 1925 (it lost 165,000 votes), the Communist Party gained, receiving 42,866 votes in 1927 as compared to 18,439 in 1925. The most remarkable gains for the Communists were in the former strongholds of the Croatian Peasant Party, in Croatia and the Vojvodina,[62] two of the richer provinces in the Yugoslav state, suggesting that the rural poor were probably not the source of Communist strength. These provinces, however, were the home of a strong sentiment for national self-determination.[63] Although the resolutions of the Fifth Plenum were still in force, there was no evidence of a united front from above, and the CPY's success in Croatia lay simply in weaning away some of the disillusioned peasants from the Croatian Peasant Party.

The very modest successes of the CPY in the elections of 1927 were not enough to appease the Comintern, for factionalism was still rife in the Party. In May, 1928, the ECCI sent an open letter to all members of the CPY calling upon the rank and file to end factionalism in the upper reaches of the Party hierarchy.[64] The Party was accused of inadequacy in using the "treason of Radić" to create a union of workers and peasants in Yugoslavia.[65] According to the Comintern, the Party had virtually split along national lines and, as a result of the constant infighting, the membership was not more than 3,000.[66] Members were urged to hold a new Party congress before the organization degenerated into a debating club, to elimi-

[62] In Croatia the number of votes received by the Communist list increased from 2,714 in 1925 to 12,606 in 1927, in Vojvodina from 1,540 in 1925 to 8,172 in 1927. Boshkovich, *Kommunisticheskii Internatsional,* No. 17 (April 27, 1928), p. 45.

[63] Burks points out that the Social Democratic Party of the Vojvodina, which entered the CYP was primarily Magyar in composition. Burks, pp. 107–8.

[64] This open letter is reproduced in full in *Kongresi i zemaljske konferentsije KPJ, 1919–37,* Tom II: *Istorijski Arhiv Koministićke Partije Jugoslavije* (Belgrade, 1950), pp. 442–52. According to Ciliga, a member of the left faction of the CPY who had been exiled to Moscow, the left faction of the Party in Yugoslavia had rebelled in 1927 and overthrown the right leadership established in 1926, but the Comintern refused to accept the change. Anton Ciliga, *Au pays du mensonge déconcertant,* Vol. I, of his *Dix ans derrière le rideau de fer* (Paris, 1950), p. 28.

[65] *Kongresi i zemaljske konferentsije KPJ, 1919–37,* p. 447.

[66] *Ibid.*

nate the intellectuals of both right and left, and to elect a genuine working-class executive committee.[67]

According to recent official histories, an antifaction faction emerged, among other places, in Croatia, under Djuro Djaković and the secretary of the Zagreb Party organization, Josip Broz Tito.[68] This group's request for Comintern intervention to end factionalism is said to have inspired a critical open letter from the Comintern. As Burks points out, the year 1928 marked the end of Serbian hegemony in the Party.[69] A new leadership was to be created drawn from representatives of the other nationalities and non-Yugoslav Comintern functionaries. The Fourth Congress of the CPY met in Dresden in October, 1928, and was supervised by the Italian Communist Ercoli (Togliatti), as the personal representative of the ECCI.[70] The old leaders of both factions were excluded from the Central Committee and a new "leftist" leadership which had been trained in Moscow was installed. The new secretary of the Central Committee was Djuro Djaković (known under the pseudonym Bosnić). According to several sources, Djaković, though resented by the former Party leaders, was, as a member of neither the right nor the left faction, admirably suited to the task of giving the Party a new course.[71] There was nothing academic or doctrinaire about Djaković's background and he was not a Serb. He had been born in a Croatian peasant family in 1886 and had acquired extensive experience in practical party work in the old Social Democratic Party of Bosnia and Herzegovina, in trade unions, and finally as a Communist delegate to the Skupština in 1920.[72]

[67] *Ibid.*, p. 452. The portion of the letter containing this last Comintern demand was the only portion reproduced for the benefit of readers of the official Comintern organ. Boshkovich, *Kommunisticheskii Internatsional*, No. 17 (April 27, 1928), p. 47.

[68] Marjanović, p. 35. *Istoriia Iugoslavii*, II, 106.

[69] Burks, p. 115.

[70] Marjanović indicates that the Party voted to exclude Marković, but that Ercoli, apparently in order to prevent further rifts, intervened in his favor. Marjanović, p. 39.

[71] Even one anti-Soviet source has a kind word for Djaković. According to Ciliga, the new leaders sent down by Moscow were "adventurers from five continents," but Djaković was "one of the few honest workers" sent by Moscow to take over the Party. Ciliga, p. 28.

[72] Iu. Pisarev, "Velikaia oktiabr'skaia sotsialisticheskaia revoliutsiia i revoliutsionnaia bor'ba narodov Iugoslavii v 1917–1920 gg.," in A. Ia. Manuse-

At the Fourth Congress the Party resolutions on the agrarian question followed the patterns established at the Fifth Plenum of the ECCI, but, foreshadowing the trend of the subsequent Sixth Comintern Congress, they were given a leftist slant. The CPY resolved, on the one hand, to adopt propaganda slogans calling for distribution of food to the peasants, a diminution of taxes, and cancellation of debts, but, on the other hand, the Party vowed to win the peasants over to the struggle (said to have direct political significance to peasants) against trusts and monopolies, high prices, war, the white terror, and fascism.[73] The Party specified that peasant committees were the best organizational form for the development of the peasants' movement. It also recommended that joint workers' and peasants' committees of action be established as embryonic workers' and peasants' soviets.

The slogan "create workers' and peasants' committees" must be advanced in opposition to the bourgeois slogan of a Croatian Sabor (Parliament). In the process of revolutionary struggle, these workers' and peasants' committees must sharpen their slogans even more, generalizing them into confiscation of the land of large-scale property owners, into the slogan of workers' and peasants' government (synonym for democratic dictatorship of the proletariat and peasantry).[74]

In contrast to the policy of 1926, the united front from above was specifically repudiated.

The Party is also obligated energetically to expose the conciliatory policy of the bourgeoisie of oppressed nations, in particular the policy of the bourgeois peasant-democratic coalition (Maček-Pribićević), to criticize mercilessly the tactics adopted by them, and to advance decisively against all illusions with regard to the revolutionary will of the leaders of the peasant-democratic coalition.[75]

This concentration upon the potentialities of revolution in Yugoslavia was reinforced by the assassination of Radić in June, 1928. At the Sixth Comintern Congress in that month a delegate from Yugo-

---

vich, ed., *Oktiabr'skaia revoliutsiia i zarubezhnye slavianskie narody* (Moscow, 1957), p. 356, n. 2.

[73] B. Boshkovich, "IV s'ezd K. P. Iu.," *Kommunisticheskii Internatsional*, No. 4 (Jan. 25, 1929), p. 43.

[74] *Ibid.*, p. 44.

[75] *Ibid.*

slavia declared that, as a result of imperialistic intervention of which the assassination was a manifestation, "a great peasant and national revolutionary movement has been born in Yugoslavia" which the CPY, after its Fourth Congress, was in a position to exploit.[76] Kolarov, speaking for the Bulgarian Communist Party at the Sixth Comintern Congress, was even more specific about the new opportunities before the CPY.

The fact that it took only a few revolver shots in the Parliament at Belgrade to destroy all that has been done to unify and strengthen the young Yugoslav state demonstrates the profound crisis in Yugoslavia. The conflict between the Serb bourgeoisie, who are trying to dominate the whole country, and the peasant masses and the oppressed nationalities has not only not been resolved but is, on the contrary, deepening. All events seem to indicate that the bourgeoisie cannot resolve this conflict and eliminate the permanent crisis flowing from it and that Yugoslavia is the Balkan state which faces the severest political and institutional crisis; it is the Balkan state which stands closest to catastrophe.[77]

The attempts of the CPY to exploit the chaotic political situation without allying itself to the political parties of the opposition did not, however, have any apparent success. An example of the state of mind of the Party is found in an article by a member of its Control Commission, Milan Gorkich (real name Yosip Chizinski). In April, 1929, Gorkich, who was destined to become secretary general of the Party three years later, drew an analogy between Radić's party and the Kuomintang. Gorkich maintained that Radić's party had joined the Krestintern in 1924 for the same reasons that the Kuomintang had allied itself to the Communist Party of China.[78] He ridiculed the Croatian Peasant Party's adherence to peaceful methods of struggle after Radić's death.

All its policies after 1925 are national-reformist. After June 20, 1928, its politicians in essence did not change. The transition of the Croatian bourgeoisie from protestations to unconditional opposition was dictated by the following considerations: in the first place, in order to preserve its influence among the peasant masses; in the second place, in order to decrease the revolutionary tendencies in the peasant national movements;

---

[76] *VI kongress Kominterna—stenograficheskii otchet* (Moscow, 1929), I, 117.
[77] *Ibid.*, p. 166.
[78] M. Gorkich, "Krest'ianstvo i samoderzhavie v Iugoslavii," *Agrarnye problemy,* March–April, 1929, p. 110.

and in the third place, in order to direct the growing flames of revolution into the channels of peaceful parliamentary struggle. This last goal was advanced, especially after the death of Radić, when the leaders of the peasant-democratic coalition forbade demonstrations for six weeks and recommended Te Deums instead of battles.[79]

In spite of Gorkich's claim that the new CPY was taking advantage of the crisis in Yugoslavia, he was forced to admit that the peasant national movement "was still basically in the hands of the bourgeoisie." [80]

On April 25, 1929, the secretary general of the CPY, Djaković, was shot while trying to escape from the Yugoslav police.[81] He was replaced at the Sixth Plenum of the Central Committee of the Party in October by Jovo Mališić-Martinović, a Montenegrin.[82] The theme adopted by this plenum was "armed insurrection against the fascist dictatorship"; the plenum maintained that this was the line established by the Sixth Comintern Congress, an altogether reasonable deduction.[83] Even more stress was placed on the need for exposing the bourgeois political parties and strengthening the independent role of the CPY.[84] A feeble armed insurrection was attempted shortly afterwards that resulted only in the virtual extinction of the Party by the royal dictatorship.

The history of the CPY during these years is a history of futility. At no time in the decade of the 1920s did the mood of the Party, Comintern directives, and internal political and economic conditions in Yugoslavia converge at the opportune moment for the CPY. These three factors seemed during this decade to be operating against one another. It would appear, on the basis of Comintern sources, that factionalism was indeed the chief source of the ineffectiveness of the Party. In particular, between 1921 and 1928 Marković's opposition to Comintern policy on the national question and his fear that a united front with the Croatian Peasant Party might result in the absorption of the CPY appear to have had strong support in the Party. From 1925 to 1927 there was really no possibility of

[79] Ibid., p. 111.
[80] Ibid., p. 112.
[81] La Fédération balkanique, No. 116 (May 15, 1929), p. 2572.
[82] Marjanović, p. 42.
[83] B. Boshkovich, "Kompartiia Iugoslavii v usloviiakh voenno-fashistskoi diktatury," Kommunisticheskii Internatsional, No. 21 (July 31, 1930), p. 54.
[84] Ibid., p. 55.

such a second alliance with Radić since, on the one hand, the position of the Croatian Peasant Party on the national question had changed and, on the other, the CPY (or more correctly the Krestintern) no longer had anything to offer Radić. Thus, during the entire "peasantist" period the Comintern's efforts to harness the force of the agrarian movement through the CPY succeeded only in heightening the doctrinal disputes in that Party.

With the end of factions in the CPY in June, 1928, it would appear that the Party was in a position to implement the policies laid down by the Comintern and see if they really applied to Yugoslavia. But two things happened. Radić was assassinated, initiating a rising wave of discontent in the country and sending the Croatian Peasant Party back to its pre-1925 tactics, and the Comintern ordered its members to return to their intransigent position of pre-1923, repudiating alliances with any political parties. So at the precise moment when conditions seemed most suitable for harnessing the peasant movement, or at least supporting it, perhaps even more suitable than in 1924, such cooperation between peasant parties and Communist parties was banned by the Comintern for private Russian reasons.

It was true, as Gorkich pointed out, that the Croatian Peasant Party rejected revolutionary methods in politics, but it had rejected them in 1924 when the Comintern had approached that party. Throughout the whole period 1924-27 the Comintern had exempted the Balkans from "capitalist stabilization" and had indicated that a "workers' and peasants' revolution" was possible there if Communist parties courted peasant political parties and infiltrated them while playing upon the "national liberation" sentiments of ethnic minorities. But in 1928 the Sixth Comintern Congress, at a time of maximum frustration for the Yugoslav peasants and their political parties, urged the CPY to prepare for revolution and shun potential political allies. The new line had unfortunate effects in Yugoslavia, none of which served Comintern ends. It divided the opposition to the royal dictatorship, thereby strengthening the forces opposed to democratic institutions, and it inspired the CPY to embark on putschist efforts which only resulted in the decimation and desertion of the rank and file.

CHAPTER X

Rumania: Communism and the Ebbing Peasant Political Movement 1924–1930

From November, 1928, to October, 1930, Rumania was ruled by the National Peasant Party. It was the second and last peasant party to gain exclusive control of its government by free elections. This made the National Peasant government a turning point in the history of Eastern Europe in two respects. For the Communists, the "peasant government" represented a significant and visible test of Comintern policy toward the peasantry and its political movement. The strategy finally adopted by the Comintern in Rumania signaled to the whole Communist world that the united front with the peasant political movement had ended. For the agrarian movement in Eastern Europe, the experiment of the National Peasant government was even more crucial as a test of "peasantism" itself, a test which the Rumanian National Peasant Party did not meet successfully. When the government failed to keep itself in power, it was a failure for the international agrarian movement as well because the latter needed political triumphs on the part of its individual members to invigorate and inspire the whole movement. After the fall of the National Peasant government in Rumania, peasantism no longer seemed to be an effective and independent third force in East European politics.

THE RISE AND FALL OF RUMANIAN PEASANTISM

Rumanian social and economic development was strikingly similar to that of prerevolutionary Russia.[1] Unlike the Yugoslav and

[1] Henry L. Roberts, *Rumania: Political Problems of an Agrarian State* (New Haven, 1951), pp. 16–17. The presence of such similarities also occurred

Bulgarian cases, but like the Hungarian and Polish, large estates continued to play an important role in Rumanian agriculture.[2] In this sense Lenin's classification of the peasantry could presumably be applied for Communist agitation in rural areas.[3] Because of a high density of population and low per capita production, the "land hunger" of the peasants could become a weapon in the hands of the Communists. There were also, as in the case of all East European countries, profound regional differences which could presumably be used to good advantage by the Rumanian Communist Party (see Table 13).

Table 13

Some Demographic Features of Rumania in 1930

Region [a]	Net repro- ductive rate	Density of population per km.	Percent of population dependent on agri- culture	Per capita pro- duction	Surplus population[b] (percent)
Rumania	1.40	61	72	48	23.1
Oltenia	1.37	63	86		
Muntenia	1.44	77	64		
Dobrogea	1.75	35	79	48	23.2
Moldavia	1.61	64	75		
Bessarabia	1.67	64	86	45	12.0
Bucovina	1.22	82	70	45	58.0
Transylvania	1.30	52	67		
Banat	.81	50	57	51	24.6
Crişana-Maramureş	1.15	65	69		

Source: Dudley Kirk, *Europe's Population in the Interwar Years* (Geneva, 1946), p. 271.

[a] The former Old Kingdom was subdivided into the provinces of Oltenia, Muntenia, Dobrogea, and Moldavia. The former Kingdom of Transylvania was subdivided into the provinces Transylvania, The Banat, Crişana, and Maramureş.

[b] Wilbert E. Moore, *Economic Demography of Eastern and Southern Europe* (Geneva, 1945), p. 72.

to Communist writers. See, for example, K. Dichesku Dik, "Oktiabr'skaia revoliutsiia i agrarnyi vopros v Rumynii," *Krest'ianskii Internatsional*, No. 1–2 (Jan.–Feb., 1926), p. 58.

[2] See Table 2, p. 9.

[3] See Roberts' analysis of the distribution of land during these years. Roberts, pp. 47–55.

The most advanced areas economically were Transylvania and the Banat. With its mineral resources, metallurgical industry, and more highly developed system of industrial production, Transylvania was the richest single acquisition of the new Rumanian state.[4] However, just as the more advanced Croatia felt that she was being subjected to the inferior Serbian Kingdom in Yugoslavia, so many of the citizens of Transylvania felt that they were being subjected to the inferior Old Kingdom in Rumania. In spite of the strong sentimental ties between the Rumanians of Transylvania and those of the Old Kingdom, there was a widespread feeling that the Rumanian government, through its policies and its disposition of confiscated industrial enterprises, was transforming Transylvania into a colony of the Old Kingdom.[5] The demands for greater provincial autonomy were further compounded by the feeling on the part of the large German and Hungarian minorities that they were not being treated fairly.

The two areas with the lowest per capita productivity, Bessarabia and Bucovina, were at the same time areas in which there was a strong Ukrainian minority. Bessarabia, perhaps because of her thwarted Moldavian nationalism, or because of the family ties between the Bessarabian Ukrainians and the Russian Ukrainians, was breeding ground for radical socialist and populist movements before World War I and the chief medium through which the Russian version of these two movements was transmitted to Rumania.[6] To some degree it was the acquisition of this territory, in which the peasants had already imposed their own radical land reform, as well as the threat of communism, which compelled the Rumanian government to institute a general land reform for the whole Rumanian state.[7]

The land reforms probably did act as a bulwark against Bolshevism

---

[4] *Ibid.*, pp. 67–68, and C. A. Macartney, *Hungary and Her Successors: The Treaty of Trianon and Its Consequences, 1919–1937* (London, 1937), pp. 269–70, 274–75.

[5] Macartney, pp. 331–34.

[6] Roberts, pp. 32–35. Roberts concludes, however, that after 1918 "the radical influences coming from Bessarabia were less than the contrary influences of Rumania upon Bessarabia." *Ibid.*, p. 35.

[7] *Ibid.*, pp. 23, 35.

in the immediate postwar period.[8] They did not, however, solve the pressing problem of overpopulation. Roberts, in his careful analysis of Rumanian statistics, indicates that even "if all land in excess of 100 hectares were distributed to properties below five hectares, their average size would rise to only 2.7 hectares; if all property in excess of fifty hectares, the average size would be 2.9 hectares." [9] While the passage of land reforms created an aura of hope, trust, and even confidence among the peasants, without concrete evidence of improvement in the peasants' lot this aura could not last.

Industrialization offered some hope, but one objection to this solution was that the expansion of industry already under way was having a negative rather than a positive effect on the development of agriculture.[10] Also, any program of industrialization required foreign capital, which was difficult to obtain without burdensome concessions to compensate for the risks created by the instability of the leu and the rather shaky financial policies of the government. The leu was not stabilized until 1929, and then by a loan of $100,000,000, an achievement which was undone by the depression of 1931.[11]

The Rumanian National Peasant Party, despite its name, was not exclusively peasantist in its approach to Rumanian economic problems. Unlike Stamboliiski, who loudly identified himself with the village against the town and with agriculture against industry, the leaders of the Rumanian National Peasant movement did not think of their party as a class organization. This was partly a consequence of its internal diversity. The National Peasants were an amalgam of the Peasant Party of Bessarabia, the Peasant Party of the Old Kingdom, and the National Party of Transylvania. The first of these, the Peasant Party of Bessarabia, was probably the most radical. It had begun to take shape at the time of the 1905 revolution in Russia under the leadership of Constantine Stere, a Moldavian aristocrat and professor at the University of Iași.[12] Stere, as a student

---

[8] Borkenau stressed the importance of the agrarian reforms in Rumania as a means of erecting a barrier to Bolshevism in the West. Franz Borkenau, *World Communism: A History of the Communist International* (New York, 1939), p. 99.

[9] Roberts, p. 54.

[10] *Ibid.*, p. 70.

[11] *Ibid.*, p. 78.

[12] Pan Halipa, "Le Mouvement agraire en Bessarabie," *MAB Bulletin*, No. 1 (1928), pp. 23–24.

at the University of St. Petersburg, had imbibed some of Chernov's neo-narodnik ideas and spent some time in exile in Siberia. Though considerably more sophisticated than Stamboliiski, like Stamboliiski he identified the national soul with peasant society and opposed westernization and large-scale industrialization.[13]

The Peasant Party of the Old Kingdom was of more recent origin, and therefore less bound by established ideological traditions. It was to a large degree dominated by village intellectuals of peasant origin, like Ion Mihalache, who tended to see the solution of peasant problems in rural cooperatives and land redistribution.[14] The Peasant Party of Bessarabia joined the Peasant Party of the Old Kingdom in 1921.[15]

The National Party of Transylvania, which was under the leadership of Iuliu Maniu and Alexander Vaida Voevod, had been founded in May, 1880, to represent Rumanians living in lands under Hungarian rule.[16] Although this party advocated extensive agrarian reforms, "it was more nationalist than peasantist in its outlook and its leaders were from the middle class." [17] It represented the interests not only of the Rumanian peasants but also of the Rumanian intellectuals, professional men, and small tradesmen in Transylvania. On October 10, 1926, the National Party and the amalgamated Peasant Party joined to form the Rumanian National Peasant Party.[18] Maniu became the president of the new organization and Mihalache the vice-president.

The motive for this union was political expediency. The Peasant Party had no foothold in Transylvania.[19] Those who were favorably disposed toward the union claimed that the National Party represented the peasants of Transylvania—which was true, since it

---

[13] For Stere's adaptation of Russian populism to Rumanian circumstances see Roberts, p. 143.

[14] *Ibid.*, pp. 148–49.

[15] Halipa, *MAB Bulletin,* No. 1 (1928), p. 29.

[16] A. Popa, "The National Peasant Party of Rumania," International Peasant Union, *Monthly Bulletin,* Oct., 1954, p. 21.

[17] Roberts, p. 140.

[18] V. Madgearu, "La Fusion du parti paysan avec le parti national en Roumanie," *MAB Bulletin,* No. 4 (1926), p. 8.

[19] Petre P. Sucui, "La Scission dans le parti National Paysan Roumaine," *MAB Bulletin,* No. 2 (1927), p. 73.

represented all Rumanians in Transylvania. But some Peasant Party leaders rejected the agreement. Dr. Nicola Lupu, who had figured so prominently in the Krestintern's plans for capturing the Rumanian Peasant Party in 1924, left the Peasant Party at the time of union in 1926.[20] Lupu charged that the policies of the National Party were no different from those of the Peasant Party's political enemies, the Liberals, and that the National Party members were religious fanatics (Uniates). Lupu's followers argued that union with the National Party had produced a hybrid and that it would have been more desirable to preserve the Peasant Party's exclusively peasant orientation, achieving political power by temporary alliances with other political parties.[21] In the late 1920s, because of the alliance with the National Party and the postwar infusion of "new blood," the Rumanian National Peasant Party did begin moving toward a less peasantist position in the question of economic development.[22] This was most apparent in the work of the prominent party leader and economist, Virgil Madgearu.[23] According to Madgearu, the National Peasant Party should support the "natural and uninhibited growth of industry." Opposition to the reigning Liberal Party should consist in an attack on the Liberals' protective tariff and identification of the Liberals as the party of financial oligarchy, financial trusts, and embryonic despotism.

[20] For a defense of Lupu's actions see Suciu, *MAB Bulletin,* No. 2 (1927), pp. 71–78. For an attack on Lupu's actions see V. Madgearu, "Essai d'une scission dans le parti national paysan roumain," *MAB Bulletin,* No. 2 (1927), pp. 68–71.

[21] There is some irony in Lupu's position in October, 1926. Earlier in the year Lupu had spoken with pride of the fact that the Rumanian Peasant Party, unlike its counterparts in Bulgaria, Yugoslavia, and Czechoslovakia, did not have a narrow class character and included workers and intellectuals. N. Lupu, "Le Parti Paysan Roumain, son origine, son existence et ses buts," *MAB Bulletin,* No. 1 (1926), p. 3. Roberts believes Lupu was an opportunist and points out that Lupu rejoined the National Peasant Party in 1933 and left it again in 1945 to form his own peasant party, which collaborated with the Communists in the National Democratic Front. Roberts, p. 141, n. 16.

[22] Roberts writes: "The principal effect of the dual origin was not, however, party instability, but the ambiguity which it imparted to National Peasant policy. This effect should not be over-emphasized because. . . the Peasant Party's policy was by no means fixed and had undergone important modifications even before amalgamation." *Ibid.,* p. 142.

[23] For Madgearu's ideas see *ibid.,* pp. 150–51.

The crisis which brought the National Peasant Party to power was to a large degree brought on by the death of King Ferdinand in July, 1927, and the death of the able leader of the Liberal Party, Ion Bratianu, in November, 1927.[24] The National Peasant Party called for a new election, refused to approve the budget (in order to block the imminent stabilization loan), initiated protest movements, and finally boycotted the National Assembly.[25] Like their agrarian counterparts in Poland and Yugoslavia, however, the National Peasants refused to countenance revolutionary action to achieve their objectives.[26]

A giant peasant demonstration was scheduled for May 6, 1928, at Alba-Iulia. Some of the more enthusiastic participants wanted to initiate a "March on Rome," but were dissuaded by Party leaders. Perhaps as a result of this massive demonstration of popular support, bearing within it the specter of revolution, but more likely as a result of the desire to form a government which could win approval for the stabilization loan, the Council of Regency accepted the resignation of the Liberal cabinet in November, 1928. Maniu was called upon to form a peasant cabinet. In the general elections in December the National Peasant Party won a resounding victory, obtaining about 80 percent of the popular vote.[27]

As might be expected, given the shift in the National Peasant Party from populism toward ideas which were "liberal" in the Western sense of the word, little was done to fulfill that part of its program pertaining to the peasant question.[28] The most important measures of the new regime were in those areas where the National Peasants opposed the Liberal program. A more elastic customs system was adopted in order to increase international cooperation and trade. The stabilization loan was concluded and the state financial system modernized as part of the effort to entice as much foreign capital into Rumania as possible.[29] A concerted effort was

[24] The crisis is summarized in "La Situation politique après le mort du Roi Ferdinand I," *MAB Bulletin*, No. 1 (1928), pp. 55–69.
[25] Roberts, p. 107.
[26] *Ibid.*
[27] *Ibid.*, p. 131.
[28] *Ibid.*, pp. 155–61.
[29] *Ibid.*, pp. 160–63.

made to decentralize the administrative structure and to give free enterprise full scope of action in the economy.[30]

After the National Peasant Party had been in power a year the opposition began to rally. While several factors, including fears of Soviet mobilization and declining grain prices, contributed to the fall from power of the Party, the immediate reason was incredibly trivial. On October 6, 1930, Maniu resigned because King Carol had, contrary to Maniu's expressed wish, brought his mistress back to Rumania with him.[31] Whatever the impelling motives, Maniu had in effect surrendered his delegated power to a rather arbitrary monarch for what was taken to be a trivial reason, damaging not only the prestige of his party but also national confidence in the effectiveness of representative government.

The development of the Rumanian National Peasant Party exemplifies the dilemma of the peasant political movement in general in the decade of the 1920s. In each and every country of Eastern Europe peasant parties abandoned the sentimental desire to do something for the peasant, finding it necessary to advance a program which rested on something more tangible than the celebrated peasant soul. Sooner or later each party had to adapt its program to the peculiar conditions existing within its own country, and in the process abandon some of the more utopian policies it had espoused when it was only a minority opposition party. In Poland an unsuccessful attempt was made to compromise with national factions and achieve needed reforms piecemeal. In Yugoslavia the national question became the emotional backbone of the Croatian Peasant movement to the exclusion of its peasantist goals. In Rumania the Rumanian National Peasant Party attempted to find a concrete economic program using the Anglo-Saxon states as a model.[32] In this last case, however, as in the case of the Croatian Peasant Party, it is questionable whether the result was still a peasant program.

At any rate, the failure of the peasant government in Rumania was at the same time a failure for the peasant political movement as a whole in Eastern Europe. By the end of 1930, of all the peasant

[30] *Ibid.*, 164–65.
[31] *Ibid.*, pp. 134–37.
[32] *Ibid.*, p. 167.

political parties in Eastern Europe, only the sponsor of the International Agrarian Bureau, the Czechoslovak Republican Party of Small Farmers and Peasants, could still claim to be both a strong party and an effective political force in its own country, although it was doubtful whether one could call the Czech party a peasant political movement in 1930.

In Rumania, as in other East European countries, the process of adaption evident in the native peasant party gave the Communists grist for their propaganda mill. They claimed that the peasant party had betrayed the interests of the peasants. Moreover, the rigid adherence of the peasant party to formal democratic procedures at a time when democratic institutions were threatened by extraparliamentary forces gave credence to Communist claims that the Communist Party of Rumania (CPR) was the only party willing to take bold action to defend the interests of the peasant. But the CPR was not able to exploit its opportunities. In Rumania, as in Yugoslavia, Bulgaria, and Poland, the combination of police repression, indigenous intellectual traditions, and unrealistic shifts in Comintern policy deprived the Party of the opportunity successfully to exploit Rumania's problems.

THE SHADOW OF A PARTY

The CPR is the only Communist party in Eastern Europe which never once played an important role in politics before 1945.[33] It was one of the smallest parties in the Comintern between 1920 and 1940, and between 1920 and 1930 the Communists never succeeded in winning as much as 2 percent of the electoral vote in Rumania.[34] One of the reasons for the failure of the Party was that it found little pro-Russian sentiment to build upon. Like Hungary, Rumania was a country where there was no Pan-Slavic tradition, and the close identification of communism with Russia was a handicap to the Communists. Although there were some Ukrainians in Bucovina and Bessarabia who were probably drawn to their brethren in the Soviet Union, the strong Rumanian majority seemed to have been

[33] Branko Lazić, *Les Partis communistes d'Europe, 1919–1955* (Paris, 1956), p. 102.
[34] *Ibid.*, p. 104.

repelled by communism because of its Russian origin. The Rumanian nationalists identified themselves as members of the Romance language family and regarded France as their cultural motherland. Although Russia had been instrumental in bringing about the liberation of Rumania in the nineteenth century, it was Russian invasions and Russian occupation armies that were remembered, and after 1917 the two countries were at odds over Rumania's annexation of Bessarabia.

Where the CPR did draw support there was some correlation between the levels of prosperity or economic development and the appeals of communism. The Communists won their heaviest support in two of the most advanced areas, Transylvania and the Banat (see Table 14). Since these provinces also had the highest proportion of national minorities to the total population, it is likely that the Comintern's program on the national question was more effective than its program on the agrarian question in winning allies. Judging from the names of the Rumanian Communist leaders during these years—among the most prominent of whom were Pavel Tkachenko, Boris Stefanov, George Cristescu, Vasile Luca, and Marcel and Ana Pauker—the thesis is borne out that the Party recruited most of its members from the minority groups.[35] The first was a Bessarabian Ukrainian, the second was Bulgarian, the last three were Jewish, and the one Rumanian mentioned soon defected from the Party.

Although conditions of illegality and the Russian stigma were handicaps, the conflict between the Comintern and the traditions of the Rumanian Marxist movement also contributed to the weakness of the party. The Comintern displayed very little concern for the CPR and normally gave great weight to the interests of the Bulgarian Communist Party.[36] Directives which were issued by the Comintern

[35] Several observers have been struck by the strongly non-Rumanian character of the CPR and by its attraction for the national minorities. See, for example, Roberts, pp. 250–51; R. V. Burks, *The Dynamics of Communism in Eastern Europe* (Princeton, 1961), pp. 155–58; 165, and D. Tomasic, "The Rumanian Communist Leadership," *Slavic Review*, XX, No. 3 (Oct., 1961), 478.

[36] Rothschild indicates that Kolarov, who was trying to establish the hegemony of the Bulgarian Communist Party in the Balkan Communist movement, proudly claimed that the directives of the Bulgarian Communist Party

for the Rumanian party seem to have been predicated solely on the needs of the international Communist movement and the Soviet Union and show little awareness of local circumstances or the needs and inclinations of the Rumanian communists.

Table 14
Distribution of Rumanian Communist Party Votes in Elections of 1928

Province	Percentage of total Communist vote [a]	Population in 1930 (as percentage of total population of Rumania) [b]
Old Kingdom	12	49
Transylvania	45	18
Banat	21	5
Bessarabia	10	15
Bucovina	9	5
Crişana-Maramureş	3	8
	100	100

[a] A. Badulescu, "Protiv tselogo mira vragov," *Kommunisticheskii Internatisional*, No. 1 (179) (January 4, 1929), pp. 12–13. The number of Communist votes was 38,343 out of a total of 2,785,620, 1.4 percent of the total vote.

[b] Henry L. Roberts, *Rumania: Political Problems of an Agrarian State* (New Haven, 1951), p. 355.

The CPR itself was reluctant to accept all the requirements of Bolshevization, finding the guidance of its own heritage more pertinent to conditions in Rumania. Above all, the Party continued until 1932 to be influenced by the ideas of the leading theorist of the prewar Rumanian Social Democratic Party, Constantin Dobrogeanu-Gherea.[37] In 1910 Gherea had maintained that the "impact of

---

played a key role in the formation of the CPR. Joseph Rothschild, *The Communist Party of Bulgaria* (New York, 1959), p. 199. The Balkan Communist Federation was established in 1920 to coordinate the efforts of Communist parties in the area, and the Bulgarians tried to use it as an instrument for magnifying the role of the Bulgarian Communist Party. The post of secretary of the Federation rotated among the three Bulgarian Communist leaders, Kolarov, Dimitrov, and Kabakchiev. By 1928, however, the Federation was already a phantom organization. *Ibid.*, pp. 231–33, 250–54.

[37] One contemporary source stated that the Party was dominated by the theory of neo-serfdom until 1926. Gori, "K itogam V s'ezda Kompartii Rumynii," *Kommunisticheskii Internatsional*, No. 8–9 (March 30, 1932), p. 52. A more recent source maintains that the theory of neo-serfdom had a strong influence on the program and activity of the CPR until 1932. *30 let*

capitalism upon a backward agrarian society such as that in Rumania produced a hybrid, in which there was a monstrous mingling of old and new." [38] The result, on the one hand, was the establishment of all the illusory apparatus of liberal-bourgeois government and law, while on the other hand, the peasant continued to be bound to an excessively small plot of land which he could not leave because of modern versions of feudal restraints (such as labor contracts and laws about the inalienability of land). The peasant found himself as much enslaved by the weight of a poverty from which there was no escape as he had been by the old bonds of serfdom. The condition of the peasant was christened neo-serfdom or *neoibăgia,* a word which became the trademark of Gherea's school. The interests of the old feudal classes were protected in Rumania by the narrow bureaucratic elite, which used democratic institutions to keep itself constantly in power.

Gherea provided a telling analysis of the consequences of Rumania's transformation once she had come into contact with industrialized countries, but he was unable to deduce a unique and compelling socialist program from it. He feared the brute passions of the peasantry and warned his followers against encouraging the peasant to mobilize on his own behalf. Nor did he see any solution in the anti-industrialization policies of the old populist movement. One could not halt the inexorable march of capitalism, he argued, and in any case it was not industrialization that was at fault. Rumanian Marxists, said Gherea, must concentrate on the elimination of feudal restraints in the land and the rural labor market and support legislation favoring the development of small farms owned by independent peasants. Gherea considered the small peasant the

---

bor'by Rumynskoi Kommunisticheskoi Partii za sotsializm, za s'chast'e rodiny 1921–1951 (Moscow, 1951), p. 11. The latter is, apparently, the "official line" in the history of the Party. In 1951, on the occasion of the thirtieth anniversary of the founding of the Party, the present first secretary of the CPR, Gheorghe Gheorghiu-Dej, said: "The opportunistic views of Constantin Dobrogeanu-Gherea were dominant among the leaders of the socialist party, and their harmful effects were also felt later on in the Communist Party. They were not eradicated in the latter until the Fifth Congress of the Party in 1932." Gheorghe Gheorghiu-Dej, *Stat'i i rechi* (Moscow, 1956–57), I, 326. It is difficult to tell where Borkenau got the impression that the "Roumanian Party was intellectually dominated by the powerful personality of Christian Rakovsky, who was the standard bearer of Russian influence." Borkenau, p. 63.

[38] Roberts, p. 176.

most efficient producer and felt that, once liberated, the small peasant would provide the agricultural basis for the rapid and uninhibited
development of capitalism, which would in its turn create the
necessary prerequisites for the proletarian revolution. But this
program was neither fish nor fowl. Gherea favored the small
peasant without favoring peasant society. He favored capitalism and
the policies which would give it full reign, but only as a means of
reaching the proletarian revolution. Therefore, those who were
drawn to one or the other feature of Gherea's program invariably
found themselves more at home in the populist or Liberal parties,
where the features they admired in Gherea's program were offered
as an expression of the party's ideology rather than its temporary
tactics.

Although the addiction of the Social Democrats to Gherea's ideas
has been noted in at least one Western study,[39] the influence of
Gherea on the Communists has usually been overlooked. Gherea's
theories were not incompatible with those of Lenin, at least in terms
of general theory, but a disciple of the Rumanian Marxist was likely
to have a different orientation in day-to-day activity and a different
schedule of priorities. The first objective to a Ghereaist was the
elimination of obstacles to capitalist development, whereas for
Lenin and the Bolsheviks it was the revolution. While a supporter
of Gherea could share with the Bolsheviks a common faith in the
tenets of Marxism, the immediate goals and tactics employed by each
would be quite different. A party which is dedicated to the art of
revolution is more likely to draw in all of the dissident elements
in an unstable society and gain a mass following than one which is
dedicated to the task of putting its country on the right track of
capitalist development. This is why the Comintern viewed the influence of Gherea's ideas in the CPR with some consternation.
The chief manifestation of Ghereaism was the pervasive belief that
the bourgeois-democratic revolution had not yet been consummated
in Rumania and that the Party had to help bring it about, and the
most obvious and recurrent proof of its presence was the numerous
attempts of the CPR to form blocs with the Peasant Party and other
"bourgeois" opposition parties.

At the time of its formation, the CPR had hoped to capture most

[39] *Ibid.*, pp. 279-81.

of the members of the powerful old Rumanian Social Democratic Party, but the Communists had only about 2,000 members by 1922.[40] The influence of Gherea was apparent in the Party's first agrarian program in 1924, which was written by his son, Alexander Dobrogeanu-Gherea, a prominent figure in the CPR.

Productive relations in the country remain servile to this very day. The regime [the Liberal government], though resting on a bourgeois capitalistic basis, placed the peasantry in a vise of neo-serfdom. . . . On the basis of this neo-serfdom a parasitical bureaucratic political oligarchy has developed which ruled the state and rules it now.[41]

Although strongly influenced by Gherea, the strategy of the Rumanian Communists was a distinct improvement over his. The Liberal government which ruled Rumania from 1922 to 1928 was said to be the embodiment of Gherea's bureaucratic elite. It was the perpetuator of Rumanian backwardness, but it did not represent feudal interests only. It was also the agent of the great capitalist powers in their imperialistic exploitation of Rumanian backwardness. To rid Rumania of neo-serfdom and foreign exploitation, one had only to support the efforts of the genuine bourgeois opposition parties against the Liberal government. Recklessly disregarding Comintern decrees which ordered the Party to exploit antagonisms within the Rumanian state, especially the grievances of national minorities, the CPR directed its venom outwards, perhaps hoping to enlist the support of some Rumanian nationalists by playing upon their nation's xenophobia. In this way the Party tried to paint itself as a patriotic party, defending the country against foreign economic aggression and its agent in Rumania, the Liberal Party.

The CPR twice made overtures to the other opposition parties—before the 1924 and the 1926 elections. On both occasions the offers of alliance roused leftist criticism in the Party. When the

[40] E. Berns, *Rumyniia i Italiia,* Tom I, Vypusk V, of E. Varga, ed., *Ocherki po agrarnomu voprosu* (Moscow, 1925), p. 76. According to one Communist source, the membership of the Rumanian Social Democratic Party on the eve of the split had been 45,089. K. Kushnir-Mikhailovich, "Velikaia oktiabr'skaia revoliutsiia i revoliutsionnaia situatsiia v Rumynii v 1917–21 gg.," *Voprosy istorii,* No. 11 (1957), p. 83.

[41] S. Timov, *Agrarnyi vopros i krest'ianskoe dvizhenie v Rumynii: Anti-neoiobăgia (Kritika neokrepostnicheskoi teorii K. Dobrodzhanu-Geriia)* (Moscow, 1929), p. 268.

Rumanian National Peasant Party came to power in 1928, the CPR found itself in a dilemma. According to its interpretation of the Ghereaist heritage, the overthrow of the Liberal Party could only mean the end of neo-serfdom and foreign exploitation and the completion of the bourgeois-democratic revolution. The right tended to follow the logic of its reasoning to this optimistic conclusion and welcomed the accession of the National Peasant government. The left faction in the Party raised a furor, pointing to the obvious fact that the National Peasant Party, with its espousal of free trade and foreign loans, fit the role of an agent of foreign capital more perfectly than the Liberal Party. Since the leftist course was slowly taking over the Comintern, the debate was allowed to flourish until all the issues had been brought into the open and everyone had taken a position; then the left was given the Comintern's stamp of approval.

But let us examine the evolution of the CPR policy step by step. At the beginning of 1924 the ascendant right wing in the Party seemed to be moving in harmony with the Comintern. In March the Party made its first overtures to the Peasant Party.[42] The Communists proposed a coalition workers' and peasants' bloc which would work for the creation of a workers' and peasants' government in Rumania, a government which would nationalize all land and industry, conclude an alliance with the USSR, and grant all minorities the right to national self-determination.[43] The Peasant Party did not respond.

At the Fifth Comintern Congress in June and July, 1924, Zinoviev was about to snare Radić, and his hopes for a Balkan workers' and peasants' revolution were expressed in his Theses on Two Perspectives.[44] Kolarov bore down heavily on the failure of the CPR to attract the peasants: "Up till now it has not understood the need for winning the peasants; it had no program of work among the peasants and has done practically nothing in the country." [45] In defense of his party a Rumanian delegate argued that neo-serfdom

[42] Berns, p. 77.
[43] Krest'ianskii Internatsional, No. 2 (May, 1924), p. 106.
[44] Piatyi vsemirnyi kongress Kommunisticheskogo Internatsionala—(18 iunia–8 iulia 1924 goda)—stenograficheskii otchet (Moscow, 1925), II, 47.
[45] Ibid., I, 753.

had so brutalized the peasants and corrupted the intelligentsia that they could not be reached by reason.[46] The delegate indicated, however, that with the help of the Krestintern the Party hoped to invigorate its work in rural areas and establish a bond with the peasants.

On the national question the leading Rumanian delegate, Cristescu, hedged, arguing that one had to treat the issue of Hungarian national self-determination in Transylvania as a matter of the greatest delicacy.[47] But the Fifth Congress was not deterred by his objections and issued its momentous orders that Communist parties must support not only national self-determination up to secession but also the reunification of Western Ukraine, Western Belorussia, Sub-Carpathian Ruthenia, Bessarabia, and Bucovina with the Soviet Union. No word was said, however, about the CPR's unique theory of neo-serfdom or its proposal for an alliance with the Rumanian Peasant Party.

In October hopes ran high in the Comintern itself for an alliance with the Rumanian Peasant Party, thus completing the Communist chain of alliances in the Balkans. Dr. Lupu attended a congress of the Croatian Republican Peasant Party as a guest of Radić, the latter having just returned from Moscow where he had joined the Krestintern.[48] The rumor was widely circulated that the Rumanian Peasant Party would enter the Krestintern as a result of Radić's prompting. If the Krestintern had succeeded, this would have given tremendous impetus to its efforts to create a strong Red Peasant International in the Balkans as a counterpoise to the Green International in the north.

On the eve of the Fourth Congress of the Rumanian Peasant Party, which met shortly thereafter, the Krestintern sent a telegram

[46] *Ibid.*, p. 577.

[47] *Ibid.*, p. 665.

[48] A. Badulescu, "K IV s'ezdu Rumynskoi Krest'ianskoi Partii," *Krest'ianskii Internatsional,* No. 10–12 (Nov.–Dec., 1924), p. 30. Stavrianos maintains that this congress of the Croatian Peasant Party was the high point of the federation movement in the Balkans. L. S. Stavrianos, *Balkan Federation: A History of the Movement Towards Balkan Unity in Modern Times* (Smith College Studies in History, Vol. XXVII, Nos. 1–4) (Menasha, Wis., 1944), p. 215.

to the Party[49] and a secret letter to its leaders.[50] In the following spring Dąbal indicated that the telegram inviting the Party to scrutinize the program of the Krestintern had been published in all the major newspapers in Rumania and was discussed in the Rumanian chamber (where it was accepted as evidence that the Party was about to join the Krestintern).[51] Dąbal also indicated that the delegates to the Fourth Congress had discussed the telegram in detail. Dąbal maintained that Lupu was most enthusiastic in his espousal of the Krestintern and that Lupu had affirmed that the Krestintern was extraordinarily useful as a means of defending the interests of the peasants on an international scale.

In the secret letter there was an astonishing proposal which suggests that the efforts of the Krestintern were about to be joined with those of the Balkan Communist Federation in a massive campaign to convert the Balkans into a federation of workers' and peasants' governments. The Krestintern invited the Rumanian Peasant Party to a conference of all the peasant and Communist parties of Balkan-Danubian countries for the purpose of uniting their efforts on behalf of their respective supporters.

The toiling peasantry are against any kind of national oppression and for the unqualified right of every people to decide their own fate. Along with this they stand for a rapprochement and alliance of all Balkan peoples into a single great union of workers' and peasants' republics in the Balkans, which will secure equal rights and independence for all Balkan peoples, eliminate national enmity, and open to those people the way to a peaceful and happy future.[52]

At first the Krestintern received no reply at all to its appeals, but after repeated urgings the Rumanian Peasant Party finally stated that it considered the Krestintern's efforts in Rumania an intolerable interference from a foreign power.[53]

While Dąbal implied in April, 1925, that there had been some

[49] *Krest'ianskii Internatsional,* No. 10–12 (Nov.–Dec., 1924), p. 148.

[50] Badulescu, *Krest'ianskii Internatsional,* No. 10–12 (Nov.–Dec., 1924), p. 38.

[51] Dąbal, "Zadachi i dostizhenie Krestinterna na Zapade," *Krest'ianskii Internatsional,* No. 3–5 (March–May, 1925), p. 36.

[52] Timov, p. 249.

[53] *Ibid.,* p. 250.

support in the Rumanian Peasant Party for the Krestintern, by October his faith in the efficacy of appeals and proclamations was shaken and he interpreted the motives of the Krestintern in appealing to the Party somewhat differently.

In the third place, we tried methods of a so-called commercial character, turning to the most reactionary people and organizations with offers to defend the peasantry. However, we clearly took into acount the fact that they would not make any alliances with the Krestintern. In this way we tried to make the peasantry aware of the fact that a world organization had been created for them, so that they would try to arrange a connection with us. Also, our attempts revealed the many enemies of the peasantry who call themselves defenders of their interests. Our protests, appeals, and telegrams to the Bulgarian Agrarian Party, to the Rumanian Peasant Party, to the Hungarian Smallholder's Party were this kind of attack. They achieved their goals.[54]

The efforts of both the Comintern and the Krestintern were dealt a staggering blow in 1924 by the loss of their only real arm in Rumania, the CPR. In July the Party was outlawed by the government. According to Communist reports, more than eight hundred members of the Party were arrested and an entirely new party apparatus had to be erected.[55] Prominent leaders like Marcel Pauker and Alexander Dobrogeanu-Gherea were forced to flee the country.[56] The only tangible repercussion was the unsuccessful putschist seizure of the Bessarabian town of Tatar-Bunar by a group of Ukrainian peasant Communists between September 14 and 18.[57]

The Third Congress of the Party met in Vienna in late August and early September, 1924, in an atmosphere of crisis. A rightist leadership including Tkachenko and Stefanov took over the remnants of the party and dutifully incorporated the decisions of the

[54] Dąbal, "1923–1925: dva goda sushchestvovaniia Kominterna," *Krest'ianskii Internatsional*, No. 10 (Oct., 1925), p. 4.

[55] *Shestoi rasshirennyi plenum ispolkoma Kominterna (17 fevralia–15 marta 1926)—stenograficheskii otchet* (Moscow, 1927), p. 250.

[56] N. Amaru, "Le Procès de Al. Dobrogeanu-Gherea c'est le procès des masses ouvrières de la Roumanie," La Fédération balkanique, No. 112 (March 15, 1929), p. 2466; "Save Marcel Pauker," *International Press Correspondence,* June 14, 1929, p. 613.

[57] According to Clark, on the basis of sources supplied by the Rumanian government, the raid was ordered by the Odessa revolutionary center, rather than by the CPR. Charles Upson Clark, *Bessarabia: Russia and Roumania on the Black Sea* (New York, 1927), pp. 264–68.

Fifth Comintern Congress into the Party resolutions. Although these resolutions were an imitation of those of the Comintern, their spirit was still derived from Gherea. For example, the tactical directives began with the statement:

The liberation of the Rumanian peasant from the yoke of serfdom, as well as the emancipation of the workers and peasants from the yoke of economic and political slavery to the imperialistic entente, slavery administered by the Rumanian oligarchy, will be possible only if there is a close alliance between the workers and peasants in the whole decisive struggle.[58]

The new Party directives required members to form cells in the villages and to infiltrate rural cooperatives, local branches of the Peasant Party, and cultural and athletic organizations. They were ordered to take the initiative in defending the interests of the poor peasant, demanding the confiscation of all large estates without compensation.

Factionalism increased when the Party went underground. Cristescu, a prominent member of the Party's Central Committee and its delegate to the ECCI, left the Party altogether when it decided to establish a conspiratorial organization and to support Bessarabia's right to national self-determination.[59] In July, 1925, the Party's Central Committee took a decisive step and formally condemned the theories of Dobrogeanu-Gherea as an expression of the theoretical errors of the Second International.[60] But the condemnation proved to be only a gesture to satisfy the Comintern.

The Comintern seemed to lose interest in the Rumanian Communists after the setbacks of 1924 and did not subject the Party to close scrutiny again until 1926. In February and March of that year the Sixth Plenum of the ECCI appointed a special commission to hear the complaints of both the right and the left in the Party and pass judgment on the Party's efforts earlier in the year to form a united front with the National Party of Transylvania as well as

[58] Timov, p. 274, n. 1. This work contains a complete copy of the directives of the Third Party Congress on the agrarian question. *Ibid.,* pp. 274–78.

[59] *Shestoi rasshirennyi plenum,* pp. 246–47, 252.

[60] *Istoriia mezhdunarodnogo rabochego: natsional'no-osvoboditel'nogo dvizheniia* (Moscow, 1962), II, 300.

with the Peasant Party and the Social Democratic Party.[61] The speaker who represented the right faction of the CPR at the Sixth Plenum defended the Party's policies by maintaining that they already fully corresponded to the directives of the Comintern.[62] The right also displayed little enthusiasm for revolutionary activity:

The left say that at a time when we find ourselves between two revolutionary waves the gap must be filled with the corpses of politicians, and with a summoning of the masses to revolutionary struggle. We should die leading the masses in revolution or in hunger strikes in prison, shouting the slogan "freedom or death." [63]

The speaker for the left faction claimed that a united front with the Peasant Party would have been a united front with "kulaks and reactionaries" and that the rightists applied these tactics because they overestimated the degree of neo-serfdom in the countryside.[64]

The Comintern was more critical of the right than it had been two years before and condemned the Party for trying to extend the united front to all bourgeois parties, essentially confirming the assertion of the left that the Party leaders had "overestimated both the feudal character of Rumania and the role of the bourgeois opposition." [65] But in 1926 the Comintern still wanted to bring the factions together rather than drive a wedge between them and so it also criticized the left for excessive revolutionary optimism. In April the editor of *Kommunisticheskii Internatsional* summarized:

The right deviation in the Party expressed itself, among other things, in a readiness to extend the tactic of the united front to almost all bourgeois opposition parties. These two deviations [left and right] were partially connected with an incorrect evaluation of the social character of the country. The right overestimated the feudal character of the country and, as a result, tended to overestimate the significance of bourgeois opposition parties in Rumania. The left, on the other hand, overestimated capitalistic degeneration, and arrived at the conclusion that Rumania stood on the brink of revolution.[66]

[61] *Shestoi rasshirennyi plenum*, pp. 248, 252, 511.
[62] *Ibid.*, p. 250.
[63] *Ibid.*
[64] *Ibid.*, p. 248.
[65] Timov, p. 269.
[66] Martynov, "Problema revoliutsii v Rumynii," *Kommunisticheskii Internatsional*, No. 4 (April, 1926), p. 65.

The third and most decisive crisis in the CPR came, however, when the National Peasant Party made its successful bid for power. George Dimitrov, who had by 1927 already become one of the chief functionaries of the Comintern, apparently sensed the imminent crisis and the CPR's probable response to it. In his advice to the Rumanians in November, 1927, Dimitrov demonstrated the limitations suffered by the Comintern in trying to learn from its own experience. The tone of his remarks also foreshadows the emerging left turn in Comintern policies in general:

The leaders of the National Zaranist [Peasant] Party, particularly since the union of the National Party with the Zaranist Party, go along with the oppositional bourgeoisie, betray the peasant masses and create at this time, by their opposition to the Bratianu dictatorship, the possibility that the masses will be dragged into the train of the Carlist movement. In these circumstances we can reckon on a fascist coup in Rumania with a Carlist cloak, which is apparently directed from the left against the dictatorship of bank capital, and is thus, to some extent, similar to the piłsudski movement in Poland. . . . The Communist Party must know how to draw the lessons from the failures of the Bulgarian Communist Party during the fascist putsch of June 19, 1923 (the so-called tactics of neutrality) and of the Polish Communist Party on the occasion of the Piłsudski putsch (actual support of the fascist action of Piłsudski under the false idea of supporting a petty-bourgeois, democratic, revolutionary movement), and not repeat such extremely dangerous errors.[67]

What the CPR was supposed to do was not clear, but presumably it should marshal its battered forces and exploit the political situation to raise a Communist revolution. The mass meeting at Alba-Iulia in May, 1928, generated considerable excitement in Communist circles, and the ECCI immediately dispatched a letter of instruction to the CPR that probably urged a revolutionary course. The Party, which was painfully aware of its own weakness, could not avoid falling into the "Bulgarian error," though the Moscow-based Rumanian Communists failed to understand this. Timov, a spokesman for the right in the Party and a veteran member of the Krestintern, wrote from Moscow, blaming the left for underestimating the revolutionary character of the National Peasant Party:

[67] G. M. Dimitrov, "The Situation in Rumania," *International Press Correspondence,* VII, No. 64 (Nov. 12, 1927), 144.

Our party, the Communist Party, did not raise a finger to try to take over the movement [the demonstration of the Rumanian National Peasant Party at Alba-Iulia] and its revolutionary influence and direct this movement along the path suitable to us. Our inactivity was due not only to our organizational weakness but primarily to our incorrect evaluation of the National Peasant Party, underestimation of its mass, peasant, petty-bourgeois, and even partly worker character. The Party saw in this struggle simply a conflict of two factions of the bourgeoisie, a struggle in which the National Peasant Party served the interests of foreign finance capital.[68]

The events at Alba-Iulia gave the Comintern an intense interest in Rumania and its feeble auxiliary there. At the Sixth Comintern Congress in 1928 Bukharin spoke with deep disappointment of the failure of the CPR to harness the revolutionary spirit of the peasants. Though acknowledging the weakness of the Party, Bukharin seemed to feel that inadequate instructions from the Comintern were responsible for the failure, and he used the Rumanian case as an example of the need to reinvigorate the Krestintern.[69] Kolarov, on the other hand, used the events at Alba-Iulia as an example of the rising tide of revolution and the precariousness of "capitalist stabilization" in the Balkans.[70] Strangely enough, only Dąbal pointed out that the errors of the CPR were the same as those of the Bulgarian Communist Party in June, 1923.[71]

Although no Comintern directives to the CPR were published, the Fourth Congress of that party was held in October, 1928, and a prominent Comintern official, Bela Kun, indicated that the right leadership was thrown out with the help of the Comintern.[72]

[68] S. Timov, "O pravoi opasnosti i primirenchestve v rumynskoi kompartii," *Kommunisticheskii Internatsional*, No. 25 (June 28, 1929), p. 43. At the time of the events at Alba–Iulia (a year earlier), another Moscow-based Rumanian Communist, Raliu, explained the inaction of the CPR solely in terms of its weakness. I. Raliu, "Krest'ianskoe dvizhenie i Natsional'naia Krest'ianskaia Partiia v Rumynii," *Agrarnye problemy*, III, No. 7 (June, 1928), 49. An interpretation more closely corresponding to the Comintern "line" on the errors of 1928 may be found in Raconescu, "A Government of the National Peasant Party in Roumania," *International Press Correspondence*, VIII, No. 82 (Nov. 23, 1928), 1554–55.

[69] *VI kongress Kominterna—stenograficheskii otchet* (Moscow, 1929), I, 55–56.

[70] *Ibid.*, p. 165.

[71] *Ibid.*, p. 445.

[72] Bela Kun, "Primernyi yrok dan," *Kommunisticheskii Internatsional*, No. 23 (Aug. 23, 1930), p. 54.

Kun also reveals the line of thought which events at Alba-Iulia had triggered in the Comintern. He said that it was now clear that Rumania was going to be the jumping-off point for the invasion of the USSR. "The Rumanian Communist Party occupies an extremely important front in the international revolutionary movement, it conducts work in a country immediately bordering the Soviet Union, a country, therefore, assigned by international imperialists to play the role of advance post in the counterrevolutionary war against the USSR." [73]

Another source, however, indicates that Kun was wrong about the CPR leadership and that the Fourth Congress established a heterogeneous and unworkable Central Committee.[74] Events between 1928 and 1932 seem to confirm the latter interpretation. The new secretary of the Central Committee of the CPR and the strongest individual in the Party was Barbu. He and the director of the trade union movement in the Banat, Koloman Müller, occupied a position close to that of the former right wing in the Party.[75] The organizational secretary, Rudolf, and Marcel Pauker, who operated from Moscow under the name Luksimin, stood further to the left, closer to the unfolding trend in the Comintern. Elek Köblos (underground name Badulescu), leader of the trade union movement in Transylvania, occupied a moderate position between the two.

On January 24, 1929, the ECCI sent an open letter to all members of the CPR, enumerating its errors.[76] This only widened the breach betwen the new leaders. The factional quarrel became so intense that the ECCI was forced to appoint a new Executive Committee for the Party before the end of 1929.[77] In August, 1930, the ECCI again ordered all factionalism to cease in the Party before the end of the year.[78] A "solid and workable leadership" (subservient

---

[73] *Ibid.*

[74] Petre Bezhenaru, "Klassicheskii obrazchik 'levogo' sektantsva," *Kommunisticheskii Internatsional,* No. 26 (Sept. 20, 1930), p. 63.

[75] Kun, *Kommunisticheskii Internatsional,* No. 23 (Aug. 23, 1930), p. 57.

[76] Gori, *Kommunisticheskii Internatsional,* No. 8–9 (March 30, 1932), p. 61.

[77] I have not been able to locate a copy of this letter, but the contents are summarized in *Kommunisticheskii Internatsional,* No. 28 (July 19, 1929), pp. 37–39.

[78] Bezhenaru, *Kommunisticheskii Internatsional,* No. 26 (Sept. 20, 1930), p. 51.

to the Comintern) was not provided, however, until the Fifth Party Congress in December, 1931.[79]

What most divided the Party was the proper interpretation of the lessons of Alba-Iulia and the implications of the new National Peasant government in terms of the future development of the Party. In an unusual step the Comintern opened the pages of Soviet periodicals to the spokesmen for the right and the left.[80] The debate lasted from February, to July, 1929, and in the history of East European communism it was as significant as Kabakchiev's debate with the leaders of the Comintern in 1923, Marković's debate with Stalin in 1925, and the controversy surrounding the "May Error" in Poland.

At the center of the controversy was the theoretician of the so-called right faction of the Moscow section of the Party, Solomon Timov.[81] However, both sides labeled one another "rightists" and Ghereaists, an excellent illustration of the ambiguity of both these terms. Essentially Timov's heresy lay in the assumption that the victory of the National Peasant Party was a positive gain and would eliminate the obstacles to industrialization and diminish the role of imperialists in the development of the Rumanian economy.

Timov had actually entered this fray even earlier at a more general level by challenging Kolarov's thesis that the Balkan countries could not be industrialized because they were colonies of the

[79] Gori, *Kommunisticheskii Internatsional*, No. 8–9 (March 30, 1932), p. 61.

[80] Timov was the most prolific writer on the subject. In addition to the articles cited above, he had already contributed an interpretation of the role of agrarianism in Rumanian politics. S. Timov, "Tsaranizm," *Na agrarnom fronte*, No. 5–6 (May–June, 1926), pp. 71–85, No. 7–8 (July–Aug., 1926), pp. 144–53. He initiated the discussion in the Party on the nature of the National Peasant government with "Problema revoliutsii v Rumynii," *Mirovoe khoziaistvo i mirovaia politika*, No. 3 (March, 1929), pp. 45–58. Other articles appearing in the course of the debate were: A. Mikhailov, "O pravom uklone v K. P. Rumynii," *Kommunisticheskii Internatsional*, No. 16–17 (April 26, 1929), pp. 40–47; A. Mikhailov, "Eshche o pravom uklone," *Kommunisticheskii Internatsional*, No. 28 (July 19, 1929) pp. 34–39; I. Raliu, "Programma pravitel'stva Natsional-Tsaranistskoi Partii Rumynii," *Agrarnye problemy*, No. 1 (Feb., 1929), pp. 75–91; T. Marin, "Polozhenie sel'skogo khoziaistva v Rumynii i znachenie pravitel'stva Natsional'no-Krest'ianskoi Partii," *Na agrarnom fronte*, No. 8 (Aug., 1929), pp. 121–35, and No. 9 (Sept., 1929), pp. 111–21.

[81] Mikhailov, *Kommunisticheskii Internatsional*, No. 16–17 (April 26, 1929), p. 44.

Western capitalists.[82] While Timov had published a book against Gherea's theory of neo-serfdom, and although he studiously avoided the use of the term, there was, as Timov's opponents pointed out, an element of Gherea's approach in his arguments.[83] Like Gherea, Timov was not primarily interested in the immediate prospect of revolution. He argued that in Rumania the postwar acquisition of industrialized territory (Transylvania) and the political and economic concessions to the peasantry had established the necessary prerequisites for industrialization.[84] These political concessions in particular had enabled the petty bourgeoisie and peasantry, the groups which supported the unhampered development of capitalism, to achieve political power.[85]

In other words, the progressive historic significance of the arrival of the National Peasant Party to power, we contend, is not due to some sort of revolutionary virtues which, of course, they do not possess but to the bourgeois-capitalistic essence of the National Peasant government, which is reactionary from the point of view of the interests of the proletariat, but progressive from the point of view of the development of capitalism. . . . This does not eliminate the problem of achieving the bourgeois-democratic revolution in Rumania, but it diminishes the period of transition to this revolution and provides most of the objective and subjective prerequisites.[86]

According to Timov, the accession of the National Peasant Party would, on the one hand, enable Rumania to eliminate the obstacles to industrialization by crushing the dictatorship of foreign capital. On the other hand, the pursuit of these policies would in the course of time create the suitable conditions for the proletarian revolution.[87]

[82] S. Timov, "Agrarizatsiia ili Industrializatsiia," *Mirovoe khoziaistvo i mirovaia politika,* No. 2 (Feb., 1929), pp. 21–32.

[83] See Timov, pp. 45–92. One recent arrival from Rumania, Timofei Marin, wrote of Timov's point of view, indicating its similarity to Gherea's theory of neo-serfdom: "In practice a similar theory brought the Rumanian Communist Party to serious opportunistic errors in the past (the united front with the National Peasant Party)." T. Marin, *Na agrarnom fronte,* No. 9 (Sept., 1929), p. 121.

[84] Timov, *Mirovoe khoziaistvo i mirovaia politika,* No. 3 (March, 1929), p. 47.

[85] *Ibid.,* pp. 49–53.

[86] Timov, *Kommunisticheskii Internatsional,* No. 25 (June 28, 1929), pp. 46–47.

[87] Timov, *Mirovoe khoziaistvo i mirovaia politika,* No. 3 (March, 1929), p. 58.

The significance which Timov attached to the removal of obstacles to industrialization places Timov in Gherea's camp. The assumption, however, that the barriers could be eliminated by the peasant political movement places Timov outside of Gherea's school, though somehow, I think Gherea might have approved. The assumption that the peasant through his political movement could play both a positive (in Marxist terms) and an independent role in the bourgeois-democratic revolution was not only a deviation from Gherea's theories but also a violation of some of the most fundamental tenets of the Comintern agrarian program. Timov's position in many ways was a testimonial to the wide appeal of the National Peasant program.

According to Timov's major critic, A. Mikhailov:

> The accession of the National Peasant Party does not deepen opposition in the camp of bourgeois Rumania, because it does not signify the destruction of the Liberal Party. The National Peasant Party, now that it has come to power, will open the gates wide to a deluge of foreign capital, following the path of capitulation before foreign capital upon which the Liberal Party had already entered. The Liberal Party, however, could not follow this course without restraint because of certain historical ties. The National Peasant government will, on the basis of this capitulation, conciliate the capitalists in Rumania and at the same time sharpen the class struggle of the proletarian and basic peasant masses with the bourgeoisie and the capitalists. Their economic legislation has already led to a quickening of class differentiation in rural areas and to a departure from it [the National Peasant Party] of broad strata of the peasantry. They have already sold the workers to foreign capital and even more successfully unleashed the sharpest class struggle in the towns.[88]

According to Mikhailov, Timov did not realize that the National Peasant Party was dominated by kulaks and was no more than an arm of Anglo-French capital.[89] Instead of eliminating the obstacles to the development of capitalism, therefore, the National Peasant government would increase the exploitation of Rumania by foreign capital. The government's accession would be marked not by a struggle between the petty bourgeoisie and the bourgeoisie but by an intensification of the struggle of the peasant with the bourgeoisie.

[88] Mikhailov, *Kommunisticheskii Internatsional*, No. 16–17 (April 26, 1929), p. 43.
[89] *Ibid.*, p. 43.

In short, the government would bring the possibility of the Rumanian proletarian revolution much closer than Timov's analysis would indicate.

At the meeting of the Tenth Plenum of the ECCI in July, 1929, Kolarov strongly condemned those who underestimated the fascist character of the National Peasant government in Rumania.[90] One of the subsequent diatribes against Timov echoed this description of the National Peasant Party as a fascist party, and asserted that the next revolution in Rumania would be a socialist revolution.[91] The Comintern gave its seal of approval to Timov's opponents.

The debate in the pages of Soviet journals ended when the editors of the Comintern journal, *Kommunisticheskii Internatsional*, awarded the laurels to Mikhailov. Timov's favorable evaluation of the nature of the National Peasant Party and his underestimation of both the power of imperialism and the imminence of the proletarian revolution were refuted.

Finally, there is the opportunistic passivity which the Comparty unquestionably displayed at the time of the events ot Alba-Iulia, when the peasant masses advanced on a revolutionary path and the Peasant Party deserted them. The Rumanian Communist Party might have yielded to the correct Leninist position of intervention in these affairs if it were not for the fact that they stood for the point of view of Comrade Timov, objectively embroidering the Peasant Party and to a significant degree confusing the role of this party with that of the peasant masses, a movement which the Peasant Party demagogically used in order to come to power.[92]

The editors explained that the principal error of Timov and the right faction was their overestimation of Rumania's bondage to foreign imperialists. This had led to ambiguity in the CPR program, which called for a joint effort with bourgeois opposition parties to drive out foreign devils and eliminate neo-serfdom before preparing for the proletarian revolution. The truth was, said the Comintern, Rumania was both a vassal of Western imperialists and an imperialistic state in its own right. It was therefore the duty of the CPR to maximize internal class conflicts as well as the external conflict

[90] *Desiatyi plenum ispolkoma Kominterna* (Moscow, 1929), I, 187.
[91] Marin, *Na agrarnom fronte*, No. 9 (Sept., 1929), p. 121.
[92] *Kommunisticheskii Internatsional*, No. 28 (July 19, 1929), p. 38.

between the interests of the Rumanian state and those of the great
capitalist nations.

There is no doubt that Rumania is controlled economically by five great
powers, but they operate through the Rumanian bourgeoisie and at present
through National Peasantism. By means of its [the National Peasant government's] measures it has already brought about an acceleration of class
differentiation in the countryside and the departure from the countryside
of a broad stratum of the peasantry. It has already sold the workers to
foreign capital and succeeded in unleashing even sharper class struggle in
the city. The necessary prerequisites for the liberation of Rumania from
the imperialistic yoke, from its role as an arm of imperialism in the struggle against the USSR, is a rising of the worker-peasant masses against the
National Peasant government, its overthrow, and the establishment of a
workers' and peasants' state.[93]

Timov's approach was unacceptable to the Comintern because
it did not generate the proper tone in the attitude of the CPR toward
the National Peasant Party. The left course was beginning to suffuse
all phases of Comintern work, and, although Timov's analysis
would seem to have described the role of the National Peasant
Party more accurately than Mikhailov's, reality had to be distorted
to provide the necessary rationale for revolution. The picture Timov
painted was not black enough. How could one justify the preparation
of revolution against a government unless it was an exploiter, a fascist government, or an agent of foreign imperialism? The Comintern's
thesis that neither external nor internal social and economic contradictions had abated in Rumania fit its needs admirably, since it
meant that there was only one possible response—armed insurrection.
Again the schematic analyses of the Comintern triumphed over a
more flexible approach to local problems. But the interpretation
of Rumanian events approved by the Comintern in 1929 was
resisted by many members of the CPR until 1932, not only because
of former traditions in the Rumanian Marxist movement, but also
because the Comintern forced the Party to accept a distorted view
of the real situation in its own country.

The actual issues in this controversy were shrouded in the labored
jargon of all Communist theological disputes. The Rumanian Communists were well aware of the handicaps thrust upon them by the

93 *Ibid.*, p. 39.

Comintern's policy on the national question and by its insistence on a revolutionary program and organization. Although the Comintern repeatedly admonished the CPR for its weakness in the Old Kingdom,[94] it continued to press the Rumanians to tout their espousal of national self-determination, which to the members of the Old Kingdom meant dismemberment of their state. Although the Rumanians were told in 1928 that their country had replaced Poland as the advance base of capitalist aggression against the USSR, the Party was asked to adopt an uncompromisingly revolutionary stance even against political parties which might be allies. As a weak and declining party, the Rumanian Communists bravely tried to offset their Russian label by exploiting a national grievance, in this case the exploitation of the country by foreign capital. The CPR paid only lip service to the Comintern's demands and tried to adjust to the relatively stable political situation in its country by emphasizing recruitment, playing down the need for revolutionary action, and supporting reformist opposition parties, hoping to shine by reflecting their light. This approach found its best rationale in a version of Ghereaism. But the Comintern was less interested in the numerical strength of the Rumanian Party than in its conformity to the new course in the Soviet Union and the international Communist movement.

After seven years of factional struggle, all the formulas of the Comintern on the agrarian question and social fascism were adopted at the Fifth Congress of the CPR in December, 1931. Timov's evaluation of the National Peasant Party was specifically rejected and the CPR accepted the task of overthrowing the existing Rumanian government. Given the tactics required in the new left period, this really amounted to no more than the allocation of another impossible task to an extremely weak section of the Comintern. All that the Comintern succeeded in doing in its tactics in Rumania during this period was to support the very disruptive forces which contributed to the growth of fascism without markedly advancing its own cause.

[94] Kun, *Kummunisticheskii Internatsional*, No. 23 (Aug. 23, 1930), p. 54, and Gori, *Kommunisticheskii Internatsional*, No. 8–9 (March 30, 1932), p. 58.

CHAPTER XI

The Exception:
The Czechoslovak Republic

In the early 1920s the Czechoslovak Communist Party was a conspicuous reminder to the Comintern that its directives could be defied with impunity. This rankled, but there were good reasons for the Comintern's self-restraint. The Czech Party operated in the most highly developed country in Eastern Europe. It was not only the largest East European Communist party, but also one of the largest Communist parties in the world. The success of the Czech Communists seemed to bear out Marx's axiom about the correlation between the level of economic development and proletarian class consciousness. The Comintern could not afford to lose so splendid a showcase and so the Czech Party was permitted to follow its own bent in more ways and for a longer period of time than any other East European party. Unlike any of them, it became a successful mass party. Among the Communist parties in Eastern Europe, only the Czech Party enjoyed a legal existence during the entire interwar period and only the Czech Party became a genuine national party, representing both the ruling nationality and the national minorities. Its success was probably a direct result of its independence and individuality. But Czechoslovakia was unique among East European countries in other respects besides the nature of its Communist movement. The country was an exception to almost every rule in Eastern Europe.

ECONOMICS AND POLITICS IN CZECHOSLOVAKIA

Czechoslovakia was the only state in Eastern Europe to preserve functioning democratic institutions for twenty years. During the interwar period the tiny Czechoslovak state earned a place in the hearts of the Western democracies, who cherished it as a precious example of the exportability of the principles and practices of democratic institutions. In retrospect it is clear that Czechoslovakia, even with her marked advantages over the other countries in Eastern Europe, did not completely escape the usual problems of that part of the world. Czech democracy was not as solid or as closely patterned after its Western counterparts as many liked to believe.

At the beginning of the republic the most promising response to the dangers which beset Czech democracy from its backward and politically volatile eastern provinces was the Czechoslovak Republican Party of Small Farmers and Peasants, a party dedicated to agrarian reform and democratic political institutions. This party occupied a prominent position in domestic politics between World War I and World War II, inspiring one historian to call the period 1922-35 the "Agrarian Era. " [1] The agrarians believed that they had discovered a "third path" to democracy between liberalism and communism, entitling Prague to assume its rightful place as the capital of East European agrarianism. Because of this claim and because of the obvious success of the Czechoslovak Communist Party in acquiring a large following, the efforts of the Comintern to apply its agrarian policy in Czechoslovakia are of special interest.

Among the factors which accounted for the extraordinary political stability of Czechoslovakia were her balanced social structure, her relative prosperity during the entire interwar period, and the high caliber of her political leaders, particularly Masaryk and Švehla.[2] The balanced social structure and relative prosperity were,

[1] M. W. Graham, "Parties and Politics," in R. J. Kerner, ed., *Czechoslovakia: Twenty Years of Independence* (Berkeley, 1940), p. 154.

[2] *Ibid.,* p. 155. Hugh Seton-Watson adds to these factors the absence of Catholic political influence, to which he attributes many of the political problems of neighboring Austria, a state similar in social and economic structure to Czechoslovakia, but less stable politically. Hugh Seton-Watson, *Eastern Europe Between the Wars, 1918–1944* (Cambridge, 1945), p. 184. In some respects Czech political attitudes and problems also resemble those of Germany more closely than they resemble those of Czechoslovakia's East European neighbors. For example, Rudolf Schlesinger chooses to treat the political history of postwar Germany, Austria, and Czechoslovakia together in his *Central European Democracy and Its Background: Economics and Political Group Organization* (London, 1953), chap. I. Schlesinger's central thesis,

however, most characteristic of the western, formerly Austrian, half of the republic, Bohemia and Moravia-Silesia.[3] It may well be that the political dominance during the interwar years of those sections enabled Czechoslovakia to escape the fate of Rumania and Yugoslavia, countries where the politically dominant provinces had not achieved the same degree of economic maturity.[4] For the qualities most conducive to the fruitful development of democracy were also concentrated in the western half of the new state.

Although the majority of the Czechs did not free themselves from the feeling of humiliation imposed by the Bohemian and Moravian Germans, their industrial, intellectual, and agricultural progress gave them self-confidence and a feeling of independence. . . . Because of previous national and social development, popular regard for the democratic way of life, and accumulation of experience in the conduct of political affairs and self-administration, it [independence] was not a transition from passive negativism to self-government.[5]

Although the social structure of the Czech lands was quite diverse, the extremes of wealth and poverty were absent and there was little of the feeling of class antagonism upon which communism could feed.[6] If Czechoslovakia had consisted solely of the Czech

couched in Marxist terms, is that in these three countries both the parties representing the workers and the parties representing the peasants lost their cohesion and stability as a result of collaboration with the political organizations of other social classes.

[3] Wanklyn suggests that there is a farming frontier in Europe running through the center of Poland, between Czech and Slovak lands, and through the center of Hungary. On the western side of this line, natural resources were developed intensively, while east of it they were developed extensively. She attributes this difference to geographic features and to the fact that there was a parallel growth of agriculture and industry in the western half. Harriet Wanklyn, *Czechoslovakia* (New York, 1954), p. 219.

[4] J. Roucek, "Czechoslovakia and Her Minorities," in Kerner, pp. 174–75.

[5] Jan Hajda, "Sociological Aspects," in Jan Hajda, ed., *A Study of Contemporary Czechoslovakia,* Human Relations Area Files, Subcontractor's Monograph No. 15 (Chicago, n.d.,) p. 52.

[6] *Ibid.,* p. 86. Hajda points out that this absence of class antagonisms created real problems for a party like the CPC, which based its appeals on such antagonisms. *Ibid.,* p. 103. Chmelar states that the conflict between the program of the Comintern and the attitude of the Czech workmen was the source of continuous crisis in that party. Josef Chmelar, *Political Parties in Czechoslovakia* (Prague, 1926), p. 44. Wanklyn indicates that the absence of rural class antagonisms in the Czech lands posed a special problem for the Communists after 1945. Wanklyn, p. 224.

lands it would have been truly a "nation of shopkeepers." Aside from the question of national minorities, the only real factors of instability were the flight of skilled labor from the countryside and the relatively high proportion of agricultural laborers among the rural population.[7]

Opposed to the political balance wheel of the Czech lands, however, were the eastern lands. Some of the indices of the relative level of economic development from the year 1930 illustrate the striking differences between the two halves of the republic (see Table 15).

Table 15

Some Demographic Features of Czechoslovakia in 1930

Region	Net reproductive rate	Density of population per km.	Percent of population dependent on agriculture	Per capita production in agriculture	Surplus population [a] (percent)
Czechoslovakia	.95	105	33	105	11.7
Bohemia	.74	137	23	155	− 7.9
Moravia-Silesia	.90	133	27	129	0
Slovakia	1.29	68	55	61	27.5
Sub-Carpathian Ruthenia	1.85	57	58	42	47.5

Source: Dudley Kirk, *Europe's Population in the Interwar Years* (Geneva, 1946), pp. 263–64.

[a] Wilbert E. Moore, *Economic Demography of Eastern and Southern Europe* (Geneva, 1945), p. 71.

Although Slovakia had some functioning extractive industries, Sub-Carpathian Ruthenia was completely undeveloped in 1919 and was little more than a Magyar deer park.[8] In these two areas one encounters all the usual problems of Eastern Europe: primitive levels of cultivation, rural overpopulation, and a relentless hunger for land among the peasants. As in the rest of Eastern Europe, these

---

[7] The problem of underpopulation in Czech rural areas is examined in detail in H. Böker and F. W. von Bülow, *The Rural Exodus in Czechoslovakia*, International Labour Office, Studies and Reports, Series K, No. 18 (Geneva, 1935).

[8] Wanklyn, pp. 304, 412.

problems were compounded by the desire of the nationalities for greater autonomy. The Slovaks already had a strong national movement, and in Ruthenia the Ukrainians and Hungarians were just beginning to voice their opposition to Czech hegemony.[9] From the outset there were also strong differences between the intelligentsia of the western and eastern provinces. For the Czech intelligentsia, the prevailing traditions were bourgeois, rationalistic, and humanitarian. For the Slovaks and Carpatho-Ukrainians as well as the Poles and Hungarians, the prevailing traditions were aristocratic and romantic.[10] The Hungarian Revolution of 1919, which inspired efforts to establish Slovakian and Carpatho-Ukrainian Soviet Republics,[11] undoubtedly fired the imagination of nationalists of all political creeds, and when the Czechs, after the formation of the new Czechoslovak state, failed to solve the problems created by overpopulation in the eastern provinces and even seemed unwilling to invest in industrial development,[12] "national liberation" movements of all sorts burst into life in the eastern provinces. As in the rest of Eastern Europe, the postwar land reforms proved to be no more than a temporary palliative.[13]

The diversity of economic, social and national groupings was re-

[9] In 1921 in Sub-Carpathian Ruthenia 63 percent of the population were Ukrainian and 18 percent were Hungarian. Carlile A. Macartney, *Hungary and Her Successors: The Treaty of Trianon and Its Consequences, 1919–1937* (London, 1937), p. 203.

[10] For an illuminating discussion of these differences see William E. Griffith, "Myth and Reality, in Czechoslovak History," *East Europe*, II, No. 3 (March, 1962), 7–8 and *passim*.

[11] See V. Maryna, "Revoliutsionnoe dvizhenie v Slovakii v 1918–1919 gg.," in A. Ia. Manusevich, ed., *Oktiabr'skaia revoliutsiia i zarubezhnye slavianskie narody* (Moscow, 1957), pp. 233–70, and I. N. Mel'nikova, "Kak byla vkliuchena zakarpatskaia Ukraina v sostav Chekhoslovakii v 1919," *Uchenye zapiski instituta slavianovedeniia*, III (1951), 104–35.

[12] Macartney, p. 131. The unwillingness of the Czechs to develop the eastern lands has been explained by the fact that the Czech lands in the 1920s were "overindustrialized." Gerhard Schacher, *Central Europe and the Western World* (New York, 1936), p. 60, and Leo Pasvolsky, *Economic Nationalism of the Danubian States* (New York, 1928), p. 268. These scholars maintain that this means that Czech industry was geared to a level of production well above the markets available to her, resulting in rural underpopulation as workers flocked to urban areas for employment. According to this argument, the Czechs therefore needed markets in eastern lands and a reliable source of agricultural goods and were unwilling to finance the development of competitors in the production of industrial goods.

[13] Böker and Von Bülow, p. 162.

flected in the number of political parties in Czechoslovakia. To a large degree this liability was turned into an asset by Švehla, leader of the Czech agrarian party. Švehla's experience in Austrian parliamentary politics may have endowed him, as it had Witos, with the art of compromise, but Švehla succeeded in applying this art, whereas Witos did not.

Švehla regarded the spirit of opposition as something in the nature of a sin and led his party into every coalition. Thus the Agrarian Party gradually became the center around which the other Czechoslovak parties grouped themselves in order to form government coalitions. The special nature of the party, its consolidation and true conservatism predestined it for this task, but in order that the heterogenous group of parties forming the government coalition might be held together in the government, there was need for the skill of Švehla, who had a unique gift for reconciling opposing points of view.[14]

One of Švehla's first victories had been the union of the Czech agrarian party with the National Agrarian Party of Slovakia (led by Milan Hodža) in the spring of 1919. The party would later expand into Sub-Carpathian Ruthenia as well.

Immediately, after the establishment of the Czechoslovak Republic, it had seemed for a time that the mood of radical reform would grant a clear majority in the new government to the Czech Social Democratic Party. But when the left wing of that party seceded and formed the Czechoslovak Communist Party in September, 1920, this was no longer possible.[15] In October the first Pětka, a coalition of five Czech parties, which was also known as the Green-Red Coalition, was established.[16] It dominated Czech politics until 1925.

Švehla's supreme achievement was to make this coalition and the succeeding Green-Black Coalition work.[17] Needless to say, this success

[14] Josef Borovička, *Ten Years of Czechoslovak Politics* (Prague, 1929), p. 105. See, also Robert W. Seton-Watson, *A History of the Czechs and Slovaks* (London, 1943), p. 329.

[15] Borovička, p. 105; Robert Seton-Watson, p. 329.

[16] The members of the Pětka were the Czechoslovak Republican Party of Small Farmers and Peasants, the Czech Social Democratic Party, the Czech National Democratic Party, the Czech Populist Party, and the Czech Socialist Party.

[17] Except for a five-month period in 1926, Švehla was premier until February, 1929, when illness forced him to resign. Agrarian premiers succeeded him until 1938.

through compromise enabled Švehla's political enemies, such as the Czechoslovak Communists, to maintain that he had bartered away the interests of the class which he was supposed to represent.[18] In his memoirs, the prominent Czech Communist Václav Kopecký notes:

> Taking stock retrospectively of the role which Antonín Švehla played as leader of the Agarian Party during the whole period of the development of the first republic, we see how accurate is the assertion that in him the Czech bourgeoisie had their most cunning politician. In him our revolutionary wokers' movement also had its most dangerous opponent. As a result of Švehla's efforts the Czech Agrarian Party, as a strong mass party, became a firm pillar of the capitalist system in Czechoslovakia and of capitalist reaction in rural areas.[19]

In actuality, the continued political success of the agrarian party did attract all sorts of interest groups eager for spoils, until it became during the last years of the republic the principal party of the wealthy.[20]

By 1925 the decline in the prices of agricultural products in comparison with those of industrial goods drove Švehla toward a policy of agricultural protection, a policy which the Marxist members of his coalition could not accept.[21] The general elections of 1925

[18] The choice of government through coalition has, in the words of Young," the disadvantage that the elector never knows, when he votes for a party, to what extent it will feel impelled to compromise with regard to the program whereby it wins his vote. On the other hand, the necessity for compromise prevents radical and arbitrary changes of policy between elections, but permits minor changes in the composition and policy of the government without a general election." Edgar P. Young, *Czechoslovakia: Keystone of Peace and Democracy* (London, 1938), p. 114.

[19] Václav Kopecký, *Vospominaniia: iz istorii chekhoslovatskoi respubliki i bor'by kommunisticheskoi partii Chekhoslovakii za pobedu sotsializma* (Moscow, 1962), p. 197.

[20] Hugh Seton-Watson, pp. 174–75, and Schlesinger, p. 77. Maslov, in his description of Hodža, indicates how Hodža's economic program became more and more conservative in the first decade of his career in the Czech Agrarian Party. For example, in 1918 Hodža wanted a third of all Slovak land to be confiscated and redistributed among the poor peasants, but, by 1930, 16 percent of all Slovak land was still in the hands of large estates and Hodža maintained that these large holdings would be preserved for a long time. Sergei Maslov, *Novaia sila V Europe i Milan Godzha* (Prague, 1938), p. 91.

[21] This Czech "scissors" crisis was in part the result of the dumping of agricultural goods into the Czech market by neighboring countries who hoped thereby to profit from the known stability of the Czech currency. Lucy E. Textor, "Agriculture and Agricultural Reform," in Kerner, p. 233.

had revealed for the first time the inroads which the Communists had made in the Czech Social Democratic Party. In 1920 the Czech Social Democrats won seventy-four deputies; in 1925, twenty-nine. The 1925 election revealed striking gains for the Catholic, conservative, and national minority parties, and it was from these latter elements that Švehla decided to form a new coalition, the so-called Green-Black Coalition. This new regime, which was to last until 1929, was dedicated to more protection for agriculture, greater provincial autonomy, and peace with the Catholic church. While this coalition was a milestone in the history of the republic, bringing as it did the major parties of the national minorities into a positive role in politics for the first time, the policies of the coalition gave it "the characteristics of a bourgeois conservative government." [22]

The elections of 1929 seemed to reflect public confidence in the moderate reform parties and the Czech agrarian party. Those parties standing for radical reform, revolution, or the exclusive interests of nationalities received fewer votes than they had in the past. Evidently the Czech agrarian party had performed a useful, popular, and perhaps necessary function in lending stability to a multi-party political system and, at least in part, in mitigating purely national conflict. Švehla's achievements had won the stamp of popular approval not only for his party but for all parties that accepted compromise as a necessary attribute of functioning democracy in Czechoslovakia.

But in making his party the nucleus of every coalition and in maintaining his political alliances, Švehla had to trim his own program. While its record in social legislation is impressive, the Czech agrarian party did not meet squarely the agrarian problems of the new republic. Its preoccupation with political power [23] tended to make

[22] Borovička, p. 105. Graham sees this coalition as a "sign of the general swing to conservatism then operative in Europe," Graham, "Parties and Politics," in Kerner, p. 157.

[23] Kopecký, who has no love for Švehla, relates a story which, although it may be apocryphal, illustrates Švehla's love for power. Švehla is alleged to have said to a Social Democratic minister of labor who was reluctant to approve some antilabor legislation; "If you want to enjoy the sweet taste of power with us, then you must not be finicky or be afraid of dishonor. If a girl wants to enjoy the sweet taste of love with her lover, she must not be afraid of losing her honor, but must go to bed boldly." Kopecký. p. 197.

the Party reflect the interests of the more influential and articulate social groups rather than those of the average peasant.

Under these circumstances the Comintern found in the Czech agrarian party a competitor considerably different from the agrarian parties in the rest of Eastern Europe. At the same time, the political environment was different from that in other East European countries. In the struggle with agrarianism in the Czechoslovak Republic there was more room for legal tactics and parliamentary action.

BETWEEN REALISM AND BOLSHEVISM

The Comintern's criticisms of the Communist Party of Czechoslovakia (CPC) in the 1920s generally followed the same theme. For example, at the special commission of the Comintern on the Czech question in 1925, Stalin stated that the Party suffered from "Social Democratic survivals." [24] This ambiguous phrase was applied in most cases to parties that did not conform to Comintern directives. In the Czech case it meant particularly that the Party paid too much attention to winning a mass following, to winning elections, and to parliamentary maneuvers, and too little attention to the directives of the Comintern and to the need for creating a cadre of dedicated and experienced professional revolutionaries. Stalin indicated that the Czechs in the Party and in the labor movement were drugged by the idea of the national state, and that only the Party members from the national minorities had adopted a truly revolutionary stance. At least one Marxist agreed with Stalin that the Czechoslovak Party was probably the least Bolshevik of all sections of the Comintern. The Austrian Social Democrat, Otto Bauer, maintained that there were only two good Social Democratic parties in Central Europe, the Austrian Social Democratic Party and the CPC.[25]

The problem of the CPC was particularly acute since it was one of the largest parties in the Comintern (see Table 16). Yet one indication of the non-Bolshevik character of the Party is the fact

[24] Stalin, "O Chekhoslovatskoi Kompartii," *Sochineniia* (Moscow, 1946–51), VII, 59–68.
[25] Branko Lazić, *Les Partis communistes d'Europe, 1919–1955* (Paris, 1956), p. 108.

that, of the enormous number of members in 1926, only 25.8 percent were active and only 30.2 percent paid regular dues.[26]

Table 16

The Strength of the Large Communist Parties in the Comintern

Communist party	MEMBERSHIP			
	1924	*1925*	*1926*	*1927*
German	121,394	122,755	132,248	124,729
Czechoslovak	138,966	93,220	92,818	150,000 [a]
French	68,187	83,326	75,000	52,372

Source: B. Vassiliyev, "The Forces of the Comintern and Its Allies," *International Press Correspondence,* IX, No. 17 (April 5, 1929), 360. Borkenau's figures are a little different. He has 65,000 in 1926 and 56,000 in 1927 for the French Party. Franz Borkenau, *World Communism* (New York, 1939), p. 367.

[a] The figure usually quoted for membership in this year is 138,000, not 150,000. Lazić, *Les Partis communistes d'Europe, 1919–55* (Paris, 1956), p. 109; Borkenau, *World Communism,* p. 367.

Unlike most of the East European Communists, the Czechs got their Marxism originally from Austrian, not Russian, Social Democracy. The uncompromisingly revolutionary tone which characterized Bolshevism was almost entirely absent from Czech communism.

At the moment of liberation it is not an exaggeration to say that communism had hardly even a foothold among the Czech and Slovak workers. . . .
Czech and German workers had a strong tradition of independent political activity in the form of the Social Democratic movement within old Austria. This experience, however, has not been a revolutionary one, and their socialism had been the characteristic parliamentary and evolutionary socialism of pre-war Europe.[27]

While the Comintern was delighted to welcome a large, well-organized party into its ranks, it was not eager to let it remain different from the Russian model. In the process of purging the CPC of its so-called Social Democratic survivals, the Comintern also succeeded in decimating the ranks of the Party, thus to some degree de-

[26] Karl Kreibich, *Kommunisticheskaia Partiia Chekhoslovakii* (Moscow, 1928), p. 51.
[27] H. Gordon Skilling, "The Formation of a Communist Party in Czechoslovakia," *American Slavic and East European Review,* XIV, No. 3 (Oct., 1955), 346.

feating its own purposes. The difficulty seemed to be that the old Social Democratic approach was more fruitful in Czechoslovakia than the new Bolshevik methods. As one non-Communist observer put it:

From the beginning of its independent existence it [the CPC] has been in the throes of continuous internal crises, which are the consequence of conflict between the romantic, unfruitful doctrine of communism and the realistic nature of the Czech workman. Even if the latter is of a radical turn of mind he does not lose his sense of everyday needs. As a result of these crisises, which involve a constant change of leaders and watchwords, the membership of the Communist organization is constantly decreasing.[28]

This decrease is illustrated by Table 17. The years of maximum decline in Party membership were the years of maximum interference from the Comintern.

Table 17
Membership in the Czechoslovak Communist Party

	Year	Members
	1921	557,774 [a]
	1922	170,000 [a]
	1923	132,000 [a]
	1924	138,996
	1925	93,220
	1926	92,818
	1927	138,000
January	1928	150,000
October	1928	48,000
February	1929	30,000 [a]
April	1929	24,000
February	1930	20,914 [a]

Source: Franz Borkenau, *World Communism* (New York, 1939), pp. 267–68.
[a] Ia. Stanek *et al.*, "Stroitel'stvo Kommunisticheskoi Partii Chekhoslovakii," *Voprosy istorii KPSS*, No. 5 (1959), pp. 135–37. Stanek indicates that the sharp drop in membership between the organizing or founding congress in October, 1921, and the First Party Congress in February, 1923, was due to a selective reregistration of all party members.

The chief spokesman for greater autonomy for the CPC in the Comintern was its leader, Bohumil Šmeral. Šmeral had been a prominent leader of the old Czech Social Democratic Party, but he had

[28] Chmelar, p. 44.

lost his prestige and influence by advocating an Austro-Marxist solution to the nationality problem during World War I.[29] After the war Šmeral moved reluctantly toward communism, perhaps because there was no other place for a Social Democratic renegade to go, but he had strong reservations about the Bolshevik program. He believed that, because the middle class was so much stronger in Czechoslovakia than in prewar Russia, and since the proletariat and peasantry could not make a revolution by themselves, Bolshevik tactics were not suitable in Czechoslovakia.[30] The "special conditions" prevailing in Czechoslovakia called for special tactics differing from those dictated by the Comintern. The Party's strength in membership in the next decade was usually due to Šmeral's realistic appraisal of the "special circumstances" in Czechoslovakia, not to Comintern-imposed policy.[31]

One aspect of Bolshevization which the CPC ignored in practice, though not in its resolutions, was the need to "go to the peasants." Although it never openly stated so, the Party probably felt that there was no need to recruit peasants since it already had a mass following. At the Second Congress of the Party in October, 1924, only 3 percent of the members were peasants, or 10 percent if one includes agricultural workers. By 1927 these figures were 2.5 percent and 14.6 percent.[32] This was not a large percentage in a country

[29] *Ibid.*, p. 46; Paul Zinner, "The Strategy and Tactics of the Czechoslovak Communist Party" (unpublished Ph.D. dissertation, Department of Government, Harvard University, 1953), p. 6; Skilling, *American Slavic and East European Review*, XIV, No. 3 (Oct., 1955), 348; Josef Korbel, *The Communist Subversion of Czechoslovakia, 1938–1948: The Failure of Coexistence* (Princeton, 1959), p. 20.

[30] Skilling, *American Slavic and East European Review*, XIV, No. 3 (Oct., 1955), p. 351. Korbel indicates that Šmeral was clearly no nationalist, which is logical considering his prewar position, but that "he was convinced that communism could not be shoved down the throat of the Czech workers, that their nationalism could not be ignored." Korbel, p. 22.

[31] Skilling, *American Slavic and East European Review*, XIV, No. 3 (Oct., 1955), 358. Zinner wrote: "If the party resisted the rough and ready ways which the Comintern was then seeking to impose on its sections [1925] it did so because of a realistic appraisal of the environment in which it operates." Zinner, p. 21.

[32] I. N. Mel'nikova, *Klassovaia bor'ba v Chekhoslovakii v gody chastichnoi stabilizatsii Kapitalizma, 1924–1929* (Moscow, 1962), p. 196, n. 235. Burks cites the 1927 figures but makes no distinction between peasants and agricultural workers, lumping them all together as peasants. R. V. Burks, *The Dynamics of Communism in Eastern Europe* (Princeton, 1961), p. 35.

where more than 20 percent of the population were dependent on agriculture.[33] One puzzling feature in the development of the CPC was that, in spite of the small number of peasants in the Party in the late 1920s, there were more than three times as many Party cells in rural areas as in the cities.[34] It seems that the Party appealed more to artisans and semi-skilled laborers (textile workers, miners, and bricklayers), who were scattered in production units employing less than 100 people throughout the country, than to the workers concentrated in large-scale enterprises in the cities.[35]

This is not to say that the Czech Party ignored the peasantry altogether. As indicated above, some peasants were recruited into the Party. A larger number joined Communist unions and an even larger number supported the Communist ticket. But the failure actively to recruit peasants was cited by the Comintern as one symptom of the non-Bolshevik character of the Party. To a large degree the indifference of the Party to peasant recruitment was a result of the conviction that another political party had already won a permanent place in the hearts of the Czech peasantry. The Communists never succeeded in breaking the hold which the Czech agrarian party had over the peasants except in Slovakia and in Sub-Carpathian Ruthenia,[36] and there those who supported the Communists were both peasants and members of national minority groups.

In Czechoslovakia, as in the rest of Eastern Europe, the Communists exploited the national minority question as well as the agrarian question, and, as elsewhere in Eastern Europe, it is difficult to determine which was more effective. Although in 1921 only 27 percent of the population lived in the two economically backward eastern provinces, 53 percent of the members of the CPC came from this area.[37] In the elections throughout this period the Commu-

---

[33] See Table 15, p. 269.

[34] Desiatyi plenum ispolkoma Kominterna (Moscow, 1929), I, 137.

[35] Hajda, p. 103. At the Tenth Plenum of the ECCI in 1929, Piatnitsky indicated that 75.2 percent of the members of the CPC worked in enterprises employing less than one hundred people. Desiatyi plenum ispolkoma Kominterna, I, 137.

[36] Mel'nikova, Klassovaia bor'ba, pp. 180, 233, and Istoriia Kommunisticheskoi Partii Chekhoslovakii (Moscow, 1962), p. 331.

[37] Ia. Stanek et al., "Stroitel'stvo Kommunisticheskoi Partii Chekhoslovakii," Voprosy istorii KPSS, No. 5 (1969), p. 135.

nists captured a higher proportion of the total vote in the two eastern provinces than in the others.[38] In his extremely useful analysis of the factors which might influence the voter in favor of communism, Burks examined the elections in Slovakia in 1929 and tried to divide the voters into industrial workers, landless agricultural workers, dwarf holders, cash croppers, and Magyars. Using a statistical technique known as multiple correlation analysis, Burks was able to demonstrate the degree of correlation between social and national groupings and the size of the vote.[39] His analysis indicates that all of the national minorities tended to vote for the Communists but that this tendency was by far the strongest among the Magyars. This testimonial to the effectiveness of the Comintern's program on the national question, as compared to its program on the agrarian question, is reinforced by Burks's other calculations, which indicate that in the elections in Slovakia from 1923 to 1929 the dwarf holders and landless peasants were not rallying en masse to the Communists.[40]

The extraordinary strength of the Communists in Sub-Carpathian Ruthenia also seems to owe more to the Comintern program on the national question than to other factors. It was not simply the extreme poverty and backwardness of the Ukrainian peasants but also their Pan-Russian ideas which made communism popular (the CPC being identified with Russian interests). Also in Ruthenia, as in Slovakia, communism was attractive to the Magyar minority (20 percent in 1921).

The first Marxist organization in Ruthenia had been the International Socialist Party, created in March, 1920, by former members of the Hungarian Soviet Republic and prisoners of war recently returned from the Soviet Union.[41] On January 16, 1921, this organization merged with the left wing of the Social Democratic Party of Slovakia and in May, 1921, both joined the newly created CPC.[42] The Ruthenians had no elected representatives in parliament

[38] Burks, p. 66.

[39] Ibid., pp. 73–76.

[40] Ibid., p. 44.

[41] I. N. Mel'nikova, "Iz istorii revoliutsionnogo dvizeniia na zakarpatskoi Ukraine v 1921–1924," Uchenye zapiski instituta slavianovedeniia, VI (1952), 8.

[42] Ibid., pp. 9–10.

until 1924, and in the interim the CPC adopted the role of defender of Ruthenia, first subjecting the government to interpellation on conditions in the area in the fall of 1921, and in November, 1922, passing through a bill for forty million koruny for relief.[43] The local representatives of the Communist Party rendered free legal aid and food doles of their own to the peasants, while at the same time reminding the Ruthenians that the Czechs were evil imperialists.[44] A prominent role in the Communist movement in Ruthenia was played by Ivan Bodnar (real name Lokat), a peasant who, as a war prisoner in the Soviet Union, had fought for the October Revolution and then had returned home to found the Carpathian Communist movement. He came from Velikiy Bychkov and had close ties with the salt miners of Solotvino (Akna-Slatina), where he had worked.[45] A prominent Hungarian Comintern Official, Mátyás Rákosi, explained the efforts of the CPC in Ruthenia as follows:

The problem of the Communist Party was clear. A party which had only several thousand industrial workers in Ruthenia had to seek support from hundreds of thousands of poor peasants. Thus it started to become a workers' and peasants' party.[46]

The CPC reaped its rewards with a spectacular victory in the elections held in Ruthenia in 1924 to select that province's first delegates to the Czech parliament. The Communists won 39.4 percent of the total popular vote and six of the fourteen seats available in the two houses of the parliament.[47] This victory was cited by

[43] Ibid., pp. 27, 36–37.

[44] M. Rakoshi, "Vybori v prikarpatskoi Rusia," Krest'ianskii Internatsional, No. 2 (May, 1924), pp. 40–41. Another Comintern source gives greater weight to the adroit manipulation of Ruthenian national sentiment in explaining the successes of the CPC in that area. Gabriel Farkash, "Pobeda kommunistov na vyborakh v prikarpatskoi Rusi," Kommunisticheskii Internatsional, No. 3–4 (May–June, 1924), pp. 402–3.

[45] "Ivan Bodnar, vozhd' prikarpatskogo krest'ianstva," Krest'ianskii Internatsional, No. 2 (May, 1924), p. 142. According to the official history of the CPC, Bodnar-Lokat led the attempts to unite Sub-Carpathian Ruthenia with the Soviet Ukraine late in 1920 at the time of the Red Army's advance into Poland. Istoriia Kommunisticheskoi Partii Chekhoslovakii, p. 66.

[46] Rakoshi, Krest'ianskii Internatsional, No. 2 (May, 1924), p. 40.

[47] Mel'nikova, Uchenye zapiski instituta slavianovedeniia, VI (1952), 45–46. Burks's figure of 42 percent of the popular vote for the Communists, which is derived from the reports of the Fifth Comintern Congress, is wrong. Burks, p. 78.

the Czech Communists as a victory of their strategy toward the peasants and prominently exhibited by the Comintern as evidence that communism was gaining a strong foothold in Eastern Europe.[48] But there is something about the striking success that doesn't ring true. In September, 1923, less than six months before, in village elections in Sub-Carpathian Ruthenia the Communists won less than 10 percent of the votes.[49]

According to government statistics, the Communist Party did hold more mass meetings and addressed more people during the intervening period than any other party.[50] But are we to believe that in six months, because of its active dissemination of Comintern theses and slogans, the CPC was able to get six times the number of votes (although the electorate was only larger by two thirds)?

Chances are that it was the gross miscalculation of the leading Ruthenian party in 1923 that made the Communist victory possible. In the village elections in September, 1923, the Ruthenian Agrarian-Republican Party, a loose coalition of five Hungarian and Ruthenian peasant parties, ran on a program of agrarian reform and self-determination for Ruthenia and garnered almost 68 percent of the vote against the Communist 10 percent.[51] In November the leader of the coalition, Kaminsky, signed a pact with the Czech Agrarian party agreeing to transform his party into a branch of Švehla's

[48] Burks apparently was taken in by this line too, although he accepts the 1924 elections as a victory for Comintern policy on the national question, which is partly correct. Burks, p. 78. As explained above, however, it was also a victory for the Comintern's policy on the agrarian question, and it was also luck.

[49] Mel'nikova, *Uchenye zapiski instituta slavianovedeniia*, VI (1952), 38.

[50] *Ibid.*, p. 45.

[51] *Ibid.*, p. 38. The exact figures for the village or communal elections are difficult to obtain. The ones used here from Mel'nikova are from the CPC newspaper, which may rightly be questioned. Macartney cites figures which are wrong on several counts. Macartney, p. 239. He says they are the results of municipal elections, whereas they were communal elections; his figures are not properly labeled and his annotation is incorrect. The figures cited by Macartney from a League of Nations document are only from one fourth of the communes participating in the elections. Elections were dispensed with in the other communes because they had only submitted a single slate of candidates, but the votes in those communes were awarded to a single slate. League of Nations Document C 821. M 310. 1923 I. p. 3. Mel'nikova's figures probably present a truer picture because most of the votes for single slates, not appearing on Macartney's list, were for the Ruthenian Republican-Agrarian Party.

party and to abandon the struggle for national autonomy, a decision which lost Kaminsky some of his former allies.[52] More important, as a result of Kaminsky's decisions, the party with the second strongest position on national self-determination inherited the Ruthenian Agrarian-Republican Party's popularity with the electorate. The Communists were able to parlay their new advantage among the peasantry along with their normal appeal among the miners and lumber workers into a resounding victory. The terms of the agreement between the Czech and the Ruthenian agrarian parties were prominently displayed as proof that the agrarian bourgeoisie had agreed to exploit Ruthenia as a colony.[53] The agrarians won only 6 percent of the vote in 1924 and never recovered the commanding position they had enjoyed six months earlier. The Communists, on the other hand, lost the advantages they had gained in 1924 only once, and that was during the great internal crisis in the Party in 1929 (see Table 18).

The petty triumphs which the CPC enjoyed in Sub-Carpathian Ruthenia did not exempt it from criticism at the Fifth Comintern Congress in the summer of 1924. A delegate from Ruthenia even joined in the chorus of criticism, arguing that Communist victories in the Ruthenian elections would have been much greater if the Czech Party had adopted an even stronger position on the national and agrarian questions.[54] One of Stalin's trusted lieutenants, Manuilsky, a Ukrainian, was given the task of spelling out the deficiencies of the Czech Communists and of supervising their corrective efforts. He attacked Šmeral and the CPC for their indifference to the debate on the dangers from the right and the left in their own party.[55] He gave

[52] Mel'nikova points gleefully to the terms of the agreement and indicates that it helped win the elections for the Communists, who now became the chief advocates of self-determination up to and including secession. Mel'nikova, *Uchenye zapiski instituta slavianovedeniia*, VI (1952), 39–40. The autonomists who left the Ruthenian Agrarian-Republican Party formed the Autonomous Agrarian Party (or Kurtiaks). They continued to demand autonomy, but their appeal apparently did not extend beyond the Magyar minority. Chmelar, p. 92.

[53] Mel'nikova, *Uchenye zapiski instituta Slavianovedeniia*, VI (1952), 42, and Rakoshi, *Krest'ianskii Internatsional*, No. 2 (May, 1924), p. 40.

[54] *Piatyi vsemirnyi kongress Kommunisticheskogo Internatsionala—(18 iunia–8 iulia 1924 goda)—stenograficheskii otchet* (Moscow, 1925), I, 416–17.

[55] D. Manuil'skii, "Cheshskii primer—urok dlia vsego Kominterna," *Kommunisticheskii Internatsional*, No. 6 (June, 1925), pp. 19–31.

the Party due credit for its success in winning members, comparing its influence on the Czech worker to the influence of the Catholic church on the citizens of Catholic countries, but he pointed out that the Party was not yet organized and disciplined for the act of revolution.[56]

Table 18

Electoral Strength in Ruthenia

Party	1924[a]	1925	1929	1935
Communist	39	30	17	26
Agrarian	6	14	34	20

Source: C. A. Macartney, *Hungary and Her Successors: The Treaty of Trianon and Its Consequences, 1919–1937* (London, 1937), p. 240.

[a] I. N. Mel'nikova, "Iz istorii revoliutsionnogo dvizheniia na zakarpatskoi Ukraine v 1921–1924," *Uchenye zapiski instituta slavianovodeniia*, VI (1952), 45–46,

At the Comintern Congress Zinoviev was unimpressed with the electoral success of the party in Ruthenia.

The results of the elections in Sub-Carpathian Ruthenia are well known to us. Many Czech comrades, Tapig, Gati, and others, especially local comrades in Sub-Carpathian Ruthenia, worked heroically, braving great dangers in the electoral campaign. But I have the impression that the Czech Party as a whole does not give the proper weight to the peasant question in Czechoslovakia, and it has been proved that it is of the utmost importance to be capable of work among the peasants.[57]

This lack of appreciation of the need for a peasant reserve in the event of revolution was expressly linked to the nonrevolutionary nature of the Czech Party. It was said to be no more than an ordinary, parliamentary, political party, a party which came to life only a few months before elections and which lapsed into inactivity immediately afterwards.[58]

In particular, Zinoviev indicated, neither the right nor the left factions fully understood the meaning of the terms "workers' and peasants' government" and "united front." At this congress Zinoviev

[56] *Ibid.,* pp. 19–20.
[57] *Piatyi vsemirnyi kongress,* I, 65.
[58] *Ibid.,* p. 84.

provided very little assistance in the matter of defining slogans, for he stated himself that the term "workers' and peasants' government" was only a slogan for attracting those who would not follow the Communists under the slogan "dictatorship of the proletariat." [59] He indicated that the former slogan was particularly useful in a country like Czechoslovakia.[60] It could not, however, as one resolution of the last congress of the CPC suggested, be interpreted as a special instrument through which there could be a peaceful transition to the dictatorship of the proletariat.[61] With obvious condescension Zinoviev said that, although there was no question of Šmeral's good will, he had not given the CPC the kind of leadership the Comintern expected.[62]

Šmeral was permitted to answer these charges. To clear himself from the outset, he picked up Zinoviev's admission of ignorance about the Czech party. According to Šmeral, the CPC had disposed of the agrarian question by appointing a permanent secretariat for research into the problem under "a comrade who knew his business." [63] He boasted that the Party had succeeded in organizing a larger percentage of the peasantry than any other party except the Russian and Bulgarian, and that in Czechoslovakia the poorer peasants were deserting the ranks of the agrarian and clerical parties for the Communists.[64] Šmeral could only have been relying on the ignorance of his audience. To the unenlightened, the victories of the Party in Sub-Carpathian Ruthenia, a peasant province, may have seemed to support Šmeral's assertions, but the Party's record there was no reliable index to its work in rural areas in general. All other evidence from the rest of Czechoslovakia belied Šmeral's claims. There were few peasants in the Party or in Communist unions in June, 1924.

Kolarov, as one of the key speakers on the agrarian question, followed Zinoviev's lead in chastising the CPC for its inattention to the peasant. Categorizing Švehla's party as bourgeois, he pointed out that the Communists had done little to wean the left wing of the

[59] *Ibid.,* p. 69.
[60] *Ibid.,* pp. 77–78.
[61] *Ibid.,* p. 74.
[62] *Ibid.,* p. 84.
[63] *Ibid.,* pp. 140–41.
[64] *Ibid.*

agrarian party, the Domovina, away from the main body.[65] Kolarov said:

Let me say a few words about Czechoslovakia, where the agrarian question and the problem of winning the peasantry have cardinal political significance. The Czechoslovak Communist Party must pay attention to the need for strengthening its propaganda and political-organizational work among the agricultural workers in all parts of the republic.[66]

He urged upon the Czechs a threefold program calling for the creation of an agricultural union, the creation of unions of poor peasants, and the establishment of ties between these unions and the newly created Krestintern.[67]

According to official Communist accounts, the CPC took its first steps toward rural agitation and recruitment that summer. As usual, it was one of the national minority sections that led the way. Already in May, 1924, the Slovak party organization had called a general conference on the question of work in rural areas and had decided to create a mass organization for the poor peasantry. The Czechs, following the Slovak example, decided to call a general conference of toiling peasants.[68] Invitations were to be issued without regard for political affiliation. Preliminary conferences were held in August for the southern Czech lands and in September for the north as well as several towns in Slovakia and Ruthenia.[69]

At the end of October, 1924, the Party held its Second Congress. Manuilsky was sent as the Comintern's watchdog to see that the party conformed to the instructions of the Fifth Comintern Congress, the decision of which a plenum of the Central Committee of the Party had already accepted in July.[70] But the party congress was necessary as a means of communicating the compliance of the leaders to all members. For the first time the Party took a firm position in favor of agitation and recruitment among the peasantry.[71]

[65] *Ibid.,* p. 749.
[66] *Ibid.,* p. 753.
[67] *Ibid.,* p. 755.
[68] Mel'nikova, *Klassovaia bor'ba,* p. 177, and *Istoriia Kommunisticheskoi Partii Chekhoslovakii,* p. 230.
[69] Mel'nikova, pp. 177–78.
[70] *Ibid.,* p. 195.
[71] *Ibid.,* p. 196.

One problem in the CPC was the fact that the new left wing emerging under the leadership of the German Neurath and the Hungarian Fried found its support chiefly among the national minorities in the Party, including the Slovaks. The Party threatened to split along national lines. The Comintern, while adopting criticism of the left wing in its resolutions on the Czech question, tried to prevent a split in the leadership. Zinoviev sent a letter to the Second Congress in which he demanded the formation of a new Central Committee composed of both "old" and "new" elements. Such a Central Committee was formed and a moderate Party veteran, Josef Haken, was elected its chairman.[72]

Resistance to subsequent Comintern interference in favor of the young members of the leftist faction was inevitable because the left did not have a large following in the Party or reflect its mood and aspirations. A parliamentary deputy and chairman of the Prague regional organizations, Josef Bubnik, was finally excluded from the Party in a storm of controversy after he had voiced his opposition to Comintern interference and the revolutionary phrases of the left.[73] As a result, the Czech question became one of the major issues at the Fifth Enlarged Plenum of the ECCI in March, 1925. Stalin and Zinoviev gave the Comintern's stamp of approval to the explusion of Bubnik, in spite of protests from Šmeral.[74] His expulsion cost the CPC nine deputies (out of twenty-seven) and more than thirty well-known and popular leaders, all of whom followed Bubnik to form a new Independent Communist Party.[75]

At the Third Congress of the CPC in September, 1925, even

[72] H. Gordon Skilling, "The Comintern and Czechoslovak Communism: 1921–1929," *American Slavic and East European Review,* XIX, No. 2 (April, 1960), 237.

[73] *Ibid.*

[74] *Ibid.,* p. 238.

[75] B. Šmeral, "Polozhenie v KP Chekhoslovakii posle rasshirennogo plenuma IKKI," *Kommunisticheskii Internatsional,* No. 6 (June, 1925), p. 9. Bubnik, by taking with him most of the leading figures in the Prague and Brno organizations, provided Jílek with a path to power. Jílek replaced Bubnik as head of the Prague organization. Bubnik's new Independent Communist Party met with little success in the elections of 1925 and soon merged with the Czechoslovak Social Democratic Party. Skilling, *American Slavic and East European Review,* XIX, No. 2 (April, 1960), 238, 241.

more members of the "new" left element were added to the Central Committee of the Party, again with the assistance of Manuilsky. Šmeral and Zápotocký were retained, but Stalin later maintained that this was not really a concession to the right wing since both men had agreed to cooperate with the left against the right.[76] One of those brought into the Central Committee at this congress was Klement Gottwald. Bohumil Jílek, elected leading secretary and chief of the organizational department, became the chief figure in the Party, while Joseph Haken retained his post as chairman of the Central Committee.[77] Jílek's coterie included Haken, Bolen, and Sturc. Although this leadership was labeled leftist in Comintern literature, the term was only a relative one, since Jílek apparently accepted Bukharin's thesis of the "stabilization of capitalism" and was later expelled for "rightist" tendencies.[78] Jílek's leadership, however, seemed to provide some stability, for it survived until the second great crisis in the Party in 1928 when the Comintern again turned toward the left.

In November, 1925, were held the first national parliamentary elections since the creation of the CPC and the acceptance of the right of Sub-Carpathian Ruthenia to representation. Although the Communists emerged as the second strongest party in the republic, the net effect of the victory was to clarify and sharpen the split in socialist forces, paving the way for the Green-Black Coalition of the following year. The outcasts from the CPC formed their own Independent Communist Party for the elections. Failing to win a single, seat they rejoined the Czech Social Democratic Party.[79] In spite of the general success of the CPC, the percentage of the popular vote going to this party in Sub-Carpathian Ruthenia declined, a fact which the Krestintern attributed to the failure of the Party to harness the "spontaneous movement of the Sub-Carpathian peasants"—and the word "spontaneous" was repeatedly used—to an effective organi-

[76] Skilling, *American Slavic and East European Review,* XIX, No. 2 (April, 1960), 240.
[77] *Ibid.,* p. 241.
[78] P. Reimann, "Kommunisticheskaia Partiia Chekho-slovakii v ogne napadeniia opportunistov," *Kommunisticheskii Internatsional,* No. 50 (Dec. 14, 1928), p. 31.
[79] Chmelar, p. 48.

zation.[80] The Czech Party was warned that this failure would deprive the Party of a valuable ally. This criticism apparently escaped the Soviet scholar Mel'nikova, who gives Ivan Bodnar (Lokat) a great deal of credit for organizing the peasants for the 1925 elections.[81] According to the Comintern, the Czech Communists were remiss in Slovakia as well.

Next door to Sub-Carpathian Ruthenia, in Slovakia, we see a classic example. Under the influence of the revolution in 1920 the peasant masses moved strongly to the left, but in the course of the last four years, owing to the passivity of the Communist party in the national question, two hundred thousand peasants passed from the socialist party into a party which, although it is clerical, fights for their autonomy.[82]

In spite of his exile to China in the fall of 1924 and his assumption of permanent residence in Moscow in March, 1925, Šmeral seems to have continued to exert some influence on the policies of the CPC.[83] He remained a member of its Central Committee until 1928. In December, 1925, in an article for the official organ of the ECCI, Šmeral contributed an analysis of the Czech elections of 1925 which displayed all the features of so-called Šmeralism which, according to the Comintern in 1928, had dominated the Czech Party from 1925 to 1928.[84]

According to Šmeral, Czechoslovakia in 1925 was an advanced country in terms of the level of industrial development, but in terms of political development it was not a model capitalistic state. The political parties of the bankers and industrialists were weak in comparison to agrarian and petty-bourgeois political parties.[85] The structure of political power in Czechoslovakia was extremely complicated owing to the number of political parties, of which only a few clearly

[80] G. Volkov, "Ugnetennaia prikarpatskaia Rus'," *Krest'ianskii Internatsional*, No. 3–5 (March–May, 1926), p. 126.

[81] Mel'nikova, *Klassovaia bor'ba*, p. 218.

[82] Volkov, *Krest'ianskii Internatsional*, No. 3–5 (March–May, 1926), p. 126.

[83] Reimann, *Kommunisticheskii Internatsional*, No. 50 (Dec. 14, 1928), p. 29.

[84] *Ibid.* Reimann's interpretation has apparently become the standard one since it is in the latest official history of the Party. *Istoriia Kommunisticheskoi Partii Chekhoslovakii*, pp. 312–14.

[85] B. Šmeral, "Vybory v Chekhoslovakii," *Kommunisticheskii Internatsional*, No. 12 (Dec., 1925), p. 59.

represented a single social class. The class struggle was therefore obscured and weakened by the political system.[86] These were some of the "special conditions" which, Šmeral maintained, warranted special tactics in Czechoslovakia.

He argued further that Czechoslovakia was a semi-colony of the Great Powers in Europe and was becoming agrarianized rather than industrialized, since this suited the interests of these powers. The attitude of the Czechoslovak government toward Slovakia and Ruthenia was cited as an example of this condition. Unfortunately, this situation did not lead to increasing class differentiation and a revolutionary situation because the Czech government granted petty concessions to the workers in the form of social legislation and to the peasant in the form of agrarian reforms.[87] Šmeral asserted that these concessions further minimized class antagonisms and antagonism toward the state, leading to a degree of political stability in Czechoslovakia. Šmeral's whole approach may have been contrived in order to justify the continuation of those policies which the Party had always pursued, for the conclusion deduced from all this was that the Party should continue to concentrate primarily upon attracting a large proportion of the working class and upon parliamentary activity.[88]

Kreibich, another rightist who pleaded that there were "special conditions" in Czechoslovakia, was probably closer to the truth when he argued that the Comintern did not understand the psychology of the Czech worker, or, by implication, the Czech people.

For Bolshevization, a specific approach to the unique situation in each separate country is necessary, and forms and methods must be correspondingly adapted to it. In the speeches of representatives of various countries there were few such specific directives corresponding to their individual problems. The distinctive features of the prewar situation in Russia in comparison with the West today and the modification of tactics resulting from these differences must be the subject of serious study. Otherwise Bolshevism will remain an idea on paper or will be conducted mechanically—with an exaggerated and forced tempo. . . .

The Czech worker was educated in the struggle against the rotten

[86] *Ibid.*, p. 52.
[87] "Pravyi uklon v agrarnoi politika nekotorykh Kompartii," *Agrarnye problemy*, No. 4–5 (April, 1930), p. 86.
[88] *Ibid.*

Austrian state and its authority. Rebellion against all authority and discipline was an integral part of the struggle for national liberation. Because of this the Czech worker cannot be influenced or won over by authoritarian means or by force from without; he needs to be convinced. . . . Nowhere had criticism of our methods brought so much harm as among the Czech proletariat. The path of mechanical subjugation to authority, the path of decree and mechanical processing with the help of commissars and agents is unsuitable, especially if the latter are themselves rather unclean.[89]

Under Jílek's leadership from 1926 to 1928 the Party apparently was unable to avoid the errors of its past, especially on the agrarian question. Fortunately the CPC did not have to contend with the question of a united front with the Czech agrarian party. Before the elections of November, 1925, the Presidium of the ECCI informed the Czech Communists that a workers' and peasants' government could not be formed in Czechoslovakia by a coalition between the Communists and either the Social Democratic or the Czechoslovak agrarian party.[90] The work of the CPC in the country was in the hands of the Communist Otto Rydlo and the non-Party peasant Václav Čech,[91] both of whom had participated in the founding of the Krestintern.

But in 1928 a Czech representative at the Sixth Comintern Congress stated that in the four preceding years his party had demonstrated little real enthusiasm for work in rural areas and little real sense of direction in it.

The theses [of the Sixth Comintern Congress] stress the fact that the Communist Party of Czechoslovakia has devoted too little attention to the peasant question. I don't think that it is a lack of real work. Each of our congresses has approved resolutions on the peasant question, but they remain on paper. It was only at the Fourth Congress of the Party in March, 1927, that we seriously concerned ourselves with the peasant question.[92]

According to this source, in the four years between the Fifth and

---

[89] *Rasshirennyi plenum ispolkoma Kommunisticheskogo Internatsionala—protokoly zasedanii (21 marta–6 aprelia, 1925)* (Moscow, 1925), pp. 227–28.
[90] *Otchet ispolkoma Kominterna (aprel' 1925–ianvar' 1926 g.)* (Moscow, 1926), p. 8.
[91] "Politicheskie partii Chekhoslovakii i krest'ianstvo," *Krest'ianskii Internatsional*, No. 11 (Nov., 1925), p. 50.
[92] *VI kongress Kominterna—stenograficheskii otchet* (Moscow, 1929), I, 291.

Sixth Comintern congresses attempts had been made to form peasant federations in Slovakia and Ruthenia and to form a united federation for the whole republic. The government imposed some obstacles to this goal by refusing to recognize the Slovak peasant federation, but the central problem was the innocent confusion of the Czech Communist when confronted with a peasant. This reporter maintained that once the peasant organizations had been formed the Czech Communists didn't know what to do with them. The secretary of the Slovak federation acquired his members simply by withdrawing all red Communist Party cards in the villages and replacing them with the green cards of the front peasant federation. This only served to confuse the recipients. In Ruthenia, the director of rural activity tried to carve out a kingdom of his own. His section became overorganized; he divided the country into three ethnic regions, each directed by an agrarian council with eighteen subcommissions, making fifty-four sections in all for one of the smallest provinces in Czechoslovakia. This kind of thing was clearly the result of indifference at the center.

More serious was the Party's inability to comprehend or reach the peasantry.

We must also correctly evaluate the class contradictions inside the peasantry, use this differentiation, and defeat the slogan of the Czech agrarian capitalists, "the village is a single family." For this slogan obscures the antagonism of interests of the different classes in the country, interferes with the neutralization of the middle peasant, and drives the great mass of poor peasants and even the rural proletarians from us.

The unpleasant fact is that up to this time we have not really succeeded in bringing into being an alliance between the proletariat and the peasant.

It must be frankly admitted that up to this time we have not been able to establish an alliance even with that stratum in the country which is the stoutest advocate of the dictorship of the proletariat, the agricultural workers, in spite of the urgency of this problem.[93]

In addition to the difficulty encountered in trying to instill the Czech peasants with the spirit of class warfare, the Czechoslovak Communists seemed unable to dilute their own communism sufficiently to create the suitable foggy environment necessary for a workers' and peasants' alliance.

[93] *Ibid.*, p. 288.

The so-called peasant journals which we create do not have a neutral character but are Communist journals. Our rural conferences are regarded by the peasants as Communist enterprises in spite of the fact that peasants from other parties participate. In the legal peasant federations of Bohemia and Moravia we are supported not by strong, fully formed factions in the countryside but, on the whole, by occasional Communists and sympathizers.[94]

Instead of a realistic appraisal of the problems encountered by the CPC, the Sixth Comintern Congress treated the Party to a new host of formulas derived from the unfolding "new course" in Russia. Kolarov declared: "In Poland and Czechoslovakia the organizations of the middle peasants and rural bourgeoisie, the agrarian party and paist, have definitely entered the camp of the bourgeoisie, have amalgamated with them and worked with them" *ergo*, the agrarian party was no more than a bourgeois party.[95] Dąbal, in describing the work of the Peasant International in Czechoslovkia, said:

In reference to Czechoslovakia I must say that, although this is a country where the agrarian bourgeoisie are in power, the Communist Party has still made no real effort in rural areas. I must say that the leaders of the Czechoslovak Communist Party have a decidedly abnormal point of view toward such work. During one conference a Party worker declared that he could not pursue work in rural areas because such work would place him in the ranks of the opposition. Another comrade "explained" that the party could not conduct work in rural areas because it was "preoccupied with Bolshevization." In areas occupied by national minorities there are great inadequacies, especially in the Sub-Carpathian Ukraine, where up to this time no regular work is under way.[96]

At the special commission on the Czech question at the Sixth Comintern Congress, the young Comintern-trained members of the CPC who were then making their bid for power [97] led the onslaught against the position of Jílek, Haken, and Bolen on the agrarian question. Gottwald, who was the leader of the attack, said:

In general it must be said that the peasantry as a whole up to this time are found in the majority of cases under the influence of the bourgeoisie. In spite of this we can find a small but perceptible shift to the left in

[94] *Ibid.*, p. 291.
[95] *Ibid.*, p. 164.
[96] *Ibid.*, pp. 444–45.
[97] These are identified by Zinner as Gottwald, Šverma, Slánský, Kopecký, and Kopriva. Zinner, p. 26.

the village (especially among the masses of Slovakia and Sub-Carpathian Ruthenia.) [98]

The major charge against Jílek, Haken, and Bolen was that they had failed to recognize the emerging revolutionary situation and the increasing differentiation between classes in the village. Gottwald, in tune with the new conception called "social fascism," indicated that Švehla's agrarian party was a protofascist organization.[99] At the same time, he indicated that the influence of the CPC among the poor peasants and in the economic organizations of the peasants was negligible.[100] The report of the commission was, however, mild in its criticisms, and it was not until September, 1928, when the drive against Bukharin began to gain momentum, that the Comintern adopted a stronger position against Jílek based on the criticisms by the left.[101]

The Fifth Congress of the CPC met in February, 1929, under the watchful eyes of Ziegler, the Comintern representative. Gottwald and other members of the Stalinist left were elected to the top posts in the Party.[102] The so-called historic right, consisting of Šmeral and Zápotocký; the so-called nonhistoric right, consisting of Jílek and Bolen; and the left, consisting of Neurath, Skala, and Toužil, were condemned.[103] For some reason Haken escaped censure and was even reelected to the Central Committee. At the congress, Ziegler especially condemned the view of Bolen on the national and agrarian questions.[104] Essentially the heresies attributed to Jílek and Šmeral were the same as some of the heresies attributed to Bukharin. Gottwald accused them of misinterpreting the nature of Czechoslovakia and of refusing to recognize the end of stabilization and the emergence of a third revolutionary period in which the danger of war

[98] Klement Gottwald, *Izbrannye proizvedeniia* (Moscow, 1957-), I, 57.
[99] *Ibid.*, p. 55.
[100] *Ibid.*, p. 56.
[101] Skilling, *American Slavic and East European Review*, XIX, No. 2. (April, 1960), 242–43. See "Otkrytoe pis'mo IKKI chlenam Chekhoslovatskoi Kompartii," *Kommunisticheskii Internatsional*, No. 37 (Sept. 21, 1928), pp. 38–43.
[102] "The Fifth Party Congress of the CP of Czechoslovakia," *International Press Correspondence*, IX, No. 16 (March 29, 1929), 320.
[103] Gottwald, I, 553, n. 14.
[104] "The Fifth Congress of the CP of Czechoslovakia," *International Press Correspondence*, IX, No. 16 (March 29, 1929), 327. See also "Posle V s'ezda Kommunisticheskoi Partii Chekhoslovakii," *Kommunisticheskii Internatsional*, No. 15 (April 12, 1929), pp. 3–11.

against the USSR was a real and important threat.[105] After a brief respite, in June, 1929, Hauser, Jílek, Muna, Neurath, Skala, and Toužil were expelled from the Party.[106] This time the CPC lost the followers of these men, consisting of one half of the members of its trade union movement and twelve (out of forty) of its deputies.[107]

The burden of eradicating the old agrarian program and formulating the new seemed to fall on the shoulders of a new member of the Czech Party's Politburo, Paul Reimann.[108] At the Tenth Plenum of the ECCI in July, 1929, he enumerated the specific errors of the old agrarian program and called upon the Comintern to make the experiences of the Czech Party an object lesson for all Communist parties.[109] According to Reimann, the Fifth Congress of the CPC had adopted the position that fascism would develop in Czechoslovakia from the left bourgeois parties (the Social Democrats and Agrarians).[110] The basic error of the old leadership in the Party (before 1929) was in trying to rally the peasant around slogans which conveyed the impression that he might achieve some of his goals through the existing regime. Instead of the slogan "nationalization of all land," said Reimann, Jílek advanced the slogan "reexamination of the agrarian reforms, distribution of remaining lands, and distribution of communal woods." According to Reimann, the slogan "organization of local self-government" was used, although if the slogan had been acted upon it would only strengthen the power of the capitalist in the Czech countryside. Instead of advancing the revolutionary slogan "elimination of all debts," Jílek had called for "cheaper credit for the peasants."

[105] "The Fifth Party Congress of the CP of Czechoslovakia," *International Press Correspondence,* IX, No. 16 (March 29, 1929), 304–5.

[106] The decisions of the Fifth Congress of the CPC were approved by the Presidium of the ECCI in April, 1929. "Resolutions of the ECCI on the Czech Question," *International Press Correspondence,* IX, No. 20 (April 26, 1929), 413. The expulsions were endorsed by the Comintern at the Tenth Plenum of the ECCI in July, 1929.

[107] Skilling, *American Slavic and East European Review,* XIX, No. 2 (April, 1960), 244.

[108] For a brief summary of Reimann's criticisms see Pavel Reimann, *Geschichte der Kommunistichen Partei der Tschechoslowakei* (Berlin, 1931), pp. 265–71.

[109] *Desiatyi plenum ispolkoma Kominterna,* I, 103.

[110] *Ibid.,* p. 102.

The new Comintern line on the agrarian question was not fully defined until March, 1930, when a special session of the International Agrarian Institute was called precisely for this purpose in Moscow.[111] Essentially Comintern slogans like "reexamination of the agrarian reforms" and "cheap or free credit to the peasants" were specifically condemned. The keynote speaker was the young, Soviet-trained economist, Dubrovskii. He indicated that for the present only such revolutionary slogans as "confiscation of large landholdings" were correct.[112] His chief concern seemed to be the denunciation of any demands which might bring out the "bourgeois instincts" of the middle peasants.[113]

At this special session Reimann again elaborated on the errors of the old leadership in his party. He claimed that the so-called right deviation in the CPC had based its position on the theory that Czechoslovakia was being agrarianized, a theory which, he maintained, ignored the close alliance between the agrarian bourgeoisie and finance capital.[114] He argued that the agrarian party's role in the conduct of agrarian reform and in raising the tariffs on agricultural goods made the agrarian bourgeoisie the strongest political element in the state, and it was this element which increased social and economic differentiation in the village. Instead of revealing the policies of the Czechoslovak agrarian party for what they were, said Reimann, the CPC had toyed with reformist proposals like "the determination of land taxes by peasant commissions, the reexamination of land reforms, etc." In particular, said Reimann, a proposal of the CPC to force large landowners to lease most of their land to poorer peasants (called compulsory rent) was wrong because it would lead to cooperation between the various rural classes rather than an intensification of the struggle between them.[115]

Following the session in Moscow, Reimann wrote that he had welcomed such a meeting, although the correct line on the agrarian program of Communist parties in the third period should have been

---

[111] "Pravyi uklon v agrarnoi politike nekotorykh Kompartii," *Agrarnye problemy*, No. 4–5 (April–May, 1930), p. 180.
[112] *Ibid.*
[113] *Ibid.*, p. 200.
[114] *Ibid.*, p. 186.
[115] *Ibid.*, p. 187.

determined at the Tenth Plenum.[116] He reluctantly paid tribute to the Czech agrarian party: "They are consummate masters of the art of social demagoguery." [117] At the same time, he condemned as social fascism the methods by which the agrarians tried to meet the growing agricultural crisis.[118] Actually, according to the Comintern, the correct line on the agrarian question was not adopted in the CPC until its Sixth Congress in 1931.[119] This congress followed the Eleventh Plenum of the ECCI, the first meeting at which the agrarian program for the third period appeared in all its glory. Kolarov, who had become the Comintern's high priest in agrarian matters as well as president of the International Agrarian Institute, outlined a program similar to that espoused by Reimann, calling for unalterable opposition to agrarian parties (all of which were fascist), elimination of reformist slogans, and a sharpening of the class struggle in the countryside.[120]

It is, of course, difficult to evaluate the effect of this shift of policy on the efforts of the CPC in rural areas. In the election of 1929 the number of Communist deputies fell from forty-one to thirty, but Gottwald attributed this to the struggle for leadership in the Party.[121] It is also true that the proportion of popular votes received by the Communists in backward, rural Ruthenia dropped from 34 percent in 1925 to 18 in 1929, but here again it is difficult to evaluate this without fully taking into account the conflicts within the Party and the exploitation of national sentiment by the other political parties involved.[122] All that one can say with certainty is that Comintern intervention in the affairs of the CPC converted it between 1928 and 1931 from one of the strongest parties in the Comintern into one of the weakest in numbers, which does not indicate very much about the effectiveness of the new policies on the agrarian question.

What is indicated by the material in this chapter is that the left turn imposed on the CPC by the Comintern conformed to the

[116] P. Reimann, "Agrarnyi vopros v Chekhoslovakii i K.P.Ch.," *Kommunisticheskii Internatsional*, No. 10 (1930), p. 46.

[117] *Ibid.*, p. 44

[118] *Ibid.*, p. 45.

[119] Zinner, p. 42.

[120] *XI plenum IKKI—stenograficheskii otchet* (Moscow, 1932), I, 354.

[121] K. Gottwald, "The Results of the Parliamentary Elections in Czechoslovakia," *International Press Correspondence*, IX, No. 52 (Nov. 1, 1929), 1327.

[122] See Table 17, p. 276.

interests of the Russian Party rather than to the concrete situation in Czechoslovakia. From the discussion of the errors of Jílek and Bolen it would appear that those leaders had concentrated upon concrete parliamentary demands for the peasants which would create an image of the CPC as a defender of the poorer peasants. At the same time, the leaders of 1925-28 pursued the tactic recommended by Bukharin of infiltrating the Czechoslovakian agrarian party in order to form a left wing, apparently with little success. In place of this line of action, the CPC, under the leadership of younger, Moscow-trained men, adopted clearly revolutionary slogans, slogans which could be implemented only by overthrowing the existing government. Simultaneously, the Party began in its propaganda to treat the existing Czech agrarian party as a proto-fascist organization. It seems improbable, in view of the material presented in the first portion of this chapter, that the left tactics were any more effective that those adopted between 1925 and 1928.

Probably the formation of the CPC had more impact on Czech politics than its activity after 1925. The splitting of the strong Social Democratic Party prepared the way for the Red-Green Coalition, and the ultimate effect of weakening the Social Democratic Party in the elections of 1925 was the formation of the Green-Black Coalition. After 1925 the example of the CPC is probably more useful as a case study in the problems of Comintern discipline than as an example of the effectiveness or ineffectiveness of Comintern agrarian policy.

In both the right and the left periods in the history of the CPC between 1925 and 1931 the most frequent admonition was to "eradicate Social Democratic survivals." What emerges most clearly from the Party crisis of 1928-29 is that the CPC remained indifferent to work in rural areas. Nothing succeeds like success, and the Party could argue that it was a working class party and a strong one. What need, then, to send comrades to the country? Some were sent, but their conduct of affairs was hardly impressive. It was only in 1931, ten years after its founding congress, that the Party could claim to have adopted what the Comintern considered a Bolshevik position on the agrarian question. The battle to Bolshevize the Czech Party had been a long and hard one, and in 1931 the Party had to begin to repair the losses suffered in the process.

CHAPTER XII

Recapitulation

The agrarian policy of the Comintern commanded attention in the 1920s because it was said to be founded upon a "scientific analysis" of the course of the Russian Revolution. This claim bore within it the explicit assumption that the pattern of that revolution could be duplicated in countries with a similar social and economic structure. The marriage of theory and example seemed irrefutable. While it is not within the scope of this study to examine the merits of Lenin's "dialectics of backwardness" as an explanation of Bolshevik success in 1917, there is little doubt that the agrarian policy of the Comintern acquired considerable credibility by being offered as one of the lessons of 1917. A part of this lesson, however, was the axiom that in an economically backward country a workers' party had to win over the peasantry. When an attempt was made to apply this axiom in Eastern Europe, the parties of the Comintern discovered that they could not compete successfully with the peasant political parties for the loyalty of the peasantry.

The existence of strong peasant political parties capable of winning political power and posing, if not acting, as the representatives of the peasant class was not the only new element to which the Comintern had to adapt in applying its lessons. Another central problem was the fact that both Lenin's theoretical bequest and the example of the Bolshevik Revolution applied only to revolutionary situations. The technique of work in an era in which revolutionary crises did not seem imminent had yet to be worked out. A third problem lay in the assumption of close parallels between the social, economic, and political structures of Imperial Russia and East European countries after 1917. There were strong similarities, but there were striking differences as well. Their political strengths and weaknesses were by no means identical. A few examples should suffice. On the one hand, the Imperial Russian state could command many of the resources available only to large, respected, and established states. On the other hand, the new East European states, at least in the short run, could draw upon a fund of good will and nationalistic enthusiasm generated by the experience of recent liberation from foreign domination. In spite of the shortcomings of the constitutional regimes in postwar Eastern Europe, these governments were probably more representative and less oppressive politically and economically than the Imperial Russian government had been. Although both areas suffered from problems common to economically backward areas, the Imperial Russian government had a special problem in its efforts to overcome the crippling effects of communal tenure, and a unique asset in its unsettled eastern frontier. Furthermore, in Eastern Europe the postwar agrarian reforms created a dramatic impression that something was done for the peasant. Neither the Russian emancipation of 1861 nor the Stolypin reforms had impressed the peasantry in prerevolutionary Russia.

The existence of all these differences was never fully recognized by the Comintern. The lessons of the Russian Revolution were treated as the bricks of which the fortress of socialism, the Soviet Union, was built. The conviction arose that the removal of one such brick might endanger the bastion of socialism in the world. Claims of "special conditions" differing from those in prewar Russia or the Soviet experience were thus treated as doctrinal heresies. There was an increasing air of unreality about the efforts of local parties to become either real political parties or effective conspiratorial organizations.

Even Bukharin's efforts to bend the East European peasant movement to his own purposes represent a trend flowing from circumstances and conditions prevailing in the Russian Communist Party during the New Economic Policy and the struggle for power rather than from a careful analysis of the special conditions prevailing in each European country. All that really sets Bukharin's peasantism off from the left course which followed in 1928 is the presence in the former of the explicit assumption that the revolutionary potential evident in the European peasantry could best be cultivated by wooing the peasantry and its parties with sweet promises. The leftists of 1928 tried to accomplish the same end by assailing the peasantry with calls to revolution.

Both Bukharin and his successors shared the same Leninist view of the peasant as a historical Jekyll and Hyde, who might at a moment's notice transform himself from a pleasantly poor and rebellious toiling Jekyll into a tight-fisted, avaricious, and property-minded Mr. Hyde. Both Bukharin and his successors shared the view passed down by Lenin that the poor peasant was a valuable, and, in some countries, necessary ally; that the middle peasant should be won over or neutralized (though the left tended to stress the latter); and that one must suspect the kulak. Both shared the view that in peasant countries like those in Eastern Europe the revolutionary strata of the peasantry had to be harnessed to the Communist movement if the obstacles to full technological development of agriculture were to be overcome by the establishment of a proletarian state. Both shared the view that the peasant would have to be cajoled and bribed with allocations of land, but that the Communist party would have to grip the reins of power firmly, permitting no real duality of the type implied by the slogan "workers' and peasants' government."

The difference between Bukharin and his successors was less a matter of doctrine and more a matter of attitude, in spite of Comintern encyclicals to the contrary. Bukharin, probably correctly, felt that the revolutionary wave had passed and would not return in the near future. Influenced by his interpretation of the role of the peasantry in the development of the revolution in Russia, Bukharin tended to give even greater weight to the role of the peasant in international revolution. But in the period of stabilization the Communist parties could only prepare for the future by electoral alliances with peasant political parties, by supporting the most radical demands of the peasantry, and by abandoning extravagant revolutionary slogans. The left, on the other hand, intoxicated with the apparent victories of Stalin's second revolution in Russia and seemingly terrified by the bogey of an attack on the Soviet Union from the West, saw visions of a new revolutionary wave. In such circumstances the left argued that it was time to stop flirting with peasant parties and time to begin arming the poor peasants. One of the curious, yet, in Communist terms, logical, anomalies of the shift in policy was that in an era of peaceful persuasion alliances with opposition parties were permissible, but in an era of putschism combining with other parties to strengthen the forces of revolution was virtually forbidden.

In both Bukharin's course and that of the left the official slogans conceal the real agrarian program of the Comintern. On the surface it would seem as though the Comintern had no program for the day after revolution. This, of course, was consistent with the heritage left by Lenin. One would look in vain in Comintern literature of the 1920s for a serious elucidation of the way a Communist government would solve the agrarian problem in any one country. Even when the collectivization program seemed to have answered that question in Russia, Communist parties were specifically forbidden to announce that collectivization was the goal of every Communist revolution.[1] The reason is a simple one: the agrarian program of the Russian Communist Party for the day after the revolution had no appeal for peasants anywhere. Even by concealing the projected solution of the agrarian question, the East European Communist parties could not make the visible Comintern agrarian program popular. They had far more success with the Comintern's program on the national question.

For this reason, and to allow some flexibility in tactics at the local level, the slogans on the agrarian question which were promulgated by the Comintern were kept purposely vague. No one knew exactly what a "workers' and peasants' government" was. At the Fifth Comintern Congress Zinoviev claimed the slogan was a synonym for the dictatorship of the proletariat. Stalin rendered the term ambiguous again in 1928. The "stages" of revolution, the "types" of countries, the qualities of imperialism and colonialism were defined and redefined, but never with sufficient clarity to make any specific course of action preordained. The advantages won in terms of local initiative by this procedure were usually lost through normal Marxist indifference to the peasant question or by last-minute special directives from the Comintern based on inadequate knowledge of local circumstances.

On the other hand, while general conceptual goals remained vague, there were specific slogans to be advanced in order to win

[1] *XI plenum IKKI—stenograficheskii otchet* (Moscow, 1932), I, 357.

the peasantry. It is these which changed considerably in the shift to the left in 1928. During Bukharin's ascendancy all of the parties involved tended to use slogans calling for reforms under the existing regime or electoral alliances with peasant political parties. Concrete demands were based on the need to attract peasants to the Communist cause, not on the need to incite peasants to revolution. Concrete slogans which could be implemented only by revolution were permissible but less desirable. In one case, the Rumanian, an attempt was made to form an electoral alliance while at the same time advancing a revolutionary program. But by 1930 the shift was complete and only slogans which could be fulfilled by revolution were acceptable. At the same time, while hope of winning a portion of the peasantry was not abandoned, hope of using the peasant political movement in some way was. The latter hope was placed to one side and plainly labeled "social fascist."

In neither Bukharin's right phase nor in the left phase following did the Comintern seem to have learned very much by experience. There was talk of the lessons of Bulgarian events, of the Radić affair, of the events at Alba-Iulia. But in fact those events were used to confirm the current Comintern line and did not seem to reflect any real response by the Comintern to changing circumstances in East European countries. While the Comintern made jabs at a sound appraisal of the particular problems of each country, for example, by establishing the International Agrarian Institute and by urging member parties to study agrarian problems, there were no serious efforts in this direction. The products of the International Agrarian Institute which I have examined were composed in most cases by Communist émigrés ill-equipped for the task and were not major contributions either to the study of underdeveloped countries or to the elucidation of more effective Comintern tactics. The member parties were no better; the usual method for conducting work in rural areas was to appoint a committee on the agrarian question and forget about it.

In view of all this, it is all the more surprising that the agrarian policy of the Comintern developed during this period provided a pattern for the future. In the establishment of People's Democracies in Eastern Europe after World War II there was at first some fumbling for a definition of the nature of the new satellite states. In these states the toleration of peasant political parties (except in Czechoslovakia), the failure to destroy democratic institutions, and the failure to collectivize agriculture led some unfortunates to speculate that these states represented a "new path to socialism." Varga, for one, perhaps harking back to the days of Bukharin, argued that this new course could be found:

In a country where feudal vestiges—large landowners—are liquidated, where a system of private ownership of means of production exists, but large enterprises in industry, transport and credit are state owned, and where the state itself and its apparatus of violence serve the interests, not of the monopolistic bourgeoisie, but of the toilers of town and country.[2]

But the assumption of the inevitability of the Soviet pattern of economic and political development proved to be too closely interwoven with Soviet claims to hegemony in world communism and had to be vindicated, especially after the Tito episode. The reassertion began in earnest with the speech of Dimitrov to the Fifth Congress of the Bulgarian Communist Party in December, 1948, and was elaborated by Soviet theorists.[3] One distinguished Hungarian theoretician wrote:

The establishment and assurance of the conditions which made possible the socialist transformation, the change of our People's Democracy into a dictatorship of the proletarian began with the destruction of the right wing of the Smallholder's Party, with the liquadation of Ferenc Nagy. Then the kulak became an enemy, then the leading role of our party and the working class was strengthened.[4]

In keeping with the Communist habit of learning no lessons except those derived from the history of the Russian Communist

[2] Quoted in H. Gordon Skilling, "People's Democracy in Soviet Theory," *Soviet Studies*, III, No. 1 (July, 1951), 21. This article and its supplement, which appeared in issue No. 2 of *Soviet Studies* for 1951, are the most thorough analyses in English of the problem of arriving at a definition of the term "People's democracy."

[3] *Ibid.*, p. 19.

[4] J. Revai, "On the Character of Our People's Democracy," in C. E. Black, ed., *Readings on Contemporary Eastern Europe* (New York, 1953), p. 82.

Party, the heresies of Bukharin were resurrected to subdue the opponents of the Soviet pattern in Eastern Europe.[5] The right deviation of the 1920s on the agrarian question was revived in order to provide a model into which the right opposition of the early 1950s could be fitted.[6]

Patterns in the agrarian question, then, had been established in the first decade of the history of the Comintern. The most striking thing about these patterns, however, is not their universal applicability but the degree to which they were shaped only by the Soviet experience.

[5] One able commentator on Soviet theoretical gyrations has remarked on the "clotting of important developments in quite separate fields into one political complex. In a totalitarian theocracy issues that seem disparate to a mere empirical temper develop a kind of paranoid interdependence. If you believe in small scale farming, that is Bukharinism, so you must believe in the primacy of light industry and a conciliatory foreign policy." Peter Wiles, "Kremlinology," *Spectator,* No. 197 (Oct. 19, 1956), p. 530.

[6] One of the best examples of this kind of thing is Partidul Muncitorila Român, *Documents Concerning the Right Deviation in the Rumanian Workers' Party* (Bucharest, 1952).

The Fate of
the Green International

To outsiders, East European agrarianism did not seem to be an impressive new "third force" in politics in 1919. Rather, to all outward appearances it was the bastard offspring of a union between Marxism and Western liberalism with a few strong character traits that suggested a Russian populist ancestry. But, however eclectic its origin, the movement soon displayed an unexpected vitality and precocity. In retrospect it is clear that many of the agrarian leaders exhibited a sincerity and dedication that was unusual in East European politics and that the movement stirred the soul of the peasant as no other political movement had. However naïve or inadequate its program, the peasant political movement made a concerted effort in the 1920s to implement its aims. But this early blooming was nourished by special conditions that would disappear in the 1930s.

In the first few years after World War I the East European peasants believed that the peasant political parties represented their interests, and they used their recently acquired power of the vote to give their parties the mandates they needed. Since the political climate favored the efforts of the parties to introduce popular agrarian reforms, they enjoyed successes which increased their popularity. Of course, in most countries it was fear of the Bolshevik menace as well as the strength of the agrarian delegation in parliament which ensured passage of the agrarian reforms, but the peasant parties usually received the credit. The early successes of the parties seemed to confirm their assertion that "agrarianism" was to Eastern Europe what "liberalism" had been to Western Europe, a creed under which the people of a country could be mustered for the battle to erect, preserve, and strengthen political democracy. The establishment and growth of the Green International at Prague was one expression of the confidence of the peasant movement.

But "agrarianism" did not weather the crises of the interwar period very well. Once the machinery of political democracy was destroyed or altered, the peasant political movement lost its power to influence events. It proved difficult to rally the peasantry for effective political action other than voting. The agrarian reforms which were attributed to the peasant parties began to lose their luster with persistent problems of overpopulation and the effects of the Great Depression. In many cases both those peasants who were satisfied with the agrarian reforms and those who were dissatisfied with them turned away from the original peasant parties, even when the polls were still open. Where the parties had won some degree of political power, their achievements were often disillusioning or disappointing.

Two different trends were perceptible in the peasant political movement after 1930. In three countries, Czechoslovakia, Rumania, and Yugoslavia, the peasant parties responded to the threat of declining peasant support and new challenges from the right by adapting their programs in order to attract nonpeasant support. The leadership in all three passed into the hands of the middle class, their programs were broadened to attract other social classes, and the peasant *mystique* was less evident in their public pronouncements; as a result, their wide popularity among the peasants tended to decline. The second trend was most marked in Poland, Bulgaria, and Hungary. Here the "peasantist" aspects of the party program were retained but became subordinated to the struggle against domestic tyranny and then against Nazi occupation, in the case of Poland, and to the struggle against the pro-Axis policies of their respective governments in the case of Bulgaria and Hungary. Although this second group probably increased its popular support among all social classes during this period, this popularity owed less to agrarian ideology than to other factors.

But it was the forces of world history rather than those of local politics that ultimately determined the fate of the peasant political movement. During World War II Eastern Europe was swept into the vortex of a storm of continental dimensions. In the reconstruction of the European state system which followed, no space was left for an independent Eastern Europe, and indigenous non-Communist movements like the peasant political parties were crushed. Using all the forces at their disposal, the Communists extinguished the agrarian movements by 1947. The Czechoslovak Republican Party of Small Farmers and Peasants had already been dissolved by decree. The leader of the Polish People's Party, Mikolajczyk, fled for his life in October, 1947; the leader of the Hungarian Independent Smallholder's Party, Ferenc Nagy, was forced into exile in May; the leader of the Rumanian National Peasant Party, Maniu, was arrested in June, as was the leader of the Bulgarian Agrarian Union, Nikola Petkov. Maniu was sentenced to life imprisonment and Petkov was executed. The peasant movements were forced into their last opposition, one which could not be conducted on native soil.

A real international organization of peasant political parties, the elusive goal sought by so many peasant leaders when they could still mount the parliamentary rostrum in their own lands, was achieved only when the East European peasant political movement was forced into exile. Stripped of any real political power, wholly dependent on the countries where they found refuge, the agrarian leaders were at last able to join together in an international organization. One might well argue, however, that it was too late.

When Ferenc Nagy arrived in Washington in July, 1947, the representatives of the various peasant political parties of Eastern Europe announced the reconstitution of the Green International under a new name, the International Peasant Union.[1] Shortly after the successful escape of Mikołajczyk, the first congress of the Union was held, and subsequent congresses have been held biennially. The exiled leaders of peasant political parties from every country behind the iron curtain have joined in this organization.

The International Peasant Union claimed in 1952 that it was "the only organization functioning under the present circumstances which represents the actual democratic strength of the captive countries as well as their homogeneous political views."[2] In 1956

---

[1] See "The International Peasant Union," International Peasant Union, *Monthly Bulletin*, No. 5 (May, 1952), pp. 3–5.
[2] *Ibid.*, p. 4.

Mikołajczyk declared that the Union "is the chief transmitter to the free world of the thoughts, aspirations, and desires of the wide masses of people who can conceive of their own and their nation's liberty only within the framework of a society in which freedom, democracy and social justice are the rule." [3] These are noble words, but the record of the peasant political movement does little to confirm them.

Perhaps, given different circumstances after World War II, the movement might have recovered some of its earlier concern for the welfare of the whole peasantry and lived up to its professed devotion to democratic institutions. Certainly in the early 1920s the movement had arisen out of the conviction of the poor and oppressed peasants that a new world was being made in which they would be able through their representatives to find social justice and avoid the indignities implicit in the industrial solution to their problems. Perhaps in this period there was among the peasants "a livelier gleam in their eyes, a ripple of boldness, above all a critical temper which knocks at every gate," as the Transylvanian writer Goga suggested.[4]

But the peasant political movement does not owe its defects entirely to the Soviet army. The vulnerability of the movement goes back to the 1920s, to the excessive eagerness of some peasant leaders to feed at the public trough, to the deferral of desperately needed economic reforms in order to indulge a private thirst for power, to the narrowness of vision on social and economic problems in the program of those who claimed to lead and direct the peasant. Perhaps the peasant ideology is not, even in its modified forms, a viable one in the backward countries of the world, but the tragic flaws in the leaders of the East European peasant political movement, perhaps inevitable flaws among the intelligentsia in backward countries, certainly helped to propel this movement on the road to impotence.

In 1928, at the First Congress of the Green International, Hodža stood before an assembly of agrarian politicians, each of whom had a

[3] S. Mikolajczyk, "The Agrarian Peasant Movement," International Peasant Union, *Monthly Bulletin*, No. 10 (Oct., 1956), p. 6.

[4] As quoted in David Mitrany, *Marx Against the Peasant: A Study in Social Dogmatism* (Chapel Hill, 1951), p. 131.

loyal following in his own country, each of whom was respected in his own land, and some of whom would still experience the exhilarating pleasure and awesome responsibility of political power. Today the Green International consists of a handful of men, shorn of political power, barred forever from their own lands, separated by more than a decade of change from their own people, yet still claiming to represent the deepest aspirations of their peasantry. There is a touch of pathos in this. It is the end of a dream.

Problems of Research

A. THE COMMUNIST INTERNATIONAL

Bibliographies are not especially helpful in studying the history of conspiratorial movements. The visible activities of the Comintern, like the visible part of a floating iceberg, represent only a fraction of the whole. Nevertheless, one must begin with that which is known before divining the rest. There is no substitute for the so-called stenographic reports of congresses and sessions of the Enlarged Plenum of the Executive Committee of the Comintern. More of the real flavor of the controversies in that body is preserved in these records than in any other source. In most cases the stenographic notes are available for the congresses in English, French, and German editions of *International Press Correspondence*. Since German was the official language of the Comintern, the German versions are the most authoritative. The recent bibliography edited by Thomas T. Hammond, *Soviet Foreign Relations and World Communism* (Princeton, 1965), provides an excellent general guide to all of the above material with bibliographic citations for each of the languages in which the publication originally appeared.

Most scraps of evidence about the daily operations of the Comintern behind its public façade must be ferreted out of articles by individual party members scattered through a large number of journals inspired by or supported by the Comintern. The official journal of the Executive Committee of the Communist International, *Kommunisticheskii Internatsional,* is the single most useful source. It provides more information than any other publication on activities of the member parties and branches of the Comintern. To locate other journals and the material in them one must rely on the standard bibliographic guides to periodicals. Some of the lesser known bibliographies are discussed below in the appropriate sections.

B. MARX AND LENIN ON THE AGRARIAN QUESTION

On Marx's attitude toward the agrarian question one book stands out above all the rest, the collection of essays by Mitrany. It is a pioneering effort, but it was derived from a series of lectures and was not intended to be a definitive study of Marx's views on the agrarian question. Such a task would require an intensive examination of Marx's voluminous published writings and the unpublished notebooks kept in the Institute of Marx-Engels-Lenin in Moscow. So far, apparently, no one has had either the interest or the patience to attempt it.

Among Soviet scholars, Popov attempted to gather together Marx's opinions on the role of the agrarian question in revolution, but I suspect the selections are not representative. More useful is an attempt to analyze the problems which Marx encountered in the agrarian question in the First International: I. A. Bakh, "Marks i agrarnyi vopros v I Internatsionale," *Voprosy istorii,* No. 5 (May, 1958), pp. 63-82.

The idea that economically backward countries might "skip" some of the well-known Marxist "stages of development" clearly played a role in Marx's thinking. In the various letters to Russian revolutionaries collected in *Perepiska K. Marksa i F. Engel'sa s russkimi politicheskimi deiateliami,* Marx frequently refers to this possibility. In particular, the various drafts of Marx's famous letter to Zasulich in 1881 reflect his uncertainty on this question. Copies of the original French drafts are available in David B. Riazanov [Gol'dendach], ed., *Marx-Engels Archiv,* I (Frankfurt, 1926), 318-40; and in Russian in David B. Riazanov [Gol'dendach], *Arkhiv K. Marksa i F. Engelsa,* I (Moscow, 1924), 270-86, and in Marx and Engels, *Sochineniia,* XXVII (Moscow, 1935). A composite letter was assembled from all the drafts in Blackstock and Hoselitz's collection of selected writings of Marx and Engels. A summary of the drafts may be found in W. Weintraub, "Marx and the Russian Revolutionaries," *The Cambridge Journal,* III (1950), 497-503, and *ibid.,* IV, 89-94. There is an illuminating discussion of this letter and the attitude of Marx and Engels toward the possibility of Russia "skipping" a stage in the article by Solomon S. Schwartz in the symposium edited by Simmons.

Lenin, unlike Marx, was constantly concerned with the agrarian question, and his collected works teem with articles on this problem. In the English version of his *Selected Works,* Volume XII is devoted to the agrarian question. The most penetrating analysis of Leninism in any language is Meyer's *Leninism.* Also useful is Owen's book on the Russian peasant movement, which includes an intelligent discussion of Lenin's attitude toward the role of the peasant in revolution.

Communist efforts to understand their own prophet have not been very successful. However, one Soviet scholar has written a balanced analysis of the development of Lenin's ideas on the agrarian question: F. Bystrykh, "Razvitie vzgliadov Lenina po agrarnomu voprosu," *Proletarskaia revoliutsiia,* No. 1 (72) (1928), pp. 3-36. But the assumption that Lenin, like other men, changed his ideas as he learned from experience, and was not born with the complete blueprints for the revolution indelibly inscribed upon his brain, apparently conflicts with the cult of Lenin. Bystrykh's treatment was recently singled out for attack because he intimated that Lenin did not advocate the nationalization of all land and the expropriation of all large estates in the 1890s in N. V. Alekseeva, "Ideia soiuza rabochego klassa i krest'ianstva v rannikh proizvedeniiakh V. I. Lenina," *Voprosy istorii*, No. 2 (February, 1959), pp. 45-58.

The Soviets also consider it heretical to suggest that any of Lenin's ideas might be derivative. Boris Nikolaevskii maintained in 1926 that Lenin's agrarian program may have been, at least in part, a result of exposure to the debates on revisionism in Germany in 1895: B. Nikolaevskii, "V. I. Ulianov—Lenin v Berline v 1895," *Letopisi Marksizma*, No. 1 (1926), pp. 81-90. This assumption was attacked by Angarskii at the time; he maintained that, although the discussions in Germany may have had some influence, Lenin's basic approach was already fully formed: N. Angarskii, "O vliianii nemetskoi agrarnoi diskussii (1895) na vyrabotku vzgliadov Lenina po agrarnomu voprosu," *Bol'shevik*, No. 2 (1927), pp. 69-75. In another article surveying the material on the agrarian question published in the multivolumed *Leninskii sbornik*, Nikonorov indicates that Lenin was very much concerned about the claims of the German revisionists and, following Kautsky's arguments, tried to prove by means of the German statistics of 1907 that agriculture was becoming capitalistic: A. Nikonorov, "O Leninskom nasledstva po agrarnomu voprosu," *Na agrarnom fronte*, No. 1 (July-August, 1932), pp. 105-18.

On Lenin's formulation of the agrarian program of the Second Comintern Congress, the nucleus of all subsequent Comintern agrarian programs, the articles by Bobinskii and the response by Kolarov are the most informative: S. Bobinskii, "K istorii agrarnykh tezisov II kongressa Kommunisticheskogo Internatsionala," *Na agrarnom fronte*, No. 1 (Jaunary, 1928), pp. 61-72; V. Kolarov, "Zametka k istorii agrarnykh tezisov II Mirogo Kongressa," *Kommunisticheskii Internatsional*, No. 1 (January 4, 1929), pp. 40-42. Lenin's preliminary draft is available in his collected works and in English in his *Selected Works*, Vol. X. The final draft accepted by the congress is available in Russian in the Bela Kun collection and in English in the Degras collection.

C. THE KRESTINTERN

The indispensable bibliographic tools for research on Comintern agrarian policy are the publications of the Bibliographic Division of the International Agrarian Institute (Mezhdunarodnyi Agrarnyi Institut). Iunovich's bibliography, which was published under the auspices of the Communist Academy, is quite useful.

The published records of the meetings of the Red Peasant International are essential sources of information about the nature and function of that institution. All of the published records are drastically abridged. Those of the First International Peasant Conference are the most complete and also the most useful. Most of these accounts were published in French and German as well as Russian. The general goals of the organization were sketched by one of its Russian officials, N. L. Meshcheriakov, in his pamphlet *The Peasantry and Revolution.* The relationship between the Krestintern and the Comintern is described in S——kii, "Krest'ianskii Internatsional i ego znachenie," *Bol'shevik,* No. 5-6 (May-June, 1924), pp. 4-11, and in Iu. Krasnyi, "Mezhdunarodnyi Krest'ianskii sovet," *Kommunisticheskii Internatsional,* No. 3-4 (N.S.) (May, 1924), pp. 163-80.

The fullest information, apart from the published records of meetings, is available in the official organ of the Krestintern, *Krest'ianskii Internatsional,* also published in German. With the demise of *Krest'ianskii Internatsional* in 1926, many veterans of Krestintern work contributed to a newsletter on peasant affairs, *Der Internationaler Bauern-Korrespondent,* published sporadically in Berlin between 1927 and 1929. The section of the Peasant International in the United States operating from Bismarck, North Dakota, distributed an English-language edition of the peasant newsletter, *Farmers' and Peasants' International Correspondent,* and published a journal of its own, *United Farmer.* The journal of the agrarian section of the Communist Academy, *Na agrarnom fronte,* and the journal of the Krestintern's research auxiliary (the International Agrarian Institute in Moscow), *Agrarnye problemy,* are also useful.

The Krestintern published a series of studies describing its activities under the title *Biblioteka revoliutsionnoe krest'ianskoe dvizhenie.* I was unable to locate two potentially useful works in this series, one on Bulgaria by Gorov and one on Hungary by Kheveshi, but Timov's book on Rumania and Boshkovich's on Yugoslavia were extremely useful. Timov offers a detailed and interesting analysis of the profound influence of Constantin Dobrogeanu-Gherea's theories on the socialist and Communist movements in Rumania and the efforts of the Comintern to combat them. Boshkovich gives the Krestintern's version of the negotiations with Radić. The whole decade of struggle between the Krestintern and the Green International is treated in a haphazard fashion in Boshkovich's book on the Green International and Kolarov's essay, "Komintern na derevom fronte," in the collection of essays on the agrarian question which he edited, *Shest' let bor'by za krest'ianstvo.*

The subdivision of the Krestintern known as the European Peasant Committee, which grew out of the Anti-Fascist Congress in Berlin in 1929, is described in: A. Kheveshi, "Evropeiskii Krest'iansii komitet," in the Kolarov collection cited above; "Le Premier Congrès Européen Paysan à Berlin," *La Fédération balkanique,* No. 132-133 (9-10A) (April 15, 1930), pp. 2878-84; "Pervyi Evropeiskii Kongress Trudniashchegosia Krest'ianstva," *Agrarnyi problemy,* No. 4-5 (April-May, 1930), pp. 161-

78. A non-Communist description of the First Congress of the European Peasant Committee by the secretary of the Green International is available in Charles Mečíř, "La Soi-disant Union Paysanne Européenne et le soi-disant Congrès Paysan Européen," *MAB Bulletin*, No. 4 (1929), pp. 295-301.

The only account in English of the Krestintern is the brief and occasionally inaccurate one in Carr's *The Interregnum*, which will be continued in Volume III of his *Socialism in One Country*, when that volume appears.

D. COMMUNISM IN EASTERN EUROPE

The only attempt to treat the whole East European Communist movement in terms of the special conditions prevailing in that area is Burks's book. Burks made a detailed statistical analysis of election returns, especially in the 1920s, in order to define the forces which impelled some East Europeans to support communism and in order to classify those who did support it. Burks's methods are highly questionable, in particular his frequent assumption that the election returns immediately after World War I are useful indices to the mood of East Europeans during the entire interwar period. Nevertheless, he displays a remarkable intuitive grasp of the psychological appeals of communism in Czechoslovakia, Yugoslavia, and Greece, and brings together data which are not available anywhere else in English. He is less successful and less accurate on the Bulgarian, Polish, and Rumanian parties. Although Burks's methods are not always sound, he suggests exciting new approaches to the history of communism which will undoubtedly inject new life into old subjects.

In most cases I have not tried to use the ever increasing supply of documents and monographs on local Communist parties by the national institutes for the study of the party, except where these sources and studies have been translated into Russian. A great deal of research on the origins of East European Communist parties was performed for the fortieth anniversary of the Russian Revolution. A useful guide to most of this material, including publications in both Russian and native languages, is *Velikaia oktiabr'skaia sotsialisticheskaia revoliutsiia i pod'em revoliutsionnogo dvizheniia v Bolgarii, Vengrii, Pol'she i Chekhoslavakii—ukazatel' knig i statei vyshedshikh v svet 1951-1958 gg.* A reasonably complete guide to all Soviet periodicals and book-length material on communism in the Slavic countries in Eastern Europe is the recent *Sovetskoe slavianovedenie*, published by the Institute of Slavic Studies of the Academy of Sciences of the USSR. The collection of essays on the October Revolution and the Slavs edited by Manusevich is useful. At the first congress of each of the East European Communist parties after World War II, the party chiefs gave a brief résumé of the history of their party.

The only East European Communist party to receive definitive treatment so far is the Bulgarian, in Rothschild's book, which covers the period up to 1936. The volume in the Bela Kun series, *Kommunisticheskie partii vsekh stran,* on Balkan communism by Kabakchiev, Boshkovich, and Vatis includes a section on the Bulgarian Party, but is not very useful. Trotsky was in Bulgaria during the war and with Kabakchiev composed a series of essays on Bulgaria's problems and the problems of the newly formed Communist Party. The official history of the Bulgarian Communist Party has been translated into Russian under the title *Istoriia Bolgarskoi Kommunisticheskoi Partii.* It is useful for placing events and developments, but suffers from the usual defects of official Communist party histories.

The documents of the Bulgarian Communist Party are available in the Karakolev collection. Two important accounts of the period treated here are Birman's study of the events of 1918 and 1919 and Tsonev (Gavril Genov) and Vladimirov's account of the September Revolution of 1923. The former is a scholarly study written from the Communist point of view, but using archival material not available elsewhere. The latter is an eyewitness account by one of the leaders of the September insurrection. The evidence used by the Tsankov government to document Communist-agrarian ties is available in *La Conspiration bolchéviste contre la Bulgarie.*

There is an outline of the history of the Communist Party of Yugoslavia by Marjanović which is quite useful. The brief history by Boshkovich (Filipović), the first man to hold the post of secretary general of the Party, appears in the book by Kabakchiev, Boshkovich, and Vatis on Balkan communism. It is not very useful. The most controversial leader of the Communist Party of Yugoslavia, Marković, has published a book in German on the first two years of the Party's history. The only impartial treatment of Marković's debate with Stalin is Suzanna Sommes Williams' Master's essay at Columbia University. The documents of the Party have been published with less of the elaborate editing than is common in most Communist countries in *Kongresi i zemaljske konferentsije KPJ 1919–1937.*

In the case of Rumania, apparently there is no official party history, though Timov's book on Ghereaism is very informative. As in the case of Bulgaria, Trotsky put his wartime travels to good use and collaborated with Rakovskii, an old veteran of the Balkan and international socialist movement, to produce a series of essays on Rumanian socialism. Two articles—V. Kushnir-Mikhailovich, "Velikaia Oktiabr'skaia Sotsialisticheskaia Revoliutsiia i situatsiia v Rumynii v 1917-21 gg.," *Voprosy istorii,* No. 11 (November, 1957), pp. 65-85, and A. N. Glugovskii, "Velikaia Oktiabr'skaia Sotsialisticheskaia Revoliutsiia i pod'em revoliutsionnogo dvizheniie v Rumynii v 1917-1918 godakh," in *Vsemirno-istorieheskoe znachenie Velikoi Oktiabr'skoi Revoliutsii* (Moscow, 1957), pp. 460-84—are also useful in understanding the early history of the

Communist Party of Rumania. The brief section in Roberts' book on
Rumania on the early history of the Party gives few details but capably
outlines the problems facing the Party during the first decade of its existence. A collection of Party documents published in Russian was of some
use: *30 let bor'by Rumynskoie Kommunisticheskoi Partii za sotsializm, za
mir za schast'e rodiny 1921–1951.* The selected published works of
Gheorghe Gheorghiu-Dej in Russian are still in progress and are useful,
if only for the footnotes.

For the northern countries there is considerably more literature. Dziewanowski's book is a useful guide to the development of Polish communism. However, Dziewanowski tried to cover so much ground in so little
space that many questions are ignored or glossed over. It is, unfortunately,
no more that it claims to be, an outline. Reguła's book, which could not be
fully used here, is the most detailed non-Communist history of the early
development of the Polish Party. A number of Party resolutions during
the interwar period have been published in the Khrenov collection and
there is some helpful information on the founding of the Party in the collection of essays edited by Misko.

The Communist movement in the eastern regions of Poland has received
some attention in Vakar's study of Belorussia and Dmytryshyn's book on
the Ukraine. The best detailed treatment of the Ukrainian peasant
movement Selrob is Girchak's book on Shumskiism. The memoirs of former members of the Communist Party of the Western Ukraine and Selrob
edited by Gerasymenko and Dudykevich contain valuable information
and provide some insight into Communist operations there. Excerpts from
the "trial of 56," the leaders of the Belorussian peasant movement Hramada, are available interspersed with righteous indignation in *Zapadnaia
Belorussia na skam'e podsudimykh protsess Belorusskoi Krest'iansko-Rabochei Gromady (23 fevralia–22 maia, 1928).* An indispensable source
for the study of the Communist Party of Western Belorussia and the
Hramada was recently published. It includes many Party documents in
the original Belorussian, while those originally appearing in languages
other than Belorussian are translated into Russian: *Bor'ba trudiashchikhsia Zapadnoi Belorussii za sotsial'noe i natsional'noe osvobozhdenie i vossoedinenie s BSSR* Vol. I (1921-29). A recent study of the Communist
Party of Western Belorussia by Poluian and Poluian exhibits surprising
candor in its treatment of such delicate topics as factionalism and Communist infiltration of peasant political movements.

The Czechoslovak Party was the only Communist party in Eastern
Europe that was legal during its entire career and the information
about it is, therefore, rather voluminous. Reimann provides one of
the most detailed Communist accounts of the early history of the
Party, but this account only goes up to 1929 and about half of the
book is concerned with the formation of the Party. Reimann con-

centrates almost exclusively on inner Party quarrels, and the book is essentially a long diatribe against Šmeral and Jílek with little information about local Party work. The official history of the Party has been translated into Russian as *Istoriia Kommunisticheskoi Partii Chekhoslovakii,* but this book suffers from the usual deficiencies of official histories. A recent work by Vesely, a Czech historian and veteran Party member, rehabilitates Šmeral, though his errors are underscored. The memoirs of Kopecký, recently translated into Russian, are rambling, but they have value because they are blunt and personal, unlike the official histories.

Zinner sketches the important stages in the development of the Party in his doctoral thesis at Harvard, though he is more concerned with the immediate postwar period. This work has been revised and recently published as Paul E. Zinner, *Communist Strategy and Tactics in Czechoslovakia, 1918–48* (New York, 1963), but the book came out too late to be used here. The volume by Kreibich on the Czechoslovak Communist Party in the Bela Kun series was not very useful.

By far the most perceptive accounts of the Czechoslovak Communist Party are those found in three articles by H. Gordon Skilling: "The Formation of a Communist Party in Czechoslovakia," *American Slavic and East European Review,* XIV, No. 3 (October, 1955), 346-58; "The Comintern and Czechoslovak Communism: 1921-1929," *American Slavic and East European Review,* XIX, No. 2 (April, 1960), 243-47; and "Gottwald and the Bolshevization of the Communist Party of Czechoslovakia (1929-39)," *Slavic Review,* XX, No. 4 (December, 1961), 641-55. Of all the monographic literature appearing in Russian, by far the most valuable is that by I. N. Mel'nikova. Using provincial archives, she has provided a unique account of the development of the Communist movement in the Sub-Carpathian Ukraine: I. N. Mel'nikova, "Iz istorii revoliutsionnogo dvizheniia na zakarpatskoi Ukraine v 1921-24," *Uchenye zapiski instituta slavianovedeniia,* VI (1952), 5-58. Her monograph on class struggle in Czechoslovakia is less exotic in its choice of subject matter but is still one notch above the usual Communist works of scholarship. Data on the membership of the Party from 1921 to the present, which are not available elsewhere, may be found in Ia. Stanek, Ts. Khvoika, and K. Satran, "Stroitel'stva Kommunisticheskoi Partii Chekhoslovakii," *Voprosy istorii KPSS,* No. 5 (May, 1959), pp. 131-51.

E. AGRARIANISM

The literature on the peasant political movement in Eastern Europe and the Green International is sparse in Western languages. Peselj's doctoral thesis is the only detailed analysis of the peasant political movement as a whole. He treats the political, social, and economic doctrines of the movement in the Balkans and includes a brief history of each peasant party down to the present time. He gives almost no information on the development of the Green International. He is weakest on the Rumanian agrarian movement and, of course, is quite partial toward his own peasant movement, the Croatian Peasant Party, with which he is still involved as personal secretary to Vladko Maček. Two personal interpretations of the meaning of agrarianism are: Branko M. Peselj, "The Concept and Sources of Peasant Ideology," International Peasant Union, *Monthly Bulletin,* No. 9 (September, 1951), pp. 9-12, and George M. Dimitrov, "Agrarianism," in Felix Gross, ed., *European Ideologies,* pp. 391-452.

The best single source of information on the history of the Green International and member parties is the official organ of the Green International, *Mezinárodní Agrární Bureau Bulletin,* Prague, October, 1923-38 (referred to in the notes as *MAB Bulletin*). This publication is indispensable to any student of interwar Eastern Europe who does not possess all the East European languages. Every article is printed simultaneously in French, German, and the native tongue. The only complete holdings in the United States are at the agricultural library, Cornell University. A supplementary source of information, but one which is not always reliable, is the official successor to the Green International, the *Monthly Bulletin* of the International Peasant Union.

For the ideology of the Bulgarian Agrarian Union, Petkov's collection of excerpts from the major writings and speeches of Stamboliiski is the best single source. There is also a sympathetic biography by Panov. I. V. Chastukhir gives a Soviet account of the formation of the Union in "Krest'ianskoe dvizhenie v Bolgarii v 1889-1900 gg. i vozniknovedenie Bolgarskoi Zemledel'cheskogo Narodnogo Soiuzy," *Voprosy istorii,* No. 9 (September, 1956), pp. 90-100. The Russian Social Revolutionaries in exile were strongly drawn to Stamboliiski and one of them, V. I. Lebedev, published a book giving a strongly favorable description of Stamboliiski's peasant paradise.

Livingstone's doctoral thesis is a superb study of the first twenty-five years in the history of the Croatian Peasant Party. Drawing upon all available sources, he has written a sensitive and revealing history of the Party. The ideology of the Croatian Peasant Party has been outlined in Herceg's book, which Stjepan Radić called the bible of his party.

For Rumania, Roberts' book provides an incisive analysis of the evolution of the Rumanian Party in the decade of the 1920s. The Polish and Czech agrarian movements await definitive treatment. The origin and development of the Polish peasant movement has been outlined in a series of articles by Peter Brock: "Bolesław Wysłouch, Founder of the Polish Peasant Party," *Slavonic and East European Review, XXX,* No. 74 (December, 1951), 139-63; "The Early Years of the Polish Peasant Party," *Journal of Central European Affairs,* XIV, No. 4 (October, 1954), 219-35; and "The Politics of the Polish Peasant," *International Review of Social His-*

tory, I (1956), Part I, 210-22. For Czechoslovakia, Hodža's "agrarian democracy" apparently attracted as much attention from the Russian Social Revolutionaries in exile in the second half of the 1920s as Stamboliiski's peasant paradise had in the first half. An extremely favorable description of Hodža's career and his theories was written by Sergei Maslov. The influence, if any, of the influx of Russian Social Revolutionaries on the peasant political movement of Eastern Europe and on the development of the Green International is a subject which deserves further exploration.

Selected Bibliography

A. OFFICIAL DOCUMENTS

1. Comintern Congresses

First Congress. *Pervyi kongress Kommunisticheskogo Internatsionala protokoly zasedanii v Moskve so 2 do 19 marta 1919 goda.* Moscow, 1921.

Second Congress. *Vtoroi Kongress Kommunisticheskogo Internatsionala—stenograficheskii otchet.* Moscow, 1921.

Fourth Congress. *IV. vsemirnyi kongress Kommunisticheskogo Internatsionala (5 noiabria–3 dekabria, 1922) izbrannye doklady, rechi i rezoliutsii.* Moscow, 1923.

Fifth Congress. *Piatyi vsemirnyi kongress Kommunisticheskogo Internatsionala—(18 iunia–8 iulia 1924 goda)—stenograficheskii otchet.* 2 vols. Moscow, 1925.

Sixth Congress. *IV kongress Kominterna—stenograficheskii otchet.* 6 vols. Moscow, 1929.

2. Plenums of the Executive Committee of the Comintern

Third Plenum. *Rasshirennyi plenum ispolnitel'nogo komiteta Kommunisticheskogo Internatsionala (12–23 iunia 1923 goda).* Moscow, 1923.

Fifth Plenum. *Rasshirennyi plenum ispolkoma Kommunisticheskogo Internatsionala—protokoly zasedanii (21 marta–6 aprelia, 1925).* Moscow, 1925.

Sixth Plenum. *Shestoi rasshirennyi plenum ispolkoma Kominterna (17 fevralia—15 marta 1926)—stenograffcheskii otchet.* Moscow, 1927.

Seventh Plenum. *Puti mirovoi revoliutsii—sed'moi rasshirennyi plenum ispolnitel'nogo komiteta Kommunisticheskogo Internatsionala (22 noiabria–16 dekabria).* 2 vols. Moscow, 1927.

Tenth Plenum. *Desiatyi plenum ispolkoma Kominterna.* 3 vols. Moscow, 1929.

Eleventh Plenum. *XI plenum IKKI—stenograficheskii otchet.* Moscow, 1932.

3. Conferences of the Red Peasant International (Krestintern)

First Conference. *Pervaia mezhdunarodnaia krest'ianskaia konferentsiia 10/10–10.16, 1923 rechi, tezisy, vozzvaniia.* Moscow, 1924. No. 3 of *Biblioteka Krest'ianskogo Internatsionala.* In French: *Premiére confer-*

ence internationale paysanne tenue a Moscow 10–15 octobre 1923. Paris, 1924. In German: *Die erste Weltkongress der Bauern vom 10 bis 16 Oktober, 1923* Berlin, 1924. No. 7 of *Bibliothek des Internationalem bauernrates.*

Second Conference. *Internationale Bauernberatung: Stenogramm und Beschlüsse.* Moscow, 1927. In French: *Conseil paysan international: Stenogram et resolutions.* Paris, 1928.

4. Plenums of the International Peasant Council of the Kestintern

Second Plenum. *Zadachi i dostizhenie Krestinterna za zapade.* Moscow, 1924.

B. OTHER WORKS

Agrarnye problemy. Moscow, 1926-35.

Akademiia nauk SSSR. Institut Slavianovedeniia. *Sovetskoe slavianovedenie: Literatura o zarubezhnykh slavianskikh stranakh na russkom iazyke, 1918–1960.* Moscow, 1963.

Barker, Elizabeth. *Macedonia: Its Place in Balkan Power Politics,* London, 1950.

Bashmakov [B——off], A. *Mémoire sur le mouvement communiste en Bulgarie durant les années 1921 et 1922 (D'apres des sources authentiques).* No publishing data.

Besedovskii, G. Z. *Na putiakh k termidoru.* 2 vols. Paris, 1930.

Birman, M. A. *Revoliutsionnaia situatsiia v Bolgarii v 1918–1919 gg.* Moscow, 1957.

Bor'ba trudiashchikhsia Zapadnoi Belorussii za sotsial'noe i natsional'noe osvobozhdenie i vossoedinenie s BSSR. Vol. I (1921–29). Minsk, 1962.

Borkenau, Franz. *World Communism: A History of the Communist International.* New York, 1939.

Boshkovich, Boshko [Filip Filipović]. *Krest'ianskoe dvizhenie i natsional'nyi vopros v Iugoslavii.* Moscow, 1929.

Boshkovich, Boshko, ed. *Zelenyi Internatsional i ego kulatskoe litso.* Moscow, 1933.

Boshkovich, Boshko, *et al. Bor'ba za krest'ianstvo.* Moscow, 1926.

Bouroff, M. Tz. *La Réforme agraire en Bulgarie, 1921–1924.* Paris, 1924.

Brdlík, Vladislaw. *Die Sozialökonomische Struktur der Landwirtschaft in der Tchecoslovakei.* Berlin, 1938.

Buell, Raymond Leslie. *Poland: Key to Europe.* New York, 1939.

La Bulgarie sous le régime de l'assassinat. Paris, 1925.

Burks, R. V. *The Dynamics of Communism in Eastern Europe.* Princeton, 1961.

Carr, Edward Hallet. *The Bolshevik Revolution, 1917–1923.* 3 vols. New York, 1950-53.

—— *The Interregnum, 1923–1924.* New York, 1954.

—— *Socialism in One Country, 1924–1926.* 2 vols. to date. New York, 1958– .

Ciliga, Anton. *Au pays du mensonge déconcertant.* Vol. I of his *Dix ans derriére le rideau de fer.* Paris, 1950.

Clark, Charles Upson. *Bessarabia: Russia and Roumania on the Black Sea.* New York, 1927.

Cole, G. D. H. *A History of Socialist Thought.* 4 vols. London, 1956.

La Conspiration bolchéviste contre la Bulgarie. Sofia, 1925.

Degras, Jane, ed. *The Communist International, 1919–1943: Documents.* 2 vols. to date (up to 1929). London, 1956– .

Deutscher, Isaac. *The Prophet Unarmed: Trotsky, 1921–1929.* London, 1959.

—— *Stalin: A Political Biography.* New York, 1949.

Dmytryshyn, Basil. *Moscow and the Ukraine, 1918–1953: A Study of Russian Bolshevik Nationality Policy.* New York, 1956.

Dudykevych, B. K. *See* Gerasymenko, M. P.

Dziewanowski, M. K. *The Communist Party of Poland: An Outline of History.* Cambridge, Mass., 1959.

Erlich, Alexander. *The Soviet Industrialization Debate, 1924–1928.* Cambridge, Mass., 1960.

La Fédération balkanique. Vienna, 1927-31.

Felinski, M. *The Ukrainians in Poland.* London, 1931.

Fischer, Ruth. *Stalin and German Communism: A Study in the Origins of the State Party.* Cambridge, Mass., 1948.

Frangeš, Otto von. *Die Sozialökonomische Struktur der jugoslawischen Landwirtschaft.* Berlin, 1937.

Gargas, Sigismund. *Die Grüne Internatsionale.* Halberstadt, 1927.

Gerasymenko, M. P., and B. K. Dudykevych, *Borot'ba trudiashchykh Zakhidnoi Ukrainy za vozziednannia z Radianskoiu Ukrainoiu, 1921–39.* Kiev, 1955.

Gerschenkron, Alexander. *Economic Backwardness in Historical Perspective: A Book of Essays.* Cambridge, Mass., 1962.

Gheorghiu-Dej, Gheorghe. *Stat'i i rechi.* 2 vols. Moscow, 1956–57.

Girchak, Ie. E. *Shumskiizm i rozlam KPZU.* Kharkov, 1928.

Gopner, S. I., ed. *15 let Kominterna (1919–34).* Moscow, 1934.

Gottwald, Klement. *Izbrannye proizvedeniia.* Vol. I– . Moscow, 1957– .

Graham, Malbone W. *New Governments of Central Europe.* New York, 1926.

—— *New Governments of Eastern Europe.* New York, 1927.

Gross, Felix, ed. *European Ideologies.* New York, 1948.

Groth, Alexander. "Parliament and the Electoral System in Poland, 1918–1935." Unpublished Ph.D. dissertation, Faculty of Political Science, Columbia University, 1960.

324 SELECTED BIBLIOGRAPHY

Hajda, Jan, ed. *A Study of Contemporary Czechoslovakia.* Human Relations Area Files, Subcontractor's Monograph No. 15, University of Chicago, n.d.

Herceg, Rudolf. *Die Ideologie der kroatischen Bauernbewegung.* Zagreb, 1923.

Hobson, Asher. *The International Institute of Agriculture: An Historical and Critical Analysis of Its Organization, Activities, and Policies of Administration.* Berkeley, 1931.

In der Maur, Gilbert. *Der Weg zur Nation: Jugoslawiens Innenpolitik, 1918–1938.* Vol. III of his *Die Jugosawlien einst und jetzt.* Berlin, 1936–38.

Der Internationaler Bauern-Korrespondent. 1927–29.

International Peasant Union. *Monthly Bulletin.* New York, 1950– .

Istoriia Bolgarii. 2 vols. Moscow, 1954–55.

Istoriia Bolgarskoi Kommunisticheskoi Partii. Moscow, 1960.

Istoriia Chekhoslovakii. 3 vols. Moscow, 1956–59.

Istoriia Iugoslavii. Ed. by L. B. Valev, G. M. Slavin, and I. I. Vdal'tsov. 2 vols. Moscow, 1962–63.

Istoriia Kommunisticheskoi Partii Chekhoslovakii. Moscow, 1962.

Istoriia mezhdunarodnogo rabochego i natsional'no osvobozhditel'nogo dvizheniia. 3 vols. Moscow, 1958–62.

Istoriia Pol'sha. Ed. by A. Ia. Manusevich, I. A. Khrenov, and F. G. Zuev. 3 vols. Moscow, 1955–58.

Iunovich, M. *Literatura po mirovoi politike za 10 let (1917–1927).* Moscow, 1929.

Iwanska, Alicja, ed. *Contemporary Poland: Society, Politics, Economy.* Human Relations Area Files, Subcontractors Monograph No. 22, University of Chicago, 1955.

Jousse, Pierre. *Les Tendances des réformes agraires dans l'Europe centrale, l'Europe orientale et l'Europe méridionale, 1918–1924.* Niort, 1925.

Kabakchiev, Khristo, Boshko Boshkovich, and Kh. D. Vatis. *Kommunisticheskie partii balkanskikh stran.* Moscow, 1931.

Kabakchiev, Khristo, and Leon Trotsky. *Ocherki politicheskoi Bolgarii.* Moscow, 1924.

Karakolov, R. K. *Bulgarskata Kommunisticheska Partiia v rezoliutsii i resheniia.* Vol. II (1919–23). Sofia, 1951.

Kerner, R. J., ed. *Czechoslovakia: Twenty Years of Independence.* Berkeley, 1940.

—— *Yugoslavia.* Los Angeles, 1949.

Khrenov, I. A., ed. *Kommunisticheskaia Partiia Pol'shi v bor'be za nezavisimost' svoei strany.* Moscow, 1955.

Kirk, Dudley. *Europe's Population in the Interwar Years.* Geneva, 1946.

Kolarov, Vasil, ed. *Shest' let bor'by za krest'ianstvo.* Vol. II of *Agrarnyi vopros i sovremennoe krest'ianskoe dvizhenie.* Moscow, 1935.

Kommunisticheskii Internatsional. Moscow, 1919–43.

Kongresi i zemaljske konferentsije KPJ, 1919–1937. Vol. II of *Istorijski Arkiv Komunistička Partije Jugoslavije.* Belgrade, 1950.

Kopecký, Václav. *Vospominaniia: Iz istorii chekhoslovatskoi respubliki i bor'by kommunisticheskoi partii Chekhoslovakii za pobedu sotsializma.* Moscow, 1962.

Kreibich, Karl. *Kommunisticheskaia Partiia Chekhoslovakii.* Moscow, 1928.

Krest'ianskii Internatsional. Moscow, 1924–26. German ed. *Die Bauerninternationale.*

Kun, Bela, ed. *Kommunisticheskii Internatsional v dokumentakh, 1919–1937.* Moscow, 1933.

Lazić, Branko. *Lénine et la III Internationale.* Geneva, 1950.

—— *Les Partis communistes d'Europe, 1919–1955.* Paris, 1956.

—— *Tito et la révolution yougoslave.* Paris, 1957.

Lebedev, V. I. *Novym putem.* Prague, 1923.

Lenin, Vladimir Ilyich. *Sochineniia.* 38 vols. 4th ed. rev. Moscow, 1941–50.

Livingstone, Robert Gerald. "Stjepan Radić and the Croatian Peasant Party, 1904–1929." Unpublished Ph.D. dissertation, Department of History, Harvard University, 1959.

Lorimer, Frank. *The Population of the Soviet Union: History Prospects.* Geneva, 1946.

Lozovskii, A., *et al. Istoriia Kommunisticheskogo Internatsionala v kongressakh.* 6 vols. [1st–6th Congresses.] Moscow, 1929.

Macartney, Carlile Aylmer. *Hungary and Her Successors: The Treaty of Trianon and Its Consequences, 1919–1937.* London, 1937.

——*October Fifteenth: A History of Modern Hungary, 1921–1945.* Edinburgh, 1957.

Maček, Vladko. *In the Struggle for Freedom.* New York, 1957.

Machray, Robert. *Poland, 1919–1930.* London, 1932.

Manusevich, A. I., ed. *Oktiabr'skaia revoliutsiia i zarubezhnye slavianskie narody.* Moscow, 1957.

Marjanović, Jovan. *Potsetnik iz istorije Komunističke Partije Juslavije, 1919–1941.* Belgrade, 1953.

Markert, Werner, ed. *Jugoslawien.* Cologne, 1954.

—— *Polen.* Cologne, 1959.

Marković, Sima. *Der kommunismus in Jugoslawiens.* Hamburg, 1922.

Marx, Karl, and Friedrich Engels. *The Russian Menace to Europe.* Ed. by Paul W. Blackstock and Bert F. Hoselitz. Glencoe, Ill., 1952.

Maslov, Sergei. *Novaia sila v Evrope i Milan Godzha.* Prague, 1938.

Mel'nikova, I. N. *Klassovaia bor'ba v Chekhoslovakii v gody chastichnoi stabilizatsii kapitalizma, 1924–1929.* Moscow, 1962.

Meshcheriakov, N. L. *Krest'ianstvo i revoliutsiia.* Moscow, 1927. Published in English as *The Peasantry and Revolution.* Berlin, 1928.

Meyer, Alfred G. *Leninism.* Cambridge, Mass., 1957.
—— *Marxism: The Unity of Theory and Practice.* Cambridge, Mass., 1954.
Mezhdunarodnyi Agrarnyi Institut. Bibligraficheskii otdel. *Agrarnaia literatura SSSR.* Moscow, 1929–31.
—— *Ezhegodnik agrarnoi literatury SSSR.* Moscow, 1926–28.
—— *Index bibliographique de la question agraire.* Moscow, 1927–32.
Mezinárodní Agrární Bureau. *Bulletin.* Prague, 1923–38.
Misko, M. V. *Oktiabr'skaia revoliutsiia i vosstanovlenie nezavisimosti Pol'shi.* Moscow, 1957.
Mitrany, David M. *The Land and Peasant in Rumania.* New Haven, 1930.
—— *Marx Against the Peasant: A Study in Social Dogmatism.* Chapel Hill, 1951.
Mollov, Janiki S., ed. *Die Sozialökonomische Struktur der bulgarischen Landwirtschaft.* Berlin, 1936.
Moore, Wilbert E. *Economic Demography of Eastern and Southern Europe.* Geneva, 1945.
Na agrarnom fronte. Moscow, 1925–31.
Nollau, Günther. *International Communism and World Revolution: History and Methods.* New York, 1961.
Owen, Launcelot, A. *The Russian Peasant Movement, 1906–1917,* London, 1937 (repr. 1964).
Panov, A. *Stamboliiski v politicheskiia zhivot' na Bulgariia.* Sofia, 1921.
Pasvolsky, Leo. *Bulgaria's Economic Position.* Washington, D.C., 1930.
Perepiska K. Marksa i F. Engel'sa russkimi politicheskimi deiateliami. 2d ed. Moscow, 1951.
Peselj, Branko M. "Peasant Movements in Southeastern Europe, an Ideological, Economic and Political Opposition to Communist Dictatorship." Unpublished Ph. D. dissertation, Department of Political Science, Georgetown University, 1950.
Petkov, Nikola D., ed. *Aleksandur Stamboliiski: lichnost' i idei.* Sofia, 1930.
Petrovskii, D., ed. *Partiia Kommunisticheskogo Internatsionala.* Moscow, 1928.
Poluian, V., and I. Poluian. *Revoliutsionnoe i natsional'noosvoboditel'noe dvizhenie v Zapadnoi Belorussii v 1920–1939.* Minsk, 1962.
Rakovskii, Kh., and L. Trotsky. *Ocherki Politicheskoi Rumynii.* Moscow, 1922.
Reimann, Pavel. *Geschichte der Kommunistichen Partei der Tschechoslovakei.* Berlin, 1931. Vol. IV of the series *Beitrage zur Geschichte der Arbeiterbewegung.*
Reguła, Jan Alfred. *Historija Komunistycnej Partji Polski v swietle faktov i dokumentow.* Warsaw, 1934.

Roberts, Henry L. *Rumania: Political Problems of an Agrarian State*. New Haven, 1951.

Rochester, Anna. *Lenin on the Agrarian Question*. New York, 1942.

Rosmer, Alfred. *Moscou sous Lénine: Les origines du communisme*. Paris, 1953.

Rothschild, Joseph. *The Communist Party of Bulgaria: Origins and Development, 1883–1936*. New York, 1959.

Schapiro, Leonard. *The Communist Party of the Soviet Union*. New York, 1960.

Schmitt, B., ed. *Poland*. Berkeley, 1945.

Serge, Victor. *Mémoires d'un revolutionnaire*. Paris, 1951.

Sering, Max. *See* Zering, Max.

Seton-Watson, Hugh. *Eastern Europe Between the Wars, 1919–1941*. Cambridge, 1946.

Seton–Watson, Robert W. *A History of the Czechs and Slovaks*. London, 1943.

—— *A History of the Roumanians*. London, 1934.

Sharp, S. L. *Poland: White Eagle on a Red Field*. Cambridge, Mass., 1953.

Simmons, Ernest J., ed. *Continuity and Change in Russian and Soviet Thought*. Cambridge, Mass., 1956.

Sokalski, Wojciech. "The Polish Peasant Party, 1926–31." Unpublished Master's thesis, Department of Public Law and Government, Columbia University, 1948.

Souvarine, Boris. *Stalin: A Critical Survey of Bolshevism*. New York, 1939.

Spulber, Nicholas. *The Economics of Communist Eastern Europe*. New York, 1957.

Stalin, I. V. *Sochineniia*. 13 vols. Moscow, 1946–51.

Stravrianos, L. S. *Balkan Federation: A History of the Movement Towards Balkan Unity in Modern Times*. Smith College Studies in History, Vol. XXVII, Nos. 1–4. Menasha, Wis., 1944.

Swire, Joseph. *Bulgarian Conspiracy*. London, 1939.

Taylor, J. *Economic Development of Poland, 1919–1950*. Ithaca, 1952.

Timov, Solomon Samuilovich. *Agrarnyi vopros i krest'ianskoe dvizhenie v Rumynii: Anti–neoiobăgia (Kritika neokrespostnicheskoi teorii K. Dobrodzhanu–Geriia)*. Moscow, 1929.

Tito, Josip Broz. Komunisticka Partija Jugoslavije. *Political Report of the Central Committee of the Communist Party of Yugoslavia*. Belgrade, 1948.

Tivel' A., and M. Kheimo. *Desiat' 10 let Kominterna v resheniiakh tsifrakh*. Moscow, 1929.

Todorov, Kosta. *Balkan Firebrand: The Autobiography of a Rebel, Soldier and Statesman*. New York, 1943.

Tomasevich, Jozo. *Peasants, Politics, and Economic Change in Yugoslavia*. Stanford, 1955.

Tomasic, Dinka A., and Joseph Strmecki. *National Communism and Soviet Strategy*. Washington, D.C., 1957.

[*Trinadtsatyi*] *30 let bor'by za sotsializm, za mir, za schast'e rodiny 1921–51*. Moscow, 1951.

Trotsky, Leon. *Stalin*. New York, 1958.

—— *The Third International after Lenin*. New York, 1957.

—— *See also* Kabakchiev, Khristo, *and* Rakovskii, Kh.

Tsonev, G. [Gavril Genov], and A. Vladimirov. *Sentiabr'skoe vosstanie v Bolgarii 1923 goda*. Moscow, 1934.

United Farmer. Bismarck, N. Dak., 1926–31.

Vakar, Nicholas P. *Belorussia: The Making of a Nation; a Case Study*. Cambridge, Mass., 1956.

Vasil Kolarov: Biobibliografiia. Sofia, 1947.

Velikaia oktiabr'skaia sotsialisticheskaia revoliutsiia i pod'em revoliutsionnogo dvizheniia v Bolgarii, Vengrii, Pol'she Chekhoslovaki—ukazatel' knig i statei vyshedshikh v svet 1951–1958 gg. Moscow, 1959.

Vesely, I. *Osnovanie Kommunisticheskoi Partii Chekhoslovakii*. Moscow, 1958.

"Vie économique," Vol. II of *La Pologne, 1919–1939*. Neuchatel, 1946–47.

Wanklyn, Harriet. *Czechoslovakia*. New York, 1954.

Williams, Suzanne Sommes. "The Communist Party of Yugoslavia and the Nationality Problem." Unpublished Master's thesis, Department of Public Law and Government, Columbia University, 1955.

Wolfe, Bertram D. *Three Who Made a Revolution: A Biographical History*. New York, 1948.

Wolff, Robert Lee. *The Balkans in Our Time*. Cambridge, Mass., 1956.

Zagorov, S. D., Jenö Végh, and Alexander D. Bilimovich. *The Agricultural Economy of the Danubian Countries, 1935–45*. Stanford, 1955.

Zapadnaia Belorussia na skam'e podsudimykh protsess Belorusskoi Krest'iansko—Rabochei Gromady (23 fevralia—22 maia 1928). Minsk, 1929.

Zering, Max, ed. *Agrarnaia revoliutsiia v Evrope*. Berlin, 1925.

Zinner, Paul E. "The Strategy and Tactics of the Czechoslovak Communist Party." Unpublished Ph. D. dissertation, Department of Government, Harvard University, 1953.

Zweig, Ferdynand. *Poland Between Two Wars*. London, 1944.

Index

Agrarian Commission, *see* Comintern, Congresses: Second

Agrarianism: agrarian ideology, 40–48; literature on, 318–20

Agrarianization, 155, 197, 289, 295

Agrarian parties, *see* Bulgaria, Bulgarian Agrarian Union; Czechoslovakia, Czechoslovak Republican Party of Small Farmers and Peasants; Poland, Belorussian Workers' and Peasants' Hramada, Independent Peasant Party, Polish Peasant Party Piast, Polish Peasant Party Wyzwolenie, Ukrainian Peasant-Workers' Socialist Union; Rumania, Rumanian National Peasant Party, Rumanian Peasant Party; Yugoslavia, Croatian Peasant Party

Agrarian Party of France, 148*n*

Agrarian question: agrarian policy of Comintern, 4, 5, 22*n*, 35–40, 51–151 *passim,* 153, 156–57, 173, 181, 212–13, 221, 237, 295, 298, 313; Marx's views on, 28, 311–12; agrarian program of Lenin, 29–32, 35, 38–39, 76, 311–13; peasantism of Zinoviev, 60–64, 67, 76, 77, 83–87, 108–9, 116, 179; peasantism of Bukharin, 81–84, 90–96, 112, 116

Agrarian Question, The (K. Kautsky), 29

Agrarian reform: in Eastern Europe in 1920s, 8–11, 24, 306–8; in Bulgaria, 161; in Poland, 182–84, 187–88, 191–92; in Yugoslavia, 217; in Rumania, 239–40; in Czechoslovakia, 267

Agriculture: proportion of population engaged in, in Eastern Europe, 7 (*table*), 13 (*table*); land affected by agrarian reforms, 11 (*table*); in Bulgaria, 160–61; in Poland, 182;

in Yugoslavia, 216–17; in Rumania, 238

Alba-Iulia, 243, 257, 258, 259, 260, 263, 302

Alexander, King of Yugoslavia, 219*n*

Alma-Ata, 117, 134

Anglo-Soviet Trade Agreement, 55

Anti-Fascist Congress, 314

Association of Belorussian Schools (Poland), 208

Atanasov, Nedelko, 100

Austria, 65; Austrian Landbund für Österreich, 148*n*; Austrian Social Democratic Party, 274

Austria-Hungary, 10

Badulescu, *see* Köblos, Elek

Balkan Communist Federation, 87, 99, 100, 132, 253

Banat, 238, 239, 246, 247, 259

Barbu (member of Communist Party of Rumania), 259

Basel, 28

Bauer, Otto, 274

BCP, *see* Bulgaria, Bulgarian Communist Party

Belgrade, 17

Belorussian Cooperative Bank (Poland), 203

Belorussian National Club (Poland), 191

Belorussian Soviet Socialist Republic, 205, 206

Belorussian Workers' and Peasants' Hramada (Poland), 99, 131, 191, 199, 200, 201*n*, 202–9, 214; membership of, 204 (*table*)

Besedovskii, G. Z., 65

Bessarabia, 238, 239, 245, 246, 247, 252; Peasant Party of, 240, 241

Białystok, 55

Blagoev, Dimitur, 166–69